JAZZ

A Da Capo Press Reprint Series

THE ROOTS OF JAZZ

Edited by NAT HENTOFF

and ALBERT J. McCARTHY

JAZZ

New perspectives on the history of jazz by twelve
of the world's foremost jazz critics and scholars

DA CAPO PRESS • NEW YORK • 1974

Library of Congress Cataloging in Publication Data

Hentoff, Nat, comp.
    Jazz; new perspectives on the history of jazz by twelve of the
world's foremost jazz critics and scholars.

    (The Roots of jazz)
    Reprint of the 1st ed. published by Rinehart, New York, 1959.
    "Selected discography": pp. 345–371.
    1. Jazz music. I. McCarthy, Albert J., joint comp. II. Title.
ML3561.J3H44   1974   785.4'2'0973   70-171383
ISBN 0-306-70592-3

This Da Capo Press edition of *Jazz* is an unabridged republication
of the first edition published in New York and Toronto.

Published by Da Capo Press, Inc.
A Subsidiary of Plenum Publishing Corporation
227 West 17th Street, New York, N.Y. 10011

JAZZ

EDITED BY *Nat Hentoff*

AND *Albert J. McCarthy*

New perspectives on the history of jazz by twelve
of the world's foremost jazz critics and scholars

Rinehart & Company, Inc., New York, Toronto

Grateful acknowledgment is made to *The New Yorker* for permission to reprint a brief excerpt from an article by Whitney Balliet, which appeared in the July 19, 1958 issue of *The New Yorker*.

Published simultaneously in Canada by
Clarke, Irwin & Company, Ltd., Toronto

Preface

The nature of writing on jazz has begun to change markedly. In place of appreciators whose main means of analysis were adjectives, there are now historians and critics who are applying the disciplines of historical and critical traditions in other fields to jazz. At its best, this writing can be termed creative in that its discoveries and insights can help deepen a listener's enjoyment of the music and can help clarify his awareness of its roots and the reasons for its uniqueness.

An inevitable result of the increasing historical research in the past decade has been the realization that several areas of jazz history have been neglected, or at least have not been seen in accurate perspective.

This book is an attempt to examine a number of those areas. It is not a formal history in that it does not aim at covering *all* of jazz. It does deal, however, with some subjects—such as the early history of jazz in the Midwest and Southwest—that no previous history has adequately explored.

Nor is this book only history. Gunther Schuller's chapter on Duke Ellington, for example, is the first extended study of Ellington's musical materials and how he works with them. It is a continuation of a relatively new tradition of jazz musical analysis that has finally come into existence in the writings of André Hodeir, Dr. Louis Gottlieb and Schuller.

All of the articles have been commissioned specifically for this book. This is not an anthology of previously published writings. On a few occasions, we have allowed a small amount of overlap between contributions of various writers so that the same material can be seen from different viewpoints.

The book's intent is to help place jazz—its history and its language—in fuller perspective. Further research in the years ahead may well shift the outlines of chapters in jazz history even more, but we feel that the substance of the findings in most of these articles should prove illuminating for a long time to come.

The Editors

Contents

THE ROOTS
OF JAZZ

Ernest Borneman

In 1944–45, the publication of a series, "*The Anthropologist Looks at Jazz,*" in the American *Record Changer*, stimulated a considerable amount of controversy and further thought on the subject of the roots of jazz among jazz historians throughout the world. Its author was Ernest Borneman, a Canadian citizen who had studied comparative musicology under Von Hornbostel at the University of Berlin, and West African languages under James at the London School of Oriental Languages. He had paid his tuition from money earned by playing in dance bands on the side.

Borneman has since then become Head of International Production Unit, Canadian Film Board, and Head of UNESCO Film Department, Paris. He has recently produced a remarkable series of programs on Negro films, Negro music and Negro dancing at the National Film Theatre in London.

In this chapter, Borneman writes a particularly lucid introduction to the subject of where jazz came from.

When the anthropologist hears the jazz enthusiasts talking cheerfully of "Negro music" or the "African roots of jazz," he often wonders what in the world they can be talking about. What Negro music? What roots? What part of Africa? What kind of jazz?

Africa is one of the world's largest continents. It has a greater variety of genetic and lingual groups than any other comparable land mass. Not all Africans are Negroes, and not all Negroes are Africans. African music isn't necessarily Negro music, and Negro music isn't necessarily African.

The ancient tribal music of West Africa—the music of the coastal belt that stretches from Senegal down to the Gulf of Guinea —differs more profoundly from that of the Berbers in the north or the Bushmen in the south than the music of any two European nations has ever differed in recorded history. To speak of African music as though there were a common denominator between the music of Riff Kabyles, Congo Pygmies and Masai is like talking about American music without trying to distinguish between that of Eskimos, Indians and Pennsylvania Dutch.

The more we learn about Africa, the more we become aware of how little we know. What emerges from the whole pool of data accumulated during the last seventy-five years by anthropologists, Africanists and musicologists in search of African music is a pitifully small store of reliable information. But one thing of which we can be fairly certain is the surprisingly functional nature of seventeenth-century West African music and the absence of any "art music" in the European sense of the term. Each type of song was used by one group within the community, and by that group alone, to exert an effect on another group or on the gods who controlled the affairs of the group. Thus arose the eight basic types of song which regulated the community's pattern of culture:

1. Songs used by the young men to influence the young women: songs of courtship, songs of challenge, songs of scorn.
2. Songs used by mothers to calm and educate their children: lullabies, play songs, song games.
3. Songs used by the older men to prepare the adolescent boys for manhood: initiation songs, legends to perpetuate the history and tradition of the community, epic songs, ballads of famous ancestors.

3

4. Songs used by the religious heads of the community to inspire feelings of mystery, solemnity, awe or submissiveness.
5. Songs used by the chiefs to keep the community under control and preserve its coherence: songs to arouse common emotions and a sense of joint participation.
6. Songs used by the warriors to arouse courage in battle and instil fear in the enemy: battle songs, ballads commemorating past victories, legends of dead heroes.
7. Songs used by priests and medicine men to influence nature: fertility songs, rain songs, songs to hurt and kill, songs to arouse love and heal disease.
8. Songs used by workers to make their tasks easier: work songs to stress the rhythm of labor, group songs to synchronize collectively executed work, team songs sung by one team to challenge and satirize the other.

West African music has turned out to be one of the most complex, subtle and sophisticated forms of unwritten music in existence. How, then, is it to be explained that it has for so many years been considered "primitive" by Europeans? Why, for instance, has the role which harmony plays in West African music so frequently been denied by all but a diminutive minority of musicologists?

Surely, it must be obvious to even the most cursory listener that all four factors which we consider essential to musical construction—melody, harmony, rhythm and timbre—are to be found as consistently in West African as in European folk music. Why, then, have so many musicologists missed the obvious conclusion: that the element which makes West African music different from ours is not the absence of any of these four characteristics but simply the different relationship between them?

The sole explanation of the musical astigmatism that seems to affect us when we listen to West African music is our inability to orientate ourselves in a world in which all the familiar elements of musical architecture have been put to a totally unfamiliar purpose. The whole structure seems lopsided to us; something, we think, must be missing.

But it is not missing; it is simply in a different place. If we put a melody and a rhythmic figure together—a cornet solo, for instance, and a passage of flams, paradiddles or other drum figures for timpani, in any march arrangement that comes to mind—we naturally think of the drums as accompaniment to the cornet. In West Africa, the relationship would be reversed: the drum figure would be considered as the lead and the cornet melody as an accompaniment.

It is for this reason that travellers have usually reported the West African melodic sense to be stunted. This, on investigation, proves far from true. There is, in fact, little to choose between the melodic development of European and West African folk music. But the subjugation, in West African music, of melody to other than melodic or harmonic considerations usually gives the European listener the impression that something in the music has been lost.

What this means in terms of the orchestra should be obvious: whereas our own music has pivoted for centuries on the increasing complexity of harmonic elaboration and the development of a body of melodic instruments capable of being sounded together, West African music has concentrated its efforts essentially on an architecture of rhythmic and coloristic patterns and on the development of a body of percussion instruments capable of being sounded together. Almost every principle of musical form which we have developed over the centuries has its counterpart in West Africa; but whereas we have applied it to melody and harmony, reducing rhythm and timbre to the status of poor relatives, the Africans have applied it to rhythm and timbre, leaving melodic and harmonic development in a subservient form.

West African music, in essence, is built on three formal principles:

1. that of *theme and variation,* which operates by stating a rhythmic pattern and proceeds by developing it through a series of increasingly complex variations;
2. that of the *suite,* which consists of a series of rhythmic patterns sounded successively to build to a cumulative effect;
3. that of *rhythmic counterpoint,* which operates by sounding a number of rhythmic patterns together and includes devices corresponding to our augmentation and diminution, as well as the rhythmic equivalents of such practices as inversion, cancrizans, stretto and ground bass.

Timbre is used primarily to define the function of each theme in the rhythmic polyphony; secondarily, to impart meaning by association with lingual significance; thirdly, to suggest mood in approximately the same sense as we suggest mood by chordal effects.

The particular importance of timbre in West African music was first summed up by Erich von Hornbostel in suggesting that one "compare significant tone in Fanti dialects with vocal vibrato of Fanti singers and check if vibrato effects are noticeable as scalar or harmonic alterations when singing European songs in the diatonic scale." The insight here shown into the relationship between the characteristics of African language on one side and the development of new scalar and harmonic conceptions on the other, has proved the key to the study of African survivals in American music.

We knew forty years ago, when the Hornbostel hypothesis was first suggested, that for more than three hundred years most West African languages had evolved not only from vowels and consonants but also from a third element of articulation which was based simultaneously on variations of pitch, timbre and timing. We have known for some decades that the West African drum language was not a primitive sort of Morse code but a phonetic reproduction of the sound of words; only languages dependent on pitch, vibrato and timing lend themselves to such treatment. The time element was the easiest to reproduce on a drumhead; changes of pitch were effected by changes of pressure on the drum skin; changes of vibrato were effected by vibrating the knees while holding the drum tightly clasped to the drummer's lap, or vibrating the arm while holding it in the armpit.

Thus language and music were not strictly divided, and the average standard of musical talent was correspondingly high. Children learned to discern subtleties of rhythm, melody and tone color as parts of their language. It is this semantic use of melody and timbre rather than the vaunted "African sense of rhythm" which really divides the West African musical tradition from the European one.

When we want to stress a word, we raise our voice—that is to say, we go up in pitch. But in those African languages where a change of pitch on any given syllable may alter the meaning of the entire word, you are left with only one device to emphasize your point: *timbre.* You can alter the *tone color,* the *voice production,* the *vibrato* of the syllable you wish to stress. This combination of pitch and timbre in African language is what the philologists call "significant tone." It has had the most profound effect on the history of American Negro music.

At first sight this appears to be a concept of music formidably different from our own. But viewed in their historical perspective, the differences between West African and European music prove to be far smaller than their common properties. And this is hardly surprising if we remind ourselves that the Mediterranean is a comparatively young lake and that Africa and Europe probably hung together as late as the Upper Paleolithic period.

It seems likely now that the common source of European and West African music was a simple non-hemitonic pentatone system. Although indigenous variants of the diatonic scale have been developed and preserved in Africa, modern West Africans who are not familiar with European music will tend to become uncertain when asked to sing in a tempered scale. This becomes particularly obvious when the third and seventh step of a diatonic scale are approached. The singer almost invariably tries to skid around these steps with slides, slurs or vibrato effects so broad as to approach scalar value.

If it were a matter of slides and slurs alone, we might think—as I myself thought for many years—that we were here dealing simply with a clash between a pentatonic and a diatonic civilization. But the increase in vibrato amplitude, paired with a decrease in frequency upon reaching the third or seventh step of the scale, tells a different tale. It speaks of a clash between two stages of the same diatonic tradition —a clash that has been complicated by the semantic use of timbre and vibrato effects in African speech.

The result of this clash has been the development of a series of characteristic Afro-European scales in places as far apart as West Africa, Suriname, Brazil, Cuba and North America. Out of two of these scales the whole harmonic tradition of American jazz has emerged.

The first of them is the "spiritual" or "shout scale," comprising the tonic, mediant, dominant and part-sharpened subdominant. The other one is the "blues scale," a diatonic major with added or alternative minor thirds and diminished sevenths. At first sight the spiritual scale looks like a somewhat perverted pentatonic, while the blues scale appears to consist simply of subdominant modulations with alternatives of major and minor. On closer inspection, however, all the variable intervals reveal themselves not as regular half-tone modulations but as slurs, glissandi and vibrato effects of precisely the same kind that you can still create experimentally in any part of West Africa by asking a good native singer to tackle a diatonic scale.

As the slaves came to America from all over West Africa and from all levels of West Africa's social hierarchy, so the settlers of the new continent had come from all over Europe and from all classes of European society. Their music contained liturgical and patriotic music, folk songs, drinking songs, ballads, French and Italian opera and the roots of the new symphonic movement developing just then out of the suite and the sonata. The juxtaposition of two musical worlds so wildly ill-assorted could have led to almost anything—and, in fact, did lead to so many varieties of music that no one so far has been able to list more than a tiny fragment. What has survived was not necessarily the best. What has vanished is irretrievable.

Musical contact between slaves and masters was as varied, multiform and unpredictable as their social relationship. Field hands and house servants had anything but equal opportunities to hear the music of their masters. The Dutch, Danes and British were Protestants; the French, Spanish and Portuguese were Catholics. Each brought not only an entirely separate musical tradition, but an entirely different attitude towards morals, ethics and social relationships.

Thus spirituals came into existence solely on the English-speaking, protestant plantations; there is no such thing as a spiritual with French or Spanish lyrics. The Catholic civilization of Louisiana yielded an entirely different slave music: Creole songs and dances that had much more in common with those of Cuba, San Domingo, Martinique and Trinidad than with the "ant'ems" and "ring shouts" of the neighboring plantations owned by Protestants.

But everywhere the influence of white music upon black was paralleled and often surpassed by that of black upon white. Through lullabies and nursery rhymes translated from dimly remembered African tongues, the slaves altered the whole mythology of the white South. Through animal stories (Brer Rabbit), they modelled the childhood imagination of ten generations of upper-class Southerners. Even the white man's religious ceremonialism underwent a gradual change during these years: From Wesley's and Whitefield's 1738 mission to Georgia, through the Red River Camp Meeting of 1799 and the first liturgies of the African Methodist Episcopal Church of 1816, to the Holy Rollers and Holiness Faith Healers of Southwest Virginia, there runs a cultural thread of African origin which left its mark on the behavior pattern of the entire Protestant South. From snake worship, through trance and spirit possession ("getting religion, coming through"), to the song-and-dance patterns of white spirituals and ring shouts, there runs a give-and-take relationship which leaves the Negro by no means the white man's debtor.

It is due to the character of these mutual influences that African music was at all preserved in America. The white plantation system, terrible as it was for those who suffered under it, must yet be considered as a beneficial influence from the purely musical point of view.

Slavery in America, not unlike serfdom in old Russia, was chiefly responsible for the preservation of the people's artistic tradition: the Russian masters encouraged their serfs to dance, just as the Southern masters encouraged their slaves to make music. The master's motive, of course, was not compassion but a combination of pleasure in watching their dance and astuteness in realising that they would do more work if they were allowed to enjoy themselves. Both the Russian serf and the American slave thus obtained in *circenses* what they lacked in *panem:* an ideal state of affairs for the master since he did not have to pay for the *circenses.*

The whole Russian theatre, Haskell once said, owed its origin to the serf. This meant that the ballet became a part of the people, not merely an entertainment provided from without. In Russia, ballet therefore remained in closer contact with folk dancing than in any other country. It could not be destroyed, as it had been in France, by any wave of artificiality, nor could it become the passive instrument of a group of poets.

Similarly, in America, the whole tradition of syncopated popular music owed its origin to the slave. This meant that Afro-American music became a part of the people, not merely an entertainment provided by black-face comedians for a white audience; and that, in the South, popular music continued to preserve a greater contact with Negro folk music than in any other part of the U.S. It could not be destroyed, as the music-hall tradition had been in England, by the coming of the commercialized song industry; nor could it become the passive instrument of a group of businessmen as it did in the North, along Broadway and Tin Pan Alley.

But inevitably all those African songs and dances died out which had no functional need in the pattern of slave-and-master relations. There remained only those songs and dances which fitted into the economic pattern of the new world: work songs, love songs, lullabies, play songs, song games, animal songs, wedding and funeral songs, and a few odd songs to make magic—such as voodoo songs, medicine songs and bewitching songs of other types. Among the songs that died out swiftly were the initiation songs, the legends to perpetuate the history and tradition of the African home community, the epic songs and ballads of famous ancestors, the ritual songs to arouse a sense of group participation, the battle songs, ballads of past victories, legends of dead heroes, and all the other Africanisms that found no parallel in American Negro culture. (Though ballads like *John Henry* have taken part of the place once taken by the legends of dead heroes, and the "bad man ballad" temporarily took that of the epic.)

Of the three main branches of Negro folk music that survived in America—work songs, spirituals and blues—the work songs are most closely related to the African archetype. They are similar to African songs in tune and intonation; rhythmically they differ only in so far as the rhythm of the work itself was different from that of African agriculture.

As early as 1860, Richard F. Burton reported from Central Africa that "the fisherman will accompany his paddle, the porter his trudge, and the housewife her task of rubbing down grain, with song." In 1861, E. Casalis reported of the Basutos that they never worked without music. "To increase the pleasure they find in the regular movements of the hands and feet they hang about their person garlands composed of little bells . . ." and when the women grind their corn in unison, they sing an air which perfectly accords with the rhythm of the tinkling rings and bells. The men, while pounding animal skins to soften them, sing a song which, "though most discordant, is yet in perfect time." If the work is performed solitarily, the songs are soli; if it is done collectively, the songs are choric.

In America, indigo, rice, corn and cotton left their mark on the work songs of the slaves. Roads, levees and railroads are remembered in the work songs of free and chained Negroes. Ballads, blues and jazz tunes have been based on the work-song pattern, from the anonymous *John Henry* to King Oliver's *Lift 'Em Up Joe* and Leadbelly's *On a Monday*. The history of Louisiana commerce has been preserved in the street cries of the hucksters, vendors, *marchands d'oignons,* charcoal, watermelon and Spanish moss sellers of New Orleans. The memories of the Civil War are preserved in the chitlin seller's street cry:

Here's your chitlins fresh and sweet,
Who'll join the Union?
Young hog's chitlins hard to beat,
Methodist chitlins just been boiled,
Right fresh chitlins they aint spoiled,
Baptist chitlins by the pound,
Here's your chitlins fresh and sweet,
Who'll join the Union?

The culinary essence of the Creole country is remembered in the bilingual street call of the *marchand d'oignons:*

Des onions sont à bon marché,
C'est li ci, c'est li ça,
La commerce tournera le dos
C'est li ci, c'est li ça.

Onions for sale!
Sometimes they're high, sometimes they're low.
Onions for sale!
Sometimes they're cheap, sometimes they're *good* cheap.
Onions for sale, onions for sale!

The early years of jazz are remembered in Louis Armstrong's charcoal cry:

My mule is white, my face is black,
I sell my coal two bits a sack.

Meanwhile, on riverboats and clipper ships, the boat songs of the great African rivers survived in the guise of canoe songs and shanties. In South Carolina, paddling songs exactly preserved their West African pattern of two measures to each stroke, the first measure accented by the beginning of the stroke, the second by the backward swing of the paddles.

African boat songs of this type have survived almost unchanged in such spirituals as *Swing Low, One More River To Cross,* and *River Jordan.* The flat-bottomed cotton boats of the eighteenth century, "pettiaugers" and "cotton boxes," were run almost entirely by Negroes. While the crew sang in unison at their work of rowing, poling, and steering, the Negro "patroon," who knew all the changing channels of the rivers, sang out the position of sand bars, shoals and river bends as he directed the huge lumbering flatboats down the tributaries of the South Carolina rivers, down the Mississippi, the Ashley-Cooper, the Coosa-Alabama, the Tombigbee, the Chattahoochee and the Pearl River. From the Ohio to the Rio Grande, Negro rivermen, roustabouts and levee workers thus laid the rudiments of the marine work songs which became known as shanties or chanteys on the oceans of the world.

Between 1812 and 1860, clipper ships out of Baltimore carried "chequered crews," one half white and one half Negro, and it was on these ships that white sailors first picked up the Negro shanties. Joanna C. Colcord, who grew up among sailors, says that while Englishmen or Irishmen were admitted to rank as chanteymen ahead of the white Americans, they were far outstripped by the American Negroes, "the best singers that ever lifted a shanty aboard ship." And Stanton C. King, official Government chanteyman, relates that in his youth, when on a voyage from Philadelphia to Japan and back to New York, there was need of a song leader, the Negro stewardess, wife of the cook on the vessel, came out of the galley and led the men in chantey singing.

When steamboats appeared on the rivers and oceans, Negroes still continued as windlass and capstan chanteymen. Mark Twain, in *Life on the Mississippi,* speaks of "the half crew of Negroes" who "were roaring such songs as *De las sack, de las sack,* inspired to unimaginable exultation by the chaos of turmoil and racket." Some of the best-known songs of America were first sung by the Negro rivermen of this period. *Swannee River* was based on a Mississippi capstan chantey named *Mobile River.* Shenandoah was first known as a Negro windlass chantey named *Shanadore.* The Sally of *Sally Brown* was identified by Cecil Sharp as the Sally who "lives on the Old Plantation. She belongs to the Wild Goose Nation." *Molly Was A Good Gal* was variously known among Negro chanteymen as *Noah's Ark, Mother Dinah* and *Sing Sally-O.*

The *Camptown Races* was based on a Negro chantey named *Sing and Heave. The Black Ball Line* was first sung by Negro cotton crews as *He-Back She-Back,* or *Santa Anna. Blow, Boys, Blow* was known as *A Yankee Ship on the Congo River. Down the Ohio* was a Cincinnati levee song first raised by Negro roustabouts. *Roll the Cot-*

ton Down came from South Carolina. *Row, Michael, Row* was the South Carolina source of *Blow, Boys, Blow*. *Rock Me Julie* was a Mississippi River song of the 1830's. *I'm Going to Texas* was a Negro firemen's song on the Red River.

On the plantations, meanwhile, there survived the old *dokpwé* songs of Dahomey, which gave rise to such varied forms as the calypsos of Trinidad, the *corvée* songs of Haiti and the corn songs of America. In the cotton belt, such songs as *Pick a Bale of Cotton* and *Round the Corn, Sally*, first noted in 1867 in *Slave Songs of the United States*, preserved the African custom of bands of singers following the men as they worked in the fields, clapping their hands in rhythm to the song and inciting the workers to greater labor. In the rice country, too, the singers followed the workers, clapping their hands and stamping their feet in time to the work. On Thursdays the fields were generally cut down by hand with small reap hooks, the long golden heads being carefully laid on the tall stubble to dry until the next day, when the Negro workers skillfully tied them into sheaves with wisps of the rice itself. Saturday the sheaves were stacked in small cocks to dry through Sunday; on Monday they were loaded on to the flatboats to be floated down to the marketing place—and every one of these operations were accompanied by work songs.

The "hollers"—thin, wailing cries, sometimes on a single note with the index finger vibrating the larynx—were directly borrowed from African sources to serve as means of communication between slave workers. Out of their tradition a great many work songs and blues developed in later years.

The French work songs were pushed out by the English work songs as the English slave owners pushed the French out of the Colonies. A few French work songs can still be heard in the Creole patois of Louisiana, but most of the surviving work songs are sung in New World Negro idioms based mainly on English words. They are almost completely uninfluenced by European tunes; they are powerfully rhythmical because they were sung by the slaves, sometimes chained, who had to work in rhythmical unison; they tell the story of the damming of the Mississippi, of the hewing of rocks, of the digging of furrows, of the picking of cotton, of the planting and cutting of sugar cane—of the building of the whole Southern agricultural economy. The phrases of the songs are separate from one another, each being, for instance, an accompaniment of the lifting of the hammers, while the intervals between them synchronized with the descent of the hammers and the pause just after they had reached the ground.

Thus the Negro work song became another example of the Negro's attempt to make the agonies of slavery bearable by integrating them with the images of his African past. There was no getting away from the miseries of plantation labor, so the work was infused with the songs of better days, and soon the songs were to influence the music of the slaves and their descendants. Thus oppression somersaults into cultural infiltration, and yesterday's slave becomes today's cultural mentor.

Spirituals, the first original songs created by Protestant Negro slaves on American soil, can very easily be dated from the changes and fluctuations in the theological attitude towards slavery. Up to the middle of the seventeenth century, the churches of all denominations strongly discouraged missionary activities among slaves in the belief that slavery and Christian brotherhood were incompatible and that slavery could therefore be defended only if its victims were, and remained, savages. From the middle of the seventeenth century to the beginning of the eighteenth century this attitude became increasingly suspect, and under the growing challenge of the Pennsylvania Quakers, Baptist and Methodist churches began to reconsider their attitude towards the question of slave proselytism.

By the middle of the eighteenth century, this reconsideration had led to a diametrical reversal of the original attitude. Now it was held that the conversion of savages to the light of God was by itself a justification and, in fact, the *only* Christian justification for slavery. The Methodist revival movement began to address itself directly to the slaves, but ended up not by converting the Africans to a Christian ritual but by converting itself into an African ritual.

It is from this revival movement, which flourished from about 1790 to 1883, that the bulk of white spirituals originated. Such Africanisms as spirit possession in the form of "coming through" and "getting religion" (which survives in the bulk of white American sectarian cults from the Holy Rollers to Aimee McPherson) can be traced back fairly accurately to this period.

We can therefore place most spirituals into a definite period of American history if we divide such varieties as hymns, ring shouts, revival chants, camp-meeting songs and funeral marches into three basic patterns of origin:

1. *Adaptations of African ritual music to Christian liturgy.* Here the form and attitude of African worship survives in the guise of Christianity. Thus the Dahomey River God ceremony was incorporated into Baptism. Spirit possession became possession by the Holy Ghost. The gods of West Africa became fused with the Trinity and the College of Saints. The bad spirits merged with Lucifer and Sammael. The snake gods of West Africa survived in the snake of Eden and the beasts of the Apocalypse.

Negro Christians took great care to preserve the semblance of propriety in these rituals. Dancing, for instance, was considered worldly and evil. Yet dancing was an inseparable part of African ritual. By way of compromise, dancing was defined biblically as "crossing of feet," and as long as no feet were crossed, dancing thus became permissible. The shuffling step of the ring shout was developed, a ritual which is wholly African in derivation and yet manages to derive a Christian justification from the Biblical descriptions of angels "shouting" in heaven. According to the May 30, 1867, *Nation:*

> The true "shout" takes place on Sundays or on "praise nights" through the week, and either in the praise house or in some cabin in which a regular religious meeting has been held. . . . The benches are pushed back to the wall when the formal meeting is over, and old and young, men and women . . . all stand up in the middle of the floor, and when the "sperchil" is struck up, begin first walking and by-and-by shuffling round, one after the other, in a ring. The foot is hardly taken from the floor, and the progression is mainly due to a jerking, hitching motion which agitates the entire shoulder and soon brings out streams of perspiration. Sometimes they dance silently, sometimes, as they shuffle, they sing the chorus of the spiritual, and sometimes the song itself is also sung by the dancers. But more frequently a band, composed of some of the best singers and of tired shouters, stand at the side of the room to "base" the others, singing the body of the song and clapping their hands together or on their knees. Song and dance alike are extremely energetic and often, when the shout lasts into the middle of the night, the monotonous thud thud of the feet prevents sleep itself within half a mile of the praise house.

2. *Songs spontaneously created by a preacher and his congregation.* Here the natural rise and fall of Negro speech, intensified by the highly rhythmical and dynamic "strain" of Negro preaching and counterpointed by the antiphonal interlocutions and exclamations of

the congregation, yielded new words and tunes at almost every church meeting, and though many of the songs thus created were as quickly forgotten as they were created, many others have survived and have been garnished, pruned, transcribed and arranged until they became part and parcel of the permanent store of American folk music.

3. *Negro variations on European ecclesiastical tunes.* Here the words rather than the music provided the initial attraction to the Negro listener. Christianity, as a Jewish religion, was an ideology of protest against centuries of political and economic oppression. Palestine was under almost constant domination from bellicose neighbors, each one of whom suppressed the Mosaic religion and carried its believers into slavery. The Negroes saw their own fate reflected in these chronicles of faith and patience in exile: as the slaves of Rome had turned to Judaism, so the slaves of America now turned to Christianity.

And as the Negroes infused their masters' religion with meanings of their own, so they infused their masters' religious music with African structural alterations. The Anglican Hymnal, Wesleyan harmony, John Bacchus Dykes—all furnished the raw material for a new ecclesiastical music which preserved little more than a few bars of tune, a basic pattern of harmony and a vague similarity of wording. By 1867, when William Francis Allen and Lucy McKim Garrison published their first spirituals, such white hymns as *Climb Jacob's Ladder, Give Me Jesus,* and *I'll Take the Wings of the Morning* had already been so profoundly changed that they could rightfully be considered as new Negro creations.

This process of assimilation and transformation has caused one of the most absurd controversies in American musicology. White opportunists have attached theories of the special-pleading type to their gleeful discovery that the Negro, after all, had to steal the white man's music because, evidently, he lacked the Nordic talent for creative composition. Negro opportunists, hurt in their racial pride, replied with more special pleading, this time from the other side, trying to prove that the Negro, after all, was the first and the white man the imitator.

The only reasonable judgment in the early years of the controversy came from the other side of the Atlantic: "The great mass of these songs are real folksongs of American Negro origin," Hornbostel pointed out; "they are not imitations, nor are they African songs influenced by the white man, but they are songs made by the Negro in European style. Had the Negro slaves been taken to China instead of to America, they would have developed folksongs in Chinese style . . . this facility for adaptation is by no means a sign of inferiority. Only a race so highly gifted for music could do this." And again: "The American Negro songs are European in style and pattern. They are American folksongs as far as they have originated amidst American folk and culture; they are African when sung by Negroes, and only then."

The transformation is mainly one of rhythm, inflection and vibrato. "At first sight, when comparing the written music of African and American Negroes, one would think that they have nothing in common." But "you will readily recognize an African Negro by seeing him dance and by hearing him sing. . . . This way of the Negro is identical in Africa and in America."

While the whole European tradition strives for regularity—of pitch, of time, of timbre and of vibrato—the African tradition strives precisely for the negation of these elements. In language, the African tradition aims at circumlocution rather than at exact definition. The direct statement is considered crude and unimaginative; the veiling of all contents in ever-changing paraphrases is considered the criterion of intelligence and personality. In music, the same tendency towards obliquity and ellipsis is noticeable: no note is attacked straight; the voice or instrument always approaches it from above or below, plays around the implied pitch without ever remaining on it for any length of time, and departs from it without ever having committed itself to a single meaning. The timbre is veiled and paraphrased by constantly changing vibrato, tremolo and overtone effects. The timing and accentuation, finally, are not *stated,* but *implied* or *suggested.* The musician challenges himself to find and hold his orientation while denying or withholding all signposts.

Rhythmically, this process takes the form not only of syncopation, polyrhythm, stop time and multiple bar divisions, but also of shifted accents, which are not normally considered of a dynamic nature in European music. To the African, however, all accents are grist for the mill, and any phrase, once established as a definite musical figure, becomes immediately accessible as a source of rhythmic variation. Every note within the phrase, every pattern of pitch and timbre, every line of melodic or harmonic progression, any structural pattern at all is evaluated as part of a rhythmic structure and treated accordingly.

The Wesleyan and Methodist hymns, which formed the original themes of a great many spirituals, were therefore transformed by American Negroes in a fairly predictable manner: The accent was shifted from the strong to the weak beat; only one or two lines out of the total length of the tune were accepted and these were varied in repetition by shifted beats, glissando and vibrato effects, and finally by the introduction of mobile thirds and sevenths.

Inevitably, rhythmic variations had their effect on the whole structure of the song. All untrained singers, Africans as well as Occidentals, tend to sharpen the accented beats and to flatten the unaccented ones. Thus, strong beats shifted to weak ones by syncopation tend to be flattened in the process, and the African's natural tendency to diminish certain notes and chords of the diatonic scale was confirmed and encouraged. Moreover, syncopation tends to encourage glissando and portamento effects, and these were exactly the effects most natural to the African sense of variation.

But these were merely the crude rudiments of Afro-American music as they first appeared in the early spirituals. Soon further characteristics of the process of adaptation became noticeable. A new interpretation of harmony appeared. Early spirituals like *Blin' Man Lyin' at the Pool, The New Born Baby, Go Tell It on the Mountains, The Gospel Train, Swing Low Sweet Chariot, Nobody Knows the Trouble I've Seen* and *Somebody Knockin' At Your Door* still preserved the pentatonic structure, though varying it by sharpening the subdominant. This scale, then, is the "spiritual scale" whose African origins were described at the beginning of this article.

Later examples like *Oh Brother, Don't Get Weary, Troubled in Mind* and *Roll, Jordan, Roll* showed the use of a new diatonic scale with added or alternative minor thirds and diminished sevenths. "Blue fifths" were used to lead into descending phrases based on tonic or subdominant chords, "blue ninths" appeared against simple tonic harmony, and partially sharpened subdominants appeared halfway between the mediant and the dominant. As soon as the banjo, an African instrument by name as well as by origin, became tuned to diatonic harmony, parallel thirds, dominant sevenths and ninths began to replace simple triads. Soon chromatic progressions of seventh chords became as common in spiritual voicing as in barbershop guitar fingering.

Simultaneously, a new interpretation of the time signature and the bar line appeared. The African tradition of ternary division of the single beat met with the duple time signature of European hymnology and found a new compromise in a duple division grouped into three-plus-three-plus-four. As opposed to the three-against-four of the European tradition, the ternary treble part in many spirituals did not coincide with the duple or quadruple time of the "lead" or bass, but tended to distort it so that the third beat of the treble part coincided with the second beat of the "lead," while the second beat of the treble's next measure coincided with the third beat of the "lead." By the time the "lead" marked the last beat of its first bar, the treble had reached the first beat of its third bar. The bar, as it were, was split metrically rather than accentually, and this principle, in the form of "secondary rag," later became one of the basic patterns of ragtime and New Orleans jazz.

When men, women and children sang together, their voices naturally fell into a sort of three-part harmony, but the placing of the voices within these three parts rarely coincided with the traditions of European part song. The voicing, in accordance with the African tradition of overlapping call-and-response phrases, was contrapuntal rather than harmonic: each part preserved a rhythmic as well as a melodic line of its own. Rhythmically, the tenor voice marked the beat, either by accentuating or by omitting it, taking care not to delay or anticipate the beat unless the singer sang solo. The alto or soprano voices, weaker in volume than the tenor voices, were heard at their best in the empty spaces left by the male voices, that is to say, on the off-beats or in the pauses at the end of a phrase. Thus, whether singing long legato notes without marked accents or multi-note phrases with marked off-beat accents, the treble part tended to develop a much more highly syncopated melodic line than the middle part. The bass voices, meanwhile, filled in the missing impetus, both rhythmically and harmonically, by glissando and portamento effects, as well as by filling in the third or fifth chords.

Further rhythmic accents were placed with handclaps and footbeats. The handclaps generally marked the off-beats while the feet marked the strong beats. Some members of the congregation would further stress the off-beat by clapping their hands a little after the weak beat, giving a dotted duration to it as the jazz drummer does in the press roll. A stop-time effect was frequently obtained by omitting all rhythmic accents except handclaps for a number of bars.

Another method of syncopated voicing was found in curtailing the end of one line and the start of the next so as to insert short solo passages whose timing stood in direct or in implied contrast to the adjoining lines of music. After a while, these solo passages became standardized and traditional and were then used contrapuntally against the melodic line in a manner not dissimilar to that which the walking bass motives in boogie-woogie piano playing or of riffs in swing music arrangements were to take many decades later.

Thus spirituals and ring shouts came to provide one of the main sources of Negro jazz. Lucy McKim Garrison's letter to *Dwight's Magazine* in 1862 contains the first reliable cross reference between spirituals, ring shouts, camp meeting songs and jubilee hymns, and her 1867 collection of Negro songs contains ecclesiastical examples of blue notes, shifted accents, ragged time, rhythmical counterpoint and all those other characteristics out of which ragtime, jazz and the rest of secular Negro music grew during the next five or six decades. Ten years before the first ragtime was published, such Negro spirituals as *Good Lord'll Help Me on My Way* had ragtime accompaniments in their published piano transcriptions.

When ragtime gave way to jazz, jazz turned to the spiritual for inspiration as ragtime had done half a century before. Songs like *Nearer My God to Thee, Flee as a Bird, Just a Closer Walk with Thee, Just a Little While To Stay Here, Sometimes My Burden Is Hard To Bear, Lord You're Certainly Good to Me* have thus served as fountainheads of jazz from Bolden's time to the present day.

NEW ORLEANS
AND TRADITIONS
IN JAZZ

~~~~~~~~~~~~~~~~~~~~~

Charles Edward Smith

Charles Edward Smith was one of the very first American writers on jazz. He began writing in 1930. His best-known book is *Jazzmen* (Harcourt, Brace, 1939), co-edited with Fred Ramsey, Jr., and now available in a Harvest paperback. Smith reviews books on jazz regularly for *The New York Times Book Review*, and free-lances for magazines. He also writes long, detailed booklets for Folkways Records' sets of folk music and jazz. One of Smith's particular areas of specialization has been the music of New Orleans, although he is expert in many other aspects of jazz.

"Is there any music?"
"Music? You don't need none."
"How am I going to play?"
"You're going to come in on the choruses."
—Picou, c. 1895, *Hear Me Talkin' To Ya*

In 1956 an impressive reception was accorded the Louis Armstrong All-Stars at the Polo Grounds at Accra in Ghana. They looked out open a sea of humanity that stirred restlessly, like the slow pulse of the slack tide. Many had come from tribal villages hundreds of miles distant and had never before heard Western music. Near at hand could be seen the beautifully designed fabrics that made the scene riotous with color. As the people waited, crowd noises died down and the ritual drums "talked," introducing the All-Stars, some of whose ancestors, hundreds of years ago, had brought the fertile seed of jazz from these same shores.

To be sure, jazz is an *indigenous American* music, as are the blues, hollers and spirituals. Of songs that sustained the slaves during the torturous "middle passage," little more than musical elements were allowed to survive, along with a knowledge of instruments. Since religious customs, language and language arts were discouraged, musical and related elements from tribal life often went into the process of regenerating types of Western European music, rather than carrying on traditions from West Africa.

Documentary material on plantation life indicates that from Colonial times the musical gift of the slaves was welcomed. It enhanced their well-being and productivity. Dancing went into American Negro background, also, because it was—as it is in West Africa today—a part of the life and the music. Of the highly developed skills in plastic arts, little remained to testify to them—a grave marker in a Georgia cemetery,[1] craftsmanship as displayed in the interior woodwork of the Ursuline Convent in New Orleans.[2]

There were few attempts to enfold tribal religious beliefs into

[1] Illus. in *The Story of Jazz,* by Marshall W. Stearns (Oxford U. Press, 1956).
[2] Illus. in *New Orleans City Guide,* American Guide Series (Houghton, Mifflin, 1939).

Christian rituals, as in many Latin-American countries, and—whatever their similarity to religious songs of the Caribbean area, for example—the spirituals of the South were the unique product of an indigenous American strain. In the Colonies and in what was to become the Louisiana Territory the tribal music of West Africa gradually disappeared, but meanwhile, chanting its death, the Africans planted the seed of a new and American music.

Even before Emancipation the seed became the shout, the sermon and the song, out of which jazz grew. In its present state, however, jazz does not suggest any *direct* ties to Africa. Speaking of the interior (tribal) African communities and their reaction to jazz— in contrast to urban centers that have both Western instruments and Western music—Wilbur de Paris, jazz trombonist on tour for the U.S. State Department, remarked, "Their reaction was one of curiosity—the down-to-earth African doesn't have a record player. And after all," he added, "their melodic construction is different than ours."

From even such a cursory summary as the above, it is clear that West African heritage, in its most significant aspect, that of music, may best be studied from an anthropological and musicological approach. Not surprisingly, few Negro Americans feel cultural ties to Africa. Their roots are in the South. Their music is American and no tradition relates it back to African music in the same way that certain aspects of American singing relate back step by step to traditions of the British Isles. Nevertheless, the powerful influence of African music on American, from field calls to concert music, insures that the African heritage will one day be a matter of pride to us all.

"Is it possible to believe that the African carried this rich musical tradition to America unconsciously?" Alan P. Merriam inquires in a study of "The African Background." [3] He goes on to say:

> Of course he was conscious of it in this sense; it was only "unconscious" in the sense that it was not necessarily verbalized as to its harmonies, scale steps, or to its artistic values in terms of deep discussions of what constitutes creative activity.
>
> Let me summarize: There is nothing mysterious about learned cultural behaviour. And most certainly the African was well aware of his music which, in Africa and later in the New World, played such an important part in his life.

---

[3] *The Record Changer*, pp. 7, 8. Nov. 1952.

Underlying all early jazz, and at the core of jazz style, was the impact of oral tradition upon written music. Garvin Bushell, in what is perhaps *only a little* too sweeping a statement, said:

> There wasn't an Eastern performer who could really play the blues. We later absorbed how from the Southern musicians we heard, but it wasn't original with us. We didn't put that quarter-tone pitch in the music the way the Southerners did. Up North we leaned to rag-time conception. . . . Most of the Negro population in New York . . . were trying to forget the traditions of the South. . . . *You could hear the blues and real jazz in the gutbucket cabarets where the lower class went.*[4]

When Mr. Garvin asserts, "By and large, the Negro musicians from the Southeast were technically better than the musicians from the Southwest and Louisiana" (he *excepts* the Creole-trained musicians), he is unwittingly basing his judgment on musical standards of the time, which alone had prestige. *Though they were to rock the world, standards of musicianship based on oral tradition had as yet (in the early 1920's) no accepted worth or renown, except on a very limited scale.* Blues-based timbre was classified as roughness of tone by some New Orleans musicians, not all of them of Creole background. (Ultimately it was canonized by young jazzmen of a much later period in the term "funky.") Fullness of tone, born of blues and brass bands, so distinctive in New Orleans playing, was described in terms of "loudness," even by New Orleanians, *e.g.,* "King Oliver was so powerful he used to blow a cornet out of tune every two or three months."[5] When asked why he clung to the difficult Albert system of fingering on clarinet, Edmond Hall replied, "The tone of the Boehm is not as big as the Albert."

Half a century after Kid Bolden was on the way to becoming King Bolden, first in a hierarchy of *hot,* Aaron Copland was to describe the type of music that began in New Orleans in the last century:

> On the firm basic pulse of the rhythm section the melodic instruments were able to weave an independent melodic and rhythmic counterpoint, such as needs careful listening to if all the subtleties of tone color and rhythmic variety are to be heard.[6]

[4] My emphasis—C.E.S. Quoted from the interesting study, "New York Jazz in the 1920's," by Nat Hentoff, published serially in *The Jazz Review,* 1959.

[5] Louis Armstrong in *Swing That Music* (Longmans, Green, 1936), p. 25.

[6] *Our New Music,* by Aaron Copland (Whittlesey House, 1941), p. 96.

Contrary to some reports, music by Negro dance bands was available on phonograph records prior to the release of performances by New Orleans jazzmen such as Oliver. Comparison with jazz was possible, for those who cared to take the trouble. Early jazz collectors, without benefit of critics, discovered the uniqueness of jazz, as did countless young musicians. There were very fine drummers associated with the ragtime and post-ragtime periods in the North, yet Warren "Baby" Dodds, Zutty Singleton and their colleagues were and are accepted as *the* pioneers of jazz drumming. Indeed, the basic instruments of jazz were all pioneered in its home city. Though the piano was not to join the band until jazz took hold in the North, Ferdinand "Jelly Roll" Morton not only brought the piano into jazz but developed a piano style based in part on New Orleans band styles, as is demonstrated in *The Incomparable Jelly Roll Morton* (Riverside RLP 12–128) and *New Orleans Memories* (Commodore 30001).

Though he had begun to learn rudiments and reading while at the "Waif's Home"—as the municipal home for boys in New Orleans was then called—Louis Armstrong never underestimated the unwritten discipline related to the blues and the beat. He seems to have realized it was providential that he should have remained to master the horn within the milieu of oral tradition. And he leaves no doubt as to the processes by which jazzmen learned their craft. "I think it turned out for the best," he wrote, "that I did not go East at that time [when offered a job with Fletcher Henderson in New York at the age of 18]. I still had a lot to learn about jazz playing *and there in New Orleans, and later on riverboats and on Chicago's South Side, I was living and working all the time around men who could teach me what I needed."* [7]

Jazz, whether close to the concert hall or the barrelhouse in style, tends to become sterile when it strays too far from its oral traditions —including improvisation, as fundamental to jazz as to West African music. This is so even though, on the basis of what is readily measurable, a superficial case can be made out for jazz as having derived largely from western European music. It is when one begins to ask what distinguishes jazz from other music—and this goes for blues, spirituals and many work songs as well—that one realizes that the measurable factors are to be discerned more often in subtler elements

[7] My emphasis—C.E.S. Op. cit. pp. 34, 35.

of style and technique than in large, complex developments of form. But the latter, too, relate to devices in blues, spirituals and work songs such as breaks (brief cadenzas) and riffs (repeated two- or four-bar phrases, *e.g.,* riff arrangements). Such elements, the subtler and the readily apparent, assume considerable importance in assaying to what extent traditions now basic to jazz derived from West African sources.

An unfortunate result of much early research has been the promulgation of the fallacy—by no means yet laid low—that almost the sole contribution from West African music has been rhythmic. In his introduction to *African and Afro-American Drums* (Folkways FE 4502), Harold Courlander notes, with regard to African influence on jazz, "The factors that have to be taken into account go far beyond the element of rhythm. Melodic structure and harmonic concepts must be considered. So must the style of presentation. . . ." Even the lyric form of blues, as well as of some spirituals and work songs, suggests correspondences with structure and metaphoric usage in West African songs.

The singing of work songs is not only occupational but cultural. It didn't take plantation owners of the old South long to realize that African work gangs, *in contrast to most other ethnic groups,* were accustomed to work to common rhythms, supplied by their own voices and accented by the tools with which they worked. The typically African use of antiphonal style and overlapping parts is also often present in spirituals and blues. It may well have been that Afro-American work songs, preserving traditional ways of singing, made possible the distinctive character of spirituals and blues. Certainly, in the work songs, as Harold Courlander remarked, "The African elements are generally discerned more clearly than in any other forms." [8]

In speaking of West African music, Melville J. Herskovits wrote: "The pattern whereby the statement of a theme by a leader is repeated by a chorus, or a short choral phrase is balanced as a refrain against a longer melodic line sung by a soloist, is fundamental. . . ." [9] And regarding elements in jazz deriving from West Africa, Alan P. Merriam states, "Certainly one of these is the riff, represented in

---

[8] Quoted in my introduction to *Folk Music, U.S.A.* (Folkways FE 4530).
[9] *The Myth of the Negro Past,* by Melville J. Herskovits (Harper, 1941), p. 265.

African music by the phrases repeated over and over by members of the chorus in alternation with the melodic line sung by the leader." [10]

Jelly Roll Morton defined the use of the riff as background and foundation; he regarded the use of breaks and riffs as fundamental to jazz. An example of the riff as used in folk music is *Help Me Mama* on a 78-r.p.m. disc by the Staple Singers of Chicago (Vee-Jay 856, 78 r.p.m., or Vee-Jay 45–856, 45 r.p.m.). An excellent example of its use in jazz is the support given Jimmy Rushing's voice in *Goin' to Chicago Blues,* in *Count Basie Classics* (Columbia CL 754). The riff is employed in Jelly Roll's piano solo of *King Porter Stomp* and employed structurally in Fletcher Henderson's arrangement of the same tune for the Benny Goodman Orchestra.

With regard to instruments, the West Africans were far from impoverished. Basic blowing and percussive patterns were all there at the coming of the slavers. Seemingly improvised devices for musical purposes—as Courlander points out in notes for *Sonny Terry's Washboard Band* (Folkways FA 2006)—were not the result of sudden inspiration in music of the Deep South. Many homemade instruments —the washtub bass, the valveless horn, the pie pan and the washboard—had their counterparts in West Indian and African instruments. A variety of trumpet and trombone mutes that owe their modern development to jazz began with a search for surfaces that would modify the blowing sounds, assuring timbres not unlike those achieved by folk instruments. Buddy Bolden employed such makeshift mutes as half a coconut shell, a bathroom plunger and an old derby hat; King Oliver used a child's sand pail.

To be sure, down-to-earth sounds (as distinct from more refined noises) are typical of much folk usage, both instrumental and vocal, but—especially as one comes to appreciate our musically gifted cousins of the Caribbean, and the differences and similarities between their music and ours—the suggestion of African antecedents in jazz, *speaking of jazz as a music of instruments appropriate to it,* is hard to escape. If jazz awarded an "Oscar" (this must not be construed as a suggestion), it might fittingly be in the form of an African earthbow. This apparent development of the spring snare (for catching animals) was the ancestor of the washtub bass (Courlander), *which, in turn, determined the new ways Jimmie Johnson of the Bolden band*

[10] Op. cit.

was to play the string bass, plucking and slapping as well as bowing.

Two decades ago Bunk Johnson was swinging his hefty paws in the cane fields of Louisiana. George Lewis, a lean, wiry man who played occasionally for brass bands when he wasn't unloading banana boats on the levee, was unknown outside New Orleans. Both men played in what appeared to be an older style than that of traditional jazz—not imitatively but because the changes in jazz, beginning with Chicago in the 1920's, had passed them by. The relationship of Bunk's band to earlier styles is suggested when one compares it to Keppard's recordings of 1926. (Keppard's *Stockyard Strut* is in Folkways' *Jazz, Vol. 5, FJ 2805.*) Meanwhile Oliver, younger than the others by a few years, had already contributed fresh ideas to orchestral jazz; his recorded output of 1923 was to furnish the cornerstone of classic jazz. The music of the Creole Jazz Band, with its irresistibly moving tempos, the swiftly paced and fluid clarinet above the brasses, was more definitely related to jazz-in-brass than Bunk's ensemble, which, like Keppard's, bears some resemblance to descriptions of Bolden's ensemble style.

The Bolden style has been described by many musicians, some of whom actually worked with Bolden, and whose memories, by and large, may be assumed to be trustworthy. A summary of it would have many points in common with the following graphic description of Bunk's ensemble style:

> All the parts are played in a sort of pseudo unison, or at least the parts are in similar rhythmic values. Of course they never are in true unison nor are they hit off rhythmically together, and naturally almost every sin known to European musical culture is committed—lack of precision, out of tunefulness, smears, muffs—in other words we have with us once again the well known "sloppy New Orleans ensemble"—but an ensemble of whose unpredictable rhythms, vitalizing accents, and independence of parts (even when played isometrically) are more thrilling than any symphonic group. There has been much talk about New Orleans counterpoint, but the performance of Bunk's orchestra, among others, suggests that possibly New Orleans ensemble style is more of a heterphony than a polyphony.[11]

In the 1890's many elements, musical and social, brought jazz into being. The blues, brass bands and the stimulating effect of piano

[11] William Russell in *Jazz Music,* October, 1943.

rags were part of it. When a Supreme Court decision upheld state segregation laws in an interpretation of the Fourteenth Amendment to the Constitution, many Negroes reared in a Creole (French-American) culture turned towards "uptown" and the sounds of the country, towards Bolden and the blues. The opening up of Storyville, its bordellos and its cabarets, gave an unexpected boost to this new uninhibited music, despised by the arbiters of culture and later castigated in the press. In the 1920's jazz continued to be held in low repute, but just as the sporting-life district of New Orleans gave it show windows to the South and the Southwest, the speakeasies of Prohibition gave it show windows on a national scale.

Studies in country-music backgrounds, such as those undertaken by Frederic Ramsey, Jr., under a Guggenheim Fellowship, and in early New Orleans jazz (a Tulane University Project enlisting the help of William Russell, the father of jazz musicology—who was, incidentally, a student of Arnold Schönberg—and financed by the Ford Foundation) are bound to relate to projects more closely allied to anthropology, such as Harold Courlander's field trip in Western Alabama, sponsored by The Wenner-Gren Foundation and, like Mr. Ramsey's study, represented in a Folkways series. Also to be noted is such independent research as that of Samuel B. Charters.

In a study of jazz origins, many details would suggest influences from outside New Orleans, or at least not exclusively New Orleanian. For example, the music of New Orleans bands that inspired the exuberant "second line"—a sort of dancing congregation with kids toting instrument cases—had its parallel in music remote from it, such as that of Brazilian street marches. Also related to it, but nearer at hand, was the music of country brass bands, of which Frederic Ramsey, Jr., wrote,

> The rhythm set up by these bands is not a tight, regular march step; it is more of a flowing anticipatory emphasis and counter-emphasis, ideally suited to a free style of dance. The Negro brass bands indulge in very little "concertizing" in the grand manner: "Any piece we strike," says George Herod, "they'll dance by it." [12]

Many minstrel shows were from New Orleans, or wintered there, and undoubtedly this made for an interchange of musical ideas long

[12] *Music From The South. Vol. I: Country Brass Bands* (Folkways FA 2650).

before Bolden got to calling his children home. New Orleans was a music-publishing center, though on a lesser scale than some cities, and phonograph records were made there, as in many urban centers. The triumph of the Onward, over other brass bands, in band competition in 1891—first locally and then, in New York, out-playing bands from other states—was noted proudly in *The Freeman.* Edmond Hall's father was in that band, probably relatives of other present-day jazzmen as well.

There were two types of minstrels, one more roughhouse than the other; the rougher type of minstrel was the first to employ jazz musicians very widely. It was the whistle-stop, crossroads minstrel that gave work to such people as Butterbeans and Susie, Ma Rainey, etc. W. C. Handy worked with a minstrel company that prided itself on its musicianship, Mahara's Minstrels. P. G. Lowery, a cornet virtuoso, once wrote of Handy in *The Freeman:* "W. C. Handy's street work is smooth, his triple-tonguing is brilliant, and he certainly plays a song to suit me."

But though Handy played with a relatively well-behaved minstrel group, he was the man who brought the blues, fused with elements of ragtime and minstrels, into popular songs. Since his songs were related to jazz, publication and early popularity of them undoubtedly helped to prepare the public for things to come. His use of the word "blues" in a song title in 1912 (whether or not he was the first to use it is immaterial) did more to "sell" the blues than anything previous to that time. The songs of jazz (Memphis) and the sounds of jazz (New Orleans) met in the minstrels.

It should be of interest to all concerned with the history of American music, and processes of acculturation, to remark pertinent news items in *The Freeman* during 1914, the year that Handy's *St. Louis Blues* was published. A Northern producer was coming out with "The Smart Set," which a minstrel group down Georgia way was to lambast in slapstick as "The Smarter Set." In January, Eiler's New Orleans Minstrels—an "All Colored Show," under canvas, traveling in "two elegant Pullman cars"—advertised for musicians and performers who could "double" in baseball. In February an editorial complained that "There is no colored star in a white theatre except Mr. Bert Williams in vaudeville . . .", and a report came from the Dixie Theatre in Atlanta that "Irene Cook, Ruby Taylor, Bessie Smith and Ada Lockhardt are all doing well and making good."

In March the Silas Green Company (minstrels) advertised their band: "They plays the blues, that's all!" and in the same month it was announced that a soloist featured blues on the calliope with J. C. O'Brien's Famous Georgia Minstrels. But Wolcott's "A Rabbit Foot Company" was having none of it. "When it comes to real music," opined Freddie Pratt, "we can well boast, that we don't have to play the so-called 'blues' as we are far above that standard of musicianship." But Freddie, with the bounce of a born press agent, was back on May second with, "Our orchestra is screaming them with those 'Jago Blues,' and the Gold Band is rendering 'Poet And Peasant' with desired effect."

In June, on the Negro vaudeville circuit later known familiarly as T.O.B.A., Rose Morton of Ferd and Rose Morton

> . . . puts over the "Blues" to the satisfaction of audiences who for some reason take very kindly to this type of singing. Mr. Morton . . . plays a good piano, classics and rags with equal ease. His one hand stunt, left hand alone, playing a classic selection, is a good one. They do an amusing comedy bit, singing "That Ain't Got 'Em." This is sung in duo style. They make a hit of this, which is Morton's own composition. In fact, he composes most of his own songs and arranges his other work. As a comedian, Morton is grotesque in his makeup and sustains himself nicely. . . . They are a clever pair, giving a pleasing show.

Meanwhile, Jones & Jones provided "genteel comedy and blues" for C. W. Parks, Jim Jackson was with Silas Green and Abby Sutton, a "coon shouter," was at Frank Lala's Storyville cabaret. The social columns in December noted that A. Moteger, director of the Tuxedo Brass Band, in which Louis Armstrong, Zutty Singleton and many other jazzmen were to play, entertained friends at a gumbo dinner. In 1958 the successor to this group, The Young Tuxedo Brass Band, recorded *Jazz Begins* (Atlantic 1297).

Alphonse Picou, born in 1879, first heard jazz when he was a boy, played by the Excelsior Brass Band. In an interview [13] he said, "Was it ragtime? No, no, it was nothing but marches they was playing—brass marches—parade music." Later he heard rags in jazz. This, plus other documentary reports, confirms that brass bands shared importance with blues at the very beginning of jazz.

The brass bands—and bands related to them, in minstrels and

[13] *Hear Me Talkin' to Ya*, Shapiro-Hentoff (Rinehart, 1957), p. 18.

on riverboats—provided the instruments used in early jazz. Even the practices of the funeral band had a direct bearing on the genesis of jazz. During the ceremony musicians played written music and, if they could not read, as was often the case, played it by ear. After the ceremony, the music was group improvisation in the jazz-march genre. Moreover, dirges and parade marches had a lasting effect on jazz, both in a search for form and in a projection of sonorities.

Traditional ways of brass-band playing continue in the present decade because the brass bands (and their repertoire, like that of country brass bands, as Frederic Ramsey, Jr., has noted) represent a continuity of the nineteenth century, when ancestors of several of the bands' members played in groups that pre-dated even the original Tuxedo. A further reason for this unbroken tradition is that bands such as the Eureka Brass Band (Folkways) and the Young Tuxedo (Atlantic) are constituted chiefly to play for funerals and parades, at the behest of fraternal clubs, many of which function as burial societies. *Thus, though jazz changed radically beginning with the Chicago period of almost forty years ago* (some New Orleans men who were a part of all that went back home), *the music of the brass bands went on as it had in the past, changing only gradually.*

Though only Negro brass bands play regularly for funerals now, funerals with bands of music were not limited to Negroes in the last century. At the height of the great brass-band period, blaring brasses sometimes participated in the Elevation of the Mass in Catholic churches. The prevalence of fraternal and burial societies—the famous New Orleans "clubs"—has been the subject of numerous studies. Like the lawn parties, they provided this type of brass-band music with its own cultural setting, thus reinforcing the intimate cultural ties of jazz itself, for the men who played for funerals and parades also furnished music for social events sponsored by these same clubs— from Buddy Bolden in the 1890's to Buddie Petit in the 1920's.

The tradition of funeral-parade music in New Orleans dates back to the eighteenth century when slaves under the French were allowed to bury their dead with music. The custom is not limited to any one country. In the last century Italian funeral bands, having played dirges for the trip to the cemetery, played gay folk dances on the return. In the Scottish highlands, following the interment, there was sometimes a skirl of bagpipes loosened up on a peat-bog potion. But only in the southern part of the United States, centering in New

Orleans, did the music take on the special characteristics that we know today as jazz.

The dirges were distinguished by moving sonorities and measured rhythms, thick-textured harmonies and the plaintive tonality of a wailing clarinet out of blues (Young Tuxedo). It is only in the setting of the New Orleans brass band that this last would seem appropriate. A little of the blues rubbed off on brass bands, in which musicians seem to push at the edges of tonality and timbre, giving the written harmony an unusual beauty not present in the score.

In New Orleans funerals the brass band was, and is, preceded by an honor guard with flags. The band itself did not enter the cemetery. At the gates the men separated into two sections, facing each other on either side of the entrance, playing the marches that, as Louis Armstrong remarked, "would just touch your heart, they were so beautiful." [14] As they played the slow, sweet dirges with an almost hesitant deliberateness that moved forward in immense solemnity, in blocks of sound, the funeral procession passed through.

The return to town of the band, deservedly publicized for its "jazz in brass," was not a part of the ceremony in any way, nor did the men get paid for it. Yet it followed a ritual of its own, once the band was a respectable distance from the graveyard: the peremptory roll on the snares, the ready-get-set blasts from the trumpet, the wonderful wail of jazz!

The lawn parties with jazz were not the sedate social affairs with string trios duly noted in the social columns of *The Freeman*. They were usually held in alleys behind houses; a dance floor was laid on, and a temporary shed with a tarpaulin top. Also sponsored by clubs, truck-borne hayrides toted musicians and guests out to camps on Lake Pontchartrain, where friendly cutting contests were the order of the day. Boardwalks led out to the camps, where were bungalows set on piles, most of them long gone now. At adjacent camps, different bands would be blowing. "We'd play a tune," Edmond Hall recalled, "and they'd come right back at us. That's the way it went."

Even more famous were the cutting contests of the bands on advertising wagons that, long before Ed Hall's time, went so far as to lock wheels to compel a reluctant band to blow. There is a story about a cornetist who, after being cut to ribbons, threw his horn

[14] *Hear Me Talkin' to Ya,* p. 14.

away (possibly to pick it up sheepishly later!). The wagons, as is well known, gave a trombone style its name—"tailgate"—from that part of the wagon over which the trombonist draped himself and his horn, so that the slide wouldn't poke out the eyes of friends and colleagues. The wagons, by 1920, were largely limited to Sunday-afternoon jaunts to advertise Monday-night dances. Edmond Hall reported that such remarks as "I could *cut* him!" were said in a good spirit, not maliciously. Two or three bands, on wagons, would meet. Each would play the same tune, and it was assumed that the people listening would come to the dance that had the best music.

In discussions of New Orleans jazz, some confusion arises, even among critics trying to assess the music in retrospect from recorded examples, because of differences in style—tonal conventions, intonation, vibrato, rhythmic tension—as between one musician and another. The Creole-trained musician usually learned to read music before he learned to play by ear. Some blues-based musicians did not care to have Creole-trained musicians in their groups, but this was possibly social rather than musical. The blues-based played for the blues-begotten, for the yard and field Negroes, the levee and railroad workers, who were paid off in cabarets like the Red Onion, a low-class honky-tonk a stone's throw from a dance hall where Bolden often played.

The art of group improvisation—like the blues, the life blood of jazz—was associated with this uptown section of New Orleans in particular. As in folk music, two creative forces were involved, that of the group and that of the gifted individual. But affecting the development of jazz throughout its early decades (1890–1920) was the stratified character of the Negro community, torn by social upheavals of the period. Reactionary legislation following the Supreme Court's decision in Plessy *vs.* Ferguson, and a sanctioned red-light district with cabarets, broke down barriers and to some extent assured jazz the best of both backgrounds, that of blues and that of legitimately trained musicians. And, of course, through all this, brass bands were, in effect, a cultural catalyst.

Backgrounds of jazzmen are still discernible, especially in the styles of clarinetists. "There are two types of reed playing out of New Orleans," Teddy Wilson remarked. "One is mellow and legato, that rippling style of Noone and Bigard. The other—and Ed Hall is the greatest exponent of it—is more a biting style. It might be termed a *punchy* style." It might indeed! Moreover, with the outstanding New Orleans clarinetists, from Johnny Dodds to Edmond Hall, *both* aspects of reed playing may be discerned, though Dodds mainly used his wailing style on discs with Louis Armstrong. Aliveness of rhythm is a feature of both styles, but one may hazard a guess as to where a specific type of *attack* or *accent* comes from by its relation to the beat, the blues beat being more dynamic.

The precursors of Dixieland style were influenced by such bands as that of Bolden, both in musical materials and in an approach to improvisation. Though not yet known by that 'name, Dixieland was a going concern by 1900. Since this article concerns itself primarily with basic jazz style, and since the writer has discussed the history of Dixieland elsewhere (*e.g.*, in *Jazzmen*), it will be in order to review it here only briefly.

In their staccato style the Dixielanders appear to have been influenced by syncopated ragtime. This was in contrast to such men as Bolden, who transformed medium-tempo rags into stomps, as they sometimes did slow blues, thus assuring them a strong jazz beat. (There's more to the beat than 2/4 or 4/4 time. Baby Dodds said that he sometimes used 2/4 time with Oliver, but one would never think of identifying the Creole Jazz Band with Dixieland.) Dixieland was a "pushing" style and countless groups were influenced by it, *e.g.*, Bix's small-group discs, various Chicago bands—and, of course, many later groups.

From all accounts a feature of group improvisations was that, at its best, the role of each musician was clearly defined. This clarity of parts, in a music that to untrained ears sounds like a strident mishmash, is something that the Origional Dixieland Jazz Band achieved to a surprising degree. Combined with their curious frenetic rhythm, that now has a slightly archaic quality, it was something new and unique, even in New Orleans, and created a sensation when the band, playing at Reisenweber's in New York in 1917, recorded for Victor. George Wettling, the veteran jazz drummer, said of their style of group improvisation, "Nobody had it before or since—it just jelled together some way and made you feel something."

Bix Beiderbecke, Pee Wee Russell and many other jazzmen who grew up during that era knew the Dixieland records by heart; Bix once left a job in upstate New York to go to New York City and hear the Dixieland band in person. It has become fashionable in recent years to low-rate Dixieland style. Indeed, a species of square swing has been promoted as the real thing. Jack "Papa" Laine, who hired the Dixielanders when they were in knee pants, probably wouldn't recognize the interlopers! But the influence of Dixieland may still be discerned, especially as it has filtered through Bix and Pee Wee, various Chicago combos and Red Nichols groups.

Another strong influence upon the musicians indicated above, and certainly upon the musicians who came to maturity in Chicago during the 1920's, was the band of King Oliver, with Louis Armstrong and Johnny and Baby Dodds, and a band strongly influenced by Oliver's, the New Orleans Rhythm Kings.

The most interesting of many traditional styles in jazz, in some respects, is the one of which Eddie Condon said, in the title of his entertaining memoirs, *We Called It Music*.[15] It was dubbed "Chicago style" and deservedly so, for its hell-for-leather push recalled the Dixieland band and it had something of the solid beat and blues color of Oliver. It was also, inevitably, affected by the music of the Wolverines and the Rhythm Kings. The Condon and Commodore recording sessions of the 1930's, among others, did yeoman service for group improvisation, but seldom—until the Yerba Buena band got under way in San Francisco around 1940—was group improvisation to receive such positive affirmation as that given it by such groups as the Condon-McKenzie Chicagoans (In *Chicago Style Jazz,* Columbia CL 632). An inspired group related stylistically to the latter and playing jazz with guts was Muggsy Spanier's Ragtime Band of 1939. Though short-lived, it was a landmark in traditional jazz and brought together a veteran of the New Orleans Rhythm Kings (Brunies) and a veteran of the music it influenced, Chicago style (Muggsy), as well as younger men (*The Great Sixteen,* RCA Victor LPM-1295).

Though its development coincided with the reappearance on the jazz scene of Bunk Johnson and other almost forgotten New Orleanians, traditional jazz in San Francisco amounted to a new style. Its weaknesses, often negligible in performance, were a lack of rhythmic ease and the difficulty of getting back to the group concept. The San Francisco movement drew upon minstrels as well as ragtime, musical materials as well as styles. The Yerba Buena and, more

[15] Henry Holt & Co., Inc., 1947.

recently, Turk Murphy's San Francisco Jazz Band, profited from orchestral recordings of Jelly Roll Morton, one of the first men in jazz who successfully combined orchestral writing with improvisation.

A creative artist in the manipulation of blues-jazz timbre, Jelly blended orchestral color with the freshness of an early Impressionist painter seeing color in depth for the first time. He devised new combinations of instruments and new sounds. Since his best-known records were issued in the mid-1920's, his influence on East Coast jazz is not surprising.

The first important break from the New Orleans style of group improvisation—after King Oliver, whose work anticipated a new, more harmonic approach to ensemble—was in an increased emphasis upon individual talent. Playing at the Vendome Theatre or at the Sunset Cafe, Louis Armstrong in Chicago faced different audiences than he had in New Orleans and on the river. Not only were different demands made upon his talent; he himself wished to develop in new ways. Inevitably, this involved a use of new materials. As this writer remarked in a study of the blues and jazz vocal:

> In his singing—even as he changed from cornet to trumpet in instrumental work—one may see how a sort of shouting style, rough and wonderful, with young Louis on a tonal bender, gave way to a unique scat chorus based on instrumental phrasing, and one may see how the latter showed the way to jazz treatment of popular songs.[16]

A further break from New Orleans was *in an approach to orchestral color that plotted the area in which group improvisation might operate.* On records reissued in 1959, for example, Jelly's music is vibrant with color and excitement. His concept of orchestral sound was dynamic. This is how he described it:

> With plenty swing it becomes beautiful. To start with, you can't make crescendos and diminuendos when one is playing triple forte. You got to be able to come down in order to go up. If a glass of water is full, you can't fill it any more, but if you have half a glass, you have the opportunity to put more water in it, and jazz music is based on the same principles.[17]

[16] "The Blues Was the Mother" in Newport Jazz Festival Program (*Down Beat,* Chicago, 1958).

[17] *Mr. Jelly Roll,* by Alan Lomax (Duell, Sloan & Pearce, 1950), pp. 64, 66.

In ensemble passages, Jelly's orchestral approach retained close ties to group improvisation. It was unlike the loose and gutty ensemble of Louis Armstrong's Hot Five, yet Jelly put a premium on vigor and spontaneity within the group, and was happiest when he had achieved it, as on *Black Bottom Stomp* in *The King of New Orleans Jazz* (RCA Victor LPM 1649).

Though Fletcher Henderson was to become one of the top arrangers of jazz, his band of the late 1920's played forceful, driving jazz that was more arrived at than arranged. To a great extent, as John S. Wilson wrote, he "created the pattern for big band jazz and made it possible through his conception of sections." [18] Carrying this thought a bit further, one should note that, as with King Oliver, the drive of the Henderson band was not just a function of the drummer or of the rhythm section, but of the entire band. Not until the advent of Count Basie's Orchestra was the gateway to swing to be opened much further. (One of the few in-print examples of Fletcher Henderson's Orchestra in the 1920's is *Sugar Foot Stomp* in *Jazz, Vol. 7,* Folkways FJ 2807.)

Following the decline of big-band swing and the emergence of modern jazz in such styles as bop and cool, small groups—which could best accommodate these rhythmic, melodic and harmonic experiments—were again in the forefront of jazz, with growing importance attached to original writing and orchestration. By the time Miles Davis, J. J. Johnson, Gerry Mulligan, Kai Winding, Gil Evans and their colleagues produced *The Birth of the Cool* in 1949 (Capitol T-762), the swing era had come to a close and the kids— not the ones who had shrieked it to success—had begun to dance to rhythm and blues.

Jazz of the 1950's represented a triumph of the small group and the individual artist. Both older and younger musicians shared in this triumph, which was supported by record companies, night clubs, festivals, concerts and, to some extent, radio and television. By 1957 it occasioned little surprise when Pee Wee Russell, who had played at the Arcadia Ballroom in St. Louis with Bix in 1926, and Jimmy Giuffre, who came in with the cool cats at mid-century, got together for CBS-TV and *The Sound of Jazz* (Columbia CL 1098). In fact, they had already traded choruses at Lenox, Massachusetts, in the famous jazz seminars held at the Music Barn.

During the 1940's the long-play, 33-r.p.m. record superseded

[18] *The Collector's Jazz* (Lippincott, 1958), pp. 153–54.

the 78-r.p.m. disc, making it possible to get more than a half hour
of music on one record. The long-play record, which could be pack-
aged to appeal to specialized audiences, was a godsend to jazz. It
also enabled musicians to take longer choruses, which wasn't always
a blessing.

In contrast to the literary view which identifies jazz with the
hipster and the beat generation, jazz has recently entered a period
of re-affirmation and rediscovery. Young musicians learned that men
such as J. J. Johnson, Tony Scott, Gerry Mulligan and Miles Davis—
to name only a few—had never left the beat. In the early work of
Thelonious Monk, piano rags echoed amongst strange-sounding
chords, and his compositions, like those of Charlie Parker, often
reflected a sensitive feeling for the blues. The Modern Jazz Quartet,
though usually photographed without a smile, were seldom without
a sense of swing. Julian Adderly, one of the most powerful altoists
on the scene today, who was influenced by both Lester Young and
Charlie Parker, said, "I'm a mainstream man, that's all." As the
work of Miles Davis indicates, hot intonation is once again a virtue,
though not at the loss of newer concepts. Recent albums include
tracks that utilize hot intonation, others that exemplify the deliberate
understatement called "cool."

Without some sort of group improvisation, if only in the spontaneity of interpretation that a competent arranger will inspire,
identity with jazz roots becomes tenuous, though other jazz elements
may be present. Of course (to paraphrase Aaron Copland) freedom
is interesting only in relation to form. In jazz the latter may exist
in the context of oral or written music, or in a combination of both.
Musicianship—technical knowledge—is no guarantee of esthetic impact, and, in fact, an esthetic result (in this writer's opinion) is not
something measurable. Yet form is required to transmit an esthetic
result.

Every art has its own disciplines, and this is no less true of jazz,
even though it often functions in the general field of entertainment.
For example, in Columbia's jazz album of *Porgy and Bess* (CL
1274), Miles Davis' hauntingly imaginative interpretations of street
cries, in the matrix of Gil Evans' sensitive background writing, are
completely devoid of easy artistry. And it should be added that,
whether blowing for scale or for keeps, a jazzman without a sense
of humor is an anomaly!

Sometimes, in blowing sessions which involve little or no arrangement, more attention is paid to the solo choruses than to those of the group. Has the ease of notation made jazzmen lazy in this respect? Many young musicians tend to scoff at older concepts of group playing, yet seldom do modern musicians get together, without music, and come up to the standards set by contemporary arrangers for small groups.

> The idea of *group* improvisation [wrote Aaron Copland] was reserved for the jazz age. What gives it more than passing interest is the phonograph, for it is the phonograph that makes it possible to preserve and thereby savor the fine flavor of what is necessarily a lucky chance result.
>
> When you improvise it is axiomatic that you take risks and can't foretell results. When five or six musicians improvise simultaneously the result is even more fortuitous. That is its charm. The improvising performer is the very antithesis of that tendency in contemporary composition that demands absolute exactitude in the execution of the printed page. Perhaps Mr. Stravinsky and those who support his view of rigorous control for the performer have been trying to sit on the lid too hard.[19]

That would be Aaron Copland, calling the children home!

Acknowledgments: Sterling A. Brown; Harold Courlander; Edmond Hall; Nat Hentoff; Neil Leonard, Jr.; Alan P. Merriam; *Down Beat;* The Schomburg Collection, N.Y. Public Library; and The Institute For Jazz Studies. Unless otherwise credited, quotations are from my own talks with jazzmen.

[19] *Music And Imagination,* by Aaron Copland (Harvard U. Press, 1952).

RAGTIME

∿∿∿∿∿∿∿∿∿∿∿∿∿∿∿

Guy Waterman

Guy Waterman was a professional pianist in the Washington, D.C., area from 1949 to 1953. He is currently an economist with the Chamber of Commerce of the United States, and writes on ragtime and jazz for *The Jazz Review*. His two articles for *The Record Changer* ("A Survey of Ragtime," Vol. 14, No. 7, and "Joplin's Late Rags: An Analysis," Vol. 14, No. 8) are among the most important pieces yet printed on the subject.

Concerning this chapter and its lack of a discography, Waterman notes: "Ragtime differs from jazz in its emphasis on the written rags. There is very little 'straight' recording of rags. I listed, with full citations footnoted, the two major recordings of interest. The list of major rags at the end was intended to replace the discography, which would be appropriate for jazz."

Ragtime, as it will be discussed here, differs from perhaps all other jazz and related music in that it is a body of written compositions. Jazz, as we usually think of it, is an improvised or arranged music, the only permanent illustrations of which take the form of recordings. Ragtime, in the context of this chapter, consists of printed music for piano.[1]

This difference is mentioned at the outset because it is more than a surface one. It reflects a difference in the orientation of the music. Jazz, whether written down in arrangements or improvised from the simplest resources (*e.g.,* a twelve-bar blues), starts with a melody and its supporting harmony. The creative process involves what is done with that melody and harmony. In ragtime, the creative process is in the writing of the whole piece in all its parts, horizontal and vertical. Ragtime lies more in the orientation of concert music than of jazz. Like all generalizations, this one obviously should be qualified; in its essential respect, however, it is valid.

It should be stressed that this distinction applies to ragtime "as it will be discussed here." It is well known that in the whole range of jazz there has been little final agreement on definitions and in many cases not even a consensus as to what is roughly meant by certain terms. For many people, including many authoritative people, the word ragtime means a particular style of playing which was used fully as much in early jazz piano as in the rag compositions. To some, ragtime is simply another name for early jazz. There is no special mandate for the definition used here, other than that which should presumably be the test for all definitions, namely, that it is *useful*—it facilitates analysis. We want to analyze this particular body of music and, in so doing, to shut off—or at least treat as different—other types of music. To do this requires that we use some terms for this music. If a term other than "ragtime" were desired, it could be substituted.

Briefly, the period of ragtime composition covers the first two decades of the twentieth century. While Roy J. Carew has traced the characteristic rhythm of ragtime (discussed below) back to an 1848 publication, it is customary to refer to the first ragtime publication

[1] The writer wishes to acknowledge his debt to Roy J. Carew, who made available both his extensive collection of printed music and his invaluable personal recollections concerning the years when the music first came out.

45

as William Krell's *Mississippi Rag,* which appeared in 1897. In the same year, Tom Turpin's *Harlem Rag* appeared. In 1899 and 1900 a steady stream of published compositions bearing the title "rag" began to appear. For the first five years or so, the style was extremely simple and light. Toward the end of the first decade, more "serious" or "high-class" rags came out. The leading composers at this time were Scott Joplin, James Scott, and Joseph Lamb. Shortly after 1910, ragtime became a national fad, in a watered-down, rickyticky form suitable for mass audiences. This fad gave way to another, jazz, around the year 1920. The major composers published right on through the 'teens, and there were even a few rags in the early 1920's, but by 1925 ragtime composition had stopped altogether.

It will be convenient in this description of ragtime to center attention on the rags of the most important composers. These are Scott Joplin, James Scott, Joseph Lamb, Artie Matthews, Tom Turpin, and only occasionally others. This list may appear to select some and reject other composers arbitrarily, but the selection is actually based on the perusal which this writer has made of the field plus competent advice from those who have done more intensive research on the great flood of written material in the period.[2]

To the jazz audience, ragtime is a relatively little-known field. This is because the jazz audience is accustomed to dealing with recordings, not with the printed page. The number of rags which have been recorded "straight" is quite limited. It might be well to approach ragtime, therefore, by analyzing first the resources with which it works—the ragtime "orthodoxy," so to speak.

Rhythmically ragtime is most noted for its characteristic right-hand rhythmic phrases: ♫ ♩ ♪ and ♫♫ ♪ .

These characteristic phrases run through virtually all published rags. Pages of Joplin abound on little more rhythmically. A good illustration of these rhythms is to be found in Tom Turpin's *St. Louis*

---

[2] If perhaps an analogy may be drawn, it might be pointed out that, in regard to the classical period of concert-music composition, a similar sifting-out process is used. Typically we study Haydn, Mozart, and Beethoven and pay virtually no attention to any other composers in the period. It is generally felt that this selectivity is valid. Or, to use another analogy, future jazz historians may well select from the early bop period a handful of really creative musicians—Dizzy Gillespie, Charlie Parker, Thelonious Monk and maybe a few others. However, we are obviously too close to that period to make any such prediction with safety.

Rag, which fortunately is available in an excellent recording of rag-time piano rolls.[3] The first strain of this rag is almost wholly built on the phrase: ♩♪♪♪♩♪♪♪ . The second strain then uses this phrase: ♪♪♪♪♩♪♪♩ . The third strain uses this phrase: ♪♪♪♩♪♪♪♩ .

In ragtime the sixteenth-note runs stopping on a syncopated beat are common. As one exaggerated example, take the sweeping line in Joplin's *Chrysanthemum,* first strain:

The left hand in ragtime is normally cast in a supporting role. The well-known oom-pah pattern of alternating single notes and chords is used. The left hand virtually never engages in syncopation. There are important exceptions, of course—*Cascades,* for example, third strain. When syncopation is used, however, it is usually more decorously done. James Scott's frequent left-hand syncopation always knows its place—that is, it is inserted in the eighth or sixteenth or perhaps seventh and eighth measures of a strain, where it will not interfere with the orthodox ragtime momentum.

This rhythmic phrasing is virtually never more complicated. It is of the essence of ragtime style that it can be trusted not to throw in less regular rhythmic patterns. One of the surest giveaways of Jelly's *jazz,* not ragtime, posture is his hitting the left hand a sixteenth note early. This can be seen in his "transformations" of *Maple Leaf Rag*

[3] Riverside Records (RLP 12-126).

and *Original Rags*. No rag writer would dream of such a blatant New Orleans crudity. Many of the revivalists fail to get an appropriate rag sound because of left-hand syncopation alone.

Ragtime's orthodoxy extends to the larger rhythmic scene—that is, to the organization of the whole strain. Virtually all rag strains are sixteen bars divided into four equal parts.[4] Many strains are organized as so many simple pieces in the classical period of Western art music (Haydn, Mozart, Beethoven): A, B, A, C, "B" being a semi-cadence, "C" a full cadence. This organization of tunes was carried over into jazz and became one of the essentials of jazz orthodoxy. In fact, while exceptions to the rule are rare in ragtime, they are still rarer in jazz, once the early New Orleans stage is over. The reason lies in the requirements of improvisation, the need to be able to assume without the slightest mental reservation that the chorus will be over exactly sixteen (or thirty-two or twelve) bars from now, not seventeen or fifteen.

We have noted the strict orthodoxy of ragtime in rhythmic phrasing and in the internal structure of the sixteen-bar strains. Moving to a still larger "rhythmic" dimension, the structure of the whole rag, we again find a remarkable degree of orthodoxy. A heavy majority of all rags are organized on the basis of four strains, either ABCD or ABACD, with a less common structure being ABACDC. In nearly all cases a repeat will be indicated for all strains except the return of a strain. There is remarkable agreement on this organization. For example, of thirty-nine Joplin rags (including collaborations), twenty-seven are built ABACD. Joplin's rags, as the archetype of the music, are unusually steadfast (until his late experimental period). In the whole Joplin literature only two rags, *Euphonic Sounds* and *Palm Leaf Rag,* have less than four themes and only two have more (coincidentally, the first and the last). Turpin generally used four strains. James Scott was willing to hold himself to three on occasion. Three of Artie Matthews' five *Pastimes* are organized ABACD, one ABCD and one ABC.

In developing the four-strain structure into a coherent whole, several approaches came into usage. The A theme will ordinarily be a straightforward "statement" type of theme. It is a complete-in-

---

[4] One minor departure from sixteen-bar and eight-bar structure involves the use of twenty-bar strains, a device which Tony Jackson was said to use and which is found in occasional rags.

itself type of home base, to which it will be possible to return after B. It is the theme which will be thought of as giving that rag its individuality. If asked to play *Fig Leaf Rag* or *St. Louis Rag,* one would play the first theme automatically. It is sometimes used as a special-effects type of theme, with the other strains being more typical two-beat (see *Maple Leaf Rag*).

The B theme will be a lighter, milder, less filled-in treatment. Often it will be prefaced by an unaccompanied right hand on the dominant. Often, though not always, the melodic line will have a tendency to soar, so that the effect of returning to A is a kind of coming back to the meat of things. As one device for achieving this type of effect, rag writers, quite unconsciously I am sure, saw fit to lead off theme A with a tonic chord but B with a dominant chord. This would certainly seem to be appropriate in light of the experience of tonal composers in legitimate, diatonic music. In some rags, the B strain modulates to the key of the dominant—Scott Joplin's *Chrysanthemum,* for example. In *The Strenuous Life,* Scott Joplin even modulates to the dominant chord of the dominant key, an awkward change. Perhaps the best way to point up the relationship between themes A and B in a rag is by analogy with the first and second themes of the standard sonata first movement. The contrast is precisely the same. The feeling of rising to the dominant key for the second theme is the effect which rag writers strove for without actually taking the plunge, except occasionally.

To note the relationship between the first and second themes, it would be useful to consult *Weeping Willow Rag* as very typical. Other typical illustrations include *Frog Legs Rags, Harlem Rag, Red Peppers Rag,* and *Pickles and Peppers.*

The Function of the final two strains extends the development of the rag. Where strain B rises to a lighter vein than A, strain C instead sinks into a slightly darker color. Normally it modulates down a fifth; it will generally tend towards the lower register of the treble. In some rags it is analogous to the trio of a march—quiet, melodious, simple. It is more apt, however, to have a kind of rhythmic excitement—subdued, contained, waiting to burst out.

The release, of course, comes with strain D. This is ordinarily a blaze of triumph. Sometimes it comes back to the original tonic (in *Maple Leaf,* for example); this can produce an electrifying effect.

But usually it remains in the new key, dispersing most, if not all, of its subdominant atmosphere, however.[5] Often it will have more of a riff quality than the other strains. It is, in general, certainly far more relaxed than C, perhaps more than all the other three. It gives the rag finality in a wholly positive vein.

For illustration of the relationship of these four themes to one another, Turpin's *St. Louis Rag* serves admirably, especially since it is available on LP. *St. Louis Rag* is atypical in the harmony which opens theme A and in the lack of a return to A after B; otherwise, however, it is a "perfect" rag. With reference to the tonal flavor of C and D, *St. Louis Rag* illustrates well how both themes use the same key, yet C is distinctly subdominant while in D no subdominant flavor is present.

Frog Legs Rag by James Scott is another in the mold, with one difference. The A strain is a straightforward detailed ragtime theme, followed by a soaring B theme (the kind of thing which brings out the best in Scott), followed by a return to A. The one departure from the norm is that the key of C and D then lies up a fifth rather than down. Strain C, however, serves the function previously suggested—that of being more subdued and suggestive, waiting for the final outburst. It is true that Scott's fury lies just under the surface in this kind of strain. The calm is threatened by the surge in bar six, but saved by the fact that seven and eight do not flare up as they do in equivalent passages of Scott's other rags (see *Grace and Beauty, Hilarity Rag,* etc.). Instead, bars seven and eight descend tamely in a sixteenth-note run. Theme D is then a typical blaze of triumph ignited by Scott's boundless energy.

It would be erroneous to suggest that this ABACD organization had anything like the universal acceptance of some of the other trappings of the ragtime orthodoxy. Plenty of departures may be found, especially in James Scott. Even old Tom Turpin's 1899 *Harlem Rag*

---

[5] It may legitimately be asked why the third and fourth themes may be in the same key, yet the subdominant flavor present in C is virtually absent in D. The answer is not very subtle: the listener's ear has forgotten the original key. This fact about tonality has always been used. The classicists establishment of a dominant key has always relied on sheer distance; not until the dominant had been harped on for some bars, usually in association with *its* dominant, would the ear forget the original tonic. But once it has been established, the listener become wholly attuned to the dominant as the new home base. Similarly, in ragtime the separation of D from A (or B) by C makes possible a triumphant flavor in D—distinctly not subdominant.

is out of the cast, except that it does rise to the dominant for theme B and sinks with the final tonic.

Joplin in late years (from 1909 on) was moving towards considerably more varied and interesting structures, almost towards classical forms. This probably was *not* deliberate or conscious on his part. That is to say, he probably did not create within deliberately achieved classical forms as his objective; rather, he probably approached classical forms simply by developing ragtime as he saw it. For his creative mind this appeared to be the direction in which the music *had* to move after its tremendously productive years just before 1910. Both in ragtime orthodoxy as it had emerged then and in Joplin's new directions afterwards, form was the servant of substance, not vice versa.[6]

Magnetic Rag, it could be argued, points toward the sonata form essentially. The return to A has all the attributes of the classical recapitulation. The two preceding themes (C and D) resemble, as closely as ragtime could, a development section. C actually breaks through the sixteen-bar barrier, which, as has been mentioned, is a most rare incident. The D theme is in the tonic's own minor, in contrast to the normal use of the relative minor in ragtime and jazz. In keeping with the classical concept of key relationships significant to a development section, Joplin goes from B flat major into B flat minor. In the return, the classical method of "dominant preparation" (harping on and around the dominant of the key which is to be restored) is used fully. The key of theme D, it is especially worth noting, has been viciously exploded with the fourth beat of bar fourteen. The mere fact of destroying theme D's key within its own sixteen-bar framework suggests something like a development section.

Having examined the ragtime orthodoxy from the horizontal

---

[6] One writer observes: "It has become increasingly clear that 'form' need not be a confining mold into which tonal materials are poured, but rather that the forming process can be *directly* related to the musical material employed in a specific instance. In other words, form evolves *out* of the material itself and is not imposed upon it. We must learn to think of form as a verb rather than a noun." Gunther Schuller, "The Future of Form in Jazz," *Saturday Review,* January 12, 1957: p. 62. Schuller's comment has to do with the direction of modern jazz but applies to any music, including ragtime or concert music, or, for that matter, *all* of jazz. The healthy interest of today's jazz frontiersmen in the form is *not* in form for its own sake, but as one of the musical resources at their command.

standpoint (rhythm and over-all structure), it may also be useful to note the well-known orthodoxy of ragtime harmony.

Much of ragtime harmony is based on standard tonic-dominant changes. There is extensive use of the common change: tonic to sub-mediant to super-tonic to dominant back to tonic. There is, of course, tonic to sub-dominant. Frequently the final four bars will run as follows: IV—IV minor—I—VI—II—V—I.

Frequently at the midpoint of a strain the harmony will move into the mediant minor, and then slide neatly into the dominant in preparation for return to the second half of the strain.

These harmonies, it is clear, are substantially identical to those used in early jazz. In fact, it is safe to say that from the standpoint of harmony alone, everything found in early jazz is found in ragtime, except that early jazz tended to place far more emphasis on the standard blues chorus and internal harmonies appropriate to that series of chord changes. It was well into the 1920's before jazz had need of more complex harmonic resources.

This is not to say that ragtime and early jazz have an identical concept of harmony. In the last-four transition from IV, for example, ragtime would typically use the VI minor, rather than the VI major seventh. More basic, harmonically, was the use of the cadential 6/4 chord in the middle of a tune where jazz always used the super-tonic, because of the preference in jazz for going up by fourths wherever possible. This is seen clearly in the tenth album of the Jelly Roll Morton Library of Congress series, in *My Gal Sal*. Here, in an old barbershop quartet, in so obvious a 6/4 situation, Jelly still substitutes the super-tonic, even the first time through, when he is ostensibly playing it straight. This makes the D the ninth of the super-tonic instead of the top of the 6/4 chord. What Jelly ever expected the whiskey tenor to do with that super-tonic is hard to guess. No orthodox tenor ever successfully got on top of a ninth chord.

Ragtime never had such an aversion for the 6/4 chord, particularly in the middle of a strain. The difference reflects the fundamental difference in orientation of ragtime itself. The foregoing description of the resources with which ragtime works is necessary to full appreciation of it. In every music there are these conventions which must develop before the music can become fully creative. For the listener to understand and fully absorb the profound experience of a really creative musical achievement, familiarity with the tools with which the music works is an essential first step.

But, having discussed the resources which the listener will need in approaching ragtime, it is perhaps appropriate to point out where the creative music within the field is to be found. Most of the significant names have already been mentioned. There is good ragtime to be found in the compositions of Tom Turpin, Charles Hunter, Charles L. Johnson, Henry Lodge, Paul Pratt, and some others. Arthur Marshall and Scott Hayden participated in some notable collaborations with Joplin. Every indication is that Louis Chauvin was one of the most creative musicians of the time. Unfortunately, however, there is precious little of Chauvin on the printed page. Of known stature are Joseph Lamb and Artie Matthews. Joseph Lamb entered ragtime publication between 1905 and 1910. Eight of his eleven published rags appeared after 1912. The style had already been staked out by Turpin, Joplin, and others. Lamb had no pioneering to do, but he did contribute some of the most powerful ragtime composition in the field. His *American Beauty Rag* is perhaps best known and is available on a recorded piano roll. It illustrates the imprint which is on every Lamb rag, the full, hard-hitting, rhythmically alive style. Lamb possibly made more use of the full range of the piano's register than any other significant rag writer. While his melodic invention was perhaps somewhat limited, he did not run out of ideas within the framework of classic ragtime.

Artie Matthews was quite a different composer from Lamb. Matthews came along well after the peak period of ragtime composition. He is known almost exclusively for five rags, all of which go under the title of *Pastime Rag,* No 1, No. 2, etc.; and for the single composition, *Weary Blues,* which became widely used in jazz. The *Pastimes* are extraordinary little pieces of ragtime invention. They are not in the classic ragtime vein of Lamb, Joplin and Scott; nor do they follow the trend towards the stepped-up style of ragtime that is sometimes called "St. Louis." Moving against the trend of the times, Matthews chose a retiring, light style into which he poured one charming contrivance after another. It is not always heavy ragtime, neither in the sense of the sound which is achieved nor in the sense of the depth to which it aspires. But it is a major contribution to the field. Number 5 is very successful in grafting Spanish rhythms onto ragtime, just as Jelly Roll's "Spanish tinge" was applied to jazz.

With due respect to Lamb, Matthews, Turpin and the others, there is no question but that the most creative individuals to work within the framework of ragtime were Scott Joplin and James Scott.

Joplin is most well known for the rags which he produced prior to 1909. He was one of the first to enter ragtime composition, with *Original Rags* in 1899. His *Maple Leaf Rag* of the same year was the all-time best seller in the field, and remains the best-known rag today. Between 1901 and 1904, Joplin produced fourteen rags which, with the writing of Turpin, Hunter, and others, created the style. These early Joplin rags are almost incredible in their inexhaustible supply of musical expressiveness. They include such gems as *Sunflower Slow Drag, The Entertainer, Easy Winners* (said to be Joplin's favorite), *Elite Syncopations,* and *Weeping Willow Rag*—uniformly high-class and extremely characteristic rags. Two with a slight march-like flavor, but otherwise quite in the vein, are *Peacherine* and *The Strenuous Life. A Breeze from Alabama* and *Chrysanthemum* hint at an experimentalism which was to run riot in Joplin's later years. *The Cascades* is slightly patterned after *Maple Leaf* in form, but is otherwise quite different.

In 1905, Joplin concentrated on the writing of a ragtime opera, *A Guest of Honor.* No trace of the effort remains. It evidently was not a success, either financially (it never received any backing after one performance in St. Louis) or artistically. It was not until after 1910 that Joplin left the standard rag-writing fold again.

In 1907–08, Joplin produced nine rags, which represent a slightly different approach than that used in the earlier period. Here ragtime, the style having been established, was now capable of moving on to real artistic effort. Joplin was in the forefront, using the style which he had helped create to achieve a really "serious" music. To examine fully the nine 1907–08 rags would be a major job. They need only be listed here—and strongly recommended for those who can obtain the scores, recordings or rolls. They are: *The Non Pareil, Gladiolus Rag, Searchlight Rag, Heliotrope Bouquet, Rose Leaf Rag, Lily Queen, Fig Leaf Rag, Pineapple Rag* and *Sugar Cane Rag.*

About this same time, James Scott emerged as a ragtime writer of major importance. Scott's *Frog Legs Rag* burst on the scene in 1906 (he had published three marches a few years earlier). This was followed by *Kansas City Rag* in 1907, and a flood from 1909 through

1911 which included *Sunburst Rag, The Ragtime Betty, Great Scott Rag, Grace and Beauty, Hilarity Rag, Quality Rag* and *Rag Time Oriole*—in short, a stream of creative ragtime comparable to Joplin's in quality, though different as night from day in personal approach.

Joplin's was a reflective spirit, seeking to control the essentially bouncy spirit of ragtime and direct it into longer phrases, sustained sixteenth-note runs, working towards four long phrases to the strain. Scott, on the other hand, used the established ragtime style to exploit its more dynamic qualities. Scott exploded in shorter and shorter phrases and splashes of color, with a furious energy that could not be controlled. There are few passages in Scott which sound truly in repose.

As has been indicated previously, Joplin ragtime is of interest not only because of the classical rags which he produced, along with Scott and Lamb, before 1910; but also because of the last period, which for Joplin begins with *Euphonic Sounds* and *Solace* in 1909. This last period of Joplin's is a curious one, representing a kind of mixture between throwbacks to the very early two-beat Turpin style (see especially the collaborations with Hayden, *Felicity Rag* and *Kismet Rag*) and the most ambitious musical efforts in the ragtime literature: *Euphonic Sounds, Magnetic Rag* and perhaps *Solace, Scott Joplin's New Rag, Reflection Rag,* and certainly the second Joplin opera, *Treemonisha.* In the final Joplin period there is growing preoccupation with form and structure, including experimentation with quasi-classical forms, such as the rondo in *Euphonic Sounds* and the sonata-like treatment in *Magnetic Rag.* As might be expected, his concern for structure was associated with interest in tonality. An additional quality of these late Joplin experiments was an attempt to abandon explicit rhythmic statement without losing the implicit momentum. It cannot be said that the final period was altogether successful. Nevertheless, it is a most fascinating chapter of the ragtime story and achieves some notable results in *Euphonic Sounds* (particularly the amazing second theme), *Magnetic Rag,* and widely scattered passages in *Treemonisha.*

The creative ragtime of Joplin, Scott, and the rest will probably enjoy an increasingly wide listening audience. The size of the audience has been narrowly constricted hereto by two facts: the relatively limited number of good piano rolls which have been put on records, and the unfortunate failure of Revivalist jazz pianists to learn the approach necessary to ragtime (rather than jazz). While little more can be expected from recorded piano rolls, ragtime's tremendous musical potential would appear to make better-informed playing of rags inevitable before long. For a music whose actual creation stopped some thirty-five years ago, ragtime has a bright future from the listeners' standpoint.

References

Riverside Records has two twelve-inch long-playing records containing an extraordinary level of fine ragtime: "The Golden Age of Ragtime" (12–110) and "Ragtime Piano Roll Classics" (12–126). Included are an unfortunately rushed version of *Euphonic Sounds,* which probably could never be adequately produced through player piano, *Fig Leaf Rag, The Entertainer,* James Scott's *Grace and Beauty,* Joseph Lamb's *American Beauty Rag,* Tom Turpin's *St. Louis Rag,* an exhilarating number called *Smokey Mokes* and others. Many Revivalist "live" recordings have been made but few are satisfactory, because the standards of jazz dominate rather than those of ragtime. Principal Revivalist pianists who have recorded ragtime are Ralph Sutton, Wally Rose, Burt Bales, and the fine jazz pianist Don Ewell.

Anyone with access to the original sheet music of ragtime is, of course, fortunate.

Rudi Blesh and Harriet Janis have written a most useful book, *They All Played Ragtime* (Knopf, 1950), which might be described as a social history of the subject; it contains next to nothing of musical value, but it is a literally invaluable chronicle of the facts of ragtime publication, including extensive appendices listing countless rags. Two musical analyses of the subject by this writer appeared in *The Record Changer,* Volume 14, Numbers 7 and 8: "A Survey of Ragtime" and "Joplin's Late Rags."

Following is a list of forty rags. The selection is designed to isolate the most "significant" rags. Any such delineation is obviously somewhat arbitrary. It is felt, however, that this kind of listing may be interesting and, possibly, illuminating.

Forty Selected Rags

1897   *Harlem Rag* (Turpin); *Mississippi Rag* (Krell).
1899   *Maple Leaf Rag* (Joplin).
1901   *Possum and Taters* (Hunter); *Sunflower Slow Drag* (Hayden-Joplin).
1902   *The Entertainer* (Joplin).

1903   *St. Louis Rag* (Turpin).

1904   *Cascades* (Joplin); *St. Louis Tickle* (Barney-Seymour).

1905   *J.J.J. Rag* (Jordan).

1906   *Dill Pickles* (Johnson); *Frog Legs Rag* (Scott).

1907   *Fine and Dandy* (Johnson); *Heliotrope Bouquet* (Chauvin-Joplin).

1908   *Black and White Rag* (Bottsford); *Fig Leaf Rag* (Joplin); *Sensation Rag* (Lamb).

1909   *Euphonic Sounds* (Joplin); *Ragtime Betty* (Scott); *Temptation Rag* (Lodge).

1910   *Dynamite Rag* (Robinson); *Grace and Beauty* (Scott); *Hilarity Rag* (Scott).

1911   *Ragtime Oriole* (Scott); *Sunflower Rag* (Wenrich).

1912   *Slippery Elm Rag* (Woods).

1913   *American Beauty Rag* (Lamb); *Billiken Rag* (Stark); *Pastime #1* (Matthews); *Pastime #2* (Matthews).

1914   *Climax Rag* (Scott); *Magnetic Rag* (Joplin).

1915   *Agitation Rag* (Hampton); *Ragtime Nightingale* (Lamb).

1916   *Pastime #3* (Matthews); *Springtime Rag* (Pratt); *Top Liner Rag* (Lamb).

1917   *Reflection Rag* (Joplin).

1918   *Pastime #5* (Matthews).

1920   *Pastime #4* (Matthews).

JELLY ROLL
MORTON

〰〰〰〰〰〰〰〰〰〰〰〰

Martin Williams

Martin Williams, a co-editor of *The Jazz Review,* is also chief reviewer for *The American Record Guide* and is a regular contributor on jazz to *Evergreen Review.* He has written for *Down Beat,* the British *Jazz Monthly* and other publications in the field. His anthology, *The Art of Jazz,* is an Oxford University Press book.

Mr. Williams' range of interests extends through all of jazz. For example, in addition to his detailed notes for the Riverside Library of Congress Jelly Roll Morton series, he has written valuable essays on Thelonious Monk (*Evergreen Review,* No. 7) and on "Extended Improvisation and Form," (*The Jazz Review,* December, 1958). He has probably done more than any other writer in the past decade to re-evaluate the musical importance of Jelly Roll Morton.

Jelly Roll Morton, the colorful character, seems to be one of the abiding clichés of jazz. It may come from writers' efforts to get people interested by hooking them on the "character," and it is certainly encouraged by one kind of look at a life full of wandering, pimping, bragging, wild ostentation in dress and possessions. And the braggart, the blowhard, the exaggerator, the liar (often just the audacious kind of liar who does not really expect to be believed)— they were Morton, too, and these images encourage the cozy, implicitly patronizing account of him. But in that life and those wanderings, amid all those delusions and painful paranoid railings, was a kind of larger integrity, and always the music in him ultimately triumphed and led him on. The journalistically conceived clown stands in the way of our hearing that music.

Morton was an exasperatingly contradictory man, a puzzlingly complex man; and, like many of his generation in jazz, he had a large and therefore fragile ego that hardly encourages everyone to try to understand the man and, what is more important, his music. From his life, one grasps what seems enlightening, one wonders at much, one can only repeat a great deal. But the ultimate point is the music. Our knowledge of his life and his world is important only insofar as it enlightens us about his music. And, hearing it, we know that it expresses more of the man and his deeper feelings than his public masks, his pride, his snobbery, his pontifications and his prejudices can show us.

In most accounts, Morton's music is placed in a neat category called "New Orleans style," and there the explanations stop and the enthusiastic adjectives start.

That category is not so neat. The usual definition is that New Orleans style is something the Original Dixieland Jazz Band was attempting to play, the style Kid Ory was first to put on records in 1921, the style King Oliver's Creole Jazz Band recorded in 1923, certain of Johnny Dodds' groups (The Wanderers, The Boot Blacks, The Black Bottom Stompers) recorded later, and the early Armstrong Hot Fives reflected.

Such an effort to place Morton historically is far too general to be very enlightening. There were many kinds of music played in New Orleans and a number of these, from the propriety of A. J. Piron to the crudeness of Sam Morgan, we would be willing to call jazz, pre-jazz, near-jazz. They were hardly all alike. Furthermore, despite the similarities, it should be obvious that there are certain very basic differences in conception between Morton's orchestral music and Oliver's. Oliver's music was improvisational blues played by an integrated group of instrumentalists, whose greatest virtue came from the individuals involved and the way they blew together in this style; Morton's is an individually, compositionally conceived music of orchestrational variety and form. Rhythmically and compositionally, Morton's music represents an earlier stage in jazz than Oliver's does (and Morton had learned a great deal of what was going on outside New Orleans in his travels). But for the moment he does represent, Morton was, as far as we can tell, an innovator and a "modernist," whose music showed more sophistication, consciousness and formal musical knowledge than Oliver's, and who had definite intellectual theories about what he was doing. At the same time, Morton never abandoned the expressive and earthy realities of jazz and the blues for the comparative blandness of a Piron (at least the Piron on his Victor records) or a Jim Europe.

So far as we can tell—so far as written documents, published scores, and recordings enable us to tell—Morton was the first great master of form in jazz. In this respect, he belongs perhaps with the Fletcher Henderson of the mid-1930's, and certainly with Duke Ellington, John Lewis and Thelonious Monk. By the late 1930's, Ellington had absorbed into his music the innovations which Louis Armstrong, as an improviser, had announced. And Lewis (by assimilating and transforming form from Europe) and Monk (by working more directly with the implicit resources of jazz itself) found form within terms of the innovations represented by Parker, Gillespie, and Monk himself.

With what resources-at-hand did Morton work? Buddy Bolden's? If we are to accept Bunk Johnson's re-creations, Bolden's sense of form was a strong one, and strikingly like Morton's (and, incidentally, Monk's). We can say, I think, that despite his exemplary handling of single-theme compositions, Morton's conception represents an extension of the form established by the great ragtime composers, but it also incorporates rhythmic, harmonic, and variational elements of the jazz movement and the blues. A conception later than Joplin's or perhaps Bolden's, earlier but more "learned" than Oliver's.

There are some curious likenesses among these leaders of form: Morton, Ellington, Lewis, Monk. All are pianists (or at least play piano) and all have been called poor pianists (which in some— usually irrelevant—senses, several are). All are major composers, of course, perhaps *the* major composers in jazz. All may show, at least part of the time, an orchestral (rather than horn-like) conception of the piano, which can make them all usually unorthodox but extremely effective accompanists. All, as we shall see, have taken strikingly similar approaches to the problem of improvisation *vs.* form, freedom *vs.* discipline, individuality *vs.* total effect. And, for Morton and Ellington at least, before their messages of form had really taken effect, revolutionary improvisers had arrived and, one should admit, almost fadish thinking about style by jazzmen had made them seem passé. Ellington's sense of form was overtaken by Parker's innovations, but Ellington had a lot to do with planting the seeds. And there are signs of another revolution as Monk's sense of form is beginning to be recognized, and Monk is planting the seeds. Morton is unluckiest of all, for he had hardly begun recording and regular publication before Armstrong's revolution was already in effect. He began almost as an anachronism, a leader in a style already becoming unstylish. But perhaps the seeds of Armstrong's revolution are to be heard in him. And obviously it is not against Armstrong that Morton should be judged artistically.

One other thing that all these men (Morton, Ellington, Lewis and Monk) share is a crucially important movement—ragtime. Ellington was steeped in its Eastern, later "stride" branch. Monk has got it indirectly from Ellington and more directly from James P. Johnson and Fats Waller. Lewis got it indirectly, but he has professed an admiration for James P. As for Morton, his relationship to ragtime was direct, and it was to the Midwestern-Sedalia-St. Louis version.

In itself, ragtime proved to be a kind of blind alley, but its contribution to jazz, and to form in jazz, is probably immeasurable. It was the most formal, most "European," most melodic—even, in a sense, most "highbrow" movement yet associated with jazz. And the fact that in so short a time those folk themes, ring shouts, church themes, European dances and military strains could be so transformed, so formalized as to create a unique, identifiable body of pianistic music is almost incredible. And almost sooner than it had happened, exploitation, excess, popularization, decadence, and its own implicit limitations had largely destroyed it. Meanwhile, for the greater movement, for jazz, its work had been done and would abide for fifty years.

Although Morton respected the best ragtime men and said so, he apparently saw what was happening and what was missing. The music had become, in the hands of pseudo-ragmen, a kind of showman's piano for vapid displays of fingering; and in the hands of publishing-house hacks, it was a style in which to compose "charming" banalities. Joplin aside, for many more legitimate rag composers it had become a rigid form in which one decorated or reworked the commonplaces of the style. Morton was part of a movement which saved things from decadence; ragtime as a form was structurally, rhythmically and emotionally limited, and Morton seems to have known it.

The printed scores of Morton's typical multi-thematic pieces— *Wolverines, King Porter Stomp, The Pearls, Kansas City Stomps, Grandpa's Spells,* etc.—show: three themes, a developing or contrasting melodic and tonal relationship among them (often as ABC or ABAC), plus one or two choruses of variation on the third theme. A very few ragtime scores survive which include written variations; in performance, spontaneous variations (or at least decorative embellishments and fills) were sometimes made, but neither is essential to this music. Written variation-on-theme is obviously essential to Morton's. And we know that in performance improvised melodic variation is a part of its substance.

There are other differences: in rhythm, harmony, and emotional range.

One could describe Morton's smoothing out of ragtime rhythms as the result of the addition, to the clipped 2/4 of ragtime, of tango-derived, syncopated quarter notes and of polyphonic bass melodies borrowed and transformed from certain marches and European folk dances. One could also describe his harmonic progress as based on his formal knowledge of music and the intuitive freedom with which he could make changes, relate tonalities, and arrive at substitutions —something which neither Oliver nor James Scott knew as much about by comparison. And his emotional range was perhaps the result of his feeling for the blues. But these categories make very arbitrary separations, they overlap in practice, and they do not complete the picture even on the level of "sources."

Many of the ragtime composers were well schooled, some undoubtedly better schooled than Morton. And most of the resources that Morton used were there in the European music to which he was exposed—ready to be used, as it were, and present for a long time. But, as the history of jazz has shown repeatedly, the Promethean task is always a matter of showing that such things will work as jazz, showing how they will work, and assimilating and transforming them into the idiom. And making a musical resource work as jazz is never easy, never the result only of formal musical knowledge or of will. It takes what we can only describe as an intuitive genius into the nature of jazz.

The rhythm in Morton's scores—the bass line and the way in which phrases are placed upon it—gives enough rhythmic and melodic variety (and this was a crucial point to Morton in his theories) to constitute an intermittent but interplaying polyphonic and polyrhythmic part—of anticipated downbeats, delayed accents, syncopated Spanish rhythms, trombone-like melodies.

In *Mr. Jelly Lord,* Alan Lomax invited us to see Morton's music as an ingenious combination of "Downtown" and "Uptown" elements as the largely European (but "folk" and therefore rhythmic) music of the colored Creoles, plus the "earthier" music of the uptown Negroes, ex-slaves, some of whom had migrated from nearby plantations.

Similarly, one might see it as an alliance between ragtime and the blues, with importations from French, Spanish, Baptist hymn, and martial music—the latter at least analogous, of course, to rags.

Unfortunately, most discussions of the constant flirting of jazz with "Latin" music soon bog down into a listing of compositions, beginning with Joplin's and coming up to Horace Silver's *Señor Blues.* In the first place, the source of the syncopated 2/4 (which led towards 4/4) of jazz may well be the tango. The source of the behind-the-beat delays and "around-the-beat" accents on which Armstrong based his innovations (and which are so important to Morton's *New Orleans Blues* or *New Orleans Joys, The Grave, Mamanita,* etc.) could also be the tango. Finally, the very placement of the melodic phrases in, for example, the third theme of Morton's *Wolverine Blues* corresponds exactly with the placement of the heavy beats in a tango—but *Wolverines* is not a jazz tango. Clearly, "the Spanish tinge" goes deeper than certain compositions, than an occasionally brilliant effect (which one hears not only in Morton's but in Oliver's rhythm section), than Morton's own comments might lead one to believe.

And from the blues? Rhythmic uniqueness and variety, depth, honest passion, and spontaneous variation and improvisation.

Between the waning of ragtime and the ascendancy of the "jazz" music of New Orleans, there was an overlapping popular movement in American music called "the blues craze," which was announced by the publications of W. C. Handy. In some ways, Handy's approach was more formal even than ragtime's had been; it was at least a little arty. He took folk blues, harmonized them (with a system in which the "bent" quarter tones of the blues "scale"— notes found in *every* music in the world except Western concert music, by the way—could be imitated by certain "dissonances" on the tuning of the European piano) and built them into often splendidly organized multithematic compositions on the model of rags. Even in Handy's somewhat fussy approach, rhythmic variety, "breaks" (suspensions of a stated pulse), and passion were captured.

As will be evident from Morton's recreations on his Library of Congress recordings of the kinds of blues that were played in the lowest dives in New Orleans, there was a lot of structural and, more important for the moment, rhythmic diversity. There were blues in the chipped 2/4 of ragtime; in the smoother and syncopated 2/4 of Creole jazz; in a 4/4 swing suggestive of the rhythmic conception of Armstrong; and even in the quarters broken into eighths of boogie woogie, suggestive of the bop style. Handy's version of his own blues used a mechanical, corny version of rag rhythm and a rather dance-band-arty approach. When others played them, a rhythm almost like New Orleans Creole jazz often emerged.

Even in the most formally compositional blues, there can be emotion unknown to ragtime. There would be no jazz without the blues, and if one dismissed them and their effect from one's mind, jazz would become a sterile and meaningless music. But without ragtime, what a melodically limited kind of rhythm-making jazz might be. The European tradition of form, discipline and order probably affects jazz more directly today than ever before, but these ideals have always crucially affected it through ragtime.

The blues had rhythmic variety, passion and, chiefly because of Handy's work, a certain public respectability. Like most folk music, the blues were performed with improvisation. Combining the melodic-compositional emphasis in rags and the improvisational-variational emphasis in blues, we have the basis for Morton's principle of thematic variation. It was an almost brilliant stroke, for it combined and developed the virtues of both forms, the dangers of neither. It made variation meaningful, but channeled and controlled it; it kept the music fresh and alive, but gave it order and purpose. It also opened up many possibilities for future developments. Later conceptions might have allowed more freedom, but at this stage, and with polyphonic structures, it was precisely this discipline of Morton's that helped immeasurably in transforming impulse and craft into art.

Morton's "theory of jazz" which he gave to Alan Lomax is not so much a theory as it is a specific response to the definition which used to be in certain Webster dictionaries (something about loud, fast, blatant, cacophonous noises) and similar Aunt Sallies. But it does give certain principles which were important to him and, perhaps more to the point, does affirm that his mind was the kind which thought about practice and abstracted principles. The fact that he acknowledges that he worked out his style at medium tempos (which permitted him to work on note-doublings, embellishment, and accentual displacements) not only indicates a fundamentally rhythmic approach to jazz but coincidentally indicates the basis on which most subsequent innovations were also worked out—hear the recordings made at Minton's in the early 1940's; hear the Armstrong of the late 1920's and early 1930's. Much has been made of Morton's "Always keep the melody going some way." The remark does acknowledge that thematic variation is Morton's way, but it is actually an afterthought to his insistence on continuous, proper, and interesting harmonization—a principle apt to shock reactionaries, surprise modernists, and shake up theorists in jazz if they are willing to consider it a bit.

Much has been made of Morton's insistence that riffs are for background, not for themes. No one could doubt that the great effectiveness of riff melodies is often bought cheap, but Morton himself wrote some riff melodies, and the very riff he used to demonstrate his point was the final theme of his rewriting of Santo Pecora's *She's Crying for Me* into *Georgia Swing*. At any rate, one could hardly doubt the effectiveness of riffs behind soloists. Nor could one question that his principle that a jazz pianist should imitate an orchestra has the confirmation of time; from Morton through Bud Powell, Hines through Erroll Garner, pianists follow band and horn styles.

As Morton put it, "breaks" are "one of the most effective things you can do in jazz." In a sense they are a culmination of the rhythmic resources of the music (unless "stop time" carries things a step further), but Morton is probably the only man, musician or critic, who has made them a principle. They continue to be used today (often at the beginning of choruses instead of as a climactic device), and the subtle sense of time and suspense they need is the bane of many a "revivalist" and an excellent test of a musician's swing.

Morton's assertion that jazz can be played soft, sweet, slow, with plenty of rhythm (or, as André Hodeir later put the same principle, "swing is not the same as getting hot"), is, of course, crucial; and the problem of swing at slow tempos is currently plaguing the young Eastern "cooking" jazzmen. In his demonstration of the point, Morton used a double-time break, a cornerstone of styles from ragtime through Parker—and the "funky" player's current coverup.

Morton was, as I say, a modernist and an innovator for the time his work represents. That is why he so frequently ridiculed "ragtime men." He was part of a movement which saved Afro-American music from degeneration at the hands of pseudo and second-rate ragtimers and continued its development. (He obviously respected the *best* ragtime and its composers, however.) And that is also why he frequently scorned blues instrumentalists ("one tune piano players"). His work was more sophisticated, formal, knowledgeable, resourceful, varied than theirs. And it was a product of intelligence and theory as well as emotion and intuition.

Morton's real reputation depends on a brilliant series of orchestral recordings he made for the Victor company between September 15, 1926, and June 11, 1928—a short enough period, but greater fan reputations have been made on far less finished work.

These recordings are the real successors to the striking series of piano solos he made for Gennett, Paramount, Rialto, and Vocalion between 1924 and 1926. He had made other orchestral records before, none of them really worthy of him as a pianist nor promising the orchestrator and leader who was to reveal himself. But in them he tried out the devices and effects which he spent the rest of his life perfecting.

The only success of the early recordings is the simplest in scoring, the Paramount *Big Fat Ham* and *Muddy Waters*. It is polyphony plus solo interludes. Jasper Taylor's excellent (if over-recorded) drumming falls into just the right rhythmic role for Morton's music. There is fine group swing, the right balance between discipline and expressiveness in the playing, with the Keppard-Oliver-like trumpet and the clarinet understanding and displaying this relationship excellently. But one failure is Morton's attempt to use a saxophone as an extra polyphonic voice, something he was to try again and something (partly because few of these saxophonists ever got any swing) he seldom made much of.

Otherwise, an inept clarinetist, an amateurish trumpeter, a rhythmically awkward ensemble usually spoil these recordings. The Morton-directed version of *London Blues* by the New Orleans Rhythm Kings ably alternates harmony, counterpoint, solo, and breaks along the lines he later perfected; and the later Okeh *London Blues,* re-orchestrated in polyphony, which is spoiled only by bad clarinet, shows the effective variety and thoughtfulness of Morton as an accompanist for the first time on records. Among the remaining records, the Gennett version of *Mr. Jelly Lord* (1926) features a three-man reed section which plays, and swings, in harmony.

As I have said, Morton's achievement, before the Victor orchestral recordings were made, was his piano, and we should take a closer look at that style.

In 1944, William Russell wrote an analytical review of Morton's rediscovered *Frog-i-More Rag* solo for the magazine *The Needle,* which, I think, is a definitive one:

> Jelly Roll's piano style and musical greatness are nowhere better demonstrated. . . . All the most typical features . . . are abundantly evident: his wealth of melodic invention and skill in variation; the tremendous swing . . . his feeling for formal design and attention to detail; his effective use of pianistic resources; the contrasts of subtle elegance with hard hitting drive; the variety of harmony, and yet freedom from complication and superficial display. . . .

Jelly Roll had a more formal musical training and background
than many New Orleans musicians. . . . At times the close-knit
design is marked by an economy of means that amounts to understatement. *Frog-i-More* follows the usual form of Morton's stomps—
introduction, a short three-part song form, and a trio section. A
definite musical idea is used for each new part. Since the opening
idea for the first strain, an ascending succession of 7th chords, does
not immediately establish the tonality, a curious effect of an extension of the introduction is created. The contrasting second strain is
unusually forceful, employing a repeated-note motive and powerful
left hand bass figures in Jelly's full *two-handed* style. After a modified return of the first strain a characteristic Morton trill bridges
over to the trio. . . .

Jelly took great pride in his "improvisations" (on theme) . . .
listen to the trio section to discover Jelly's phenomenal skill in
variation. And if one were to study the four different versions of
The Pearls or the half-dozen recordings of *Mr. Jelly Lord,* and perhaps also take time to compare some of these variations with the
published versions, he would begin to get an idea of Jelly's unlimited
imagination and mastery of motival variation. . . . The beautiful
chorale-like melody of the *Frog-i-More* trio is first played very
simply, in a style reminiscent of the sustained trio of *Wolverine
Blues.* . . . On paper the tune, with its constantly repeated motive,
presents a singularly four-square appearance, but Jelly's performance is a revelation of rhythmic variety by means of such devices as
shifted accents, slight delays, and anticipations. . . . As raggy as
Jelly's performance of this chorale is, it nevertheless is in perfect
time; the regular pulse can be felt throughout with no loss at all in
momentum. . . . The melodic invention of this finale is as notable
as its immense rhythmic vitality. . . . Jelly's rhythmic impetus
and melodic embellishment give the effect of a fantastic and
frenzied variation. Actually, each bar is directly related to its
counterpart in the first simple statement and all of Jelly's characteristic and fanciful "figurations" are fused with the basic idea as
though they belonged there originally . . . with Jelly Roll, no matter
how exuberant rhythmically or varied melodically the final choruses
become, there is never any doubt of their musical logic and that
each note grows out of the original motive. Nor is the typical flavor
of the unique Morton style ever . . . lost.

When Morton recorded his music and reminiscences (and
fabrications) for the Library of Congress (beginning May 21, 1938),
he gave us documents that are revealing, exasperating, and delightful.

His invention is extended, unhampered by such things as the time limits of recording for ten-inch 78 r.p.m. There are unique revelations of his resources and great inventiveness on the extended versions of *Wolverines, The Pearls, Creepy Feeling.* But this man, aging, inwardly discouraged behind the pride and bravado, sick, sometimes faltered in fingering and time.

One of the most revealing things is the performance of Joplin's *Maple Leaf Rag,* first in St. Louis-ragtime style, then in his own. The performance speaks for itself of his innovations in tempo, rhythm, polyphony, improvisation. Guy Waterman has said of Morton's re-organization of Joplin's *Original Rags:*

> "The most obvious indications of Jelly's jazz approach stem, in the right hand, from the improvisation and, in the left hand, from the anticipated downbeats and the octave runs of four sixteenth-notes, Jelly's trademark. Actually, however, these devices do not explain the full transformation which Jelly brings about. [There is a] gulf which separates ragtime, as the early rag composers understood it, from jazz as Jelly epitomized it. This gulf has more to do with the type of beat which the two develop and the nature of the momentum which builds up. The difference is reflected in the entire organization [of the performance]." [1]

Two other performances on the Library series are worth examining for what they show us about what we may call Morton's principles of structure. The first is an extended version of *Kansas City Stomps.* As published, *Kansas City Stomps* consists of an introduction (a "tune up" motif) and three themes, thus: A (E flat), A (an exact repeat), B (E flat), B (an exact repeat), C (A flat), C' (a melodic variation). Both A and B are sixteen-bar themes (out of ragtime, church music, marches) and C is an unusual twelve-bar melody with stop time at bars one and two, seven and eight, making two six-bar units possible.

In this performance, Morton plays: introduction, A, A' (a variation), B, B' (a variation), A" (another variation), C, C' (a variation), introduction (as a modulational interlude), A''' (a third variation). Thus, an implicit rondo is completed, with each return to each theme a variation on that theme.

Then there is the challenge of a single theme. *Hyena Stomp* is a simple sixteen-bar melody of pronounced rhythmic character. As

[1] *The Jazz Review,* December, 1958.

a comparison of the (shortened) printed score and the orchestral version will show, the basic outlines of the way Morton handled variations on it were compositionally pre-set—but that is true of much jazz, and, as is also true in jazz, the way the outlines are *used* in performance can be another matter.

The basic motive of the theme is stated in the first two measures, then modulated through a chorus of sixteen bars, which serves as an introduction. There follows a second sixteen-bar chorus, in which the melody is again stated in bare form. In these first two statements the harmony (full and beautifully appropriate) is made clear and an almost lyric mood is set with that riff, but there are hints of the kind of rhythmic variation to come. There follows a series of six variations. Each is based on a musical idea, which Morton works out; each is related to what immediately precedes and follows it, either as contrast or complement; each is also part of the total pattern of the performance; and each is orchestrally or instrumentally conceived.

Chorus three is primarily rhythmic, an appropriate contrast to the careful harmonic-lyric emphasis of the first two. Morton simplified the melody and harmony drastically in a kind of "barrelhouse" destruction of the piece, in which the swinging momentum and a partly polyphonic bass line are first introduced, and from which he rebuilds it in various ways. The fourth chorus is an elaborate lyric transformation—melodically the most complex—of the theme, lightly dancing after the heavier motion of what has preceded it. From this point on, as we gradually return to and build on the pronounced rhythmic momentum introduced in the third chorus, we hear a melodic simplification from this peak and dynamic building. The fifth chorus is an excellent stroke. It still refers to the melody, but it also transforms (by simplification) the fourth, forming a kind of two-chorus unit with it. The next chorus (six) is a contrast, but one which had been subtly prepared for. It is a variation in the bass (a rather complicated one for the time) under a simple treble statement, and in the preceding chorus there has been much activity in his left hand, readying our ears for this one. In the seventh chorus, we are reminded of trumpet figures, and these gradually build into an ensemble variation in the eighth. Morton leads into and makes his climax, the dynamic-rhythmic ideas continue to build excitement and the rhythm swings freely and simply.

Instrumentally the style of the variations is:

Chorus 1   ensemble in harmony
Chorus 2   ensemble, in hints of polyphony
Chorus 3   polyphonic
Chorus 4   clarinet solo, lower register
Chorus 5   clarinet, upper register, trombone in polyphony
Chorus 6   trombone solo, broken polyrhythms behind
Chorus 7   trumpet into riffs, hints of polyphony
Chorus 8   unison brass-like riffs, still on theme

On the basis of the various ways that Morton handles his simple theme, we have heard some remarkable things, but there is even more in some of the details.

For instance, as we have seen, our chorus unit is sixteen measures. But Morton used variations which unified two groups of choruses (four and six, seven and eight). At the same time, each chorus, by the nature of the theme, may fall into two eight-bar units. These, in turn, may fall into units of four bars. Then there is the fact we began with: the basic melodic motif can be stated in two bars; to some, such a thing is evidence of melodic crudeness. Morton was quite aware of these "limitations," took interesting advantage of them and made them principles of his structures. The final chorus, for example, consists of an unbroken eight-bar line followed by two four-bar units, all held together in tone. Also, the first melodic fragment in chorus one is not exact; an improvised shift of metre is then "corrected" in bars three and four. And in the two clarinet choruses Morton handles bar lines with further ingenuity: the first is based on a parallel repetition of two-bar units; the second begins with contrasting two-bar units. Thus Morton builds variations in continuity within choruses, combines some of these into double choruses, and within this, works out small structures of two, four and eight bars, all of which contribute by contrast, parallel, and echo to a total development and unity.

Any such an attempt at scrutiny as the foregoing is bound to make a music that is warm, passionate and spontaneous seem a contrived, pat set of devices. The point of it, of course, is to illustrate general and subtle principles of style. In any given performance, the application of Morton's ideas will be different. But once one grasps the nature of these ideas and their relationships, the excitement, beauty, and uniqueness of Morton's work will, I think, possess him even more strongly and lastingly.

Behind the success of the Victor recordings are a maturity in Morton's conception, a group of musicians equipped both to play well and to take Morton's exacting instructions and leadership, careful rehearsal, and a series of splendid orchestrations.

Like the question of how many of his compositions Morton stole or otherwise obtained from others (a question hardly confined to him; it might be raised about many major jazzmen), the question of how much musical knowledge he actually had and how much help he had with scoring is perpetual. One can get testimony, often from excellent jazzmen, that Morton knew little of music and played badly. One can get just as much reputable testimony that he was an excellent musician, ahead of his time in several respects, and could play extremely well. The only answer, of course, is his playing—*with* its faults, and with an evident evolution and refinement, especially in harmony. The answer to the complaint that Morton did not make his own orchestrations is the obvious fact that a single musical intelligence and taste is behind them. Doc Cook, Tiny Parham and others have been mentioned as helpers with scoring, but none would have worked on the New York recordings. The answer undoubtedly is that, even if Morton had needed help, the conception was nevertheless his.

The ensembles for the Victor recordings were sometimes written —always at least sketched in advance. Obviously those with harmonized parts were written or at least carefully rehearsed, but so were some of the polyphonic ensembles. They are the disciplined perfection of integrated, interweaving New Orleans contrapuntal playing, surpassing others we have on records, and, at the same time, precisely because they are pre-sketched, the death cry—unless someone realizes what a model they might be for the further development of the kind of polyphony that is unique in jazz. The release of alternate takes of the recordings confirms that in ensemble nearly everyone except Morton often played *ad lib* upon a pre-sketched outline of his part.

The solos, more often than not, were improvised. There are exceptions: Johnny Dodds obviously plays (or plays from) two written choruses on *Hyena Stomp,* and Omer Simeon obviously allowed himself little freedom on *Shreveport Stomp.* On the other hand, the recent release of a very different and superior take of the excellent trio recording of *Wolverine Blues* (Label "X" LVA 3028) confirms that, for that performance, Johnny Dodds improvised entirely, using the chord structure alone, as Morton varied the trio theme behind him. And, as several of Omer Simeon's and George Mitchell's solos on the alternate takes demonstrate, Morton would often work out with the instrumentalist a sketch or plan which the latter, in turn, was free to fill in or work with ad-lib. Surely the similarities between Morton's way of working with his musicians and that of both Ellington and the Modern Jazz Quartet confirm that, variously arrived at, there has been only one really successful solution to the problem of improvisation and total form, of spontaneity and discipline, in jazz.

One thing that immediately strikes one about the Victor recordings is the magnificence with which the players in the various groups work together. Such unity (and it is beautifully recorded) would be rare for a group which had been playing together for many months, regardless of the stylistic sympathy of its members with one another. For pick-up groups, even ones so carefully selected as these were, it is almost unthinkable. And one should remember that such discipline as Morton exacted may easily produce negative results in the playing of jazzmen of any school.

Smokehouse Blues, from the first recording date, is exceptional, if only for the polyphony of its last chorus and because it is so movingly and passionately played; one must wait almost until Morton's last years for so moving a blues. The orchestration is largely soloistic, however, and the soloists were equipped for it. They were equipped not only to play expressively but also to let any emotional subjectivity contribute to the performance as a whole rather than detract from its development—a task few jazzmen have been able to fulfill unless they were willing to submit their talents to the direction of a Morton or an Ellington. Morton's own solo does not seem to fit rhythmically with the rest of the recording, but before one decides that his time was failing him (as it sometimes did), one should be aware of the deliberate variety that is a part of so many of these recordings, and aware that the successful use of it is a crucial part of Morton's achievement. *Black Bottom Stomp,* an excellent case in point, was also made at this first Victor date.

As a composition *Black Bottom Stomp* (also called *Queen of Spades*) is hardly one of Morton's best: neither of its themes is distinguished and one treatment of the second is by an obvious arpeggio made on a rhythmic pattern that was already a cliché in ragtime. However, the piano version shows that the composition itself employs some fairly sophisticated use of alternate endings and extension.

In the orchestration the variety of effects and rhythms would seem much greater than one should dare try in such a brief performance. Briefly, the introduction is stated in harmonized call-and-response patterns by the horns. The first theme enters in harmony but the clarinet breaks away from it at the ends of phrases for contrapuntal commentary. The trumpet then follows for solo "call" statements which trumpet, clarinet and trombone answer in harmony. The second theme is introduced in a contrasting polyphonic chorus with breaks and a sprightly, less raggy rhythm with John Lindsay's bass strongly audible beneath the interplay among the three horns. The variations on the trio are (1) clarinet, (2) piano, (3) trumpet against Charleston-esque stop time, and (4) banjo in rhythmically patterned arpeggios, with the string bass reappearing strongly. The horn trio re-enters for very light, dancing polyphony. The last chorus is again polyphonic in a strong but never lumbering stomp rhythm, with Lindsay's third entry now augmented by the bass drum, audible for the first time. As usual, the climaxes, the excitement are entirely melodic-rhythmic—no one shouts or screams; there is no "Dixieland" frenzy.

Without going into the patterns of echo that occur, and leaving out details of breaks, etc., these are some of the things that happen in a three-minute performance of a two-theme composition by seven instruments. One's immediate reaction might well be that it must be extremely cluttered, contrived and even a bit pretentious. Actually it is none of these things: it flows from beginning to end with the inevitability that only an artist can achieve, and no device or detail draws any attention to itself. All are intrinsic parts of a knowingly paced whole. Could anyone else in jazz, except Ellington, put so much into a three-minute performance with such success? Morton's music seems always to reflect a deep understanding of the value and purpose behind device and effect, and he constructed works rather than demonstrations—but perhaps that is a definition of "artist." The Red Nichols-Miff Mole version of *Black Bottom Stomp* (Riverside 1048), made a few months after this one, is a rhythmically unsure, ineptly played and comprehended parade of lumbering and superficial effects; Morton's is a musical experience.

The strongest contrast to such complexity is a recording like *Jungle Blues,* which is its opposite in almost every respect. It is a deliberately "archaic" piece, whose basic ingredients are nothing more than a very primitive blues bass line and a simple riff. Before he has finished, Morton has formed the riff into three distinct themes (and they are good ones), handled the heavy "four" of the bass with some variation, occasionally relieved it briefly and, as he usually could, spun the performance to the brink of monotony, ending it exactly one moment too soon.

Between the complexity of *Black Bottom* or *Grandpa's Spells* and the comparative simplicity of *Jungle Blues* or *Hyena Stomp* lies the range of an artist.

One decided success in the Victor series is *Dead Man Blues.* It begins like several of his other recordings, with some very bad jokes, but at least the Chopin "funeral march" theme is not an auto horn, boat whistle, or goat's whinny. (Such things are apt to seem either pointless or annoying to us, even if they are sparsely used and humorous in intent. Perhaps more important, they indicate an approach to one's audience that is more real than arty.) *Dead Man* attempts a difficult combination of sprightliness and seriousness. If it did nothing else, it would display three very good themes and show the easy swing of George Mitchell's never-obvious lead and the strength of Omer Simeon in both counterpoint and solo. Mitchell's two solo choruses are excellently constructed melodically, and a superb transition into the trio [2] at the same time. The three trio choruses develop with a beautiful simplicity of outward form. The first two have three clarinets in harmony, first alone, then with a trombone quietly singing blues in counter-melody behind them. Then comes the counterpoint of the last chorus, with lines so brilliantly interweaving—the trumpet playing lead but giving the effect of an integrated part at the same time—that they seem to us the fruition of some twenty years of a style. It is a chorus which might in itself make reputations for its orchestrator and its players and, as a part of the whole performance, is one of the most superb climactic under-

---

[2] This theme was not used in previous versions of *Dead Man;* Oliver had recorded the same strain as *Camp Meeting Blues* in 1923.

statements in recorded jazz. Morton knew, as Bach did, that if polyphony does not give a sense of forward movement, it comes to nothing—to use the usual comparison, a horizontal structure must be linear and lines must move.

Dead Man redeems *Sidewalk Blues,* wherein Morton was perhaps a bit too preoccupied with the excellence with which he got this ensemble (even when augmented to ten pieces) to swing, and a bit careless with the quality of his melodies in the introduction and trio and with some of his trombone lines.

Some kinds of failure are necessary to an artist, particularly if they show him just what he does best. To have followed *Dead Man* by the excessively corny and banal added parts for two violins on *Someday Sweetheart* is perhaps a bit like John Lewis' having recently followed *Sait-on Jamais* with *European Windows;* for, if Morton's intentions were more "dance band" and Lewis' more "concert hall," both tended, perhaps equally, towards "acceptability." Of Morton's other "experiment" in the Chicago recordings—that of again adding the extra voice of an alto—even in polyphony, one cannot really call it failure. Stomp Evans swings more and, for all the modified slap-tonguing in his solos, his part interferes far less in the polyphonic sections. Indeed, on the trio of *The Pearls* he seems to contribute to an interesting texture and ensemble swing.

To single out moments from these recordings is obviously unfair, especially since I am claiming such unity of conception for many of them. But, with that in mind, there are things in them which should be mentioned: the chorus on the trio of *Cannonball Blues* when the banjo carries the theme against the double-time piano variation; the conversation in "twos" on *Wild Man* between clarinet and piano, then clarinet and alto, in which intermittently one will egg the other into double time; the announcement which *Steamboat Stomp* makes that Morton's orchestral style has dealt with the problem of fast tempos; the apparently innovative conversation of breaks among bass, trombone and ensemble (is there anything comparable in jazz until Ellington's *Jack the Bear?*) in *Grandpa's Spells;* and the entirely infectious movement and swing of *Doctor Jazz.*

It was exactly a year and a day later that the next session was held, in New York. I think that the location probably accounts for the final fulfillment of Morton's rhythmic conception, which we hear on *Georgia Swing, Kansas City Stomps, Shoe Shiner's Drag* and

Boogaboo. Many Northeastern players were using (and continued to use) an older rhythm, rather closer to ragtime, than could be heard elsewhere, and Morton could take direct advantage of that fact; that is, it was easier to get these players to swing *his* way than it would be with Red Allen or J. C. Higginbotham, on later recordings. *Shoe Shiner's Drag* was, as we know, apparently impressive enough to be remembered by Lionel Hampton, but the real "work" from this date is probably *Kansas City Stomps.* At a medium tempo, it features excellent polyphonic writing and playing on several themes, and it sustains throughout the swing of some of the Chicago recordings, which have slower tempos, but with their same easy understatements in climaxes—and *Georgia Swing* is almost as good. Ward Pinkett is a fine trumpeter for Morton to have chosen: his sense of time and accent is almost equal to George Mitchell's, and his abilities with mutes imply exactly the variety which Morton knew how to use.

The last of the great Victors is a quartet based on Oliver's *Chimes Blues,* which Morton called *Mournful Serenade.* None of his subsequent recordings is supposed to be as good as the earlier ones. But the point is that he had too much taste and insight merely to repeat and decorate, to reiterate and complicate what he had already done—a lesson he could well have learned from what he had seen in the degeneration of most ragtime and the later explorations of Joplin. Twenty-five sides had given his conception, complete with as much perfection as an artist can ask for. It was time to try other things, and among those other things are some real successes.

The first date announced the things he would work on. *Red Hot Pepper* successfully modifies the earlier manner towards a big-band scoring, and the blues, *Deep Creek,* is a string of solos (on more than one theme) with opening and closing ensembles. Certainly many of Morton's big-band arrangements suffer by comparison with the kinds of things that Redman, Henderson and Ellington did, but Morton's best were done in 1928 and 1929, and their best a bit later. *New Orleans Bump* (Monrovia, 1929) is certainly successful at the same kind of thing his successors were to do; it is another excellent example of pushing simplicity to the brink of monotony, but saving it by a hint of variety and by knowing exactly when to stop. In many more of these scores there are fine moments: the clean swing and passion of the last chorus of *Pontchartrain;* the well-paced and varied textures of *Burning the Iceberg* (the familiar integration of section harmony, polyphony and solo now working in the new conception) despite its rather anachronistic basic rhythm; the handling of the first theme in its various appearances on *Pretty Lil* (by an immediate reduction in the second chorus, later by solo variation, etc.). And if the scoring or the handling of elements on a later record is not quite on that level, there may well be other things: the superb interplay of piano and guitar on *Little Lawrence* or the very effective piano breaks and solo on *Tank Town Bump.* And when one of these records fails, it does not fail because what is on it is pedestrian or banal. Even when the arrangements are based on familiar chord structures of melodic patterns, Morton may handle them with a freshness that will discover something alive and different, if not artistically complete, in them.

Finally, a performance like *Blue Blood Blues* shows that Morton knew exactly what the theme-string of solos-theme approach might achieve, and that recording is still one of the best of its genre— possibly *the* best before some of the small-group recordings of the late 1930's.

A decidedly minor artist (or, for that matter, minor craftsman) may be a major influence—even on a major artist. But it is also quite possible for a major artist to have little influence on his immediate successors. The kind of after-the-fact argument which elevates a man on the basis of influence often avoids a crucial evaluation.

I would like to present Morton on his own terms. If one cannot quite see his achievement on those terms, if one needs comparisons from the work of those around him to help, there is the evidence of the inept, unswinging, monotonous recordings of his own pieces made by Red Nichols and Miff Mole, The Original Memphis Five (Riverside RLP 1048); or the more recent ones made by Turk Murphy (Columbia CL 559) and Pee Wee Erwin (United Artists UAL 4010). One can also learn much by comparing the versions which some of the Southwestern bands made of his things in the 1920's— the Bennie Moten version of *Midnight Mama,* for example (Label "X" LX3004), is poor indeed.

But it is in the Southwest that one can gather the most verbal evidence of Morton's influence. Interview after interview brings testimony that Morton, his compositions, his musical training, or his scores were an inspiration—Andy Kirk, Jimmy Rushing, Don Redman, Ben Smith have all attested to it. Then, in *King Porter,* we can see a direct and clearly identifiable influence of Morton's work on jazz. In the variations on the trio, we hear figures which are typical of Morton, which Henderson's arrangement used and passed to Goodman—a kind of scoring for brass (and Morton clearly had brass in mind in such sections) which set a pattern used by almost everyone during the "swing" period (even Ellington: hear *Bojangles* for the clearest instance). And one can hear it still in the arrangements of Ernie Wilkins, Quincy Jones—and everyone who writes big-band jazz scores.

But the real challenge that Morton's work represents is not a result of Morton the composer, the orchestrator, the theorist, the formalist; it is the fact that in him jazz, by the mid-1920's, had produced an artist.

BLUES TO
DRIVE THE
BLUES AWAY

〜〜〜〜〜〜〜〜〜〜

Paul Oliver

It's ironic that most of the best writing on American blues has come from Europe. American magazines like *Down Beat* and *Metronome* have seldom printed articles on the blues, and even the professional folk music and folklore journals have largely ignored the subject. In Europe, magazines like *Jazz-Hot* (France) and *Jazz Monthly* (England) devote a sizable amount of space, in the course of a year, to the blues. Among the leading European writers on blues are Yannick Bruynoghe (Belgium), Jacques Demêtre (France) and Paul Oliver (England).

Oliver is an artist, writer and teacher, and his paintings have been displayed in many British exhibitions. He has been a lecturer on the history of art at the National and Tate galleries in London and has lectured widely on art and music at universities and other educational institutions, both in England and on the Continent. As a result of his special interest in American arts, in 1955 he was awarded a scholarship to the Seminar in American Studies in Salzburg, Austria.

For sixteen years, Oliver has concentrated on collecting and studying blues and Negro folk music. He has written scores of articles on the blues and blues singers in *Jazz Monthly, Jazz Journal, Jazz Music Mirror, Discophile,* and *The Jazz Review;* and has broadcast frequently on the BBC. His book on the blues, *Blues Fell This Morning (The Meaning of the Blues)* is soon to be published in England by Cassell, and he has contributed chapters to several books on jazz.

People, if you hear me hummin' on this song both night and day,
People, if you hear me hummin' on this song both night and day—
I'm just a poor boy in trouble, trying to drive my blues away.
                                                    —Walter Davis: *Worried Man Blues*
                                                    (Bluebird B-5129).

In the form and content, the sentiment and delivery of his verse,
Walter Davis epitomises the blues. He sings as a man who wishes
to rid himself of the blues as a state of mind and who feels the need
to give expression to his emotions. Addressing his words half to
himself, half to those who listen to him, he creates a song that
loosely conforms to a traditional pattern, improvising the while
an accompaniment that complements and amplifies the meaning of
the phrases that he sings. This is the blues as a folk music: the
blues that would have developed and thrived whether jazz had been
born or not. It has profoundly influenced jazz and it is unlikely that
jazz music would have followed the course it has, had it not been
continually fed by the blues. Today the blues means, for many persons, the collective improvisation of King Oliver's Creole Jazz Band
or the unison work of a Count Basie section; for others it is an
extemporisation by George Lewis or Charlie Parker, the singing of
Bessie Smith or Billie Holiday. For half a century blues has been
woven into the fabric of jazz, but the bulk of the material has remained apart from it. Though its nature has sometimes changed
with the passage of the years, the blues still remains fundamentally
a folk music.

Many theories have been propounded to account for the growth
of the blues and widely differing dates, covering a period of more
than a century, have been given for the first appearance of the song
form. Our knowledge of the blues is dependent, however, on the
written observations of early collectors of Negro folk song, on the
recollections of aged musicians and singers and on examples that
have been made available on phonograph records. No collectors
turned their attention to the blues before the turn of the century,
and serious, informed study was not to be made until a score of
years later. Often the reminiscences of singers have proved prejudiced
or unreliable, and few were interviewed at a date when some light
could be thrown on the origins of the blues as a result of their state-

ments. Until 1920 no records were made that were remotely related
to the blues; it was not until the mid-1920's that recordings of Negro
folk singers were made available, and these to the colored market
only. In subsequent years commercial records were made of street
beggars and itinerant singers, of vaudeville and tent-show artists,
of folk entertainers and urban singers representing many forms
and styles of blues, but it was not until the 1930's and 1940's that
field recordings were made of Southern rural laborers and of working gangs in the state prison farms and penitentiaries. As these are
frequently cited as examples of the antecedents of the blues, it is
important to realise that they are of relatively recent date, for though
there is every indication that they represent traditional song forms
that may recall patterns existing during the days of slavery, they
may well have undergone a process of change. It is not unreasonable to assume that many styles and forms of blues or related song
forms have never been committed to paper or wax and that others
may have died before they could be recorded. Any conclusions
drawn, therefore, from the material that is at hand must be tempered with caution and the realisation that the origins of the blues
may forever remain obscure.

When Negroes were imported into the Americas, they undoubtedly brought certain aspects of their culture with them, as is
proven by the survival of these in Dutch Guiana and the West Indies,
where they were allowed to flourish with relatively little hindrance.
Africans who were imported and pressed into slavery in the Deep
South were forced to abandon much of their culture and to adapt
themselves to a new ethos: they had to learn a new language, follow a new mode of life. The visual and plastic arts were suppressed,
and if any African arts survived, they would have been in the field
of music and song. In some areas drumming and dancing were permitted; elsewhere they were forbidden.

A sense of rhythm is common to all peoples; it is not essentially
characteristic of Negroes, and the creation of music of any particular
form is acultural, not inherent in any one race. Group labor songs
were sung by slaves when at work, much as they had been sung in
Africa. But if there had been no such tradition, one would doubtless
have been born because of the circumstances of the work. Too much
emphasis can therefore be placed on the African origin of the American Negro, who was becoming an integral part of the society of the

United States, even if he did remain at the bottom of its structure. More than any other factor it was, in all probability, his peculiar position in American society that stimulated the Negro to create his blues: he was forced to conform on the one hand, yet rejected by virtue of his color on the other.

Joyfully the Negro embraced the Christian religion. He interpreted the Bible stories literally and adapted the Wesleyan Methodist hymns and the white spirituals to suit the needs of his intensely emotional form of worship in song. Some Negro spirituals were highly dramatic, strongly rhythmic; others were sad, slow songs which told of the wanderings of the lost tribes of Israel, in whose plight the slaves saw their own echoed: these were the blues in feeling, if not in kind. Work song and spiritual were frequently one and the same, the laborers following the sung exhortations of their leader as they did the preacher in their choral responses. In structure the spirituals generally followed the white hymns, but their singers were uneducated and happily unfettered by conventional rules of music. They delighted in long cadences, in bends and turns of the notes they sang, which gave added expression to their words, though fundamentally they often employed the pentatonic scale—allegedly African in origin, but common in fact to folk songs of simple peoples all over the world.

Instrumentally, Negroes showed early talent with the fiddle— and with the banjo, which has an authenticated African ancestry. White reels and jigs were imitated and new ones invented with strongly syncopated rhythms, giving birth to the banjo rags of the second half of the nineteenth century. At that time, Negro ballads extolling the virtues of colored heroes and closely patterned on the sixteen-bar or eight-bar ballads of Anglo-Saxon origin began to appear; and with the abolition of slavery, Negro balladeers had more time in which to sing them. Group labor had largely disappeared, and individual Negro farmers and sharecroppers cultivated their own small plots, working alone. Their work songs became looser and their long, meandering hollers—part sung, part cried, part yodelled—were heard in the Southern fields. Individual workers became known by their particular hollers, which they improvised interminably, repeating the lines until new ones came to mind.

Blues as a recognisable form seems to have developed as a blend of these individual elements. In its repeated lines and falling, crying notes it owes much to the hollers, direct forerunners of the blues. But the discipline imposed by the use of instrumental accompaniment gave the music shape. Early blues seem to have had verses of eight and sixteen bars in common with the ballads; and the three-chord European harmony of both ballads and spirituals is that on which the blues is based. At the close of the century the guitar became extremely popular, and the long, whining notes that are more easily achieved on this instrument than on the staccato banjo allowed instrumentalists to copy the shadings and flattenings that the field hands favored in their hollers. The moans of their voices were imitated by sliding the strings and by the use of what later became known as "blue notes"—minors introduced into a song in a major key, where a preference for diminished thirds and sevenths became apparent; resulting, it has been suggested, from the superimposition of an African pentatonic scale on the diatonic. In the process of development a more sharply defined form evolved, based on the familiar tonic, subdominant, dominant progression—the "twelve-bar blues." In this, the most common but by no means the only blues structure, the verses are constructed of three lines, each four bars in length. The first four bars are played on the tonic chord, though the last half of a bar may move to the seventh of that chord: thus, in the key of E, much favored by blues singers, there will be three and a half bars in E, half a bar in E7. The next two bars are played on the subdominant chord A, returning to the tonic chord for the closing two bars of the second line, while the final and third line consists of two bars on the dominant seventh B7 and two bars again played on the tonic. This three-line structure permits the singer to conceive a line and then to repeat it while inventing a third. Usually his words occupy approximately two bars of the line, permitting an interval of two bars during which he may extemporise an "answering" phrase on his guitar—if need be, only on the tonic chord. Such intervals vary greatly in length, however, and the solo player is free to extemporise as long as he wishes, his blues verse being ten, a dozen, fifteen bars if he so desires. In this traditional structure lies both the strength and the weakness of the blues. As a musical form it is limited in scope, but within its limitations it is capable of infinite variations, according to the originality and inventiveness of the blues singer. It is a form which is readily available to the instrumentalist of only limited means, who need but strum three or four chords to provide himself with a setting for his vocal improvisations. With practise he can extemporise melodic phrases within the "breaks" or non-vocal passages; and as his skill develops, he can pick instrumental patterns of great complexity, which express his ideas and complement his voice to the full. There is in the blues form an inevitability, a perfect musical resolution which allows the artist to follow its progression almost without conscious thought and to extemporise vocally and instrumentally with perfect freedom.

Blues is an intensely personal form of folk music, and the singer, in giving emphasis to his words, may make use of unorthodox and largely subconscious devices as he sings, just as he is given to the use of unconventional techniques on his instrument. As did the singer of spirituals, work songs and hollers, the singer of blues may moan, murmur or, in moments of emotional excitement, shout his words. He will punctuate his phrases with glottal stops and vocal snaps; will enjamb or elide words and syllables. Sometimes he will sing in the abstract but not meaningless syllables of a "scat vocal"; sometimes he will make falsetto cries and whoops, spoken asides and comments to his guitar. In the phrases "hollering the blues," "crying the blues," "shouting the blues" and many others used by singers may be detected different qualities of blues vocal expression. Some singers may have the rough, earthy voice of a Tommy Mc-Clennan, others the burred intonation of a Brownie McGhee, while still others may sing in the shrill tones of a Lee Brown. For the true blues singer does not strain to make his voice falsely rough or unnaturally "pure"; he sings in his natural voice, and his artistry lies in his ability to express himself to the full, using the means within his reach.

Because the blues is an improvised music, it is essentially transitory; the life of any one blues is short if it is not preserved on a record. But in this too, the blues gains strength, for the blues singer is ever seeking to create anew. There are undoubtedly certain blues stereotypes, and most blues singers have their stock in trade of melodic or rhythmic phrases and favorite verses. But the truly creative blues singer invests even these with new life by giving them new meaning, and he constantly creates new blues that draw directly from the enrichment of his own experience. Unlike the ballads of an earlier tradition, the blues seldom tell of the exploits of folk heroes, for the singer is usually the central character in his theme.

In his blues he comments broadly on the social scene, but almost invariably from a purely personal point of view. In some respects it is a selfish music; selfish and self-centered. It is a hard-bitten music, too, with little room for sentimentality and a certain lack of the higher virtues, as in Peetie Wheatstraw's *Hearse Man Blues:*

> I went around the casket and looked down in my baby's face [twice]
> Then I was soon wonderin' what good woman will take her place.

> The church bell begin to tone, hearse wheel was rollin' slow [twice],
> And I take my baby to the place where I will see her no more.

> Then I watch the undertaker slowly let her down [twice],
> My baby don't go no further—I know she is six feet in the ground.

In spite of its personal nature, the blues is curiously objective, often brutally realistic. Yet the blues is sung as a statement of fact, and seldom in a spirit of bitterness or anger. The blues singer sings to get the blues off his mind. He sings of love and infidelity, of sex and of loneliness. He sings of drinking and drugs, of murder and mutilation, of disasters and death. If his blues are frequently based on melancholy themes, it is because he sings as a member of an underprivileged class, as a member of a social group that is stigmatised by its pigmentation. There are few blues that tell of race riots or of lynching, partly because they could well be an inducement to further trouble, but primarily because they are outside the immediate world of the singer. The blues singer is an individualist who sings primarily for himself, but his appeal to others in his race lies largely in the fact that, in singing of a common predicament and of common experiences, he sings also for them. His hearers share his blues, for his troubles are also their own. With him they, too, can lose the blues and with him they can laugh. For there is laughter in the blues, though it is not of the easy, complacent kind. Sometimes it is aggressively bawdy, sometimes it is laughter through tight lips; but whatever and however the blues singer sings, he is only fully understood by those who live within his world. Barbecue Bob's *Bad Time Blues* (Co 14461) is an example:

> Bad time is upon me, everywhere the panic is on [twice],
> I feel so disgusted, all the good times done gone.

> Everybody is cryin' they can't get a break [twice],
> Tell me what's the matter? Everything seems to ache.

I can't make a nickel, I'm flat as I can be [twice],
Some people say money is talking, but it won't say a word to me.

I had a big check when the Devil was a boy [twice],
If I got a real job, I'd pass out with joy. . . .

Where was the blues born? Some say Tennessee, some say
Louisiana, and the claim has been made for many another state.
Mississippi is perhaps most frequently cited, and on grounds of
the density of its colored population there would appear to be some
justification. But it is more than probable that the blues had a
more or less simultaneous origin in many different areas, arising
from identical circumstances. The spirituals, the ballads, the work
songs and the hollers had a wide distribution through many states,
and the logical evolution of the blues from these may have been
equally widespread. Regional differences would have occurred, without doubt, but the great migration of Negro workers which commenced in the 1870's and gained considerable strength at the turn
of the century would have spread the music rapidly. By 1910 the
northward migration that was to last for another score of years
was well under way, and the over-all distribution of the blues was
effected without question. Even so, when recordings were made of
folk blues singers, from the late 1920's to the Second World War,
regional differences were still detectable. The high-pitched, declama-
tory but sad voices of the great Blind Lemon Jefferson or Rambling
Thomas from Texas, with their rapid arpeggio guitar breaks, contrasted with the richer voices and ballad-influenced blues of Barbecue
Bob, Blind Willie McTell or Peg Leg Howell in Georgia. Traces of
guitar rags and minstrel songs were to be found in the work of Blind
Boy Fuller, from the Carolinas, while the work songs survived in
the singing of Louisiana-born Huddie "Leadbelly" Ledbetter, who
spent many years in the state prison farms. Several regional styles
were to be noted in Mississippi, from the rough singing and unorthodox chords of Bukka White or Robert Petway to the shrill
moaning of Kokomo Arnold or Robert Johnson, whose knife blades
and bottle necks made their guitars wail in sympathy.

Many of the great blues singers and not a few of the itinerant
preachers and gospel singers were blind—and some, like Bogus Ben
Covington, pretended that they were. It was often hard for a Negro
who was not shackled to the sharecropping system to obtain work

in the South if he did not care to labor "on the jobs"—the occupations, dangerous to life and limb, that were "reserved" for Negroes because no one else would take them. For a blind Negro it was even harder, and so he would take to begging in the streets, with a guide boy to act as his "eyes." Attracting attention by playing the guitar and singing the blues, many a blind man saved himself from starvation and introduced the blues to an ever-widening and appreciative audience. But as folk artists, the majority of Southern blues singers could not depend on their playing for their employment, and they labored in various occupations. Big Bill Broonzy, from Mississippi, was a field hand; Sleepy John Estes led a railroad section gang; Big Boy Crudup was a lumber-camp water boy. Some graded the river levees, while others worked in the sawmills. When the work was exhausted and they were laid off, they "nailed a rattler" and, putting a plank across the brake rods of a moving freight train—risking death and the night stick of the brakeman—they hoboed a cheap ride to a new district.

In the lay-off periods on the plantations the field hands had time to spare, and after the harvests had been gathered in and the shucking done, picnics, parties, "sukey-jumps" and clambakes were popular. These festivities offered temporary musical employment for the blues singers, and they would also earn a casual dollar by playing at the roadside "jukes"—wood-frame saloons that offered cheap alcohol, women and rough entertainment. Two or three guitarists would form a small juke band and wander through the country together, seeking engagements. Often they would be augmented by other unemployed Negroes who played a heterogeneous collection of instruments: tubs converted into rudimentary one-string basses; washboards played with forks, nails or thimbles; jugs that produced a booming scale when blown into; swanee whistles, kazoos and mouth harps. Some of these folk bands were eventually recorded: Cannon's Jug Stompers, the Mississippi Jook Band, Phillips Louisville Jug Band were among them. They played and sang the blues, but drew from the repertoire of the minstrel bands, ballads and popular songs, too, according to the requirements of the function at which they played.

Many of the jug and washboard bands begged in the streets of the Southern towns, and the formation of groups of this kind became popular in some districts, notably in Memphis, Tennessee. In the back parlors they were joined by the city blues pianists, who entertained in the barrelhouses and ginmills back of town. In these crude saloons battered upright pianos were to be found, awaiting the thick stubby fingers of logger or miner to pound out a vigorous blues that would shake the building and set the feet of the close-packed throng slow-dragging across the floor. From Greenville to Groesbeck, Macon to Mound Bayou, Nashville to Natchez the picture was repeated a thousand times. The rolling piano blues of countless nameless men —some of whom knew but a single theme, while others learned to play with feeling and originality—could be heard in the dim, smoke-filled interiors of the bars and beer taverns. In spite of the positive tuning of the pianos, the barrelhouse blues pianists achieved the shadings and "blue notes" of their vocals by "crushing" the adjacent keys as they played. In imitation of the guitarists, who "walked the basses" in eight-to-the-bar rhythms, they set up rolling bass figures in the left hand and improvised endless blues variations in the treble. From such a background emerged the talents of Roosevelt Sykes and Walter Davis, Memphis Slim and Champion Jack Dupree, singers and pianists whose powerful yet moving blues earned them a wider fame.

Through the Southern towns and villages came travelling shows, which entertained the populace for a brief period before moving on to the next district. The vendors of patent medicines and pills could be assured of sales in Negro areas, where doctors and hospital beds were virtually unknown, and to attract attention to their wares they would employ blues singers and entertainers to put on "medicine shows." Such medicine shows have flourished for more than half a century, and by working in them many blues singers served their apprenticeship as semi-professional artists, met other singers and toured throughout the South. Guitarists like Will "Casey Bill" Weldon and Po' Joe Williams, harmonica players like Jaybird Coleman and later, Sonny Terry, worked with the "medicine men," earning in experience what they lacked in wages. Similar employment was to be found with the travelling carnivals and minstrel shows: McCabe's Minstrels, Mahara's Minstrels, Silas Green's from New Orleans and the Rabbit Foot Minstrels. These and scores of other shows, both great and small, toured the South for decades on end, travelling in caravans and trucks, carrying their "big tops" for erection on vacant lots on the outskirts of town. Among the motley assembly of "Tom Walkers" on stilts; menageries, freaks and midgets; and the girl "hoofers" on the "clothesline," could be found blues singers who attracted the crowds, commented on the scene and provided the music. Here the great Negro singers and entertainers, such as guitarist Jim Jackson or pianist Charles "Cow Cow" Davenport, came face to face with their people, and here in the travelling tent shows were made the "classic blues" singers, who stood with one foot in the tradition of vaudeville-minstrel entertainment and the other firmly planted in the folk tradition of the blues.

Of the "classic blues" singers, Gertrude "Ma" Rainey was undoubtedly one of the first, commencing her professional career at the turn of the century, when she was fourteen years old. With her husband, Will Rainey, whom she married a year later, she toured the South in the Rabbit Foot Minstrels, singing the songs that her parents, also minstrel troupers, used to perform. And she sang the blues. Ma Rainey brought a certain degree of professionalism, of conscious artistry to the blues, but it was only a row of candles that kept her apart from her audience. She felt the blues and as she sang in her rich, warm voice she endeared herself to her listeners. They loved her stocky brown frame, her gaudy magnificence, her wild hair and her songs. It was Ma Rainey who discovered and taught the child who was to be known as the "Empress of the Blues," Bessie Smith. When she commenced to record, Bessie Smith was in her mid-twenties, but she possessed a full, round voice of great dramatic intensity that belied her years. Her broad, sweeping phrases, her moaning syllables and the blue shading of her notes were superbly controlled, and though she was a professional blues singer, her audiences were profoundly moved by the sincerity of her performances. Bessie's rival, Clara Smith, though less celebrated, was at her best the equal of the "Empress." Unhappy with the inferior vaudeville material that Bessie Smith could still turn to good account, Clara rendered the blues with great sympathy and understanding.

Tank towns and whistle stops deep in the "sticks" saw the classic blues singers as they barnstormed through the country. But for the most part the singers worked, when they could, in the larger towns that offered a Negro theatre of sorts. In the vaudeville shows of the first decades of the century, the blues singers were prominently featured, and they followed the Keith-Orpheum or similar theatre circuits. The T.O.B.A. (the Theatre Owners' Booking Agency, or, as the colored troupers interpreted the initials, "Tough on Black Artists") afforded a continuous tour throughout the South and Midwest, including Baltimore, Nashville, Atlanta, New Orleans and Kansas City among the centres where the singers worked.

Sara Martin was celebrated for her striking personality on the stage, while Ida Cox continued to fill the halls for more than three decades, singing in her hard, incisive voice blues that were close to the folk tradition. Lillian Glinn and Mattie Hite, Martha Copeland and Bertha "Chippie" Hill, Sippie Wallace and Lucille Bogan were only a few of the great singers who were immensely popular with Negro audiences in the 1920's.

Many of these singers, who brought the blues into the field of professional popular entertainment, found a happy relationship with the jazz bands that had emerged from New Orleans and the Midwest and were enjoying sensational success in Chicago and New York. Blues—the blues of the street guitarists and the "black butt" pianists of the New Orleans honky-tonks—had played a considerable part in the development of jazz, and a few blues singers, but not those of the first rank, sang successfully with the New Orleans bands. Blues singers and jazz bands met in the carnival and minstrel shows, and the "classic" singers, with their part vaudeville origins, worked with the jazzmen as few folk singers could be expected to do.

Mamie Smith, a Negro entertainer with a leaning towards the blues, was the first singer in this genre to record, and following the success of her *Crazy Blues* for Okeh in 1921 there was an unprecedented rush to put the voices of blues singers on wax. Okeh commenced its "race" series designed for the Negro market, and Gennett, Paramount, Columbia and other firms followed suit, many issuing some of the finest examples of the music on record. As the popularity of the "classic blues" was assured, the talent scouts began to search for the folk singers, and brilliantly endowed if wholly unsophisticated singers of the calibre of Blind Lemon Jefferson appeared before the horns of the recording machines or were "captured" near at home by the mobile recording units that combed the South. A vast and eager buying public in the Negro market was discovered, and the blues in its most raw and also its more self-conscious forms proved to be, for a time, a commercial proposition.

While talent scouts in the South were discovering such unlikely characters as Blue Coat Tom Nelson, Keghouse and Jaybird, Daddy

Stovepipe and Whistling Pete, the record companies also found blues singers of no little ability in the teeming ant hills of Chicago's South Side and New York's Harlem. Negro migration to the North had continued unabated and the colored sectors had multiplied their population many times, though they had seldom increased in area. Much hardship was caused by the congested conditions, but families from the South shared their rooms, and the "hot-bed" apartments (where successive families rented the same room for eight hours in the day) put money in the pockets of the tenement owners. Among the hundreds of thousands of migrants were blues singers, pianists, guitarists, who sang and played the blues off their minds. To combat the pressure of high prices and demanding landlords, "house-rent" parties—or, in the euphemism of the time, "social whist" parties— were instituted. Bathtub liquor and favored delicacies like chitterlings or hog's maws were provided, and guests paid twenty-five cents for admission. On the proceeds the rent could be paid and a similar serv- ice afforded to someone else in like straits at a later date. Music for these functions was supplied by a boogie pianist—Charlie Spand from Detroit, perhaps, or Pinetop Smith from Troy, Alabama, who could entertain, play and sing the blues for hours on end. The gin- mill pianists of the South brought their "fast Western" walking-bass rhythms to the North, and the music of boogie-woogie was ideally suited to these functions. Many rent-party pianists and blues singers —together with the Southern guitarists like Blind Blake or Sylvester Weaver, who joined them—were recorded on wax, though some are represented by only a couple of sides.

Of the folk singers who were recorded, few were women. Negro women have been proportionately more faithful to the various de- nominations of the church than their menfolk. To the church the blues were "devil songs," and a large number of colored women would not be heard singing the blues. But others absorbed the idiom and sang as they worked in yard and field, with washtub and needle. Theirs was unaccompanied blues, and few women sang for casual employment as entertainers; either they were in vaudeville and the minstrel shows, or else they sang for their own pleasure and relief. Occasionally a Bobby Cadillac from Dallas or a Nellie Florence from Atlanta, with the voice of a virago, would be recorded, and in Memphis and St. Louis a number of hard-voiced women with the blues on their minds were also recorded: Bessie Tucker, Ida May

Mack, Little Alice Moore and Elzadie Robinson, for example. Moaning or strident, their blues compared well with that of the male folk singers, and if they did not play an instrument themselves, they found sympathetic support in the piano blues of a K. D. Johnson, Bob Call or Will Ezell.

But the Depression stilled the turntables of the record companies. Many of them did not survive these terrible, lean years, and countless folk singers and musicians disappeared in the anonymity of the vast segregated Negro areas of the Northern cities, while others, disillusioned, returned to the South and were forgotten. It was the end, too, of true vaudeville, and the majority of the great "classic blues" singers were heard for the last time. By the late 1930's Ma Rainey was in retirement in Georgia, Bessie Smith had died in tragic circumstances and Clara Smith had also passed on in an obscure death. Their form of blues, with its close links with vaudeville and jazz, had virtually died, though a little of it survived in the tent-show companies that still continued a struggling existence touring the rural South.

If there was a time to sing the blues with feeling and meaning, it was surely during these years of the Depression, when Negro workers were laid off first and when thousands suffered literal slow starvation. Folk blues did not die at this time, though for economic reasons it was not to be heard on records.

As the larger companies were resuscitated and others ventured forth for the first time, the blues was recorded again—tentatively at first, and then with increasing numbers of releases as it was realised that Negroes were prepared to buy the work of singers whose blues they shared. Among the first to be put on wax again was the pianist and singer from Nashville, Tennessee, Leroy Carr. He had a soft, plaintive, almost sweet voice, but an inherent feeling for the blues. His warm piano style was given a certain bite by his almost inseparable companion, guitarist Frankie Black ("Scrapper Blackwell"). No singer was better loved by his race than Carr. His blues were of the city rather than the country, and his recordings indicated a new trend to a slightly more sophisticated form of blues than the frequently rough or strident blues of the rural areas. When he died suddenly, under circumstances that have never been satisfactorily explained, he was widely mourned in the colored world. His style survived in the singing of many admirers, among them Bumble Bee

Slim (Amos Easton) and Little Bill Gaither (who called himself "Leroy's Buddy," both of whom composed blues to his memory.

A number of blues singers from the South settled happily enough in the tumult of Chicago or Harlem and remained there, adapting their styles of singing and playing unconsciously to their changed environment. Lonnie Johnson and Aaron "T-Bone" Walker, who came from the areas near New Orleans and Dallas respectively, had been brought up in urban communities, and their clever, pithy blues and superb instrumental techniques have made them familiar names in the catalogues for more than thirty years. Another celebrated singer who left a primitive Mississippi community to spend the major part of his life in the clamor of the city was the late Big Bill Broonzy, a guitarist and singer of great talent, who brought the blues to audiences in schools and concert halls, as well as cellar dives throughout the United States and Europe. Even the tough and belligerent Leadbelly, with eleven years in Southern penal institutions behind him, eventually became used to the accelerated New York life. With quiet dignity he would listen to the chatter of the Greenwich Village night clubs, and then unleash something of the power within him as he recalled with thunderous voice and twelve-string guitar the folk songs and blues of his tumultuous past. Leadbelly's companion of former years, Josh White, who is intellectually, instrumentally and vocally gifted, has continued to tour and work, to sing at folk music festivals, at institutions and expensive clubs alike—until, inadvertently, he has almost divorced his music altogether from the background of the blues.

But "urban blues" or "city blues" as terms used to identify particular music styles do not necessarily signify the modification of the blues to bring it to a wider audience. They refer to the development, specifically in the Northern cities, of an urban form of folk blues. Often this has been the creation of Southern Negroes who have settled in the North, retaining some vocal characteristics of the South but producing a different form of the blues in their new surroundings. One such singer and guitarist is Tampa Red (Hudson Whittaker), who accompanied Ma Rainey early in his career and later recorded a large number of racy and often wryly humorous blues and blues songs. Altogether more grim and serious in content were the blues of "The Devil's Son-in-Law," Peetie Wheatstraw (William Bunch), an able guitarist and pianist who had an original talent as a composer of blues based on his personal experiences. He was killed in a road accident in 1941. Others who created meaningful blues from the harsh realities of their lives were singers as diverse as the deep-throated Johnny Temple and the high-pitched Ollie Sheppard; Jimmy Gordon and Lee Brown; Charley Jordan and St. Louis Jimmy (James Oden), and the habitually drunk "Doctor" Clayton. Beside them worked a number of women singers, including Memphis Minnie McCoy, who had played guitar on the street corners of Memphis as a child and who developed a technique to rival any man; Lil Green and Georgia White; the "Yas Yas Girl," Merline Johnson; and the Harlem singer, Rosetta Howard.

Guitar and boogie piano remained the basic instrumental accompaniment for city as well as country singers, but they were often augmented by bass and drums and sometimes clarinet, saxophone or trumpet. Big Bill Broonzy's half brother, Robert Brown, succeeded in singing the blues while he played a washboard; under the name of Washboard Sam, he made a large number of recordings. The harmonica players John Lee "Sonny Boy" Williamson and William "Jazz" Gillum developed techniques of alternately singing and playing so that their melodic lines remained unbroken. In the company of such blues musicians as Big Bill Broonzy, Willie Lacey (guitar), Blind John Davis, Big Maceo Merriwether (piano), Ransom Knowling (bass), and Tyrrell Dixon and Charles Saunders (drums), they made many recordings and obtained casual engagements. Frequently these musicians recorded under their own names, to be joined by some of the others or by such singers and instrumentalists as Charles and Joe McCoy. A number of effective partnerships evolved from these circumstances: Big Bill Broonzy with his pianist, Joshua Altheimer; Lonnie Johnson with Blind John Davis; Big Maceo with Tampa Red—worthy successors of the team made by Leroy Carr and Scrapper Blackwell. Through the late 1930's and up to the end of the 1940's most of these blues singers and instrumentalists remained active, though their recording careers were broken by the war.

And the country singers? During the middle 1930's a small number were recorded, and at this time the great Sleepy John Estes, with his harmonica player, Noah Lewis, made some of his best recordings. With his tragic, broken voice Estes put on wax some of the finest examples of recorded blues, drawing from the everyday happenings of his life for his material. Such colorful characters as Po' Joe Williams and Bo Carter also appeared on discs at this time. As the war years approached, other Southern singers came before the microphones, among them the celebrated Blind Boy Fuller, with his grit-textured voice, accompanied by the brilliant harmonica player, Sonny Terry; the youthful Brownie McGhee, similarly supported by Jordan Webb; Buddy Moss, Tommy McClennan, and a number of similarly gifted singers. Before the war put an end to recording activity for a period, one small incident of far-reaching effect occurred: the folk-song collector and authority, Alan Lomax, recorded a couple of primitive blues by a young guitarist who called himself Muddy Waters. His items, recorded "in the field" near Clarksdale, Mississippi, were evidence enough of the continued existence of Southern folk blues.

After the war there was a mushroom growth of small record companies, including a large number that issued records exclusively for Negroes. Few of these flirted with the innovations of Long- and Extended-Play records, in clear acknowledgment of the Negro's continued economic inferiority. The success of the recordings of boogie pianist and blues singer Private Cecil Gant, whose issues proudly and cunningly stated his military rank, indicated that the Negro worker still looked to the blues singer for moral and racial support. Though a few disc catalogues still bore the phrase "race records," the majority of record companies had felt the quickening pulse of the Negro minority group and realised that the old term, with its implications of segregation, was held in disfavor. "Rhythm and blues," among the various new terms used to identify the still-segregated catalogues, was the one which was to become permanently employed. It was as broad in its implications as the earlier term had been, for "race records" included vaudeville and variety acts, spirituals, gospel choirs and sermons, as well as blues, among their number. Rhythm and blues records featured close-harmony quartets and quintets, both secular and religious in character; religious services and small band groups, in addition to the blues. Within the blues the emphasis was now on punching, driving small bands supporting fiercely aggressive "blues shouters."

Although rhythm and blues seems to be a postwar development, it has its roots in the blues shouting of Jimmy Rushing, vocalist for many years with the bands of Count Basie, and in the equally stentorian delivery of Joe Turner, a Kansas City bartender whose records, made in 1938 with pianist Pete Johnson, coincided with the commercial discovery of boogie-woogie. Both Rushing and Turner remained active in the postwar years, but the former's style became gentler, if anything, while Turner joyfully leaped into the exhilarating atmosphere of "R. & B." The riffs and unison saxophone work of Kansas City-style jazz played a part in the formation of the new music, in which, however, heavily accented off-beat drumming, percussive piano boogie and ringing electric guitars were markedly featured. Among the principal singers in the shouting style of rhythm and blues were a number who were experienced band singers. Wynonie Harris, known as "Mister Blues," came from Kansas City and worked with Lucky Millinder and Lionel Hampton, big-band leaders who have left their mark on R. & B. Harris' blues are highly sophisticated but wide in their appeal. Also a singer with Hampton was the late Sonny Parker, who owed much to Joe Turner in his shouting style. Among others, Charles "Crown Prince" Waterford and Jimmy Witherspoon had a similar background in the Kay-Cee-inspired form of blues shouting with strong band backing, and made their substantial contributions to the popularity of R. & B. Some of the new school of singers liked to "front" a band but continued to play an instrument between vocals—among them the prematurely bald saxophonist, Eddie "Mister Cleanhead" Vinson, and another saxophone player, "Bull Moose" Jackson, whose sobriquet aptly describes his instrumental and vocal techniques. New guitarists came to the fore, playing heavily amplified instruments so that they could be heard above the strong "shouting" bands that gave them support: the flamboyant "Gatemouth" Brown, for example; Smiley Lewis (Overton Lemon) from New Orleans; and the Memphis disc jockey turned blues singer, B. B. "Blues Boy" King.

Before he became a blues singer himself, B. B. King relayed blues records from his WDIA station for eight hours every day; and throughout the South, radio stations in Baton Rouge and Birmingham, Nashville, New Orleans and elsewhere play recordings of R. & B., alternating with programs of gospel songs, all day long. The disc jockeys have become celebrated: Vicksburg has its "Jet Pilot of Jive," Bruce Payne, who daily presents his show, the "Jet-Powered Jive Ship." Knoxville has Ace Wilson; New Orleans has "Doctor Daddy-O" (incidentally, a graduate from Chicago). And there is "Sugar Daddy," the "World's Wildest, Loudest, Craziest

Dee-Jay who invites you all to do the Sugar Bounce! Torrid Tunes for Sugar Mamas and Sugar Papas!"—who delivers the blues from the "one hundred per cent Negro" Network WBCO in Birmingham-Bessemer, Alabama. Often the material presented on these programs is of a mediocre standard, but the fact remains that the blues is much in demand; New Orleans housewives complain that they cannot get a colored girl in domestic service unless they can assure a radio to keep her company with the blues.

So the slicker styles, the shouting styles of the Northern cities have reached the Southern communities rapidly, and it is possible to hear a Dallas band with Zuzu Bollin, or a Houston band with Johnny Ace (or at least it was, until his demise in an unfortunate game of Russian Roulette) that is almost indistinguishable from those of Harlem or Cleveland. Nevertheless the singers have retained their individuality to a considerable degree, and the widespread transmission of rhythm-and-blues discs is not wholly to the disadvantage of the blues. One outcome of the energetic work of the disc jockeys has been the "rediscovery" of the Southern blues; still very much alive, and popular, too.

From Louisiana to Houston, Texas, came Sam "Lightnin' " Hopkins to farm a plot within reach of the town. He is a singer of great depth of feeling and a fine, if "primitive," guitarist. Andrew "Smokey" Hogg from Texas plays guitar in the old tradition of the Southern country blues and sings in a warm voice, while John Lee Hooker has been outstandingly successful in bringing his boogie-based guitar playing and forceful vocals to the stage of the Apollo Theatre. Smokey Hogg moved over to the West Coast, where Lowell Fulsom had brought his Texas blues. Texas, in fact, has been a fountainhead of the Southern blues ever since the Second World War.

While the more sophisticated blues bands have developed along the riffing, shouting lines of the Kansas City style, simple groups—composed, say, of guitar, boogie piano and traps, in support of a harmonica-playing blues singer—have been unpretentiously active. Among the harmonica players, Rice Miller (calling himself, unnecessarily, Sonny Boy Williamson No. 2), from Jackson, Mississippi; Chester "Howling Wolf" Burnett from Arkansas; Little Junior Parker from Houston; and Little Walter Jacobs from Chicago have been outstanding. The latter has been recorded many times with Muddy Waters, now Chicago-based and highly popular, and with Albert

Luandrew (or Sunnyland Slim), a fine boogie pianist. Together this group has put in some excellent accompaniments to other singers, including St. Louis Jimmy; and it is of interest to see this veteran singer still recording fairly prolifically. Although some blues singers have been unable to make the change and have retired from active recording—Buddy Moss, Jazz Gillum, Kokomo Arnold, Scrapper Blackwell and Walter Davis among them, all living but otherwise employed—others whose names have long appeared in the "race" catalogues are still active. Little Eddie Boyd, Roosevelt Sykes, Champion Jack Dupree, Curtis Jones, Ollie Shepard and Memphis Slim, and such veterans as T-Bone Walker, Lonnie Johnson and Alberta Hunter, still have a considerable following. And on a large proportion of America's six hundred-odd record labels, the blues still sells in quantity to a Negro market.

It had been said that such a singer as Fats Domino is the modern equivalent of a Bessie Smith. In popularity he may well be, but his music is not as vital, nor is his material so closely related to the struggle for life. Fats Domino is a singer whose blues, smoothed at the edges and charmingly delivered, attracts a white audience: it is comfortably exciting. But the blues of Memphis Minnie, J. B. Lenore, Leroy Dallas, L'il Son Jackson or Big Walter Price is too tough, too earnest to break far into the popular market.

There are those who say that the blues is dying; they are the persons who wish it to die. For the Negro intellectual the blues can be something of an embarrassment; a reminder of simple origins. For the white man the blues can also be something of an embarrassment; a reminder of the injustice of Segregation. In a sense they are both right, for the blues is unlikely to outlast the eventual complete integration of the Negro in American society except in the most vitiated form, for the real reasons for singing the blues will then have largely disappeared. The length of time that elapses before the Negro is accepted on terms of complete and unconditional equality in the United States may well be the measure that determines the life of the blues.

Today the Negro in the Southern villages and Northern cities still obtains from the blues a feeling of security, the knowledge that he is part of an in-group. When the blues dies, it will have served its purpose, and a great and valid folk music will pass into the cultural heritage of the nation. That day has yet to come.

BOOGIE-WOOGIE

^^^^^^^^^^^^^^^^^^^^^^^^

Max Harrison

One of the most impressive writers on jazz to have appeared in several years is Max Harrison, whose criticism appears regularly in the British *Jazz Monthly*. He is interested in and can be illuminating on all phases of jazz. In this book, for example, he has contributed a chapter on Charlie Parker, as well as the one on boogie-woogie. He is capable of close musical analysis, as in this chapter, but he is also able to relate his musical findings to the lives of the players and the social context of their work. Harrison, incidentally, is also thoroughly trained in classical music.

His chapter on boogie-woogie should help dispel the oversimplification that boogie-woogie is "all the same" or close to it. It is also a particularly lucid approach to jazz criticism, or so it seems to the editors; and several of his insights in the chapter can apply to other areas of jazz as well.

Boogie-woogie is an aspect of the blues. It can be generally defined as piano solo music based on twelve, or occasionally eight, bar patterns, the most immediate characteristic of which is the use of repeated, or ostinato, bass figures. Popular jazz history usually places it in the 1930's, with Pinetop Smith, who made his first records in 1928, as the patriarchal figure in the background. In fact, while the origins of this music are as obscure as those of any basic jazz form, it appears to have derived from two kinds of music that were widely distributed considerably before the turn of the century. These forms were the vocal blues and the guitar music that accompanied Negro dancing.

This is not the place to discuss the distribution of the blues, but one instance of its early dissemination may be noted. In 1876 Lafcadio Hearn contributed an article to *The Commercial,* a Cincinnati publication, in which he described the Negro life round the docks in that area. He wrote of the singing and dancing of the sailors, dock workers and their women and described the music as "sonorous and regularly slow," "plaintive," "slow and sweet" and "lengthy chants." Clearly this was the blues.

Not only in dock areas but all over the South, and especially in railway construction camps, mining towns, lumber and turpentine camps, colored people gathered in bars and back rooms to dance. In the early days music was provided by guitars, and the anthropologist Zora Neale Hurston has described the form it took:

> One guitar was enough for a dance. To have two was considered excellent. Where two were playing one man played the lead and the other seconded him. The first player was "picking" and the second was "framming," that is, playing chords while the lead carried the melody by dexterous finger-work. Sometimes a third player was added, and he played a tom-tom effect on the lower strings.

Such places were known as "jukes," the playing was called "juking" and the music was based on the blues. In time pianos replaced guitars, but their players, whose music had to fulfill the same purpose, took over many devices of guitar technique; the right hand continued the melodies of the leading guitar while the left provided a solid accompaniment.

This crystallisation between blues and guitar music on the piano keyboard probably took place in the Midwest, because it was there that so many of the logging and turpentine camps were situated. The earliest references we have to boogie tend to confirm this. Huddie Ledbetter said he first heard it in 1899 in Caddo County, Texas, and Bunk Johnson apparently first encountered it in the lumber camps of western Louisiana. Richard M. Jones remembered a pianist known as "Stavin' Chain," who played it around Donaldsville, Texas, in 1904, during the building of the Texas-Pacific railway. At approximately the same time and in the same area, Jelly Roll Morton heard Buddy Bertrand, whose *Crazy Chord Rag* he re-created in his Library of Congress recordings. In 1909 W. C. Handy heard it in Memphis, played by Sonny Butts, Seymour Abernathy and Bennie French. Morton also mentioned French in his Library of Congress sessions.

The music did not acquire the name "boogie" for some time. At first it was called "fast Western"—another indication of its place of origin—and it retained similar names when it travelled. Thus, when recalling his early days in Kansas City, Pete Johnson said all the pianists played "the same sort of Western rolling blues."

Needless to say, boogie was not recorded until the 1920's, and we can never have much idea of the pattern of its distribution from the Midwest, or of the regional differences of style it may have acquired. But whatever area it penetrated, boogie remained in the same kind of social environment. Joe Turner has given us an excellent picture of its milieu in Kansas City:

> All the working people came in early and got high and had a ball and then things would kinda quiet down and finally there wouldn't be nobody in there except the bartender, waiter and the boss, and we'd start playing about three o'clock in the morning. People used to say they could hear me hollering five blocks away. It would be in the still of the morning and the bossman would set up pitchers of corn-likker and we'd rock. Just about the time we'd be starting to have a good time, here would come the high hats and we'd set the joint on fire then and really have a ball till ten or eleven o'clock in the day. Sleep? Who wants to sleep with all that blues jumpin' around?

Boogie probably reached Chicago after the 1914–18 war, when so many colored people travelled north to escape the unemployment in the Southern states—but it took its place in a not-dissimilar scene.

Here it was played at ginmills, good-time flats, saloons and rent parties. Speaking of the latter, the New York pianist Willie "The Lion" Smith recalled:

> The parties were good for everything. A hundred people would crowd into one seven-room flat until the walls bulged. Food! Hog maws (pickled pig bladders) and chitt'lins with vinegar—you never ate nothing until you ate them. Beer and gin. When we played everyone danced.

Because boogie was created within one definite and limited set of circumstances, its range of expression was not wide. Yet it derived strength from this confinement, like a river that flows quickly in a channel that is narrow but deep. The music drew much of its power from being so closely related to the life of its audience. There was little separation between performer and audience, and often the musicians had other work that involved them in the life of their fellows: Jimmy Yancey was a ball-park groundsman, while Meade Lux Lewis and Albert Ammons were taxi drivers in the 1920's. They were in no way a class apart, seen only when playing. So close a link between musician and audience had a number of beneficial effects. Most important of these was the inspiration the players drew from contact with an audience which approved and responded to things they themselves liked, and with which they were able to feel one. In view of its comparative limitations of technique and materials, boogie would hardly have acquired the musical quality it did without this factor. How important the environment was to the validity of the music was demonstrated in later years, when it moved to the concert hall and the smart night club.

Analysis

In considering the exact nature of boogie-woogie, with regard to both style and content, it is important to bear in mind that it was the product of a limited set of circumstances and conditions. The main determinants were the kind of places in which it was played, the type of men who played it and—a factor often forgotten—the instruments on which they had to work. In places like the recreation centres of lumber camps and in ginmills, the music would need to be loud and forceful. At all times the pianos would be battered and out of tune. The audiences would not want, nor the instruments permit, many refinements of technique. Richard M. Jones said, "Music was different in New Orleans because many were too blamed ignorant to read. There were no schools." Yet this was true of most Negro music-making at that time; boogie is essentially the creation of men who were never taught how to play and who ignored the conventions because they did not know there were any.

There are a number of ways of producing volume on a piano, but an untutored player would almost always choose the most obvious—that of hitting the keys hard with tensed muscles and rather stiff wrists. This kind of touch results in the hard percussive quality of sound that is characteristic of almost all genuine boogie. It is a tiring way of playing, but the primitive pianists knew of no other method and were doubtless inured to hard work. Accusations of monotony have often been levelled at boogie, and the present writer believes that whatever the conscious objection made—for example, Aaron Copland's, that it "lacks any shred of melodic invention"—listeners unaccustomed to the idiom are in fact repelled by the unvarying percussive touch. This is because it is diametrically opposed to the conception of pianism imposed on us by nineteenth-century music. From the time of Beethoven through the work of Chopin and Liszt to the compositions of Debussy and Ravel, the general trend in piano writing was towards an increasing reliance on variation in touch, scope of harmonic vocabulary and use of the pedals, particularly the sustaining pedal. Everything possible was done to mitigate the instrument's percussive qualities. This tradition has been continued in jazz by men like Art Tatum and Erroll Garner. Pianistically the main point about a Garner ballad performance is that he makes the instrument *sing*. In sharpest contrast to all this, the boogie players used the piano virtually as a percussion instrument. This was not an abuse of its qualities, for it has enormous resources and fully admits of both approaches.

In practice the unconsciously imposed limitation of the percussive touch proved to be a beneficial discipline. Cut off from the resources of touch by his ignorance and the poor quality of his instrument, the boogie player was forced to develop variety of effect by other means. His harmonic knowledge was small and his themes were a limited number of blues. As he was called upon to produce brash and forceful music at all times, the refinements of elaborate melodic development were out of the question. (This is not to suggest that boogie does not have its share of melodic interest, but melody could never be its foremost quality.) Consequently the boogie player explored the only avenue open to him and cultivated great rhythmic virtuosity. Against the unfaltering beat of the left hand were thrown an endless variety of rhythmic punctuations and irregular accents. Thus did the rhythmic element predominate as in no other form of jazz, and it became the richest part of the boogie idiom.

The most immediate identifying feature of boogie and the one that lays the foundation of its singular qualities is, of course, the ever-present ostinato bass. Like the tonal qualities of boogie playing, this also arose from the musicians' lack of training. The "normal" type of piano bass, which is to be found in the work of such diverse pianists as James P. Johnson, Erroll Garner and Teddy Wilson, consists of a single note, octave or tenth in the lower register, alternating with a chord in the middle of the keyboard:

Example 1: James P. Johnson—Lonesome Reverie

This is one of the most convenient and frequently used pianistic resources, and gives fullness and depth of sound, a sense of movement through the contrast of lower with middle registers and an effective sense of harmonic changes. Yet however widely used, it is essentially a device of the trained pianist and could not have been employed by the early boogie men. These players had little to start with but their early-acquired knowledge of the blues and the simple harmonies that went with them. While improvising melodies and rhythmic punctuations with the right hand, they would probably tend to keep their left in a few close positions, stating the underlying chords in simple repeated patterns. At first this would almost certainly have been only four notes or chords to the bar:

Example 2

However, this is a heavy and uninteresting sound, which quickly becomes monotonous. Yet by doubling the number of notes a very different effect is obtained and we have the archetypal boogie bass:

Example 3

It is a short step between these two patterns, and it may well be that the characteristic ostinato basses of boogie arose simply from the need to impart a degree of momentum and interest to elemental basses like Example 2.

The phrase "eight-to-the-bar" was coined in connection with boogie, and it is a misleading one in that, although the presence of eight notes or chords in one bar is usually one of the essentials of the idiom, these do not always give eight beats. Sometimes the effect is of four only, and a good instance is Meade Lux Lewis' *Bass on Top*. However, once the ostinato bass was established, it assumed a number of rhythmic patterns:

  (i) The bass in even eighth notes. This does give eight beats, of course, and is found in many forms in countless boogie solos. Examples: Romeo Nelson's *Head Rag Hop*, Albert Ammons' *Monday Struggle* and Speckled Red's *Wilkins Street Stomp*.

  (ii) In dotted eighth and sixteenth notes. This is equally common. Examples: Ammons' *Chicago on My Mind* and Lewis' *Six Wheel Chaser*.

  (iii) In triplets. Here each group consists of a fourth note and an eighth note in triplet time, and there are four groups to a bar. This and the previous pattern give only four beats to a bar, and the note on the weakest part of the beat is in effect an un-accented after-beat. Pattern (iii) could be notated in 12/8 time. Examples: Montana Taylor's *Detroit Rocks* and *Indiana Avenue Stomp*, and parts of Lewis' *Honky Tonk Train Blues* and *Bass on Top*.

It is not always easy to distinguish between (ii) and (iii), but the following extract from Jimmy Yancey's *State Street Special* will make the difference clear. In the first bar the sixteenth note in the second and fourth beat groups comes *after* the last note of the right-hand triplets, but in the third bar the second note of the left-hand triplets comes *with* it.

Example 4: Jimmy Yancey—*State Street Special*

  (iv) In fourth notes and pairs of eighth notes. A less common pattern, favored by Yancey. Example: *Yancey Stomp.*

  (v) In fourth notes alternating with groups of dotted eighth and sixteenth notes. Another Yancey pattern, to be found in *State Street Special.*

  (vi) In fourth notes. With only four notes or chords, this is not really a boogie pattern. It is used only by Lewis in *Bear Cat Crawl,* a piece that owes its boogie atmosphere almost entirely to its treble figurations.

A number of other rhythmic patterns were utilised, but these are the most noteworthy. Yancey's work was particularly rich in its variety of bass formulae, and this has caused his status as a boogie pianist to be questioned. In fact, he was simply more imaginative than the rest.

The actual forms in notes these patterns took were many, although all were firmly rooted in the chords of the blues. The two basic formulae were that given in Example 3 and the walking bass in broken octaves:

Example 5

Here are four of Ammons' developments of Example 3:

(a)

(b)   (c)

Example 6: Albert Ammons basses—(a) from *Boogie Woogie Stomp*,
(b) *Shout for Joy*, (c) *Monday Struggle*

and one of Lewis':

Example 7: Lewis—Ammons—Johnson—*Boogie Woogie Prayer*

Similar figures appear in pattern (ii):

(a)   (b)

(c)

Example 8: (a) Ammons—*Bass Gone Crazy*,
(b) Ammons—*Boogie Woogie Blues*, (c) Lewis—*Bass on Top*

Here is another Lewis variation:

Example 9: Lewis—*Six Wheel Chaser*

And some more Yancey patterns:

(a)

(b)

(c)

(d)

Example 10: Yancey basses—(a) from *Yancey Stomp,*
(b) *Mellow Blues,* (c) *East St. Louis Blues,*
(d) *Slow & Easy Blues*

As its names implies, Ammons' *Bass Gone Crazy* contains deviations
from all normal bass formulae and, in addition to chromatic scales,
includes passages like the following:

Example 11: Ammons—*Bass Gone Crazy*

It should not be assumed that the same rhythmic pattern was used throughout an entire performance. Outstanding players made subtle changes in rhythm even though the same note grouping was retained. For example, Lewis' *Bass on Top* employs the broken-octave bass in patterns (i), (ii) and (iii).

With regard to right hand figurations, it is possible within the space of this chapter only to indicate general tendencies. Passages in single notes were naturally common:

Example 12: Ammons—*Boogie Woogie Blues*

But in view of the need for strength in the boogie pianists' work, these were often reinforced with double notes at various intervals:

Example 13: Lewis—*Six Wheel Chaser*

Passages in thirds were common:

Example 14: Ammons—*Boogie Woogie Stomp*

And sixths even more so:

Example 15: Yancey—*Yancey Stomp*

Piano octaves have a ringing sound well suited to the boogie pianists' task:

Example 16: Yancey—*State Street Special*

Example 17: Ammons—*Bass Gone Crazy*

Arpeggios over wide stretches of the keyboard were less common than might be expected, but here is an example from Ammons:

Example 18: Ammons—*Shout for Joy*

Among many other devices employed were repeated notes:

Example 19: Ammons—*Bass Gone Crazy*

And tremolos that were almost certainly of guitar origin:

Example 20: Lewis—*Bass on Top*

Grace notes were quite often used. In contrast with the usual classical practice they were executed as quickly as possible, not to decorate but to give emphasis to the note they preceded. Among the commonest ornaments were the groups of three or four notes —usually descending—preceding a note or chord, and the chromatic slide that often led into a tremolo:

Example 21: Ammons—*Boogie Woogie Blues*

Example 22: Lewis—*Bearcat Crawl*

Trills were often employed and Yancey demonstrates their use in *Tell 'Em About Me.* Heavy, detached chords were often used to punctuate the bass in purely rhythmic passages:

Example 23: Ammons—*Monday Struggle*

And in more connected form in riff passages:

Example 24: Lewis—*Six Wheel Chaser*

Although groups of even eighth notes and dotted eighth and sixteenth notes were common, boogie pianists seemed especially to favor triplets. Here are two instances (see also Example 12):

Example 25: Yancey—*Mollow Blues*

Example 26: Ammons—*Chicago on My Mind*

As already stated, cross-rhythms abounded and many instances might
be given. The following extracts from Meade Lux Lewis exemplify
the kind of effects produced:

Example 27: Lewis—*Honky Tonk Train Blues*

Although the harmonic basis of this music was very simple, it
abounded in pungent dissonances. The following chords are taken
from a Meade Lux Lewis solo, and in isolation appear to be evidence
of—by older jazz standards—quite an advanced level of harmonic
thought:

Example 28

In fact they are not the result of harmonic thinking at all. With its variety of rhythm and figuration, the right hand of the boogie pianist was more independent of the left than in any other style of jazz piano playing. To this extent boogie was two-voiced music—that is, the result of thinking in two horizontal streams of notes rather than in a series of chords. It was as a result of this independence that dissonances were produced. The boogie pianists thought not in terms of complex chords but in terms of rhythm and color. They would strike notes with the right hand that made sharp discords, either in themselves or in conjunction with the bass, not as part of a carefully worked-out harmonic progression but to give color to a phrase or stress to a rhythmic accent. Thus, in the following extract (from the same Lewis solo from which the above chords were taken), and in the three bars preceeding and three following those quoted, the continued repetition of C and G against a changing bass appears to be a double upper pedal:

Example 29: Lewis—*Six Wheel Chaser*

Again, it is another effect of rhythm and color. Similarly jazz musicians have always had a weakness for the rather saccharine chord of the added sixth. It occurred as often in boogie as in other styles of jazz, except that it was used not harmonically but as a percussive effect, as in this passage:

Example 30: Ammons—*Boogie Woogie Blues*

Superficial appearances to the contrary, then, boogie remained true to the harmonic simplicity of the blues, which were its origin.

Considering its rhythmic complexity, this simplicity of real harmonic structure was undoubtedly a good thing for the balance of the idiom as a whole.

Hand in hand with this harmonic simplicity went simplicity of form. As stated at the outset, boogie was based on the twelve-bar blues. The usual blues chorus is made up of four bars on the tonic chord, two on the subdominant, two again on the tonic, two on the dominant, and two final bars on the tonic. Upon this pattern countless boogie solos were based. A fairly common variant, however, replaced the second bar on the tonic chord with one on the subdominant. Examples of this are Pete Johnson's *Shuffle Boogie* and Meade Lux Lewis' *Bear Cat Crawl*. Another modification substituted the subdominant for the dominant in the tenth bar, thus giving each chorus a plagal instead of a perfect cadence. Examples are *Yancey Stomp* and the earlier choruses of the Lewis-Ammons-Johnson *Boogie Woogie Prayer*.

Choruses were sometimes made to accommodate four-bar introductions and two-bar codas. When this was done, the corresponding number of bars was taken from the beginning of the opening chorus or the end of the last. Exceptions to this are the introductions to Lewis' *Bass on Top* and Ammons' *Shout for Joy,* in both of which a four-bar introduction is followed by a full-length chorus. Tremolo chords were quite often used in introductions. An interesting example —and, incidentally, an unusual six-bar introduction—is the beginning of Ammons' *Boogie Woogie Stomp:*

Example 31: Ammons—*Boogie Woogie Stomp*

A typical non-tremolo introduction is that of Lewis's *Bass on Top:*

Example 32: Lewis—*Bass on Top*

Codas were usually abrupt and simple, and there is little point in detailed quotation. Here is the coda to *Monday Struggle:*

Example 33

Invariable exceptions to this simplicity were the codas of Jimmy Yancey. He had an unaccountable penchant for ending all his pieces in E flat, no matter what the home key. This produced results like the following:

Example 34: Yancey—*Yancey Stomp*

Example 35: Yancey—*Slow & Easy Blues*

A further modification was the use of breaks. This is not really a formal matter, but is best dealt with here. The musical purpose of the break in boogie, as in all jazz, was, by suspending the regular beat, to create suspense and expectation, and thus increase tension towards the performance's climax. Probably its most effective use in the boogie context was in *Yancey's Bugle Call. Yancey Stomp* is a good instance of breaks adding to a solo's momentum and tension. Here is the break employed:

Example 36: Yancey—*Yancey Stomp*

The practical purpose of the break was clearly to rest the left hand from playing the tiring ostinato basses.

Another form that is really a further modification of the twelve-bar pattern is the eight-bar chorus. This was sometimes the normal twelve-bar chorus, with the first four bars on the tonic chord omitted. An example is Yancey's *Slow and Easy Blues,* in which each chorus starts on the subdominant. Another eight-bar pattern consists of two bars each on the tonic chord, the subdominant, the dominant and two more on the tonic. This is the form of such blues as *How Long?* and is to be found in boogie in the *East St. Louis Blues* recorded by Yancey.

The above has been conducted, as all analyses must be, with some strictness. Only solos wholly representative of the idiom have been mentioned, and the passages quoted typify boogie practice with especial clarity. This is an artificial but necessary procedure if a precise idea of the music's essential character is to be grasped. Yet it must be remembered that boogie was only one part of blues piano playing, and in practice the idiomatic purity this analysis implies existed only in the work of a very few players. For the rest, there was no reason why the honky-tonk and house-rent pianists should have cultivated stylistic refinement, and they often employed the devices outlined above along with other elements not essential to the idiom.

The Outstanding Figures

No attempt will be made here to retell the life stories of the leading boogie pianists. This has been done often enough before, and with several encyclopaedias and dictionaries of jazz now in circulation, biographical details are readily available. The full potentialities of boogie were realised by a very small number of men, but in their hands it attained a remarkable level of expressiveness. It was their achievement that, while retaining all the essentials of the idiom, each fashioned a style of improvisation that allowed an intensely personal degree of expression. These are the "pure" boogie pianists alluded to above. Their imaginations were sufficiently strong for them to use the limitations of the idiom as a kind of beneficial discipline.

Jimmy Yancey (1894–1951): Yancey was born in Chicago and, apart from touring with a theatrical troupe in his youth, lived there all his life. Although very active at rent parties in the 1920's, he never became a professional musician and was quite unknown outside Chicago until his work was brought to light by the revival of interest in boogie during the 1930's. This revival led to Yancey's first records, made in 1939 for Solo Art. (The Solo Art label was run by Dan Qualey, a New York bartender with great enthusiasm for blues piano playing. His venture did not last long, but in 1939 he recorded some of the finest examples of boogie we have. Without his work our knowledge of the idiom would be very much poorer.) These were followed by some Vocalion sides and his magnificent recordings for Session in 1943.

Categorical judgments are generally to be avoided, but Yancey was undoubtedly the greatest exponent of the boogie idiom and was, indeed, one of the very few musicians in all jazz whose work ever attained to profundity. To make such a claim for a man who developed his art at noisy rent parties and ginmills will seem ridiculous to those unacquainted with the records. Yet by nature Yancey was a retiring and introspective man, who had the rarest of gifts for communicating his thoughts with power, directness and simplicity. As noted in the analytical section, he used a greater variety of basses than other boogie players; he would often omit, or syncopate, the second beat of each bar and even omit the fourth. This created an effect similar to that of the swaying habañera rhythm. There is a relationship here with the "Spanish tinge" in jazz, upon which Jelly Roll Morton was so insistent, but the connection should not be too highly stressed. Like most other boogie pianists, Yancey played right-hand patterns of great rhythmic variety; but whereas others set these patterns against an unchanging basic rhythm, he adapted his left-hand parts to complement the treble figurations in a more positive way. This resulted in a close and always shifting relationship between the hands that gave an extraordinary richness of cross-rhythms. Such a process entailed abandoning any set bass patterns of the kinds notated above (in Examples 5 to 9) for bars on end, but never for a moment did Yancey lose the fundamental pulse of a performance. Coupled with this rhythmic complexity was a blues melodic style of the utmost simplicity. The force of Yancey's music derived from the combination of these two factors. His touch was the most purely percussive of all the boogie pianists, yet such was the finesse and delicacy of his playing that his work always had an air of grace and finish. All this was achieved without much invention in terms of actual musical material. Similar phrases occurred in different solos and expression was obtained through the effect of the style as a whole and the way in which ideas were presented, rather than by the constant invention of new patterns. His number of actual themes was also limited. Thus *Midnight Stomp, Yancey Stomp, Janie's Joys* and *Yancey Limited* are based on the same theme. *The Rocks, Five O'Clock Blues* and *Jimmy's Rocks* are closely related. *Slow and Easy Blues* is the same as *Boodlin'*, and *The Mellow Blues* the same as *Sweet Patootie. State Street Special* is a variation of *Lean Bacon.*

Of his Solo Art recordings, *Jimmy' Stuff, The Fives, Two O'Clock Blues* and *Lucille's Lament* are the most satisfactory. One doubts if Yancey was in practice when these were made, but the last two titles are beautiful blues. Less successful were *La Salle Street Breakdown* and *Big Bear Train,* which have rather monotonous final choruses.

All six pieces recorded at the Victor session later the same year are outstanding examples of Yancey's work. *State Street Special* and *Yancey Stomp* are admirably forceful and vigorous and, in their performance, are marked improvements on the earlier versions under alternate titles. The former is especially worthy of study for the way one idea contrasts with and complements another. *Slow and Easy Blues* and *The Mellow Blues* are two simple but very expressive pieces. The sides he recorded for the same company in 1940 are equally remarkable, and *Yancey's Bugle Call* was mentioned on a previous page for its masterly use of breaks. On *Death Letter Blues* and *Crying in My Sleep* he sings with great sadness in a voice that is rough but a perfect complement to his playing, giving, one suspects, an accurate impression of the man. *Death Letter* is a blues that has brought out the best in a number of singers but, with the advantage of his playing, Yancey's version is unlikely to be surpassed. He gave further evidence of his understanding of the vocal blues in his records with Faber Smith, with whom he recorded for Vocalion. On *East St. Louis Blues* and *I Received a Letter* he provided rugged but highly sympathetic accompaniments.

Yancey was at his greatest on the Session recordings of 1943; more moving solos than these will not be found within the idiom. *At the Window* is a slow blues, extremely melancholy but without the slightest suggestion of self-pity. *Death Letter Blues* is even finer than the early version, and Yancey's singing here has a quality of resignation that is perfectly matched by the accompaniment. With performances like this one realises that Yancey achieved such moving results because he was not attempting to create a mood outside himself; his playing was an extension and corollary to the circumstances of his own life. For this reason he was never hampered by his rather limited vocabulary of phrases but, on the contrary, was almost always able to impart fresh meaning to them.

Meade Lux Lewis (born 1905): Lewis was born in Kentucky and began music by studying the violin. In Chicago he was inspired by Yancey and took to the piano. He may even have had some informal lessons from the older man. Unlike Yancey and Ammons, he did make a few records in the 1920's. These were mainly accompaniments to singers Rob Robinson and George Hannah, with just one solo—*Honky Tonk Train Blues.* Train blues occurred constantly in the boogie repertoire and probably had their origin in the earliest days of the idiom. Honky-tonk trains were used for excursions, run by railway companies, that took colored industrial workers to visit their relations in the South. They were done as inexpensively as possible, and the trains consisted of baggage cars with no seats. But a piano was provided for entertainment and at one time Albert Ammons worked on one of them. Lewis, whose father was also a railway employee, named his first solo after them.

After these recordings Lewis fell into obscurity for several years, until the discovery of an old copy of his solo stimulated the revival of interest in boogie. When this occurred, he recorded two new versions of it, together with several other solos, for Decca and Victor in 1936. Two years later he recorded some excellent sides for Solo Art, but his finest work unquestionably was created at his Blue Note sessions. Most notable are the lovely four-part *Blues, Six Wheel Chaser, Melancholy, Tell Your Story, Solitude, Bass on Top* and another version of *Honky Tonk Train,* all recorded in 1939–40. Although they lack the emotional depth of Yancey's work, these pieces show Lewis to have been the most pianistically inventive of boogie players. His technique and creative skill enabled him to produce solos of unique complexity, with an unparalleled variety of textures and figurations. In his best moments Lewis played with a rhythmic force and momentum that imparted overwhelming vitality to solos like the Blue Note *Honky Tonk Train.* Instead of producing new ideas in each chorus, he showed great resourcefulness in developing his basic material throughout a whole performance. Thus *Bass on Top* grows from a simple rhythmic motive, stated at the outset with two added sixth chords in the right hand, that is elaborated in succeeding choruses with mounting drive and tension. More than the complexity of his work, it was this ability to develop material at length that gave Lewis a place in boogie as singular as Yancey's. And this compositional faculty imparted a degree of shape and integration to his best records that is unique within the idiom. It is interesting to note that, although Lewis' solos, like all boogie, were always cast in the blues form, they did not all have a conspicuous blues feeling. Thus *Six Wheel Chaser* is an exuberant, stomping dance of almost elemental power that, played with such crushing force and energy, reflects the idiom's environment far more closely than Yancey's most characteristic work.

Albert Ammons (1907–1949): Ammons was closely associated with Lewis throughout the 1920's and 1930's and, like him, was influenced by Yancey. A native of Chicago, he led a small band at the Club de Lisa in that city from 1934 on and made his first records with it two years later for Decca. Because boogie is so fundamentally a pianistic idiom, it could never be properly adapted to a band, yet these recordings of Ammons'—*Nagasaki, Boogie Woogie Stomp, Mile-or-Mo Rag* and *Early Mornin' Blues*—came nearer to success than the many later attempts. Ammons integrated his playing with the small-band style quite well, and in addition to his driving piano there are good trumpet solos by Guy Kelly and alto solos by Dalbert Bright.

Like Lewis, Ammons made his finest solos in 1939–40 for the Solo Art and Blue Note companies. The Blue Note sides are *Boogie Woogie Stomp, Suitcase Blues, Bass Goin' Crazy, Boogie Woogie Blues* and *Chicago on My Mind*. Outstanding among the Solo Art titles are *Monday Struggle, Mecca Flat Blues* and *Bass Gone Crazy*. Although lacking Yancey's depth and Lewis' subtlety, Ammons was the most powerful of boogie pianists and, in some respects, the most immediately impressive. The solo version of *Boogie Woogie Stomp* is played with tremendous attack and builds to an almost ferocious climax. At such tempos Ammons' ideas were simpler than those of his associates, but the authority of his playing imparted to some of his solos a headlong quality that made them sound as logical and inevitable as those of Lewis. The slower tempos of *Chicago on My Mind* and *Suitcase Blues* allowed him a greater degree of elaboration, and both of these are reflective, thoughtful improvisations in which the melodic grace of the right-hand variations is enhanced by the rocklike solidity of the basses. *Suitcase* is by Hersal Thomas, a Chicago pianist of the 1920's, who made only a few records for Okeh during 1925–26 before his death. Ammons' interpretation is happier than the composer's, but retains the flavor of the original. That this is the case, even though fourteen years separate the two recordings, leads one to speculate on Thomas' importance as a formative influence in the early Chicago days. With so few of his records to hand and no biographical information, it is impossible to draw any conclusions; but for this reason, as well as for the quality of his *Suitcase* and *Hersal Blues,* Thomas' is a name to remember.

Clarence Lofton (1896–1957): Lofton was born in Tennessee and presumably went to Chicago in the middle 1920's. In 1927 he recorded one accompaniment, to a singer called Sammy Brown, and this was followed in 1930 by a session with Louise Johnson. Lofton here showed himself to be an excellent blues accompanist, and he consolidated his reputation in his 1935–36 sessions with Bumble Bee Slim and Red Nelson. He recorded the first titles under his own name for Vocalion in 1935. These are *Strut That Thing* and *Monkey Man Blues.* No more solos were recorded until the 1939 Solo Art session, and this was followed by the Session date of 1943. This is the total extent of Lofton's recordings—about forty sides.

Although he was one of the greatest boogie pianists, Lofton was stylistically a primitive. In contrast with the careful integration of the best Yancey, Lewis and Ammons solos, his work is idiosyncratic and conveys little impression of structural organisation. This is not to suggest that his pieces were not firmly based on the blues, but he had something of the country blues singer's disregard for precise considerations of form. Thus in *Pinetop's Boogie Woogie* the first three choruses are eleven, ten and twelve bars long respectively, and later choruses are fourteen bars in length. In the Solo Art version of *I Don't Know* can be found choruses of nineteen and twenty bars and one, apparently, of nineteen and a half. We can be sure Lofton did not set out deliberately to indulge in formal eccentricities, but that these deviations are the result of playing just as he felt. He recognised no guide but his own productive and highly individual imagination, and sometimes, when struck by a new idea in mid-chorus, he would start to develop it immediately, without regard to what had gone before! The result of all this is a kind of freshness and abandon that, apart from the other characteristics of his style, makes his work as immediately recognisable as that of his peers.

There is about some of Lofton's records a sombre, nearly sinister aspect. This is particularly so in *South End Boogie* and *Had a Dream;* the former, especially, has a gauntness that is almost forbidding and must be a reflection of his Chicago environment.

Streamline Train was his most famous piece, and is of surprising complexity and variety. The Solo Art version is the finest. *The Fives* is another great performance, and builds with more logic and organization than most of his pieces. *In de Mornin'* has an unusual stuttering right-hand part that recalls Hersal Thomas.

Some Minor Figures

The outstanding musicians discussed above, far from being isolated, were part of an enormous amount of activity. The background to their achievements was provided by scores of minor pianists, all of whom had something to contribute but lacked the ability to form styles as personal as those of the giants. It is obvious from the first recordings of boogie we have that the idiom was firmly established by countless anonymous players of earlier times; in the same way the achievements of the outstanding musicians were possible only because of the work of their lesser fellows. A few of the minor pianists are cited below. Many others might have been included, but the records mentioned here give an adequate idea of both the variety and limitations of the mass of boogie pianists. Only in one or two cases do they have the stylistic "purity" of the great players. In most instances their work combines boogie characteristics with elements not essential to the idiom, in the manner referred to at the end of the analytical section.

At one time Pete Johnson was ranked with the great exponents of boogie. Together with Lewis and Ammons, he was the boogie pianist to acquire the greatest fame. In retrospect his records show him to have been an outstanding player, but his work lacks the personality of the other men's. He represents the Kansas City school of boogie, and at slow tempo his phrases often had a sweetness that was quite attractive. His best records were made in 1939 for Solo Art. Some of them, like *Climbin' and Screamin'* and *Let 'Em Jump,* are tense, exciting performances from the rhythmic point of view, but the right-hand improvisations show a strictly limited invention. *Shuffle Boogie* has a fine, striding bass and *B & O* is an average train blues. *Pete's Blues* is very simple, with a four-in-bar left-hand part. Its melody is pretty, but languid and rather aimless. *Buss Robinson* and *Re-Pete Blues* are very similar. In some cases Johnson's treatments were too rigidly stylised and in his version the lyrical cadences of *How Long?* are damaged.

Johnson also recorded two excellent titles, *Goin' Away Blues* and *Roll 'Em Pete,* with Joe Turner, the fine singer with whom he worked in Kansas City. His Blue Note records, also made in 1939, are less satisfactory, for several of them were accompanied by guitar and bass, which served only to obscure the left-hand patterns. The unaccompanied titles, *Holler Stomp* and *You Don't Know My Mind,* are easily the best.

The St. Louis group was, in the 1920's, a flourishing one, producing blues and boogie pianists with a variety of approaches. Henry Brown's work exhibits a mixture of boogie and non-boogie elements typical of the lesser pianists. The right-hand figures impart a definite boogie feeling and atmosphere to his *Henry Brown Blues* and *Deep Morgan Blues,* but the left hand plays a boogie bass in only a few choruses of the former title and not at all in the latter. His *Eastern Chimes* employs a particularly firm left hand with four solid chords to the bar. Brown played with the assurance that comes from having performed these pieces many times before. His work is enjoyable for its simplicity and restraint, although *Eastern Chimes* is rather sombre. In his day Brown had some reputation as a blues accompanist and recorded with minor singers like Alice Moore, Mary Johnson and Robert Peeples, as well as with trombonist Ike Rodgers.

Most of the St. Louis players made their records in Chicago, but Wesley Wallace first recorded in St. Louis itself. His initial visit to the recording studio was to accompany Bessie Mae Smith, but he is of interest here for *Fanny Lee Blues* and *Number 29,* recorded in Chicago. His playing had more spontaneity and thus less finish than Brown's, and he employed boogie basses consistently. *Number 29* is one of the best of all train blues. The left hand is in 3/4 time throughout, with six eighth notes to the bar. The right hand is sometimes in 3/4—for example, the dotted half notes at the beginning that recur at various points—and at other times in 4/4. Wallace makes verbal comments and tells of a journey from Cairo to East St. Louis, illustrating his story with figures suggested by the train whistle and other noises.

Jabbo Williams' records illustrate another, wilder aspect of St. Louis boogie, and his playing was cruder than that of any other pianist mentioned here. He matched a regular boogie bass against ever-changing treble phrases that were arrestingly wild and undisciplined. Some idea of his style can be gained from the description of *Jab Blues*—one of his most remarkable solos, taken at a very fast tempo—as "sounding like a player piano out of control." *Polack Blues* and *Fat Mama Blues* should also be mentioned. Williams sang in an abandoned but engaging manner, especially on *Polack Blues*.

Most impressive of the minor Chicago pianists was Montana Taylor. His *Indiana Avenue Stomp* and *Detroit Rocks* are examples of unalloyed boogie and contain an abundance of ideas performed with marked vitality. Taylor returned briefly to the scene in 1946 and recorded eight magnificent titles for Circle.

Will Ezell, who is said to have come from Texas, recorded music that may be considered typical of what was to be heard at rent parties and ginmills. Indeed, two of his records, *Pitchin' Boogie* and *Just Can't Stay Here,* convey the atmosphere of such places convincingly. Over the foundation of the boogie bass, cornet and guitar mingle with Ezell's treble figures, his singing and, on the former title, his exhortations to the imaginary dancers. His other records are solos, *Playing the Dozens* being the only one to employ the boogie bass consistently. Boogie elements are present in *Barrel House Man,* but the ostinato bass is used only in one section. Contrasting with this is *Bucket of Blood,* a stomp in the Morton tradition with halting rhythms and glissandi. This shows Ezell's technical limitations and the uncertainty of his touch. Far more impressive are *Mixed Up Rag* and *West Coast Rag.* These owe nothing to the blues and are sequences of ragtime melodies. In both pieces, especially the former, the themes are well contrasted and the transitions from one section to another are handled with greater skill than might be expected from a musician who was primarily an entertainer for noisy crowds. Ezell performed both these pieces with impressive drive. *Heifer Dust* has the stuttering treble part that once again suggests Hersal Thomas' influence.

A musician of similar type but who generally worked in different circumstances was Cow Cow Davenport, born in 1894. He was expelled from a theological seminary for playing jazz and thereafter toured the T.O.B.A. vaudeville circuit until about 1930, playing ragtime and singing blues. He was most successful when teamed with the singer Dora Carr, and wrote many songs, including *Cow Cow Blues, I'll Be Glad When You're Dead, You Rascal You* and *Mama Don't Allow*. His recordings exhibit a ragtime rather than a blues slant and his playing was very accomplished. This is particularly so in the fast *Atlanta Rag,* in which one theme succeeds another in a performance that gathers tension as it proceeds. Less interesting are *Cow Cow Blues* and *State Street Jive,* which are repetitive and fail to develop their initially good material. Within the context of this chapter, Davenport's most interesting recordings are *Slow Drag* and *Chimes Blues.* The former combines a heavy four-in-a-bar bass with a right-hand part that has distinct blues inflections. *Chimes Blues* is outstanding in that its seemingly disparate boogie and ragtime sections are knit together in a thoroughly cohesive performance.

Charlie Spand was a considerably less polished musician than Davenport, but his work had far more connection with the blues tradition. He played loosely constructed, rough-hewn boogie with a rather heavy touch but with considerable expressiveness. Both his singing and playing are still entertaining on such records as *Mississippi Blues* and *Moanin' the Blues.* On the latter title there is a guitar accompaniment, probably played by Blind Blake, and guitar patterns mingle intriguingly with the piano treble. Other representative Spand recordings are *She's Got Good Stuff* and *Big Fat Mama Blues.*

Spand recorded quite often, but there were several worthy pianists who left only a few tracks. Charles Avery accompanied the singers Lil Johnson and Charles Anderson on records but made only one solo. This was *Dearborn Street Breakdown,* a vigorous piece of boogie playing with good ideas. Leroy Garnett was a similar case. He provided accompaniments to Joe Wiggins' singing and left two solos: *Chain 'Em Down,* an instance of boogie and broader jazz elements being mixed to particularly good effect; and *Louisiana Glide,* which might be described as barrelhouse ragtime.

Despite their varying degrees of pianistic accomplishment, most of the minor men played with energy and drive, generally employing the percussive touch mentioned in the analytical section. In direct contrast was the work of Pinetop Smith. Like Davenport, he toured the T.O.B.A. circuit—as a soloist, with Butterbeans and Susie, and with Ma and Pa Rainey—as well as working in night clubs as comedian, tap dancer and pianist. He was shot dead in a Chicago brawl in 1929, shortly after he had recorded eight titles for Vocalion. The best of these are *Jump Steady Blues, Pinetop's Boogie Woogie* and *Pinetop's Blues.* In them he played with a delicacy that places him apart from all other recorded boogie pianists. Indeed, a consider-

able part of the appeal of Smith's work comes from the contrast
between the refinement of his phrases and the solidity of his rhythm.
His invention was limited—the last two titles contain many virtually
identical ideas—but these solos have a praiseworthy clarity of texture
and organisation. Nonetheless there has been an unfortunate tendency
to exaggerate Smith's importance. He was a distinct musical personality and his influence on Lewis and Ammons, although not as
great as Yancey's, is not denied. Yet the widespread notion that he
was the fountainhead of boogie is absurd. The refinement of Smith's
work, especially when contrasted with the musical "toughness" of,
say, Garnett's *Louisiana Glide* or Williams' *Polack Blues,* probably
makes his work more acceptable to those unfamiliar with the idiom;
this might account for his overvaluation.

Decline and Fall

Several references have been made to the boogie revival of the
1930's. In the latter half of that decade the idiom acquired great
popularity. A number of outstanding pianists, especially Lewis,
Ammons and Pete Johnson, appeared in concert halls and expensive
night clubs. At first the results seemed to be wholly good. A group
of obscure but creative musicians was brought to light and the great
Blue Note and Solo Art recordings were made. Before long, however, commercial imitations and dilutions began to appear. Every
dance band featured synthetic boogie, popular songs based on the
idiom were soon common and some of them were worthy forebears
of the moronic rock songs of the 1950's. This was not only Yancey's
and Lewis's most creative period, it was also the time of *Beat Me
Daddy, Eight to the Bar, The Booglie Wooglie Piggy* and *Scrub Me
Mama with a Boogie Beat.* A host of imitative pianists arrived who
had mastered the external details of the style, but approached it
from outside and for commercial reasons—not because it was natural
to them, as it was to Yancey and Montana Taylor. Among them were
Freddie Slack, Deryck Sampson, Cleo Brown, Sammy Price and
Honey Hill. Even some of the outstanding established jazz musicians
attempted to adapt the style to large and small combos, always without success. Although they were played with real jazz feeling, pieces
like Count Basie's *Red Bank Boogie* and *Basie Boogie* were as
artificial stylistically as the work of the outright imitators. The most
successful attempts were those of James P. Johnson, whose *Im-*

provisations on Pinetop's Boogie Woogie and *Boogie Woogie Stride* were brilliant if not authentic performances.

The commercial exploitation of so potent an idiom was almost inevitable, and was not, in the long run, very important. Of greater significance was the effect of the boogie vogue on its genuine exponents. As stated already, boogie drew much of its strength from the fact it was a living part of the environment in which it was created. To say this is not to denigrate the gifts and hard work of Lewis, Ammons and the rest, but to recognise that the concert hall-night club milieu quickly sapped the idiom's vitality. Ample proof of the vulnerability of boogie when removed from its natural surroundings is afforded by the later recordings of the most celebrated pianists. As late as 1944, Lewis' Asch and Blue Note sessions yielded fine music, but by the time he made the J.A.T.P. recordings, unfeeling repetition of mechanical formulae had replaced the teeming invention of earlier years. Similarly, Ammons' Mercury recordings of the late 1940's and Johnson's work on Apollo and Jazz Selection are as empty as Lewis'. The latter's Clef recordings, such as *Shoobody* and *Bush Street Boogie,* are lamentable when compared with his earlier work.

It is illuminating to contrast this with the cases of Yancey and Lofton. Despite their records, they never broke into the concert-night-club circuit, but remained in obscurity throughout their lives. However regrettable this may be from the human angle, it enabled their playing to retain its vitality and freedom from mechanical formulae until the end.

It would be pointless to blame Ammons, Lewis and the rest for bringing about the death of the music they helped to create. Even without their exploits boogie would have lost its place as a vital part of jazz. This is because the environment from which it drew sustenance has disappeared. Rent parties and good-time flats are long extinct; and in his later years Lofton found that, because he had never accumulated enough money to join the union, he was chased from the countless joints in which he had once been welcome. He used to say of the young pianists around the South Side, "I gotta help these boys along, so when us old fellows are gone there be more coming up," but it's very doubtful if he had many "pupils" in his later years. Now that the conditions that gave birth to boogie no longer exist, it would be foolish to expect another revival, even if the musicians were available. Only the records remain.

CHICAGO

~~~~~~~~~~~~~~~~

John Steiner

Dr. John Steiner has been immersed in the history of jazz in Chicago for many years. Professionally, he was with Miner Laboratories, a chemical research and consulting firm in Chicago, from 1937 to 1952; and since then, he's been Director of Chemical Research Laboratories. With Hugh Davis, he organized S.D. Records, originally a hot reissue label, in 1944. He took over the management of the New York Recording Laboratories in 1946, and became owner in 1948. From time to time, he's issued records of historical importance on Paramount and other labels. He maintains that he still has unreleased recordings by "Keppard, Noone and Dodds that are too far ahead of their time to be issued as yet." Dr. Steiner's chapter on jazz in Chicago may be cataloguish occasionally, but it is also the most comprehensive introduction to the subject ever assembled.

As for the "Chicago style" (the jazz derived from listening to the early New Orleans emigrants), there used to be spirited debates in the specialist magazines as to whether such a phenomenon existed. Allowing for generalization, one of the best descriptions of that "style" by a man who did believe it was measurable was given by George Avakian in his notes for *Chicago Style Jazz* (Columbia CL 632):

> The tension, urgency and fire of Chicago style are external as well as internal matters. An "explosion" at the end of every chorus sends the succeeding one off to a catapult start; those two-bar flares are played by everyone, even in choruses which are otherwise solos. Stop-and-go devices, shifting rhythmic patterns (including a kind of double-time known as the "Chicago shuffle"), varying dynamics, and all-out finishes capped by "double endings" (the addition of two extra bars to the last chorus) are used to create a supercharged atmosphere. The ensemble holes are filled like Nature tackling a vacuum; the solos are almost agonized. Phrases are short, jagged, almost spit out. There is a Chicago tone, too—tart, slightly off-pitch, with a buzzy, rough edge. Strong notes stop mattering; driving, on-the-beat excitement is what counts.

The aphorism that art reacts to its time and place was never more substantiated than in the case of Chicago jazz. In the initial period maturing artists brought from New Orleans a growing music. It was first presented by the small jazz bands. But soon, changing needs that required show bands, radio bands and grandiose ballroom orchestras restricted, confounded and dispirited the originators.

Before its dilution and further dispersion, an upcoming, impressionable, iconoclastic generation of musicians found in the "pure" New Orleans jazz a challenging *métier*. Logically enough, they were constrained to change it to their own conceptions, needs and conveniences. A part of the challenge for the newer generation of musicians in Chicago was to develop even greater liberties of expressiveness, and to develop for themselves new, often bizzare individualities. For a time many of them felt that success balanced effort; it might be uphillish, but there was compensation both in money and in satisfaction.

Then for both groups came a new time and new conditions, the Depression, a constricting economy, changing patterns of metropolitan life. The opportunities evaporated. Only a few jazzmen had the tenacity, talent and idealism to remain "Chicago jazzmen" until today.

The Chicagoans' pliability and open-door policy have led to constant revision, re-evaluation and adaptation of the style to their particular time and place, so that now it may be largely white Dixieland with a rotation of solos to those listening at Jazz, Ltd; or Dixie & Hokum to those at the 11-11 Club; or a mixture of Dixie types if you're at Danny Alvin's Basin Street. To those following the Grosz-Chace herd (mostly a rehearsal-recording, homeless band of enthusiasts) it may come out as McKenzie whimsies on Harlem harmonies. Or it may be a melee of Dixie, blues, Red Peppers and even Ellington to the devotee of the Hodes Fivers. Or it can be essentially the Oliver sound from the Franz Jackson Stars at the Red Arrow.

The Chicagoans themselves pretty well agree that after the Emigration, the style was best preserved by the Condon, the Summa Cum Laude, the McPartland-Freeman and the McPartland-Pee Wee-Sullivan bands. At any rate, every one of these band shares the principles of producing uncluttered, unambiguous, moving (and that can mean lilting, exciting, soothing, comical, fierce or gay), creative, spontaneous and inspired-sounding small-band jazz music.

When you consider that the jazz in Chicago today was derived from New Orleans' special music of less than fifty years ago; when by count you find that half the present jazzmen in Chicago are from out of town and half the original Chicago jazzmen have left; when you hear a few Chicagoans blending with Harlem (Rex Stewart, the late Walter Page, Joe Thomas, Herman Autry), New Orleans (Ed Hall, Eddie Edwards), Mexico (Emil Caceres), New York (Miff Mole, Joe Bushkin, Dick Cary, Joe Dixon, Johnny Windhurst, Cutty Cutshall, Bob Haggart), Texas (the Teagardens) and Boston (Bobby Hackett, Max Kaminsky, Brad Gowans) as the Condon nucleus has been doing these past years, maybe it's time to drop the tags and, like Eddie says, call it music.

The Emigrants

". . . all of them was from some part of the South and had come to Chicago to better their living," said Big Bill Broonzy. Bill's observations, specifically concerning the early blues singers and guitar strummers, coming by dozens in the period 1912 to 1924, apply also to the instrumentalists arriving at the same time. The colored population of Chicago rose from about forty thousand in 1910 (2 per cent of the total) to well over one hundred thousand in 1920 (4 per cent of the total).

Population drift brought Bill and such compatriots as Georgia Tom and Tampa Red, Sunnyland Slim and Memphis Slim, Black Bob and Barbecue Bob, Blind Blake, Blind Beck, Blind Lemon and Sleepy John, Casey Bill, Kokomo, Lonnie Johnson, Roosevelt Sykes, Freddie Shayne, Big Maceo, Peetie Wheatstraw, Jim Jackson, Washboard Sam—and probably fifty other career, itinerant bluesmen who composed and sang songs on street corners and in bars, usually augmenting meager tips with occasional work at shoeshine stands, as janitors or delivering jugs.

Fewer in number were the girl singers, who worked principally as show acts or vocalists in small tavern bands. Among them were Chippie Hill, Hociel Thomas, Georgia White, Lil Green, Mama Yancey, Rosetta Howard, Leathia Hill and Memphis Minnie. Many of the girls migrated a step further, into the singing of popular songs for theaters, cabarets and floor shows. Some of these were Mae Alix, Twinkle, Alberta Hunter, Cora Green, Florence Mills, Monette Moore.

The blues, a music come from the land, had one especially unique characteristic, its personal nature. The performer was often his own accompanist and was often, too, composer of both melody and lyric. As Lonnie Johnson modestly sketched:

> "Of course you know how the blues will be. You think of some words and that is how the melody must go. Then you play it awhile one way or another to see how you and other people like it. If they ask for it again or if somebody wants to record it, then you've got a blues. I recorded 125 songs against the same chords.

The bluesman was largely self-tutored, and consequently his music was unsophisticated, but unencumbered with affectedness or traditional restraints. Although his accent or something in his style might reflect influences of his origin or travels, the personality in his music was unique—a respected hallmark.

The Pianists

Another member of the earliest Chicago jazz hierarchy was the pianist, and he, too, was usually a vocalist. World-traveled Glover Compton, a pianist-entertainer who came to Chicago in 1910, and Local 208's elder statesman, Charles Elgar, remember no jazz hornman or anything like Dixieland jazz in Chicago before 1911. But there had been for several years some rag players and blues noodlers, their names now long forgotten, who might be considered precursors of the jazzmen. Possibly in 1910, but more likely about 1912, both Jelly Roll Morton and Tony Jackson began playing piano and entertaining in the bars of the "Section" along State Street near Thirty-fifth. At times when the more sensational Morton was featured, he might continue at the piano by the hour, attracting a growing audience that filled the place and gathered outdoors, swelling until, Gideon Honore avers, it would impede the passing of trolleys. More than one old-timer remembers that special police were assigned to an opening of the likes of Jackson or Morton. Their special province was Elite No. 2. Even Hines, on his arrival in the early 1920's, found No. 2 most hospitable.

Boogie-woogie was a separate department of pioneer jazz. Blues players and "boogies" worked together in all kinds of circumstances and with clear understanding; yet to a marked degree they specialized.

Jimmy Yancey, one of the oldest of the boogie-woogie players, claimed no more than: (a) his compositions, which were often relatively sophisticated in their rhythms, and (b) his pupils, of whom he was boastfully and justifiably proud. Jimmy thought that he had encountered boogie-woogie prior to War I. Little Brother (Eurreal Montgomery), who became a pianist by letting his fingers learn for themselves, started professionally in 1917, at the age of eleven, near Shreveport. Brother relates that practically all Southern pianists used various patterns of rolling bass on occasion.

Pinetop Smith, who learned much from Yancey, taught Albert Ammons and Meade Lux Lewis, who lived in the same apartment building. The younger boys would visit frequently at the Yancey flat, sometimes when Jimmy Flowers or Romeo Nelson, or possibly the still younger Tom Harris or Charlie Castner, were also present. Such gatherings might last the most of a weekend. A rent party at Mecca Flats would attract Freddie Shayne, Jimmy Blythe and Dan Burley. In a nearby tavern "The Crippled One," Clarence Lofton, might be hosting Will Ezell or Leroy Garnett or Charlie Spand as they passed through with a show or came around to give the town a whirl.

Owning a piano meant an opulence and stability that few bluesmen attained. A portable instrument is a simpler thing, both ways. Piano practice cannot be as casual as strumming a guitar. For this reason the pianists were often from relatively better families, often better musically instructed and informed. But guitarists had the more extensive repertoires—at least more lyrics. When, during the Depression, some of the boogie-woogie players could not afford their own pianos, they joined the staffs of State or Maxwell Street taverns, janitoring or noodling on piano during the afternoons and playing for drinks and tips in the evenings. Many became virtual wards of the proprietors. Sammy Williams, broader in scope than most boogie-woogie pianists, may have established a record for staff tenure with his twenty-five years at Gibby's.

As the Original Dixieland Jazz Band had carried jazz into world markets, so boogie-woogie, twenty years later, found world-wide appreciation and large commercial exploitation upon its exposure via the Boogie-Woogie Trio's cross-country tour in 1939–44. They were extensively recorded and their solos were transcribed into print. The Trio was composed of Chicago's Albert Ammons and Meade Lux Lewis (joined later by Albert's drummer, Jimmy Hoskins), Pete Johnson of Kansas City and his singer, Joe Turner. When Ammons and Johnson subsequently became a duo, Chicagoan Joe Williams, later of Basie fame, became their vocalist.

Jack Gardner, working closely with the trio in 1940 when all were part of the Harry James package, became one of their best imitators. Don Ewell, playing opposite Yancey at the Beehive, was soon one of Jimmy's best latter-day disciples. The highly original piano of Art Hodes is strongly flavored by low, bluesy boogie-woogie. Frank Melrose was of much the same persuasion. Bob Zurke could finally match Ammons' precision and drive.

Many late practioners of boogie-woogie treated it as a velocity exercise or muscular display. In the hands of the original players it had been more beautifully a blues song with a kind of rocking accompaniment. While boogie-woogie, largely brought to fruition in Chicago, walked the world, it died on the South Side. Today not a single prominent boogie-woogie pianist lives there. True, boogie-woogie has entered the mainstream of jazz, but there has been no concentrated effort to explore or redevelop the idiom further. Not a significant new artist or new composition has appeared since War II.

The Section

Returning to Glover Compton's days, Compton thinks that about 1912, a New Orleans clarinetist (possibly George Bacquet) sat in with him at Elite No. 1, causing a minor riot by his sensational display. But a jazz band had not yet been heard in Chicago despite the years of jazz popularity in New Orleans. Before War I a variety of novel entertainment was available in the Section to town prowlers and to the after-theater crowds from the Loop, only a ten-minute El ride away. The area was generally run down as a result of the inroads of industry along the railroad tracks passing nearby; but it was to begin an upward climb which continues, with fits and starts, today.

Within that half mile along State Street, cafés (saloons), cabarets (saloons with singers and sometimes food), cabaret-theaters with vaudeville acts such as the Blatz Beer Garden (soon to become the Pekin Cabaret-Theater) and the Dreamland Café, the Elites, and ten or twenty bars comprised a white-light section adjacent to several red-light sections—a daring, exotic avenue. Even before jazz, the Section became second to the Loop in night attractions. But a stigma became attached to the raucous entertainment features of the Section and was associated with it so enduringly that, even in recent years, many Negroes have been reluctant to acknowledge the importance of musical events there.

With ample material still available for research, no study has ever issued from the South Siders on the musical revolution which passed before their eyes. The broad sociological chart of the South Side by Drake and Cayton, *Black Metropolis* (Harcourt, Brace, 1945, 800 pages), contains no mention of jazz or jazzmen, although almost every civic, labor, religious and economic leader is mentioned. One comment relates pointedly to their attitude towards the entertainment world: "Negro civic leaders and many middle-class people protest against the tendency to regard Black Metropolis as an exotic rendezvous for white pleasure seekers." Yet "exotic" jazz brought better understanding between the races as well as fruitful, noble careers to many a Negro.

The Importations

In their letters back home to New Orleans, the Chicago Negro Local 208's first president, George Smith, drummer in the band at the Grand Theater, and Charlie Elgar, leader at Fountain Inn, related that conditions were good. They imported friends as needed in their bands, but initially not jazzmen. However, this was opening the door for jazz. Compton spread similar word to Louisville, and when the Cafe de Champ was opened by boxer Jack Johnson, he sent for his pianist friend, Will Taylor of Louisville, to entertain there. Compton then bought a home and brought his mother to Chicago. Tony Jackson, feeling that conditions were good and apt to remain good, sent for his sisters to join him. Trombonist George Filhe and pianist Marvel Manetta, dissatisfied with working conditions in New Orleans, journeyed to Chicago in 1913. With cigar making as their second livelihood, the move was not too daring. Manetta, soon after his arrival, expressed displeasure with metropolitan life and apparently became the first of numerous jazzmen to return South after a try at a jazz career in Chicago. Ed Garland arrived in 1914; by 1918 he had developed into one of the town's best tuba and string bassmen.

The rapidly mounting popularity of jazz meant importing men because the South Side, largely a new community of porters and special-service people, had not yet developed its own talent resources. Traveling shows, often originating in New Orleans but more often in New York, frequently ended their treks in Chicago. When the traveling musicians found work, they stayed. By 1915 the T.O.B.A. circuit had been organized and was using the Monogram Theater, with pianist Lovie Austin's house band. The Orpheum circuit supplied talent to several South Side theaters. Glover Compton, returning from a stint of several years at San Francisco's Barbary Coast and the World's Fair, joined fatman drummer Ollie Powers at the Panama in a band that soon had Johnny St. Cyr. When Elgar left the Fountain Inn on the far Southwest Side, George Filhe took in a brassier band. Bill Johnson's Original Creole Band, on the Orpheum circuit, is reported to have been at several theaters and clubs in Chicago in the period of 1912 to 1918, the latter year being the time of their appearance with Trixie Friganza in the "Town Topics" revue at the 8th Street Theater. Several musicians identified with Johnson's Creoles apparently settled in Chicago as he passed through on his tours. Mike Fritzel is said to have approached Johnson to take the Creoles into Fritzel's Arsonia Cafe at Madison and Paulina. When Fritzel found Johnson unavailable, he commissioned Filhe, who had been working for him intermittently, and Elgar, now important as a booker, to import a New Orleans band. In 1915, trumpeter Emmanuel Perez, clarinetist Lorenzo Tio (replaced in about a year by Alphonse Picou), trombonist Eddie Atkins, pianist Frank Haynie and drummer Louis Cotterell, came as a group from New Orleans into the Arsonia.

Pay

Not many jazzmen became wealthy by music alone. The remarkable genius of Goodman earned him top billing as "Ben Goodwin, The Eleven Year Old Clarinet Wizard" and ten dollars nightly for several years. Oliver and Noone were leaders doubling on early- and late-hour jobs to earn independence; neither did. Playing jazz became a second job for many. Gid Honoré, Art Hodes and others taught music; trumpeter Jimmy Ille and Frank Chace were music salesmen; trombonists Floyd O'Brien and Don Thompson tuned pianos; Darnell Howard had a photo studio; Danny Alvin, Max Miller and Bill Reinhardt ran their own saloons; Marty Grosz is a cartoonist; Don Gibson became a Fuller Brush Man; Preston Jackson and Johnny Dodds ran boarding houses; Charlie Pierce ran a butcher shop; Frank Snyder sells TV at the Fair Store; Jim Barnes was in hats at Marshall Field. Pianist Roy Wasson and trombonist Sid Dawson earned so much more at sales work that they had to give up playing regularly.

Several fine Chicago jazzmen were active in jazz circles for a time, but then they were diverted from a maximum jazz exposure by the security and bigger salaries of big-band and studio work—notably Gene Caferelli (trumpet in the late 1920's), Joe Masek and Bob Durfee (saxes in the 1930's and 1940's), Sid Nierman (pianist, currently) and Ralph Hitchcock (bass, past twenty-five years).

When with marriage, family responsibilities and advancing years many decided to leave professional music, some found conventional employment a bore; others found it a relief. But it was sometimes more rewarding financially. Dave North for many years has run his father's print shop with great satisfaction; Frank Lehman became an executive in the phone-book organization; Ralph Rudder became a dentist; Scoops Carey an attorney; Bud Hunter founded a music school; Dash Berkus, drummer, manages the North Star Inn; Ralph Blank, pianist, manages an FM station; Bill Priestley, cornet, became an architect; Jim Lanigan an engineer; Volly de Faut raised dogs.

When, sixteen years ago, Murph Podalsky left jazz, he had a twenty-year service stripe; now he is worth about a million from dealing in land and homes. Murph characterizes jazzmen as "the happiest independents in povertyville." But even when the jazzmen left professional activity, all, including Murph, continued wanting to play every chance they could get—for kicks, for charity, for anything.

In this period the arrival in Chicago of cornetist Tig Chambers and trumpeter Sugar Johnny Smith was reported, and also that of clarenetist Lawrence Duhé (Dewey), trombonist Roy Palmer, bassist Ed Garland and guitarist Louis Keppard (Freddie's brother). These musicians gravitated together into what may have been the first hot jazz group in the Section. Their initial long-term job was at the Dreamland Cafe at Thirty-fifth and State, where they replaced a dance group led by violinist Mae Brady. In 1918, when Lil Armstrong joined this group on piano, Fred "Tubby" Hall was their drummer and the violin and alto sax were played by Jimmie Palao, formerly with Johnson's Creoles. Bassist Ed "Montudi" Garland was soon replaced by newcomer Wellman Brieux (Braud).

The Sugar Johnny Band—or the Duhé, as it was known by others—transferred shortly to an upstairs poolroom-bar-dance hall across State Street called the De Luxe Cafe. Lil recalls that they replaced Tony Jackson and Charlie Hill, the two pianist-entertainers previously ensconced, to begin a band policy at the De Luxe. That jazz was on the upswing is suggested by the band's routine of seven nights weekly there. Soon they were doubling five mornings (1 to 6 A.M.) at the nearby Pekin Theater-Cabaret.

Many jazz artists were soon to be able to find two jobs nightly whenever they chose as the market for jazz grew. When Sugar Johnny died in the late winter of 1918–19, Mutt Carey became the band's trumpeter for a few frosty weeks until he found the weather intolerable and returned to New Orleans. He told Oliver (who was about to entrain to join Bill Johnson's Creoles) about the opening with Duhé's band, and after Oliver arrived in Chicago, he fronted both bands. The Oliver story is exhaustively told in the monograph by Walter C. Allen and Brian A. L. Rust, (*King Joe Oliver* 1955, Walter C. Allen, Belleville, New Jersey).

After about a year and a half at the Arsonia the band under Perez, with Filhe replacing Atkins (who returned to New Orleans), also moved into the Section, and they, too, are reported to have played at the De Luxe.

Jazz in The Loop

So jazz came to the South Side. Meanwhile a parallel development had begun in the Loop area as well. According to legend, in early 1915 the rhythm dancer and comedian, Joe Frisco, told proprietor Smiley Corbett of Lamb's Cafe that he had heard a white band as fantastic as the Johnson Creoles during an earlier New Orleans engagement. Corbett sent for the outfit, Tom Brown's Band from Dixieland, and in early summer, upon their arrival, they gave new tone to a rostrum previously a haven of string ensembles.

The question seems still unresolved whether this band of Brown's or some of the first Negro jazzmen (Johnson? Sugar Johnny?) were first given the shocking opprobrium of being called "jazz" players.

Negro artists were then regarded by an affluent and aloof segment of the all-white Loop cabaret clientele as interlopers—although, if they were well behaved, semiclassical, and out of view, they were countenanced at private parties because of their lower cost. The sound of jazz was to some unfamiliarized ears too loud and cacophonous, or simply distastefully new.

Imitators, like Brown, of the type of Negro "noise" that went on in the Section were *ipso facto* musical white trash. The subject was too controversial for newspapers to touch in a serious or objective manner, according to Warren Smith of the *Chicago Tribune,* except when the audiences were referred to as abandoned mobs (this was in reference to a campaign for a closing-curfew law). Finally, in a music-union conflict, Brown's imported band and their music were used as a scapegoat, and thereupon the unapproved, out-of-town Dixieland Band was stigmatized as a purveyor of ignoble "jazz" music.

But "jazz" implied not a taint, but a new and vivid coloring in the mind of the public. Here was a name for these novel sounds. "Jazz" began to mean something new in music. Many thrilled to the jazz music's gaiety and impact. "Jazz" distinguished these sounds from the sedate music they had known before. It meant musical liberation. And so the word caught on. Soon a banner over the door of Lamb's Cafe read "Jazz Band."

Lamb's prospered and other spots wanted to share the glory. The next white group recruited contained the nucleus of the New Orleans Jazz Band. They left New Orleans on Thursday, March 2, 1916, according to their trombonist, Eddie Edwards, arriving in the snow-coated city the following evening and going directly to work. Besides Edwards, there were Nick LaRocca, Alcide Nunez, Harry Ragas and Johnny Stein. They opened at the New Schiller Cafe, about a mile north of the Loop. Shortly they went to the De Labbie in the Loop, leaving Stein at the Schiller and replacing him with Tony Sbarbaro. Subsequently they went northward again, to Casino Gardens, where an argument between LaRocca and the ill-chosen manager, Nunez, resulted in a breakup. Larry Shields was then brought in on clarinet. Apparently the band, then called the Original Dixieland Jazz Band, played some neighborhood vaudeville houses before entraining in 1917 for New York.

The Happy Schilling band came to Chicago from New Orleans about the same time the ODJB left. Emile Christian of New Orleans, then on trumpet, is reported to have played at the Green Goose in 1917, under banjoist Bert Kelly.

New Orleans jazzmen were carried on the summer-excursion steamers playing the Mississippi as far north as they could, usually to Minneapolis-St. Paul. Although jazz is picturesquely described as journeying up the river, not an instance is known of either a New Orleans or St. Louis jazzman arriving in Chicago by the slow river route. On the contrary, Fate Marable, pianist-leader on the boats, took several musicians *down* the river on the boats, recruiting several better-educated hornmen to improve the versatility of his winter bands based in New Orleans, including Boyd Atkins, reeds, from Paducah; Bert Bailey, trumpet and reeds; and Bob Schoffner, trumpet, both from St. Louis. These men later migrated to Chicago.

Several New Orleans men tried to convert Chicago musicians to their New Orleans style. In dismay at the inadequate results, New Orleans drummer Ragbaby Stevens, at Campbell Gardens, about 2100 West Madison, sent an invitation home to George Brunies to join him. George was reluctant to leave until Paul Mares, acting on Stevens' telegram, went North and soon wrote back to the effect: Come on in, the water's fine.

Brunies arrived in the early winter of 1920. Mares and Brunies were heard and admired by many Chicago jazzmen-in-the-making. Reciprocally, the two sometimes jammed with the Pettis-Schoebel-Snyder group at the Blatz Beer Garden, at North and Halsted. There they met young Muggsy Spanier, also sitting in. When faced with the usual summer layoff, a group consisting of Jack Pettis, alto; Elmer Schoebel, piano; Lew Black, banjo; George Brunies, trombone; Paul Mares, trumpet; and Ayres, drums, found a Mississippi riverboat job. They met their New Orleans buddy, clarinetist Leon Rappolo, in Davenport, and with him a kid trumpet player, Bix Beiderbecke.

On returning to Chicago in the fall, the same band was booked by Husk O'Hare, first into the big Cascades Ballroom (Sheridan & Wilson) and then into Toddle Inn roadhouse at Fox Lake. Nearby was drummer Ben Pollack, probably on his first professional job. Soon the band was booked into the Friar's Inn, a basement cabaret at Wabash and Van Buren, now an autopark. The club was obviously more fanciful than accurate in billing the band as Friar's *Society* Orchestra. The "Friars" were originally composed of Midwesterners Schoebel, Pettis, Snyder and Black; and New Orleaneans Brunies, Mares, Arnold "Deacon" Loyocano (bass) and John Provenzano (clarinet). Rappolo was soon called up from New Orleans on clarinet and Steve Brown (Tom's brother) joined on bass. After an O'Hara-booked recording session in 1921, Schoebel was offered the leadership of a band at the Midway Ballroom, near the University of Chicago, and when he left, Mel Stitzel took the piano chair. Then, changing their name—both for recording and, ultimately, at the Inn —to the New Orleans Rhythm Kings, they went down to Richmond to record the famous *Tin Roof Blues* (a retitling of R. M. Jones' *Jazzin' Babies*. Later Kyle Pierce came in on piano, and Chicagoan Pollack replaced Snyder for the third set of records, on which Jelly Roll Morton, in the studio for a date of solos, sat in with them on some titles.

In 1924, at the conclusion of the Friar's engagement, Mares returned to New Orleans. Brunies remained, taking Pierce; Gene Cafarelli, trumpet; Bill Paley, drums; Dale Skinner, reeds (all from Chicago); and Chink Martin, bass (imported from New Orleans), into the nearby Valentino's Inn. There he was heard (and seen) by Ted Lewis, who invited him to an audition at what is now the United Artists Theater, Randolph and Dearborn. Thus Brunies joined Lewis for a seventeen-year world tour and endless material for mimickry. When shortly after joining Lewis Brunies ran into his lakeboat friend, Bix Beiderbecke, in New York, Bix insisted that Brunies be used on a forthcoming Wolverine recording date.

When Ted Lewis needed a hot trumpet a few years later, Brunies recommended Spanier, who joined Lewis for a long stay. Brunies also recommended his lakeboat friends of Chicago days, Don Murray and Benny Goodman, to Lewis. Later Brunies and Spanier were together for recording dates, in the Ragtimers, and in the 1950's they played together at Jazz Ltd. and several other Chicago clubs, recording subsequently for Mercury and Standard Transcriptions. These stories of friendships and cliques and the alloying of bands are repeated time after time in the Chicago story.

The New Orleans Rhythm Kings, more than earlier New Orleans bands and more than the Negro bands, introduced jazz to the North Side youngsters and Chicago dance musicians. Pianist Murph Podalsky relates that on a spring afternoon in 1921, when he and clarinetist

Mezz Mezzrow (both professional dance musicians at the time) were walking in the 2000 block of Division Street, they were overwhelmed by a wave of vigorous sound unlike anything they had ever heard. "We had heard the Original Dixieland Jazz Band records; but this live jazz was something else!" The band they heard was rehearsing in a poolroom with door open, kitty exposed, and included, according to Murph: Mares, Brunies, Earl Wiley (drums) and probably Rappolo and Steve Brown. "This immediately converted both of us."

Two years later Murph was to arrange gratis employee meals for the NORK members, who would frequently respond to bandsmen's invitations to come along for the ride (and perhaps sit in) on the lakeboat excursions out of Chicago, across to the Michigan shore. These boats carried bands contracted by pianist-leader Bill Grimm, with Frank Lehman, banjo; Harry Gale and Jack Schargle, drums; Jimmy Hartwell, George Johnson, Glen Scoville, Don Murray and (in 1923) Benny Goodman, reeds; Frank Cotterell, Bix Beiderbecke, Harry Greenberg, and Jim McPartland, trumpets; John Carsella, trombone; and Murph Podalsky, piano. It is true that McPartland and his neighbors in and around Austin High School listened to the NORK records, but they also had opportunities such as this for first-hand contact.

Dozens of jazz students teethed on records and player-piano rolls. Albert Ammons and Cass Simpson told of fitting their fingers into dropping player-piano keys; the roll was worn ragged within a week and the tune would remain for thirty years a part of their "book." Bix's constant playing of the ODJB records as his accompaniment (revealed in interviews with his brother Charley) was repeated by others time after time, especially in the small towns, where a student could find but few fellow partisans. Bunny Berigan, up in Wisconsin, learned these records, too, and when he played with Chicagoans at college dances in Madison and Champagne, he was prepared for their Dixieland items.

The Oliver and Noone records were also consulted, and later, of course, those of Armstrong, Johnny and Jabbo Smith, but perhaps more in the spirit of enjoyment and reference than for patterns, ensemble sounds or repertoire. Until the days of the Bob Crosby band (with his arrangements of *Cow Cow, Yancey Special, Louise, Louise Blues,* etc.) the blues and boogie-woogie repertoires were almost untapped by the white bands. Thereafter, some Chicago groups were finally to draw on the Noone and Oliver concepts, using the original records in their woodshedding. For example, pianist Chet Roble, in the early 1940's, reincarnated the Noone Apex Club sound remarkably, using clarinetist Bud Phillips, altoist Boyce Brown and a full rhythm section. Today clarinetist Franz Jackson has an excellent Oliver-styled group, with Bob Schoffner, trumpet; Albert Wynn, trombone; Little Brother Montgomery or Rozelle Claxton, piano; Ikey Robinson or Lawrence Dixon, banjo; Bill Oldham, bass and tuba; and Dick Curry, drums.

The "white" Chicago style, which we will define by recorded examples, continues as a peripheral rather than a dominant factor in Chicago jazz today. On occasion the bands of plectrist-arranger-vocalist Marty Grosz and reedman Frank Chace borrow directly from the records of the 1920's. The personnel of such groups favor the first-generation stalwarts and also sometimes include trumpeters Del Lincoln, Jack Ivett and the imported Nappy Trottier, Norm Murphy and Doc Evans; trombonists Sid Dawson, Bud Wilson and Al Jenkins—none of whom can yet, by long residence, qualify as Chicagoans—imported reeds of Bob Skiver, Jug Berger and Charley Clark, among many; native pianists Tut Soper, Mel Grant, Ralph Blank, Dave North, Chet Roble and Art Gronwald, and the imported Floyd Bean; bassists Earl Murphy, Johnny Frigo, Truck Parham, and Israel Crosby; native drummers Booker Washington and Hey Hey Humphries, and imports Bob Saltmarsh and Bob Cousins, with Barrett Deems in frequent attendance. Until their death, trumpeter Jim Cunningham and drummers Baby Dodds, Danny Alvin and Snaggs Jones were also part of this scene.

The Instrumentalists

Much of the South Side's jazz history has been disclosed in the prolific writings of George Hoefer and Paul E. Miller, and it may now be summarized with a consideration of individual instrumentalists and their influence.

The Violin

Before the introduction of jazz, the violin, second in popularity to the piano, was studied by many musically inclined youngsters who were later to become jazzmen. Darnell Howard continued to use his fiddle into the 1930's. Eddie South, by spanning several idioms, has remained artistically and commercially successful for almost thirty years, solely as a jazz violinist. Even in the first jazz wave Ray Nance was studying violin and has continued it as his second instrument. Many North Siders likewise started musical studies on the violin, among them Frank Melrose, Frank Teschemacher, Ray Biondi, Boyce Brown and Bud Hunter. The violin, when it appeared in the early jazz bands, was logically enough the maestro's instrument, played by Charles Elgar, Erskine Tate, Carroll Dickerson, Mae Brady, Jimmy Bell, Clarence Black, Arthur Sims and Sig Meyers—none of whom were themselves prominent jazzmen. But the violin was gradually displaced by the newly popularized alto sax or other reeds with a stronger voice. Many incipient violinists soon switched to reeds.

The Trumpet and Cornet

Almost immediately upon the arrival of Freddie Keppard's sensational, powerful, dominating trumpet, a big brassy sound became the commercially successful element of a jazz band. Keppard, upon finding his strength, left Johnson's Creoles to organize his own band and soon became the biggest jazz draw in town. Equally artistic horns—such as those of Sugar Johnny, before him, and later Mutt Carey and Tommy Ladnier—found far less aclaim; the day of soft, delicate jazz, the day of the microphone and intimate club, was in the future.

Upon realizing that he needed another powerful horn to front his Creoles, Bill Johnson engaged "King" Joe Oliver, the next developing ultra-strong horn from New Orleans. Oliver soon ascended to leadership, and in 1924 he sent for Louis Armstrong to further strengthen his strong brass position. In the wake of the resulting immense Oliver-Armstrong success, Ruben Reeves, Punch Miller, Jabbo Smith, Lee Collins and at times Bob Schoffner and Herb Morand—as well as the North Side's Muggsy Spanier, Johnny Mendel and Bill Davison—made the trumpet the dominating voice of their orchestras. Not all of the jazz trumpets in town could or even did aspire to be blasters. More subtle, sensitive horns were played by George Mitchell, Natty Dominique, Guy Kelly, Shirley Clay, and uptown's Charlie Altiere and Jimmy McPartland, the latter pair falling under the influence of Paul Mares and later Bix Beiderbecke.

Trumpets soon flourished in Chicago. Bunny Berigan's originality was briefly felt; George Kenyon, Shorty Sherock, Marty Marsala, Carl Rinker, Jack Ivett, Pete Daily, Del Lincoln, Nappy Trottier and Norm Murphy were freewheelers; and on the South Side, King Kolax and Shorty McConnell expanded their talents under the later influence of Roy Eldridge.

The Trombone

Early Chicago jazz-trombone influences may be categorized as, first, the Negro pioneers; second, George Brunies; and third, Floyd O'Brien. Most good jazz jobs on the South Side went to George Filhe, Roy Palmer, Eddie Vincon (Vinson), Honoré Dutrey, Kid Ory, Zue Robertson and Jim Robinson, approximately in that order. The younger Preston Jackson and still younger Albert Wynn were perhaps the first South Siders of stature who developed their trombone talents in Chicago. They were followed in the mid-1920's by Jabbo Smith, Ken Stewart, Dick McKendrick and Billy Franklin, and in later years by Benny Green, more prominent for work afield. Filhe was schooled and versatile but apparently not an outstanding improviser. Ory's gustiness seems to have been part of the traditional brew also dipped into by Robinson, Dutrey and Palmer. Jackson studied under the last two, substituting at times for Dutrey while sharing his home with Palmer. Jackson and Wynn are the only ones active today. Wynn attributes his first hot inspiration to George Brunies' solo on NORK's *Tin Roof Blues*. "It was really the first true jazz trombone solo I had heard; it was a revelation to me how a trombone could be used."

Brunies (today Brunis) re-established himself in 1950, after a twenty-five-year absence, as Chicago's leading tailgate and ensemble anchorman, as well as a superb natural comedian. Floyd O'Brien, also lost to Chicago in his middle years, returned about the same time and reaffirmed himself as the top Chicago-style trombonist. Where Floyd was more subtle, George would make the opposite bank by stomping. Other Chicago trombonists of special merit have been Joe Rullo, Johnny Carsalla, Case Kuczborski, Jack Read; and more recently Sid Dawson (St. Louis), Bud Wilson (Pittsburgh), Ralph Hutchinson (England), traditionalists; and Paul Severson, modernist.

The Piano

It was not emphasized in earlier surveys that New Orleans did not supply the expected proportion of orchestral pianists. Although Jelly Roll Morton and Tony Jackson brought New Orleans influence, they remained principally solo "entertainers." Women pianists made up the deficit. Oliver used Lil Hardin (Armstrong), Lottie Taylor and Bertha Gonsoulin at various times during his early years of leadership. Other women band pianists were Lovie Austin, Lottie Hightower (wife of New Orleans trumpeter Willie Hightower), Margie Lewis and, in later years, Christine Gassi and Israel Crosby's sister, Laura. Several women became prominent pianist-vocalists: Cleo Brown, Gladys Palmer and Laura Rucker. In the same period not one white girl became prominent as a jazz pianist in Chicago. Male blues pianists abounded, and many ultimately took over piano in the bands—for example, Richard M. Jones and Luis Russell, who were imported.

For reasons not easy to decipher today, the first great piano stylist, Ferdinand "Jelly Roll" Morton, has not been greatly imitated by the Negro. Several white disciples arose, the first being Frank Melrose, Jelly's close companion for years. To a small degree Frank's brother Walter, a music publisher, also absorbed a Jelly feeling. Certainly Don Ewell became the best Jelly-styled pianist, as he demonstrated in his long Chicago tenure, but honorable mention should also go to Murph Podalsky, Roy Wasson and Art Hodes, who refer to Jelly's style upon occasion.

After Jelly Roll Morton left Chicago for California, Teddy Weatherford appeared on the scene as a sensational swinging pianist, but he was soon deposed by Earl Hines of Pittsburgh. In the later period of Hines and Weatherford the solo pianist was not expected to sing or perform acts; he was fully respected for devoting his attention to the increasing complexities of playing big piano.

Hines founded the first sizable jazz piano school. In a most imitative and direct way, Zinkey Cohn, Cassino Simpson, Gideon Honoré and Tut Soper developed in the Hines fashion. More timidly Jess Stacey, Teddy Wilson attempted to use his basic premises in their styles. Striding Chicago pianists like Johnny Fortin borrowed liberally from Hines.

Hines himself seems to have been influenced by the New Orleans horns with which he played after his arrival from Pittsburgh. Armstrong's flares and punching accents were soon a part of Hines. Noone's cadenzas and sudden changes of register and dynamics also became Hines properties.

Ragtime and blues seem to have been the major influences acting on the other early jazz pianists, notably Alex Hill, Jimmie Blythe, Art Hodes, Joe Sullivan and Jack Gardner. Classical backgrounds were put to excellent jazz use by Mel Grant, Mel Henke and Sammy Stewart.

The Clarinet

The Tio family, major influences on the New Orleans clarinet, influenced Chicago in the sense that many of Lorenzo Jr.'s pupils and others affected by him came there. Another reed influence from New Orleans, exemplified in the style of Johnny Dodds, was less imitated, but was no less important in the ultimate formulation of the Chicago style. The Tio manner was smooth, round-toned, gliding with classical grace through the instrument's whole range—a style requiring knowledge of harmony and high technical proficiency. Rappolo and, to a lesser extent, Shields sought the tonality but neglected or intentionally avoided the extensive cadenzas and scrollwork which marked Bigard's and Noone's work. Volly de Faut, Irving "Fazola" Prestopnick (with Bob Crosby for years at the Blackhawk), and more recently Pete Fountain (briefly at Jazz, Ltd.), showed some continuity of a white branch of the Tio school.

The biting, hot-inflected, wanton clarinet style, originally well stated by Dodds, contrasted strikingly with Tio's figurations. From Dodds' brash voicing, matching ideally King Oliver's searing companion horn, many young Chicagoans derived inspiration, none more than Frank Teschemacher. And none was readier to modify the Dodds style to his own conceptions. Frank was a jumble of ambitions. He wanted a personal style; he wanted to indulge broadly in experimentation; he wanted to mature. In his haste to acquire all of these things, he sometimes sacrificed precision, but never vigor. Despite Frank's short three or four years in hot bands, his few records immediately became definitive-study texts for all Chicago jazz clarinetists.

Benny Goodman in his early years effectively employed the

phrasings, the tone shadings and the stridencies of Tesch. Benny may have heard Tesch for the first time in 1925, when Benny was with Clyde Doerr at the Congress and Tesch was at Midway Gardens with Art Kassell's hot band (which included Bud Freeman and Muggsy Spanier). Yet by 1926 Goodman was demonstrating competence in the Dodds-by-Tesch idiom and establishing himself as the most proficient, most versatile Chicago clarinetist. Upon short contact with Goodman, and probably shorter (if any) contact with Tesch, Fud Livingston acquired some of the same Doddsian character and then introduced it into the East. Pee Wee Russell and Ed Hall seem to have acquired membership in this clarinet school from other sources. Maurie Bercov, Bud Jacobson, Milton Mezzrow, Rosy McHargue and Charlie Spero show Doddsian-mold marks. In recent years Bob Lovett achieved an amazing similarity to Dodds. Chicago-born Frank Chace is certainly the finest young Dodds-Pee Wee-Tesch student.

In early Chicago, Noone's spectacular work at the early-morning Apex Club provided the foundation for Johnny (Italiane) Lane and his student, Joe Marsala. Playing beside Bigard and Nicholas, Chicagoan Darnell Howard developed Tio characteristics. Bechet, representing something of a fusion of New Orleans styles, was not often imitated in Chicago.

Many clarinetists exposed to the Chicago atmosphere, such as Inge, Bailey, Rand, O'Bryant, Strong, Ball and certainly the majority of younger fellows, have relatively amorphous styles. Currently active are Jug Berger, Bill Reinhardt, Bob McCracken, Franz Jackson, Wally Wender, Armin VonderHeydt and Brian Shanley.

The Saxophone

By rugged persistence, some pretty obvious talent and also keen affection for the music, Bud Freeman long ago became and remains the personification of Chicago-style tenor sax. Bud Jacobson before him and Bob Skiver thirty years later, both playing "naturally" without imitating Freeman, fall into surprisingly similar sounds and forms. But Freeman plays the Chicago style so much more grandiloquently, uncompromisingly and consistently that others in the field are dwarfed. Before 1927 Freeman fought viciously to quicken what appeared to be a slow-developing technique. In retrospect it is clear that Bud had selected an instrument especially suited to displace the trombone in what was to evolve into the Chicago style. His Wiedoff method book may not have been the perfect jazz manual, yet he finished it off, and now he often rides the exercises to humorous and even hot ends. When Bud encountered Coleman Hawkins at the Detroit Greystone Ballroom in his formative years, it was love at first sound; he began a new phase based on Hawkins effects, agility and assertiveness. Hawkins later, in turn, borrowed from Bud.

If Eddie Miller's playing has in fact been influenced by Bud—and there is certainly reason for that suspicion—this would constitute some small repayment of Chicago's musical debt to New Orleans.

The tenor has been the most popular reed in the Chicago area, aside from the clarinet. In addition to a surprising number of excellent jazz tenors from the Hull House supply house (listed later), Chicago tenormen of particular jazz note have been Bud Hunter, the contemporary and associate of Bud Jacobson and Freeman (the Bud tag was strictly coincidental); George Demaris; Joe Masek; Shreveport-born Pud Brown; and on occasion Toasty Paul; Floyd Town; Mezzrow; and George "Snurps" Snurpus.

The tenor enjoyed a fad in Chicago long before its burst of popularity in Harlem (1943 *et seq.*), starting on the South Side in the larger bands of Elgar, Cooke and Joe Oliver, who had the services of Nicholas and Bigard. Subsequently the tenor replaced the trombone in the bands of Albert Ammons, King Kolax, Lee Collins, Punch Miller, etc., usually as a double with clarinet. Franz Jackson, Cecil Irwin, Happy Cauldwell and Bud Johnson were soloists with both large and small Chicago groups. More recently Gene Ammons, Ira Schulman, Ira Sullivan, Sandy Mosse and Mike Simpson have been active in the modern idiom.

The South Side's most famous altoist was Scoops Carey; "was" because he is now a non-playing attorney. Scoops was with Gid Honoré, then for years with Art Tatum's Three Deuces Band, then Roy Eldridge, then Earl Hines. He attributes most of the groundwork in jazz alto to Stump Evans and, soon after, Doc Poston (of Jimmie Noone fame). On the other hand, the North Siders more often recall the popularizing influences of Jack Pettis and Frank Trumbauer, both of whom appeared on the Chicago scene in the early 1920's. The theatrical appearances and music-store demonstrations of Bennie Krueger, Rudy Wiedoff and Paul Biese also stirred enthusiasm for saxophones.

As several early altomen treated the horn as a stepchild—Darnell Howard, Frank Teschemacher, Omer Simeon and Barney Bigard having virtually abandoned it—others rejected all other reeds in its favor. The top white altoists were Bill Dohler, Dan McManman and the late Boyce Brown. Several Chicago-style or Chicago-Dixie bands used the alto effectively (chronologically, Charlie Pierce, with Ralph Rudder and Tesch on alto in the same band; Noone with Poston; Mares with Boyce Brown; Freeman with Dohler; and Chet Roble with Brown). The most frequent combination has been alto and rhythm—the economy package.

There were essentially two schools of Chicago alto. The rollercoaster or virtuoso style emulated the Tio string-of-pearls phrasing. Benny Goodman and Boyce Brown leaned this way and Scoops Carey, under the tutelage of Hines and Tatum, developed into an extension of this pattern. Carey's high development of melodic eccentricity and harmonic discoveries ultimately brought him close to Charlie Parker, whom he induced Hines to hire on tenor until an alto chair could be arranged for him. Despite resemblances, Carey claims that he and Parker were mature before meeting and that they probably were mutually compatible rather than influential for each other.

The second Chicago alto style featured punchy phrases, recalling Freeman's fast style, and was preferred by Dohler, who is still the master. More modern altos in Chicago have been represented by Johnny Bothwell (now out of music), Eddie Wiggins, Lee Konitz and a new player, Joe Daley.

The Rhythm Section

New Orleans sent up to Chicago a strong steady beat which all drummers quickly assimilated. Vic Berton, the most respected Chicago drummer before 1920, was followed by Frank Snyder, Phil Dooley and Earl Wiley, who soon subscribed to Dixieland rhythm. Ben Pollack may have been the first who did not have to erase earlier military influence. Ben was soon followed by Jim Barnes, Davey Tough and Gene Krupa. These young whites were instructed by the examples of Tubby Hall and Ollie Powers, then by Jimmy Bertrand and Jasper Taylor (although the latter were not from New Orleans), then by

Paul Barbarin and Baby Dodds, then by Snaggs Jones and Zutty Singleton. Other great Negro drummers became prominent as the jazz population increased, men like Sidney Catlett (with Sammy Stewart), and Wally Bishop (with Hines). In later years, Kansas Fields, Osie Johnson and Buddy Smith were recognized as exceptional. Eddie Condon made a fetish of learning from Negro rhythm sections, and he cajoled every drummer he worked with, even Josh Billings, virtuoso of drumming on a suitcase, to tour the South Side joints with him night after night. George Wettling (Wichita) and later Don Carter, Doc Cenardo (Detroit) and Mousie Alexander learned the same lessons.

Throughout the "Chicago period," the most frequent bass instrument has been the percussive, plucked bass viol. It was used regularly by Johnson, Garland, Brieux, Brown, Loyocano and Chink Martin (imported from New Orleans in 1924 by George Brunies). As exceptions to the parade of string bass players, Bass Moore and Charlie Jackson were best known for their work on bass sax in the early period, and today expatriate Joe Rushton and newly arrived Spencer Clark specialize in bass sax, both inspired by Adrian Rollini. In the early 1920's Bert Cobb entered the picture as the first tuba virtuoso, claiming to have made the first tuba solo on jazz records (Oliver's *Someday Sweetheart*). Native sons Quinn Wilson, Lawson Buford and Bill Oldham were South Side representatives of the second generation of jazz tubaists, and all doubled on viol. On the North Side, string bass was used by Jim Lanigan, then Pat Pattison, and is still used by Earl Murphy. Bob Casey is fondly remembered as the bass cohort of the traditionalists. With the coming of swing Israel Crosby, Truck Parham, Big Crawford, Jerry Jackson and Ed Mihelich came into focus. Johnny Pate, Wilbur Ware and Johnny Frigo ruled the roost in later years.

In the early bands up from New Orleans, and throughout the Chicago period, the banjo and finally the guitar supplied a treble tonality to the basic beat. The plectrist of the early Chicago rhythm section rarely soloed. His whole function was to help give the band a massive pulsation. But only the larger or more successful bands could afford a plectrist. Soon the cymbal took over the banjo's function.

A banjo could accent the beat in a manner scarcely attainable with a six-string guitar. In an effort to combine banjo percussiveness with guitar tonality, Chicagoans Eddie Condon, Earl Murphy and Marty Grosz have chosen the four-string guitar.

Unlike their compatriots on other jazz instruments, the young Chicago plectrists—including Lew Black, Frank Lehman, Jack Goss, Dick McPartland, Mario Tanney and Remo Biondi, as well as Murphy and Grosz—attribute little influence to the South Siders. Obviously Eddie Lang and Lonnie Johnson exchanged notes, but within the Chicago picture, with which we are particularly concerned, the South Siders Johnny St. Cyr, Mike McKendrick, Junie Cobb, Lawrence Dixon, Ikey Robinson and Bud Scott don't recall instructing North Siders or indulging in much exchange of ideas.

As for miscellaneous instruments, in the first generation George Kenyon, and in the second, Cy Touff, have performed well on mellophone. Max Miller was the one outstanding jazz vibesman in Chicago.

Hokum

To achieve hot intonations, prior classical instrumental techniques often had to be discarded. Such irreverence opened the door for further experiments. Bud Jacobson produced a ludicrous tone by inserting modified Kazoo heads into his clarinet. Oliver's derby mute suggested a wide assortment of headgear for tone modification to later hornmen. Art Kassel's *Hells Bells* effect depended on a mute designed by Mel Stitzel; and Paddy Harmon devised a mute, still popular, for adding vocal quality to the wah-wah. Al Kvale ordered a batch of miniature instruments and spent years developing the ability to play them convincingly. The "hokum deal" or "act," when discovered to have commercial value, was generally accepted good-naturedly into a band's repertoire. Bill Davison did wry comedy on hot mandolin. Baby Dodds' shimmy-while-drumming also became standard for Danny Alvin. Trombonist Sid Dawson and trumpeter Del Lincoln conceived amazing mouthpiece duets, given three-part harmony by Marty Grosz' Kazoo.

Phil Dooley had a trapeze above his drums, loaded with a variety of kitchenware and, on each end, a "kitty" or donation pot. When Phil shook the trapeze, the clanging junk made a hell of a racket, reminding dancers of the musicians' needs. In the disputative 1930's, Phil had Ed Fox—proprietor in 1918 of a desegregated cafe and pool hall at Thirty-fifth and State, and employing Phil's band at the time—legally attest that Phil had originated the expression "swing" as a euphemism for naughty "jazz"; and also that Phil had first called the dancer-listeners "cats." Somehow this tied in with "swingin' the cats"!

Perhaps the most hokumized item of all was displayed by Jasper Taylor, who earlier had introduced the washboard into the drum kit. Jasper found a way to tune and play melody on a bedspring. Like Moondog's Monster Drum—a tarpaulin over a hole in the ground— Jasper's jazzy bedspring was impractically cumbersome and difficult to keep in tune.

The Mound City Blue Blowers had a substantially pure "act." Organized and rehearsed in a dismal Chicago hotel room, they created a wholly novel, bright, gay sound with kazoo, papered comb, suitcase, banjo and guitar. During their existence they traveled to London and formed memorable collaborations on records.

Boys' Bands

During the War I years, Chicago grew too fast for comfort. A short but severe depression followed, threatening to cause slums and crime. Then civic conscience awoke in some quarters to the need for social development, or at least off-the-street pastimes, for the adolescent. High schools and community houses sponsored dances. Almost every old-time jazzman recalls playing dozens of these "kid dances" at Columbus Park Refectory, Austin, Senn, Lakeview and many other high schools. Dance instruction was usually offered in the afternoons, with small bands, amateurs or even phonographs supplying the beat. The evening dances were dressier social affairs. There were post-game celebrations, proms and just plain dances—several weekly. Boys' orchestras were rehearsed in the schools for this blossoming market and were exchanged between schools.

In addition to the high-school bands, three larger boys' orchestras came into prominence:

1. The Jane Addams Hull House Band produced the Goodman brothers, Benny, Freddie and Harry; the Spero brothers, Carmen and Charles, reeds; Pip Villani, George Cecilia, Tony Pelligrini and Joe Mangano, all reeds; Al Turk, trumpet; Joe and Marty Marsala.

2. The Chicago Daily News Band produced Charles "Nosey" Altiere, trumpet; Joe Rullo, trombone; and Frankie Rullo, drums, as well as many studio men.

3. The Chicago Defender (newspaper) Boys Band under Major Smith trained upcoming jazzmen Lionel Hampton; drummers Wally Bishop and Dick Barnett; bassists Hayes Alvis, Milton Hinton and Quinn Wilson; trumpeters Charlie Allen, Leon Scott and Thomas "Tick" Gray; trombonists Ken Stewart and Billy Franklin; tubaman Bill Oldham, and at least an equal number who remained in jazz until the Depression decimated music.

A year or two later, when Major Smith had the Phillips High School Band, he started Ray Nance and Scoops Carey on their musical ways. Soon jazz instruction became a part of the curriculum of every South Side high school, and even the technical schools; Franz Jackson received his first instruction at Tilden Tech, and Benny Green at DuSable High.

Friendships

Intense friendships and mutual admirations between jazzmen— even men competing on the same instrument—have been legion, and the rewards of friendship often truly substantial. To cite some examples from around Chicago: in the road show "Keep Shufflin' " (1926), Jabbo Smith played with bassist Lawson Bufford. When the show sat down in Chicago, Jab was invited to live at the Bufford parental home. Ikey Robinson sought Jab for his *Got Buter on It* recording date with Brunswick. When the same company later commissioned Jabbo for several dates, Bufford and Robinson were on them. The three pianists Jack Gardner, Mel Henke and Max Miller greatly enjoyed each other's talents. One would invite the others to sit in on his job; thus the proprietors came to know all three, and amongst themselves they had a three-man piano circuit. When musician-impresarios Pope and Allen sent out a call for a Lee Collins benefit, eleven bands and a dozen stars appeared and collected two thousand dollars for the trumpeter. Author Studs Terkel had the same response with a Bill Broonzy benefit. This camaraderie differs from the New Orleans tradition only in its desegregation.

The Chicago jazzmen are a friendly, intimate group, socially visiting together, picnicking, gathering literally in hundreds at the immense parties at Squirrel Ashcraft's, Howe's, Priestley's, Atwood's or Bill Wright's—any jazz buff's home that is capacious enough. Everyone brings his instrument.

Numerous marriages of musician to musician, or to a member of another musician's family, reveal what a tight little island Chicago jazz is. Chet Roble married Bill Reinhardt's sister; Bill married a dancer; George Wettling and Jim Barnes married sisters; later Jim married June, the bassist; Jim McPartland married Dorothy Williams, the singer, and subsequently Marian Page, the English pianist; Jim's sister married Jim Lanigan; Bud Jacobson's daughter, Marie, married trombonist Roy Olandfield; George Zack married Bunny Berigan's widow, Donna; Bill Davison married his vocalist, Dianne; Johnny Lane and Bill Dohler married sisters; drummer Sleepy Kaplan married Rod Cless' widow, who was also Bud Freeman's sister. Guitarist Gassi married pianist Christine; Bud Freeman was married to a prior wife of Lou Garcia; Zinkey Cohn to a prior wife of Billy Minor, bandleader. "Has your bride been cleared with the local?" is understandably a common joke.

The friendships of Freeman and Tesch, then Freeman and Dohler; of Oliver and Armstrong, Morton and Melrose; of Grosz and Chace, of Spanier and Brunies; of Natty Doninique and Baby Dodds; of Preston Jackson and Roy Palmer are a few of the dozens which indicate that jazz is indeed a communicative means.

Chicago jazz has had many friends on the periphery. Proprietor Palmer Cady (Cascades, Wind Blew Inn) offered the boys a bandstand, a piano and a cut in the take—and, in addition, an understanding equalled only by Condon's. Simply because they enjoyed hot jazz—certainly not because they could play it—Joe Kayser, Sig Meyers and Art Kassel organized and attempted valiantly to crack the ballroom-schmaltz barrier. Squirrel Ashcraft, an articulate attorney for jazz, has found a higher niche, being able (and almost always asked) to fill the piano chair of any band he goes to hear.

Radio

In Chicago the 1920's were the roaringest. Publicity via nightly radio remotes, phonograph records and stage shows—movies had become secondary attractions—swelled the market for jazzmen into the hundreds. Gambling, bootlegging and lots of loose money added up to fabulous night clubs with fabulous floor shows. Golden opportunities existed in the entertainment field. Dancing continued popular; ballrooms and roadhouses were on the ascendancy. The popularity of stage shows increased so much that a show band on the stage, often with hot specialists, shared musical responsibilities with huge pit bands. Within the span of a few years two hundred musicians were drawn into studio work as Chicago became for a time the hub of the networks. Axel Christensen had a Loop school and five neighborhood schools of rag and jazz piano, and he was opening branches in neighboring towns. But there were no talkies, no TV.

Probably one of the first appearances on radio by a Negro band was the participation of Jimmy Wade's Moulin Rouge Orchestra, featuring pianist Teddy Weatherford and violinist Eddie South, in the opening ceremonies of station WBBM, in late 1923.

Trumpeter Hughie Swift reports that his band at Jeffery Tavern was the first South Side group to have nightly remotes, broadcasting via WSBC in 1926. His band included Charlie Allen, trumpet; Roy Palmer, trombone; Baby Dodds, drums. Swift was followed shortly by the broadcasts of Sammy Stewart's band, with Sid Catlett, drums; Ikey Robinson, banjo; and the remaining personnel Columbus boys who had come with Stewart and young Chicagoans. The overwhelming popularity of Ellington's daily broadcasts during the month in summer, 1929, he was at the Congress Hotel really opened the larger stations and networks to hot music. From this period and into the swing era, the Grand Terrace airings offered Earl Hines, with, as the most stable elements of his band, Omer Simeon, Darnell Howard and Cecil Irwin, reeds; Wally Fuller and George Dixon, trumpets; William Franklin, trombone; Wally Bishop, drums; and Quinn Wilson, bass. Subsequently, from the same location, came the traveling bands of Lunceford, Kirk, Armstrong, the Hendersons and Basie. Cabin Club broadcasts had a Frankie Jaxon contingent in 1928 and later Jimmie Noone's big band. Noone was then heard from Skoller's Danceland, as, subsequently, was Horace Henderson's band. By the mid-1930's the Three Deuces had a half-hour nightly of the groups of Art Tatum, Johnny Dodds and then Roy Eldridge, with intermission soloists Cleo Brown, Lonnie Johnson and Monette Moore.

There was an improbably early-morning studio program for a short season in the early 1930's by a band including Wingy Man-

none, Red Norvo and Volly de Faut. By the mid-1930's day-
time radio was devoid of hot music and thinning in other attractions.
To spark their programming, WIND hired an all-jazz house band
under versatile Max Miller, who played guitar, bass, piano, vibes
and harmonium; Bill Funky, alto; Yohannan, piano; Grahel, drums;
Vance, bass—Max' clique from Gary.

The Kapp brothers, Dave and Jack, before starting Decca
Records, were interested in a record store and in various other
musical enterprises, including the management of a sixteen-piece
radio-studio band under Frankie Jaxon's leadership, with Bob Schoffner, musical director and trumpet; George Mitchell, trumpet; Del
Bright, reeds; Preston Jackson, trombone; John Lindsay, bass;
Jerome Carrington and Charlie Beal, duo pianists, and Tubby Hall,
drums. After sixteen sustained weeks, the band was reduced to
approximately the men named and continued for a season, sponsored
by Muscletone, a cure-all nostrum.

Finally, with swing, the Loop's Blackhawk became a jazz
stand for years, with Louis Prima, Red Norvo, Mildred Bailey, and
Bob Crosby. At the College Inn, in the Hotel Sherman, practically
all traveling swing bands were aired, as well as the local groups of
Bud Freeman, Boyd Raeburn and Muggsy Spanier's Ragtimers, then
just beginning. For a time in the 1940's the Brass Rail, the Ambas-
sador East and the New Downbeat Room offered dozens of small
groups and soloists, notably McPartland, the Marsalas, Kirby, Smith,
Wilson, Waller and Allen.

Following is a list of some of the more important contributors
to or practioners of the jazz art who were Chicago-born and/or long-
term residents (thus avoiding some midground individuals not particularly identified with the Chicago scene, such as Lionel Hampton
and Jo Jones). Many significant jazzmen have been omitted because
their ages were not known. On the other hand, some may seem
unfamiliar because they were not recorded adequately; after 1930
Chicago lost its position as a recording center, and to this day
there is neither a large nor a quality pressing plant in the area.
Many Chicagoans—for example, Art Hodes, Cy Touff, Floyd
O'Brien, Max Miller, Danny Alvin and Israel Crosby—became
internationally familiar from records made outside of Chicago. (At
present, all these men are again living in Chicago.) In the listing,
the men born outside outside of Chicago are named in parentheses.

Some Prominent Chicago Jazzmen

Approximate Birth Year	The Style of Their Period	Names
Pre-1900	Rag & Early Dixieland	Berton, Mezzrow, Yancey (Mares, Brunies, McKenzie, T. Jackson, Morton, R. M. Jones, Schoebel, Oliver, J. & W. Dodds, S. & T. Brown, Ladnier, Mitchell, Jasp. Taylor, Schoffner, Tio, Ory, Noone, Keppard, Broonzy, Lofton)
1900–1905	Originators of Chicago Style	Pollack, Obrien, Jacobson, North, J. Barnes, Lanigan, de Faut (Condon, Rappolo, Mannone, Hodes, Beiderbecke, Alvin, Armstrong, Stacey, Hines, South, Reeves, Lux Lewis, Palmer)
1905–1910	Peak of Chicago Development	Freeman, the McPartlands, Rushton, the Marsalas, Spanier, Biondi, Roble, Reinhardt, Alvis, Howard, A. Ammons, Krupa, the Goodmans, Sullivan, Cless, Mendell, Murphy, Daley, Lincoln, Tough, Melrose, Simpson (Catlett, Teschemacher, Davidson, Gardner, Grant, J. Smith, Hill)
1910–1915	Last Chicagoans & First Experimenters	Soper, Ivett, Parham, Nance (Hinton, the Careys, Bean, Miller, Mince, Sherock)
1915–1920	Technicians & Adaptables	Henke, G. Barnes, Marx, Frigo, J. Jones, I. Crosby (Ewell)
1920–1925	Early Modern	Tristano, Kral, G. Ammons, O'Day, Russo (Green, Bothwell)
1925–1930	Mid-modern	Levy, Konitz, Touff, Mance, Wiggins
Post-1930	a) Current Modern b) Revival of Dixie & Chicago	Karlin, Schulman, Sullivan, Mosse Chace, Wright (Grosz, Dawson)

Classification is not as simple as this table might imply. For example, Ewell is an anomaly in the sense that he has developed along more elemental lines than his contemporaries; Gene Ammons covered swing to bop, and rhythm and blues to rock and roll; Touff seems equally at home with Dixie and modern; Marx, Frigo and Wiggins are not definitely classifiable. Discounting such exceptions, there still remain several interesting and revealing correlations:

1) The supersaturation of heavy talent in the first years agrees with reports of the greater opportunity and greater stimulus then afforded.

2) That exactly one half are men in the rhythm section would seem statistically satisfactory, but that two-thirds of these are pianists seems to point to a particularly favorable climate for their breed. Recalling that New Orleans was relatively low in piano talent, it might be speculated that a decided change was occurring, either in musical tastes or in sophistication of the artist.

3) Although time and again brothers entered the jazz field, we find that the Ammonses were the only father and son.

Chronology

The story of jazz in Chicago, or anywhere, is not as simple as a listing of dates; but for convenience the chapter headings might be put in this fashion:

Circa	
1911	Jelly Roll Morton, Tony Jackson and early bluesmen.
1915	Tom Brown's Band from Dixieland. Appelation "jass." Negro theatricals. Perez's band imported.
1916	Original Dixieland Jazz Band. Influx of New Orleans jazzmen begins.
1917	Sugar Johnny, Roy Palmer, Ed Garland, Tubby Hall, etc.
Spring 1918	Bill Johnson's Creoles, with Oliver, opens Royal Gardens. Keppard's Creoles. Dreamland, Panama, De Luxe, Thirty-fifth and State.
1922	Oliver back at Lincoln Gardens, Ladnier added. New Orleans Rhythm Kings recording. Chicagoans in development.
1923	July 8, at 11 P.M., Louis Armstrong arrives.
Circa 1925	Peak of South Side's jazz band and blues recording. Stage shows.

1927	Chicago style recordings begin. Oliver has big band. Armstrong returns from Henderson in N.Y. to be featured, to form own band and to record Hot Fives (and to be greatly imitated).
1929	Depression. Hines big band. Exodus of jazzmen to begin.
1933–1934	Chicago World's Fair reprieve. Hot men in show bands and small clubs. Three Deuces, My Cellar, Liberty Inn, Silhouette.
1936	Swing bands in hotels, theaters, ballrooms. Three large South Side show clubs.
1942	War prosperity. Traveling jazz groups. Pump Room, Preview, Capitol, Offbeat.
Circa 1947	Blue Note, Beehive, Jazz, Ltd., Helsings, Rupneck's Streamliner.
1950 and after	Continuing Dixie revival: 11-11 Club, Basin Street, Red Arrow, Firehouse concerts.

THE SPREAD
OF JAZZ AND
THE BIG BANDS

Hsio Wen Shih

Hsio Wen Shih was born in Peking. He attended schools in several northern American cities and is a graduate of the School of Architecture at the Massachusetts Institute of Technology. Mr. Shih avocationally is art director and a reviewer for *The Jazz Review*. His study of the spread of jazz and the big bands during a pivotal decade indicates a kind of approach that could be productively applied to other aspects of jazz history.

In 1917 the Navy Department closed the District and, so the story goes, New Orleans jazz moved up the river to Chicago. The story can't be wrong because it has been exhaustively documented at both ends; it is merely unedifying. It explains well enough the jazz played in Chicago until almost the end of the 1920's, but what about the music of the East, the South, and the Southwest in the 1920's that, more than New Orleans jazz, was to provide the basis for the developments of the 1930's?

New Orleans jazz was already in decline before the Depression, which killed some New Orleans musicians and forced so many others into retirement. Perhaps jazz would not have survived the Depression with only New Orleans musicians; they did not adapt easily to new conditions. Their conservatism had always been famous: Buddy Petit, Wade Waley, and Frankie Dusen had threatened to kill Morton for poking fun at their cooking beans and rice on stage at the Lakeside in Los Angeles; and Keppard had refused to be the first to record jazz because he couldn't see the advantage. He only saw that other musicians would be able to steal his ideas. Especially conservative were the *gens-de-couleur;* they got it honestly enough; a small, slightly favored minority looking apprehensively over their shoulders at a large, threatening one; and they were small tradesmen and skilled craftsmen, too, with all that kind of caution besides. They might have been happy forever, with their gumbo and their parades, their cigar-making and their music, and of course leaving New Orleans could not have helped: Adam, expelled from Eden, must afterward have distrusted innovation, too.

The only New Orleans musicians who were innovators as well as creators throughout the 1920's were both mavericks. Armstrong was a street Arab who floated up on his virtuosity and fertility of invention; Morton a Ulysses who had stifled in the coziness of home-town life, a rambler, a midnight creeper. They created the elements that started the transition from New Orleans to the jazz of the late 1920's, Armstrong showing the possibilities of solo horn and Morton creating much of the repertory of jazz while developing a balanced ensemble style. Only Armstrong survived the Crash to develop further in the 1930's; his New Orleans contemporaries were left behind.

The typical innovator of the 1920's was a very different figure,

173

and an easy one to describe. He was born about 1900, into a Negro family doing better than most, possibly in the Deep South, but more likely on its fringe; in either case, his family usually migrated North in time for him to finish high school. If he had gone to college, and he often had, he had gone to Wilberforce or a fringe school like Howard or Fisk. He might have aimed at a profession and fallen back on jazz as a second choice. He was, in any case, by birth or by choice, a member of the rising Negro middle class; he was Fletcher Henderson, or Don Redman, or Coleman Hawkins, or Duke Ellington.

They were not the only men attracted to jazz; there was a huge lesser company of eager and talented men who felt the fascination of jazz, or smelled the promise of financial reward. The converts came from every part of the country and all strata of Negro (and, for that matter, white) society. Many of the converts were already skilled instrumentalists; some, like Dewey Jackson and June Clark, had played in brass bands in schools or clubs. Others came from the older Negro entertainment world—dance-band musicians like Buster Bailey, Darnell Howard, or Johnny Dunn—and a few, like Sammy Stewart and Don Redman, had solid music-academy training. Like the New Orleans musicians, they almost always had their roots in the matrix of jazz, the compound of European and West African elements that had produced, one after the other, field hollers, spirituals, blues, ragtime—the whole range of folk music of the Negro South. They had heard the same blues, played the same rags, and, like Lil Hardin, just up from Memphis, didn't find fitting into a New Orleans ensemble too hard. Improvisation was something else again; some of them never learned and most took time to develop, but learning to improvise in the New Orleans manner couldn't have been as hard as it is to switch from a rock-and-roll group to a jazz band today. By the mid-1920's many competent soloists had developed; a few were still developing—into something more.

It was a matter of age, too. Jazz, then as now, was a young man's game. The older, established Negro musicians, like James Reese Europe, Will Marion Cook and their Clef Club circle never caught the authentic accent, although their young friend, Noble Sissle, came close simply by hiring New Orleans musicians to play in his band. Erskine Tate was another older musician who took transfusions of New Orleans men into his pit band to "play for films, and during the intermission, we would play a big Overture and a Red Hot Number afterwards," as one of the ringers, Armstrong, described.

Their attitude toward jazz wouldn't have surprised white bandleaders such as Whiteman and Goldkette a few years later. These men also saw jazz as another kind of addition to the repertory of a dance band, and hired the white counterparts of Armstrong and Stomp Evans, Bix and Trumbauer, only to smother them in arrangements so overblown that even Lombardo-loving Armstrong had doubts. By the late 1920's there was nothing remarkable about a shrewd bandleader exploiting a vogue; there was also nothing remarkable about his finding a few brilliant white jazzmen to hire: Bix, at Lake Forest Academy, and the West Side boys like Teschemacher and Goodman, had spent many nights on the Black-and-Tan South Side, learning and listening.

Musicians, Negro and white, from other parts of the country, are harder to explain. They appeared from everywhere, from 1920 on; by 1930 every city outside the Deep South with a Negro population (1920 census) above sixty thousand except Philadelphia had produced an important band: Washington, Duke Ellington; Baltimore, Chick Webb; Memphis, Jimmie Lunceford; St. Louis, the Missourians; Chicago, Luis Russell and Armstrong; New York, Henderson, Charlie Johnson, and half a dozen more.

Where did all these musicians learn to play jazz? Not from records; most of them developed before the early 1920's, when few records existed outside those of the ODJB: such an influence would be too ironic for belief.

A few musicians had been to New Orleans in their travels: June Clark worked to New Orleans on the Pullmans in the 1910's; and Buster Bailey went to New Orleans on a school holiday in the winter of 1917, first heard jazz there, and "came home and started jazzing it up in Memphis." Others heard early New Orleans migrants in the North: Darnell Howard recalls hearing Keppard in Milwaukee in 1915 and Bechet a little later in Chicago. The musicians from the river towns like Memphis or St. Louis can be accounted for, too. Dewey Jackson, for example, grew up in St. Louis and was playing with Charlie Creath on a boat by 1919, and others must have learned jazz that way, playing alongside New Orleans musicians on the Streckfus excursion boats.

There were still other musicians who grew up before 1920, before jazz records were available: Washingtonians like Ellington, Baltimoreans like Joe Turner. They had heard blues and church music, of course, and followed ragtime, but during the crucial years in their development as musicians—late adolescence, when music ceases to be a drudgery and becomes first a social asset and then a means of livelihood—where had they heard jazz in those cities? Ellington gives the answer himself: "I'd often watched Luckey Roberts who had come down from New York to play the Howard Theatre." Roberts was one of the Harlem post-ragtime pianists, and the Howard was a stop on one of the Negro vaudeville circuits that covered the South, reaching down to towns of less than five thousand Negroes, and often, under "colored ownership and management," supplying entertainment to people who would otherwise have been isolated.

The Howard was one of four Negro vaudeville houses in Washington then; there were three in Baltimore; there were two in Pittsburgh, and at one of them Mary Lou Williams was inspired by Lovie Austin as Duke had been by Roberts. These theaters always had music, and not only pianists: Lovie led a traveling band. Farther South the musicians were likely to be from New Orleans rather than New York or Chicago. Danny Barker says, "All the shows played [New Orleans] . . . if they needed a musician they knew they could pick one up in New Orleans."

The circuits extended as far west as Texas; the American in Houston, the Park in Dallas, the Aldridge in Oklahoma City, the Dreamland in Muskogee, the Lincoln and the Lyric in Kansas City —they help to account for the beginnings of jazz in the Southwest, not only as a vehicle for the spread of jazz, but also providing work for local musicians: one of the first bands in Kansas City, George Lee's, played as a pit band at the Lyric.

After 1920, with the wide distribution of recordings, the tracing of the spread of jazz is no longer necessary; a young musician could "come swingin' out of Chittlin' Switch" without ever having heard live jazz. Unfortunately recordings also make the tracing of musical influence impossible: if Lester Young claims Trumbauer as his principal early influence, it can only be accepted with wonder and doubt; if Oran Page says the principal influences on the Blue Devils were Oliver, Morton and Ellington, in that order, can the evidence of two records contradict him?

But to return to the typical innovator of the 1920's: the earliest developed example is a woman, Lil Hardin Armstrong. Born in Memphis and raised partly in Chicago, where her family had migrated, she had been a student at Fisk before she began her musical career, which was to include playing with the three greatest groups of early jazz, King Oliver, Louis' Hot Five, and the Hot Seven. She had helped Oliver "arrange his band," without written music, into the tightest pre-Morton ensemble group in the New Orleans tradition. A large part of the engineering of Louis' early successes must be attributed to her. "If it wasn't for Lil," says Preston Jackson, "Louis would not be where he is today. She inspired him to do bigger and better things." When Louis went to New York in 1929, she "loaned everybody in the band twenty dollars" to go with him. She showed, in fact, all the traits that were to be so essential to the group of musicians who followed her: self-awareness ("I encouraged him to develop himself," she said of Louis); ambition, both musical and, in the larger sense, social; musicianship; and an engaging mixture of shrewdness and adventurousness.

The world of the jazzman faced him with "dizzying temptations, overpowering pressures, insidious diversions of purpose" in the 1920's, especially after the vogue for Negro entertainment spread among the white public, who saw Harlem as a black Arcadia, a reservation of hedonists. It was all a misunderstanding, of course, at least where the music was concerned: Ellington's style of the 1920's has rightly been called the papier-mâché jungle. But the white Public was fooled, and the urbane Ellington was forced by public demand to be the mock-primitive, as the genius of Waller was diverted to comedy; and the temptations killed, in the space of a few years, Joe Smith, John Nesbitt, Bix, Bubber Miley, Long Green. A jazzman needed all those sturdy middle-class traits to resist the temptations of the environment, to develop within it as a musician, and to survive to collect the rewards.

The rewards were real enough to attract even entrepreneurs like McKinney and Moten; it was one of the few fields where the Negro had an economic advantage. Henderson, with his chemistry degree, said to his future wife in the early 1920's, "You better learn to play jazz or you won't make no money." If so many musicians came to jazz after training in one of the professions, it was because jazz was both more profitable and safer for a Negro in the 1920's; it was a survival of this attitude that decided Ellington to keep his son out of M.I.T. and aeronautical engineering in the 1930's.

The jazzmen came from all over the country: Don Redman from West Virginia, Storer's College, and conservatories in Boston and Detroit; Coleman Hawkins from St. Joseph, Topeka, and Chicago, running away from home at fourteen to escape the discipline of an ambitious mother, but still managing three years of music studies at Washburn College; Benny Carter from New York and Wilberforce University; Ellington from Washington and a rejected scholarship at Cooper Union; Fletcher Henderson from Cuthbert, Georgia, and a chemistry degree at Atlanta University.

During the next decade they were to be followed by younger men of the same type: Teddy Wilson from Austin, Texas, with a degree from Talledega College in Alabama; Sy Oliver from Cleveland, sending his wife through college and trying to find time to go back himself; Walter Page with his incomplete work for a degree at Kansas State Teachers' College; Jimmie Lunceford from Mississippi and Denver, with a degree from Fisk University.

They were a remarkable group of men. Between 1925 and 1935 they created, in competition, a musical tradition that required fine technique and musicianship (several of them were among the earliest virtuosi in jazz); they began to change the basis of the jazz repertory from blues to the wider harmonic possibilities of the thirty-two-bar popular song; they created and perfected the new ensemble-style big-band jazz; they kept their groups together for years, working until they achieved a real unity. They showed that jazz could absorb new, foreign elements without loosing its identity, that it was in fact capable of evolution.

Their most characteristic contribution was the development of big-band jazz, a process that began when the first big band was formed by jazzmen in 1922, and was completed by 1931, when the basic musical problems of big-band jazz were solved. The solutions were then accessible for imitation by the mediocre and for development by the creative. The whole swing era relied on the experiments of these years, and that long period of consolidation and exploitation, very like the one we are living through now, was to build on this base the best fruits of big-band jazz.

In 1922 Fletcher Henderson was in New York, working for

Harry Pace's Black Swan Record Company (motto: "The only genuine colored record. Others are only passing for colored."), playing
piano behind blues singers, leading small bands, writing arrangements
—a proto-A&R man, too, like Clarence Williams at Columbia or
Richard M. Jones at Okeh—when he met Don Redman, another
musical handyman, who had come from Pittsburgh with the short-
lived Broadway Syncopators, led by Billy Paige. Together they formed
an eight-piece band—two trumpets, one trombone, three reeds, and
four rhythm—to make some records for Black Swan; several months
later they were hired to play at the Club Alabam, one of the early
Broadway night clubs featuring Negro entertainers, and they added a
tuba and drums to the recording group to form what was to become
the first big jazz band. The next year the band went into Roseland
for a run that lasted, off and on, fifteen years.

The instrumentation of this band added two reeds to that of
Oliver's band, but it should not be considered a bold innovation. It
was a reduced version of the white commercial dance bands of the
1920's. The California Ramblers, then an ordinary jazzy dance band,
had a similar instrumentation at the same time. The saxophone trio
was a commonplace in stock commercial arrangements of the time,
and arrangements made in 1920 were sometimes written for three
trumpets, two trombones, four reeds, four rhythm instruments, and
a violin section—almost the exact instrumentation of Paul Whiteman's band around 1924.

Henderson was playing at Roseland for white dancers, after all.
Probably the instrumentation was not chosen for jazz at all; more
likely for the pieces like "the new arrangement of a medley of beautiful Irish waltzes" that so puzzled Armstrong at his first rehearsal with
the band. Henderson didn't record that kind of music, though he
must have played a great deal at Roseland. But his records before
1925 echo no very daring use of the new resources of instrumentation: on jazz pieces like *Copenhagen,* as well as on popular songs like
When You Walked Out, the band style was a mixture of harmonized
adaptations of New Orleans ensemble and straight homophonic writing, typical of commercial arranging of the period. The famous Henderson trademark, the clarinet trio—sometimes called a Henderson
invention—was one device from stock arrangements; the fuzzy tutti
passages were another.

Two years later, when Armstrong held the third chair, jazz

orchestral style had developed considerably. In *Money Blues,* for example, the introduction and first chorus were scored for saxophone trio with only the slightest brass punctuation; the mobility of the reeds was well exploited and there was remarkably mature rhythmic construction and phrasing. This was a striking innovation: only a few years earlier Thomas Edison had remarked, "Saxophones were never meant to play this jazzy kind of music." The saxophone trio was the spine of the dance-band sound, and if jazz could be scored for a reed section, then a base was laid for a big jazz band.

This development in reed writing should probably be credited to Don Redman, who did most of the arranging in the early Henderson band; when he left to join McKinney's Cotton Pickers in 1927, the Henderson band drifted back to their early polyphonic style until almost 1930. Redman was hired by Jean Goldkette to direct the band he had just installed in his Greystone Ballroom in Detroit, just as he had hired Trumbauer to direct his own band. McKinney had already abandoned musical direction of the band, and Redman, with the help of trumpeter John Nesbitt, took charge. He had brilliant qualifications for such a task, and over the next three years he was to show, more than he had with Henderson, his abilities and intentions.

As a child prodigy, Redman had played every instrument in the band, and his conservatory musicianship was then so rare in the dance-band world that he had to hold classes in elementary musicianship for the members of the band. He had fine orchestral imagination: with Henderson he had taken the first step in adapting dance-band instrumentation to the playing of jazz. He had, besides, a genuine instinct for material—especially popular songs—that was adaptable to jazz playing, and enormous facility in arranging: he could hear a new song at a party and make a new arrangement in time for the band to play it on the job the next night. He had a gift for writing variations, especially riffs and endings, that were related to a theme but had a strong, independent character. A phrase from the coda of *Shim-Me-Sha-Wabble* became the opening of Hodges' *The Jeep Is Jumping* and a riff from *You're Driving Me Crazy* became the principal theme of *Moten Swing.* The Cotton Pickers were his image. They were among the first to record new pop songs, and always with fine, daring arrangements. Redman had consolidated his reed-writing style during the first year with the Cotton Pickers, and many of their 1928 recordings, including *Four or Five Times, Rainbow 'Round My Shoul-*

der, and *Nobody's Sweetheart,* feature fluid reed passages that are completely modern in swing and in voicing.

Redman's arranging was widely imitated by his contemporaries, who copied not only his admirable reed writing, but also the chunky rhythm section and the occasionally ricky-tick brass writing that now betray the Cotton Pickers as a band of the 1920's. Partly through Redman's influence, the remembered remants of brass-band trumpet and trombone parts survived into the 1930's, while the newly created reed styles were hinting at a new ensemble conception.

Redman, in spite of his striking talents, never had the creative genius' need to reconstruct completely all the elements of his art. He never concerned himself with the vital relation between solos and the ensemble; he never concerned himself with the rhythm section, except in its simplest time-keeping role; he never developed more than a limited melodic invention; and worst of all, he preferred polish to all other virtues.

The Cotton Pickers' peers in Detroit were Goldkette and the Orange Blossom Band; but there was no competition except in polish. After three years of polishing, the Cotton Pickers had worn off most of their jazz qualities. When Sidney de Paris joined them for a few records in 1930, he stood out like a wolf in the flock—in fact, like Bix with Goldkette. Records like *If I Could Be with You,* perhaps under pressure from the recording director, were often no more than a smooth first chorus for reeds, a soft superficial vocal, and an ingenious coda.

Fletcher Henderson had never lacked competition in New York. By 1927 he had at least three important rivals: Charlie Johnson's band at Small's Paradise and the Missourians at the Cotton Club, both uptown, and Duke Ellington at the Kentucky Club on Broadway. All three used the instrumentation that Henderson and Redman had pioneered, but they were not much like either Henderson's band or the Cotton Pickers in style. All three were show bands; that is, they worked in large night clubs with elaborate revues, and so played behind singers and specialty dancers, as well as for dancing. Show bands needed dramatic qualities that the dance band could ignore, and to create maximum excitement all these bands concentrated their ensemble sound on brass as the dance bands did around reeds. To satisfy the demand of white customers for "low life," they all adopted the "freak" brass playing of New Orleans musicians like Oliver and Mutt Carey, using a variety of mutes to produce strange tonal and expressive effects, and thereby developing what was called the "jungle style."

The origins of these three bands were diverse. Charlie Johnson was a piano player who had formed his band around a nucleus of musicians associated with Clarence Williams' recording groups; Ellington had come from Washington with the nucleus of a band, but the brass players, who were the key to his style, were added in New York; the Missourians were a co-operative group from St. Louis, but they included DePriest Wheeler, Leroy Maxey, and Lamar Wright from K.C., and Walter Thomas of Muskogee. But the three or four years in New York before their first records had solidified the styles of all three in the same pattern. All tended to use brass for the opening chorus, where Redman would have used reeds; all depended on clarinet trios for changes of color; all used the saxophone trio, though without Redman's fluency, and seldom to carry the exposition.

In contrast to the simple arrangements of the dance bands, their arrangements had frequent changes of color and an intricacy that bordered on clutter. A few vestiges of their origins were still detectable: Johnson's band, with several musicians brought up in the New Orleans traditions, remained closest to the tight ensemble style; the Missourians, like Moten's and other Southwestern bands, played steam-roller jazz in ensemble passages, but more often stitched one solo to another with only short ensemble sections and endings: Ellington's band had grown slowly from a small group, and he retained an ability to think of his band as a collection of sounds, and to break the band down into its components and re-combine them imaginatively.

The show-band style died with the Depression, and except for the after effects on Ellington's mind, had no wide influence, but the style did produce a number of masterpieces: Johnson's *Boy in the Boat,* the Missourians' *Ozark Mountain Blues* (possibly the hottest ever recorded), and three Ellington-Miley mood pieces, *East St. Louis Toodle-Oo, Black and Tan Fantasy,* and *The Mooche.* About the Cotton Pickers one says, "What modern records!" About these, "What wonderful records!"

Even before Redman left Henderson, the instrumentation they had brought into jazz had become standard for Negro bands: King

Oliver had adopted it, and so had Jelly Roll Morton, Dewey Jackson and Bennie Moten. Sam Wooding was leading such a band in Paris, and Teddy Weatherford was soon to lead one in Shanghai. By 1930 there were more than a dozen such bands: Calloway had taken over the Missourians, and there were Luis Russell, Charlie Johnson, Claude Hopkins, Louis Armstrong, Chick Webb, Henderson, Ellington, Cecil Scott, all in New York; Earl Hines and Tiny Parham in Chicago; the Cotton Pickers in Detroit; Bennie Moten, Andy Kirk, the Blue Devils, and Alphonse Trent in the Southwest; Lunceford in Memphis.

The ten pieces of the original big bands were steadily being augmented, especially in the three most secure bands—Henderson at Roseland, Ellington at the Cotton Club, and the Cotton Pickers at the Greystone. Henderson had added Armstrong as the third trumpet in 1924, and a second trombone in 1927. Redman added a fourth reed in 1928, and a second trombone in 1930. Ellington had followed on these additions and added a third trombone in 1931, and when Redman formed his own band in 1931, he also included three trombones. This was to be the typical band of the thirties: three trumpets, three trombones, four reeds and four rhythm instruments.

Henderson, after some floundering and a period of imitating Redman arrangements, had written a series of arrangements based on the contrast of eight-bar sections scored alternately for brass and reeds. As the band grew, the brass became too heavy for such arrangements, and about 1930 he began to adapt the antiphony of the Southern Negro church. The process of breaking up eight bars into a call and a response was not new to instrumental jazz. Ellington had used it to contrast two horns on records like *The Mooche,* and it was the most common technique in instrumental accompaniments to blues singers. Fletcher's small groups behind singers always used it (Fletcher had tentatively used it in a band arrangement of *Off to Buffalo* in 1927). About 1931, with records like *Strangers* and *Sugar Foot Stomp,* he began to develop it; instead of contrasting eight-bar sections he would arrange eight bars so that a reed-section phrase covered the first six, and then fill out the remaining two with brass accents. By 1933–34, in arrangements like *Hotter Than 'Ell* and *Down South Camp Meeting,* the style was fully developed.

It was a style of no great expressive range, built out of short staccato phrases that sacrificed melodic interest to swing, but it provided a perfect foil for the many soloists in his band and, in contrast to more melodic clarinet trios, often produced performances of interest. It was a highly accessible style, easy to imitate and hard to spoil, and was soon adopted by bands all over the country.

At the start of this development, the composition of the rhythm section was also beginning to change significantly. In 1928 string basses were beginning to replace tubas and guitars were in for banjos. When the string bass replaced the tuba, the temptation to double the melody in the bass was gone, and the rhythm became both steadier and more fluid. The introduction of the guitar similarly encouraged greater flexibility in accenting. Perhaps the earliest band to take advantage of these changes was Luis Russell's, with Pops Foster, bass; Will Johnson, guitar; and Paul Barbarin, drums. As usual, both Henderson and Ellington were among the first to adopt the improvement.

Ellington, meanwhile, had been developing several ideas based on his preoccupations of the late 1920's. His sensitivity to expression, sharpened by years of playing shows, and his ability to regroup the elements of the band had led him to a series of explorations into the expressive possibilities of muted brass and of unusual voicings, which resulted in *Mood Indigo,* the first of a series of studies in the blending of overtones that included *Bundle of Blues, Tough Truckin'* and others. After Miley left the band, he continued the studies in the relation of solo to ensemble with *Clarinet Lament, Echoes of Harlem* and *Trumpet in Spades.* With *Caravan* he began a series of minor key flirtations with latin rhythms that he was to carry into the 1940's. With *Rockin' in Rhythm* he began an exploration into extended compositions that continued with *Reminiscing in Tempo* and *Diminuendo* and *Crescendo in Blue.*

During the middle of the Depression, Ellington's seemed to be the only band that did not feel the pinch. Henderson had trouble keeping his band busy through 1932–33; Redman, with a less established band, must have had even greater difficulties. Ellington and Redman both escaped briefly to Europe when the work was shortest, but many less fortunate bands collapsed, including Charlie Johnson's, the Cotton Pickers, Cecil Scott's, the Blue Devils, and even Henderson's.

Yet new bands were still starting despite the Depression. Benny Carter, a talented arranger and a brilliant soloist, started one in 1932, but could not get enough work to keep it together. Like Hawkins, he

Billie Holiday

COLUMBIA RECORDS

Troy Floyd Orchestra, Plaza Hotel, San Antonio, Texas (1928)
LEFT TO RIGHT: Willie Long, John Henry Braggs, Scott "Funny" Bagby,
Kellough Jefferson, Allen Van, John Humphries, Troy Floyd, Benny Long,
Don Albert, Si Ki Collins, Charlie Dixon.   COURTESY DON ALBERT

Jap Allen's Cotton Club Orchestra, Kansas City (1930)
LEFT TO RIGHT: Joe Keys, Booker Pittman, Clyde Hart, Ben Webster, Alton
"Slim" Moore, O. C. Wynn, Jap Allen, Alfred Denny, James "Jim Daddy"
Walker, Raymond Howell, Dee "Prince" Stewart, Eddie "Orange" White.
                                                  COURTESY SLIM MOORE

Alphonso Trent's Orchestra, Memphis (1932)
LEFT TO RIGHT: Chester Clark, Hayes Pillars, John Fielding, A. G. Godley, George Hudson, Dan Minor, Anderson Lacy, Herbert "Peanuts" Holland, Gene Crook, Alphonso Trent, James Jeter, Leo "Snub" Mosely, "Nu Nu" (Louis Pitt??), Brent Sparks, Robert "Eppi" Jackson. COURTESY ALPHONSO TRENT

Bennie Moten Kansas City Orchestra, Pearl Theatre, Philadelphia (1931)
LEFT TO RIGHT: Count Basie, Jimmie Rushing, Hot Lips Page, Willie Mack Washington, Booker Washington, Ed Lewis, LeRoy "Buster" Berry, Thamon Hayes, Harlan Leonard, Eddie Durham, Jack Washington, Vernon Page, Woodie Walder, Bennie Moten, Ira "Bus" Moten. COURTESY ED LEWIS

13 Original Blue Devils, Kansas City (1931)

LEFT TO RIGHT: LeRoy "Snake" White, Jap Jones, Theodore "Doc" Ross, Leonard Chadwick, Lester Young, George Hudson, Ernest Williams, Buster Smith, Charlie Washington, Reuben Lynch, Druie Bess, Abe Bolar, Raymond Howell.

COURTESY LOCAL 627 AFM

Jay McShann Orchestra, Savoy Ballroom, New York (1942)

LEFT TO RIGHT: Jay McShann, Leonard "Lucky" Enois, Gene Ramey, Walter Brown, Bob Mabane, Gus Johnson, Charlie "Bird" Parker, Buddy Anderson, John Jackson, Bob Merrill, Freddie Culliver, Orville "Piggie" Minor, Lawrence "Frog" Anderson, Little Joe Taswell.

COURTESY GENE RAMEY

Count Basie Orchestra, Paramount Theatre, New York (1938)
LEFT TO RIGHT: Buck Clayton, Herschel Evans, Ed Lewis, Earl Warren, Harry
Edison, Benny Morton, Jack Washington, Dickie Wells, Lester Young, Dan
Minor.   COURTESY ED LEWIS

Coleman Hawkins, Lester Young, Ben Webster.   COLUMBIA RECORDS

Duke Ellington   COLUMBIA RECORDS

Lester Young
COLUMBIA RECORDS

Birdland, Ravi Shankar,
ne of India's leading classical
usicians, demonstrates technique
Dizzy Gillespie.

Jimmy Rushing
COLUMBIA RECORDS

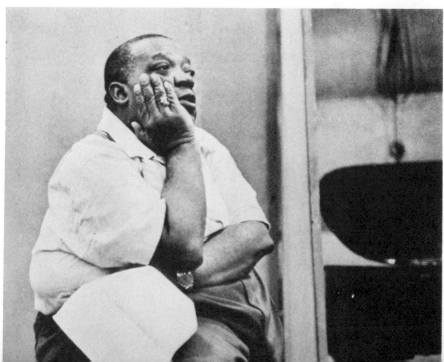

Erroll Garner
COLUMBIA RECORDS

Miles Davis, with Red Garland (piano), Paul Chambers (bass), Julian "Cannonball" Adderley (alto saxophone).   COLUMBIA RECORDS

left for Europe to weather the Depression. Two new bands did manage to thrive despite the Depression: Jimmie Lunceford's and Count Basie's.

Lunceford had formed his band before 1930, from members of a high-school band he had coached, and kept them together through their college years. They came North in the early 1930's, and in 1934 followed Calloway's band into the Cotton Club. The Southwestern origins of his band sound are traced by Frank Driggs elsewhere in this volume, but the band's musical interest depended on its young trumpeter and arranger, Sy Oliver. The band lacked the great soloists of Ellington's or Henderson's, and had to depend more on intricacies of ensemble work. To their light, two-beat swing and precision section work, Oliver brought considerable harmonic daring and a feeling for voicing exceeded only by Ellington's. He was a virtuoso at selecting unusual tempos that often revealed new aspects of well-known songs: the band played *Annie Laurie* at middle tempo and *Organ Grinder Swing* at almost ballad tempo. His eclecticism could include a Dixie opening to *Baby Won't You Please Come Home,* Redmanesque vocals and Hendersonesque flag-wavers, but he could write such original things as the brilliant accompaniment to the vocal of *Lonesome Road.*

Basie's contributions were not in scoring. He was to demonstrate the importance of relaxation in ensemble playing and the importance of the blues. The nucleus of the Basie band had played together since 1928, first in the Blue Devils and later in Moten's band, and they continued to work together in small groups after Moten's death. They had all grown up in big bands, and they were all dedicated after-hours jammers. In these small groups they adapted many of the features of both big bands and jam sessions. Their earliest records, the Smith-Jones quintet sides, are not strings of solos with a polyphonic ending, like Eastern records of the time; the ensemble passages are played as exact imitations of big-band section work, as on *Boogie Woogie,* and solos are backed with riffs, as in a Kansas City jam session.

As the big-band techniques showed in these small-group records, so the techniques, and the relaxation, of the jam session remained when the band expanded. In fact the arrangements that were not adapted from Henderson's arranging style by Eddie Durham were often merely expansions of their own small-band routines. The 1937 *Roseland Shuffle,* for example, is an expansion of the Smith-Jones,

Inc., *Shoe Shine Boy,* and has much of the same relaxed small-group feeling.

As for the revival of interest in the blues, it had never really died out, but the most creative musicians of the previous decade had not concentrated on playing blues. Redman preferred material in the thirty-two-bar popular-song pattern. Ellington and Carter had both used blues extensively, but usually transformed, like *Waltzing the Blues, Blues in My Heart,* or *Diminuendo and Crescendo.* Even the two most creative soloists, Armstrong and Hawkins, had recorded few blues in the 1930's. Basie not only played blues in their simplest form, but even played popular songs as blues—as in the arrangement he made of *I May Be Wrong* called *Boogie Woogie.*

Basie and the blues-rich Southwestern musicians who followed him to New York revitalized big-band jazz. Their influence extended even to Ellington. *Across the Track Blues* was the most direct blues Duke had recorded in a decade, and *Cottontail* was so saturated with blues that it has been mistaken for one. Lunceford's *Uptown Blues* is another example of Southwestern influence.

This cross-fertilization from the Southwest must have revitalized Ellington, especially after Blanton and Webster joined the band. The two years, 1940 and 1941, were a period when the band became looser in performance, and the time when Ellington summed up all his experiments. He produced a series of brilliant climactic works: the rich voicings produced *Chelsea Bridge;* the concerti included *Concerto for Cootie;* among the portraits and sketches were *Bojangles* and *Harlem Airshaft;* and there were Latin experiments like *Flaming Sword* and *Ko-Ko.*

Ellington and Basie, however, were not the dominant figures of the late 1930's; Henderson, as arranger for the enormously popular Benny Goodman band, was becoming the most influential musician of all. Goodman played his arrangements; Shaw competed with similar ones; Edgar Sampson wrote them for Webb; Gifford wrote them for the Casa Loma; Oliver for Lunceford and, later, Dorsey; Durham for Basie and, later, Lunceford. The increasing popularity of swing arrangements on the Henderson model led to a general similarity of style in all the big bands, Negro and white. Goodman, Shaw, the Dorseys, Barnet, Hines, Calloway, Teddy Hill, Webb were all approaching the same standards of proficiency. There is a terrifying record, an anthology called *The Great Swing Bands,* on which most of these bands are represented. If they are played without consulting notes or label, it is impossible to distinguish one from another.

It is customary to date the decline of the "band business" after the end of World War II, but, artistically, swing had died earlier. By the early 1940's the gradual elimination of stylistic variations had killed big-band jazz. It was a death by entropy.

KANSAS CITY
AND THE
SOUTHWEST

Franklin S. Driggs

Franklin S. Driggs has been an invaluable chronicler of the story of jazz in Kansas City and the Southwest. Through him, many musicians who contributed to that tradition have told their histories in English and American magazines, among them *The Jazz Review, Jazz Monthly, Jazz Journal,* etc. Driggs has spent time in Kansas City, but not nearly enough, he feels, to begin to do the research necessary to further fill out this part of jazz history. Driggs is an excellent example of the jazz scholar who needs research grants. It is astonishing that he has been able to collect so much information with such limited facilities. This chapter is an introduction to his speciality, and it may surprise a number of readers to find many names here who have never before been included in a jazz book.

The following story of Kansas City and the Southwest introduces a major source of jazz history and development that has been largely ignored. At this writing, research is still in the exploratory stage. Southwestern musicians traveled continuously throughout many thousands of square miles over a twenty-year period, touching a dozen states and many more large and small cities. This presents a huge task to the researcher in correlating their movement into a meaningful story.

Jazz began to take root throughout the Southwest just about the same time it took root in New Orleans and other parts of the country, although individual soloists and bands apparently did not develop until New Orleans had begun to shut down, after Storyville's closing in 1917. Hundreds of musicians were thrown out of work by that edict. Farther north, in Kansas City, the most popular groups were the three- and four-piece bands led by Bennie Moten and George E. Lee. At that time there was neither a great demand for nor much knowledge of jazz in Kansas City.

Ragtime pianists and brass bands were still active in the 1920's, and one of the greatest of all pianists was James Scott, who made Kansas City his home in 1914. In ragtime the riff was born, and the repeated musical phrase became the foundation for many of the most famous Kansas City and Southwestern compositions, and ultimately the heart of all the big-band music of the swing era.

The early Southwestern bands used 2/4 rhythm, which was standard in New Orleans, and they tended to play in the polyphonic ensemble style also associated with New Orleans. The bands increased in size throughout the 1920's; they had nine and ten pieces by 1927, including brass and reed sections which played harmonized solo lines, while occasionally allowing an individual soloist four to eight bars on his own. Similar developments were taking place in New Orleans and Chicago, as the strength of the New Orleans style waned.

Written arrangements came in around 1926 and 1927, initiated by advanced musicians like pianist Jesse Stone and saxophonist Ben Smith, each of whom led successful bands for several years all over the Southwest. Other bands, led by bassist Walter Page and pianist Alphonso Trent, were experimenting with string bass and using the more flowing 4/4 rhythm. Orchestral devices such as the "chase chorus," which occurred whenever two reedman, or a reed and a brassman, would solo alternately for four bars; reed harmonizing behind a tinkly piano chorus; and riffing behind a soloist were devices used with great frequency during the late 1920's. The rhythm sections blended so well that they seemed to speak as one unified voice.

The Southwestern musician tended to be well educated musically, which enabled him to meet the challenge of constantly developing styles. The solo line played by the New Orleans musician was, as a result of his polyphonic ensemble work, fairly simple and stayed close to the melody of whatever tune was being played. The solo line of the Southwestern musician tended to be more complicated, and by the end of the 1920's, more flowing; in some advanced cases, he employed chord sequences rather than melody as the basis of his solo. Saxophonists Lester Young and Buster Smith are two choice examples of musicians with flowing solo lines, who often looked towards chord patterns as well as melody. Smith can be heard on an extremely rare 1929 recording made by Walter Page's Blue Devils, playing both alto and clarinet in a flowing style that was to be disseminated all over the world more than a decade later by his chief disciple, Charlie Parker.

The essence of the mature Southwestern style was its relaxation. Instead of a note being hit directly on the beat, it might be played either just before or just after, or in a variety of combinations, while the rhythm would flow evenly in and around the beat, four beats to the bar. The music had intense drive and yet it was relaxed.

But before Southwestern musicians evolved their driving yet relaxed rhythmic and solo impetus, they had blown harder and higher than musicians from other parts of the country. They had heard Paul Whiteman and Fletcher Henderson very early; they had been impressed by their musicianship, precision and sophistication, if not by their jazz; and they endeavored to play something equally professional, or perhaps blow the other back to New York by sheer power alone.

The blues had more meaning for musicians and public alike in the Southwest than anywhere else, except the states of Mississippi, Georgia and Alabama. Many of the greatest blues singers, both urban and rural, were born and raised in Oklahoma, Texas and Arkansas, and grew to maturity before leaving for other parts of the country. Singers like Texas Alexander, Big Bill Broonzy, Jimmy Rushing and Blind Lemon Jefferson gave rise to T-Bone Walker, Memphis Slim, Al Hibbler, Joe Turner and Walter Brown, and their tradition continues today with singers like Lightning Hopkins and B. B. King. Con-

stant use of blues materials in the band library helped the Southwestern musician retain his traditions while allowing him to seek
further musical progress through harmonic and rhythmic evolution
and greater instrumental technique.

Dancing audiences throughout the Southwest insisted on a large
diet of blues in every band's repertoire, and for many years the finest
musical organizations in the country, Fletcher Henderson's and Duke
Ellington's, could not make any impression at all in the area. Both
bands played there from the early 1920's through the middle and later
1930's, but not until local units adopted Eastern rhythmic concepts
could Eastern bands make any headway in the Southwest. McKinney's
Cotton Pickers and Cab Calloway were among the few bands to im-
press Southwesterners. In Cab's case, this success was due both to his
showmanship and to the fact that his band was then (1930–31)
largely composed of musicians from Kansas City or St. Louis. None
of the Eastern bands or, for that matter, bands from any other part
of the country, played the blues with the feeling and depth of Bennie
Moten in Kansas City, Walter Page in Oklahoma City, Troy Floyd
in San Antonio or Charlie Creath in St. Louis. Although the musicians
from the Southwest for the most part realized that their Eastern counterparts were in general musically superior, and ended up by emulating
them and swinging even more, they had to comply with their audiences' demands for the blues, and for novelties and showmanship, before they could arrive at the level of progress they felt was necessary
in order to compete on an equal footing.

The Southwest includes the states of Texas, Colorado, Arkansas,
Kansas, New Mexico and Oklahoma, and for the purposes of this
chapter overlaps into Nebraska, Missouri and Iowa, states not geo-
graphically considered in this area. Each city in these states that had
ballrooms, hotels, night clubs, outdoor amusement parks and a Negro
population large enough to keep one or more big bands and other
smaller combos working, was said to headquarter a "territory" band.
That is, each band had its own territory to play in, which often lapped
over into many neighboring towns and cities whose population could
not support a band with any degree of consistency. Each territory
supported its own band, however, until population increase—which
was often coupled with industrial boom—accelerated the growth of
local amusement enterprises such as those listed above. Then the
demand for the bands grew until the local outfit could no longer

handle all the work, and a call was sent out for other bands from other territories to come in and fill the engagements.

From the middle 1920's until the Second World War, industrial developments throughout the Southwest, coupled with population shifts and increases, created a very heavy demand for dance work that led to the organization of band after band, until well over one hundred were operating with regularity in that part of the country. Bands from Florida, Georgia, Illinois, Indiana and the Carolinas also found a lot of good work in the Southwest, and many of the territory bands in the Southwest—which had, in the 1920's, generally limited their working area to a circumscribed radius close to their home city —started answering the call for work in other areas and began traveling regularly from the late 1920's all through the 1930's, creating the "traveling" or "road" band. In general only those bands musically above average did any amount of road work, the others working only in their own territory. As the 1930's wore on, even the territory outfits gave way to better bands from other areas, which then set themselves up in cities other than the ones in which they had originally been based. The term "one-night stand" arose from traveling bands' practice of working one night in each city, often going all across the country. At best the traveling band would work possibly two nights in one city, then travel by bus or car, often several hundred miles, to their next job. They would leave at two or three in the morning and travel well into the next day, sometimes barely arriving in time to shave and clean up before going on the bandstand. The veteran tenorman and arranger, Budd Johnson, recalled jumping from New Orleans to Omaha in the early 1930's with George E. Lee's band, a trip of a thousand miles, with only one or two stops in between.

Competition was very keen then, particularly in the ballroom circuit. There were several individual operators who owned a chain of ballrooms all over the Midwest and Southwest, and any band they favored worked regularly, on rotation, at each ballroom in the chain. The local territory bands were eventually reduced to working social and private dances if they could not meet the musical challenge presented by the better-established bands. One particular challenge during the mid-1920's, and a practice which held forth right into the early 1940's, was the "battle of the bands."

Each local band played opposite each visiting band at the town's local ballroom. This constituted a battle of music, not often publicized as such until later on in the 1920's, but nevertheless regarded by the musicians as such. The bandleaders in those days quite often did their own promoting. The visitors arrived in town a few hours ahead of the dance and putting up handbills advertising the dance all over town. They began taking newspaper space, which assumed the gigantic proportions of full-page ads as public interest picked up. Each leader would proclaim his band as the finest in his part of the country, and the local leader claimed that he would blow the visiting band right back to its home location without any difficulty at all. Several thousand people would be witness to many of these affairs; often there would be more than two bands, and they would play well into the morning. The spirit of the after-hours jam session grew during the same period, and carried over into smaller clubs, where only the top soloists would come to blow after their regular commercial big-band jobs. The battles of music became commercially profitable during the late 1930's, and the musicians then tended to regard them as such, but during the 1920's the musicians were after each other's musical reputations.

To musicians throughout the Midwest and Southwest, Kansas City became the center of music, for although they wanted to make the big time in Chicago and New York, more often than not it was individual musicians plucked out of road and territory bands who were brought to New York by previously established leaders, and not an entire band. Kansas City, during the later 1920's and through most of the 1930's, was controlled by one of the most powerful political machines in the history of the United States. Tom Pendergast was boss of the Democratic party in Kansas City from 1927 to 1938, and the men he chose for office held all the key positions of power in Kansas City during those years. Pendergast himself held political office as early as 1902, and ran a wide-open hotel, the Jefferson, from 1907 until 1920, with police protection. He encouraged gambling and night life; clubs as such appeared during his years of power in vast proliferation, and all had music of one sort or another. Many could house full bands, and many of the owners had political connections. It is significant that nearly all the developments in Kansas City's music took place during Pendergast's reign. Since his conviction in 1938 for income-tax evasion, relatively little of importance has occurred, and only the 1942 Jay McShann band, with Charlie Parker and Walter Brown, has made any further impact on the jazz world at large.

Little is known of the actual beginnings of jazz in the major cities of the Southwest, other than some new data discovered on a trip to Kansas City made in the fall of 1957 and partially financed by the Institute of Jazz Studies, through Marshall Stearns. Felix Payne, the former owner of the Subway and Sunset Clubs, famed all during the 1930's, began his career as a night-club owner in a back room near the river bottoms at the turn of the century. He recalled that his small operation was then no competition for Dick Stone's club on Grand Avenue, a combination dance hall and barroom which featured a wonderful pianist in Lester Brown. The other big club in those years was the Ozarks, at Seventh and Wall, which was operated by Bill Blunt and Sam Jones. At the latter, Payne heard Willie Young, a pianist and entertainer he considered the finest musician he had come in contact with in more than forty years. When Payne's own ventures began paying off, he opened the Twin-Cities Club, so named because it was on the border between Kansas City, Kansas, and Kansas City, Missouri. He was able to hire Willie Young then, and Young appeared at Payne's club regularly for several years. Young's services were much in demand for touring vaudeville circuits, but he turned all offers down, eventually leaving Kansas City and drifting westward to perish in one of California's earthquakes.

Major N. Clark Smith, a professional music teacher in the Kansas City school system for many years, is said to have been the musical father of many a jazzman who passed under his sharp scrutiny as bandmaster at Lincoln High School. Smith had come out of the Spanish-American War and had toured to Australia with a "Pick-a-Ninny Band" of youngsters in 1903 before returning to Kansas City and Lincoln High. Walter Page, Jimmy Smith, Eli Logan, Lamar Wright and many other Kansas City musicians who became integral members of famous bands during the 1920's and 1930's went through the major's music courses and received a solid foundation. Smith had a well-regarded brass band that performed for parades and the like, as did trumpeter Shelly Bradford, another early jazzman who kept active into the 1920's. They often battled a touring brass band from New Orleans, directed by Clarence Desdume, who worked all over the Southwest for more than twenty years. The brass bands did not assume the importance in the Southwest that they did in New Orleans. It was the legitimate dance band, and later orchestra, which came to be the focal point of music throughout the Southwest.

One of the first jazzman to play for dancing was violinist George Morrison. Born in Fayette, Missouri, in 1892, he moved with his family to Denver in 1900. After he graduated from Colorado University, he organized a string trio to play the Albany Hotel in Denver. Soon after that his reputation on violin took him and his band to Europe, where he played command performances before royalty. His orchestra recorded for Columbia in 1920, although it's uncertain whether the records were released. During the early 1920's Andy Kirk, tuba; Jimmie Lunceford, alto sax; and Hattie McDaniel, vocalist, all got their start with Morrison. His popularity extended to Utah, and was so great in Denver that he often had to send out a second band under his name, with Leo Davis conducting, to fill his many engagements. Andy Kirk recalled Morrison's music as being "a little stiff," but then, neither he nor Morrison had had much idea of jazz until Gene Coy's Happy Black Aces burst into Denver from Amarillo, Texas, in 1925 and "upset the town." Jelly Roll Morton came through somewhat earlier and influenced Andy's musical thinking. Andy left Morrison in 1925 to join trumpeter Terrence "T" Holder in Dallas, Texas. Morrison's activities went into the 1940's, although his orchestra did not compete against other road bands after 1930.

One of the first bandleaders in Kansas City was pianist Paul Banks, whose career began as a drummer. He directed bands until the Second World War. As a drummer he had accompanied a fine early pianist, Andy Miller. They worked the old Emanon Hall at Eighth and Washington. Banks recalled, "Those were the days when just two people could draw a crowd." Banks gave his drums to one of his brothers and started in on piano, taking lessons from Clyde Glass and Charlie Watts, among others. The last named was a student of Scott Joplin's and was considered, with Scrap Harris, the best local pianist during the ragtime era.

One of ragtime's foremost composers and performers was James Scott, who lived in Kansas City from 1914 until his death in 1938. His career was documented accurately in *They Called It Ragtime* (Blesh-Janis, Knopf, 1951). Scott's music apparently had little effect on Kansas City's musicians after 1920, although he was personally active as house director for the Eblon and Lincoln Theatres all through the 1920's. He also took bands out to fill local social-club dance dates, but never attempted to compete with established leaders like Bennie Moten or George E. Lee. He went into retirement in the 1930's, and his name does not appear on the memorial roster of Local 627, indicating that he may not have belonged to the union.

Kansas City and other cities in the Southwest had their counterparts of the Storyville section in New Orleans. Kansas City's "buffet flats"—private homes running from Truman Road to Independence Avenue—were bases for after-hours frivolity. Sporting gentlemen and some musicians recall Mother McLain's and Vinie North's as being the most popular "flats," and two itinerant pianists known only as "Tex" and "Black Satin" worked them regularly. Civic efforts closed them down in 1925, before boss rule came in with Pendergast.

Although no one I interviewed would admit it publicly, both whites and Negroes hankered for the return of what Pendergast stood for. Indirectly, of course, Pendergast was the musicians' friend, and in some quarters he is sorely missed. The most important single figure in Kansas City music rose as Pendergast did, and died in an accident a few years before Pendergast went to prison.

Bennie Moten led the biggest and best jazz orchestra in Kansas City from 1926 until 1935, and scores of top musicians went under his baton. He was born in 1894 and started playing baritone horn as a teen-ager in Lacy Blackburn's Brass Band. He stayed with the horn and the band for only a year; ragtime piano artistry appealed to him far more, and he cajoled lessons from his parents, who paid Charles Watts and Scrap Harris, both Joplin alumni, to teach their eager son. By 1918 Bennie was good enough to have his own trio, the B. B. and D. band, which played at the old Panama Cafe. The three initials stood for Bennie, Bailey (Handcock, a singer) and Dude (Langford, a drummer). They were very popular and did good business at the Panama, and, later, with a quintet at Street's Hotel.

An Okeh Records talent scout, Ralph Peer, heard Moten's combo and took them to St. Louis to record in the fall of 1923. The first titles were *Elephant Wobble* and *Crawdad Blues*. From then until 1925 they recorded a dozen more tunes, all original compositions, including trombonist Thamon Hayes' famous *South,* in later years one of the best sellers Victor ever had. On the strength of their early successes, Moten and Hayes formed a music partnership, resulting in a music store which they operated together for many years. When Peer went over to Victor in 1926, he took Moten's contract with him, and Moten's band increased in size, popularity and prosperity until the early 1930's.

During the same period another well-trained composer and pianist, Jesse Stone, had organized a band which barnstormed through Kansas and Missouri, outside of Kansas City. Stone was born in Atchison, Kansas, in 1901, and raised in Kansas City. He became a proficent musician quite early, and started working with local combos. By 1920 he was ready to go out on his own. He organized a band which he called the Blues Serenaders, and by the mid-1920's, he was established as the number one band operating in Missouri and Kansas, with the exception of Kansas City.

Stone and Alphonso Trent, first in Little Rock and then in Dallas, had the first bands in the Southwest to feature arrangements, and Stone worked through a ballroom-chain operator named Frank Rock to get the choice bookings in those states until 1928. Alto saxophonist Jack Washington (later with Moten and Basie) started with Stone, and trumpeter Eddie Tompkins also worked with him. Two of Stone's musicians were then considered outstanding. Trumpeter Albert Hinton had an unheard-of range, surpassing Louis Armstrong's, and greatly influenced young Paul Webster and Eddie Tompkins, who in turn showed the world their influence with Jimmie Lunceford after 1935. Trombonist Druie Bess had tremendous drive and power, and later worked with the Blue Devils and Fate Marable. Hinton went into decline as a result of personality defects which kept him from working regularly.

The Blues Serenaders recorded four titles for Okeh in 1927, which, with the exception of King Oliver's classic Gennett band sides, were the hottest things in jazz up to that point. *Boot to Boot* is Stone's interpolation on *Tiger Rag,* while *Starvation Blues* is a slow dirge. Stone wrote both compositions, and had written arrangements for the band to play, including written-out solo parts! Anyone who has heard the titles listed above would find this incredible, after feeling the terrific drive of *Boot to Boot.*

Stone had to disband in 1928, after his band had lost a disastrous battle of music to bassist Walter Page's Blue Devils from Oklahoma City. Stone had broken with Frank Rock earlier; he was booking the band himself and handling all the business affairs, meanwhile neglecting the music. Page, a triple threat on tuba, string bass and baritone sax, took over Stone's territory for the next three years, while Stone detoured to Texas, to assist T. Holder in the reorganization of his band.

Holder's reputation as a soloist and lead trumpeter was assured through his work with Alphonso Trent from 1922 until 1925, when he left to organize his own band. He worked out of Dallas from 1925 to 1928 and, after Trent, was considered the best leader in Texas. He lost his own band in 1928, when he was accused of mishandling its funds. His band was eventually turned over to Andy Kirk, to form the nucleus of the first Clouds of Joy, which Kirk took to national fame several years later.

Holder, with Jesse Stone's help, formed another band, and after several personnel changes it became the top band in Texas from 1930 through 1932, when he disbanded for good. He was able to organize a band of raw musicians and drill them into shape within a remarkably short period of time, a feat which other leaders often took months and sometimes years to achieve. Some of the Southwest's top younger musicians, such as altoist Earl Bostic, tenorman Buddy Tate, pianist-arranger Lloyd Glenn and trumpeter Carl "Tatti" Smith, were in this band. Holder went into obscurity in the late 1930's.

Of all the orchestras to come out of the Southwest, the most influential and the finest in over-all musicianship was Alphonso Trent's. Trent, a pianist, was born in Fort Smith, Arkansas, in 1905; he had studied music formally and graduated from college. After working resort jobs in Muskogee, Oklahoma, he absorbed the nucleus of banjoist Gene Crooke's Synco Six (including trumpeter Edwin Swazye) in Helena, Arkansas, and built a fine reputation playing in Little Rock. Afterwards he accepted a job in Dallas, which didn't pan out, and was about to return to Little Rock when a group of local businessmen offered the band a job in suburban Oakcliff. Trent's reputation on that job reached the management of the famed Adolphus Hotel, who were then looking fo a new band for their second ballroom. They decided to give Trent a two-week trial, and the job lasted better than a year and a half, breaking all previous records for both white and Negro orchestras. They went on the job with eight pieces and expanded to ten by 1926, broadcasting regularly over WFAA in Dallas.

Lionized by musicians and public alike, they were an impressive sight to see, with several changes of immaculate uniforms and an entourage of long touring cars, in which they traveled to work. The brilliance of their over-all performance as a unit tended to cast a slight shadow on the solo efforts of men like trombonist Leo "Snub"

Mosely, who had developed a fluent, lightning-fast trombone style years ahead of its time, which accurately forecast the rise of J. J. Johnson, Kai Winding and other present-day stars. Trent's entire brass section and rhythm team, the first to perform as a really single voice, were felt to be the best in the country then, and their precision section work was praised by everyone from Paul Whiteman to Fletcher Henderson.

Many lucrative offers began to pour in, and late in 1926 they left the Adolphus to tour Texas, playing many other top white hotels, the Governor's Inaugural Ball, and countless college proms. They went on the road to the Midwest in 1927.

In Lexington, Kentucky, Stuff Smith was added as vocalist and front man, and also soloed on violin on their first recordings, made for Gennett later that year. Stuff completed a vocal trio with Snub Mosely and John Fielding, the band's regular singer and road manager. Theirs may have been the first use of vocal trios in jazz; at any rate that, among other things, vividly impressed Jimmie Lunceford, who was just getting his band organized in Memphis.

Trent's band drew five thousand people to the steamer *St. Paul* in St. Louis in 1928, where they played against Louis Armstrong, who fronted drummer Floyd Campbell's band for the occasion. The boat shook so much from the people on board that it had to return early to avoid capsizing. Trent's music also made a vivid impression on Fate Marable, dean of riverboat jazz in St. Louis.

Three top soloists joined in 1928. Tenorman Hayes Pillars from Arkansas, trumpeter Peanuts Holland from Buffalo and altoman and trumpeter Lee Hilliard, who doubled into either section, all added tremendously to Trent's potential. It must be pointed out that Hayes Pillars' tenor solos were the ideal of the younger Herschel Evans, then featured with Troy Floyd's band in San Antonio. Buddy Tate, also with Floyd during the same period, recalled how Herschel would threaten to quit if Floyd wouldn't allow him to leave the stand whenever Trent was in town, so he could go listen to Pillars play.

Trombonist Gus Wilson (Teddy's brother), an advanced arranger, joined Trent in either 1929 or 1930, contributing some remarkable scores, among them *Clementine,* which they recorded. (Sy Oliver also joined the band in 1930, shortly after a fire in Cleveland had destroyed their uniforms and their entire library of arrangements.) Trent's recording of *Clementine* has the unique combination of precision and swing that so affected Jimmie Lunceford, forming the basis of many of the latter's most successful scores later in the 1930's, after Trent's band had broken up for good. Fletcher Henderson had heard them play in Cincinnati before the fire that destroyed their library—and to some extent their morale—and became extremely enthusiastic about their music, urging Trent to play New York if at all possible. Trent did play the Savoy Ballroom for a week, and society bandleader Meyer Davis heard him and offered him a choice job at the Arcadia Ballroom, then rivaling Roseland in importance. Trent turned the offer down, fearing that he would lose his best men to the then-established leaders. Other leaders had tried to woo away Trent's men before, without any real success, and it wasn't until 1932, when the band disintegrated, that they left in larger numbers.

Trent had never been booked by a professional manager, and apparently no one in the band had enough business sense to handle its members properly. Booking agencies like MCA were just getting started then. The band's work began to dwindle as other bands' music constantly improved. In early 1932 Bennie Moten had made offers to Peanuts Holland and trombonist Dan Minor, who had joined a year earlier, and Trent himself quit the band to return to Fort Smith and tend his sick parents. Minor went over to Moten, and Holland formed his own band. Gene Crooke quit in Memphis, his home town, and formed his own group, which later came to New York as Bob Pope's orchestra.

Vocalist Anderson Lacy took charge, and with trumpeter Harry Edison and guitarist Charlie Fuque (later with the Ink Spots) they kept going until the spring of 1933, when they gave up in Massachusetts. Trent returned to music in 1934 and led combos all over the Southwest—one, in 1938, featuring Charlie Christian on guitar and tenorman Henry Bridges (later with Harlan Leonard).

Jimmie Lunceford paid tribute to Trent in the *1947 Esquire Yearbook of Jazz* when he wrote, ". . . Trent's band gave inspiration to more young musicians than any other. They had a unique style and terrific arrangements. . . ." The musicians who heard them in their prime felt them to be every bit the equal of Fletcher Henderson's and Duke Ellington's bands.

When Trent was establishing himself in Texas during the middle 1920's, Bennie Moten's orchestra had already become the number one outfit. In 1925, LaForest Dent joined on banjo, and by the following year he had learned alto sax well enough to fill out the three-man reed section. Trumpeter Ed Lewis, who had begun his career on baritone horn with pianist Jerry Westbrooks, switching as a result of an accident that finished the promising trumpet career of Herman Walder, impressed Bennie at an audition arranged by Lewis' mother, a relative of the Moten family. Lamar Wright, who had been the solo trumpet since 1923, left in 1927 to join a St. Louis band then known as the Missourians. His place was taken by Paul Webster, who stayed through 1928, when the band made its first trip East, to Buffalo's Paradise Ballroom. Tiny Taylor was vocalist and director until 1929, when Bennie's nephew, Ira "Buster" Moten, and vocalist Jimmy Rushing were brought in. Bennie's tour in Buffalo lasted six months and established him in upstate New York, and his Victor recordings were number one best sellers among jazz artists. Jack Washington had also joined, coming over from Jesse Stone's band.

Moten's absence caused a mad scramble in Kansas City for the top jobs he had vacated. George E. Lee, Paul Banks, violinist Chauncey Downs and saxophonist Clarence Love all found better work then. Lee had an eight-piece band with his sister, Julia, on piano and vocals. Lee was a powerful singer himself, and was later referred to as the "Cab Calloway of the Middle West," just as Bennie Moten was referred to as the "Duke Ellington of the Middle West." Neither description was quite accurate, for Lee stressed "novelty syncopation and singing" with a lightly bouncing two-four rhythm. Trombonist Thurston "Sox" Maupins was considered by Kansas City musicians to be the equal of Fletcher Henderson's Jimmy Harrison. Maupins has a short solo spot on Lee's first and rarest recording of *Merritt Stomp,* made in 1927 for a local Negro firm run by politician and clarinetist Winston Holmes. The recording does not indicate any outstanding ability, but the solo is too short to decide one way or another. He died in 1928, while Lee went on to record again in 1929 for Brunswick, Jimmy Jones on trombone, Budd Johnson on tenor sax and Jesse Stone's arrangements.

Paul Banks and Chauncey Downs became prominent locally by 1927, and held on to their positions after Moten returned. Ed Lewis played trumpet with Banks in 1925 and Jap Allen was on tuba through 1928, when his brother Clifton's alto and clarinet were also featured. Baby Lovett was on drums and Paul Webster on trumpet in 1930.

Chauncey Downs' band had the Ashby brothers on trumpet and

sax and the vocals of Iola Burton. Neither group recorded as such, although Banks and a trio accompanied the Kimbrough sisters, Lottie and Lena, on recordings for Merritt and Brunswick. Downs migrated to Michigan and Minnesota after 1930, leading various bands there and not returning to Kansas City until late in the decade.

Bennie Moten's return was triumphal; he lost none of his earlier popularity. The other bands held their jobs, but Moten once again took the top spots like the El Torreon Ballroom and Fairyland Park. With the exception of George Lee, the other leaders did not compete with Moten, depending on novelty or ballad specialties to get by— or, in Clarence Love's case, a more sophisticated appeal.

The summer of 1929 Moten accepted an offer to play Celeron Park in Jamestown, New York, near Lake Chatauqua. They did such terrific business they were kept on the job for nine months. By that time pianist Bill "Count" Basie and trombonist-guitarist-arranger Eddie Durham had come over from Walter Page's Blue Devils.

Before going down to Camden to record for Victor, Bennie decided to take the band to New York for a holiday. The sight that hit them hardest upon arriving was their name on the marquee of the famed Lafayette Theatre in Harlem. Since they hadn't any bookings in New York, a quick investigation turned out a bogus band on stage, playing carbon copies of Moten's recorded hits. Bennie stormed into the manager's office and threatened suit, but to no avail, since the manager had gangster backing. Nevertheless Bennie was allowed a certain satisfaction when the manager told him the crooked agent who had sold the band as Bennie Moten's Kansas City Orchestra "would get what was coming to him." Moten accepted the manager's offer of the first decent available bookings and then went on to Camden to record. His band was strengthened immeasurably by the addition of Basie and Durham, each of whom had brought valuable experience and training from his stay in Walter Page's Blue Devils.

Walter Page was born and raised in Missouri and was taught the fundamentals of tuba and string bass by Major N. Clark Smith at Lincoln High. He was graduated in 1917 and in the same year heard New Orleans bassist Wellman Braud, then playing with John Wycliffe's band from Chicago. "Big 'Un," as Page was called because of his imposing size and strength, was impressed by Braud's tone and power, and decided to make music his career. He worked locally with saxophonist Dave Lewis and Bennie Moten before going on to Kansas University at Lawrence, where he completed three years of full music studies, and then went on the road with Billy King's show. He traveled all over the Southwest with King for the next three years, and was asked to take over the band when leader Ermir Coleman left to enter politics. They were stranded in 1925, and Page took the musicians to Oklahoma City, where they reorganized with the help of local businessmen and set up headquarters.

After working throughout Oklahoma, building his repertoire and reputation, Page went through Texas and added three more musicians to the band who were to be of prime importance to him—as well as to jazz, in the course of time.

Altoist Buster Smith was playing with Carl Murphy's Satisfied Five in Waco, and couldn't read; trombonist and arranger Eddie Durham had been with Gene Coy in Enid, Oklahoma; and trumpeter Oran "Hot Lips" Page had been with Eddie and Sugar Lou's popular combo in Tyler, Texas. Page also got another man, pianist Bill Basie, who had originally come from New York with the Gonzell White show, became stranded in Kansas City, and apparently worked his way down to Dallas, where he was doing a single. With these men, plus vocalist Jimmy Rushing—who was discovered singing locally in Oklahoma City while working in his father's hamburger stand—Page's Blue Devils, as he named them, were a formidable band.

The Blue Devils promptly "cut out" both Jesse Stone and George Lee from their territories in Kansas and Missouri, and were the top band there and around Oklahoma all during 1928. Page was a real battler and wanted to battle Bennie Moten and Alphonso Trent in the worst way. Moten always ducked him, and Trent had gone East by this time, but Kansas City newspapers of the time indicate that Moten did battle Page in 1928 at the Paseo Hall, and Page is said to have blown Moten out.

Moten's eyes were opened by this defeat, and he is reported to have made an offer to take over the Blue Devils intact, retaining Page as the leader but using his own name. Page refused, but apparently ran into some bad bookings, and was raided by Moten, who took Basie and Durham early in 1929. Towards the end of that year Jimmy Rushing and Lips Page left also, and although Page obtained exceptional replacements for them, he was to have tough luck from that time until he finally gave up the band in late 1931 and joined Moten himself, turning his own band over to vocalist Ernest Williams and trumpeter Snake White.

After Trent's, Page's band was considered the finest jazz orchestra playing in the Southwest. He had taken musicians who couldn't read, taught them how and cued them in with a whistle on the stand until they knew when to play without being told. Page often battled the bands of Vincent Lopez and Lawrence Welk, then struggling for a place themselves. They were not jazz outfits, and stressed novelties—and, in Welk's case, polkas. Welk had a feature on *Tiger Rag* in which the trumpeter played his solo on two instruments simultaneously. This sort of novelty stunt enabled many a lesser band to stay in business and to ward off their musical superiors.

The Blue Devils made one rare recording, which was released on Vocalion. The books list the date as the fall of 1929, although Jimmy Rushing insists it was made in 1928. The titles were *Blue Devil Blues,* sung by Rushing, with a trumpet solo by Lips Page and a clarinet chorus by Buster Smith; and *Squabblin',* a riff instrumental credited to Count Basie, with solos on piano, trumpet, alto and clarinet (the last two by Buster Smith), and featuring Page's walking string bass and a series of breaks on baritone sax, also by Page.

Buster Smith's loping clarinet and alto solos on *Squabblin'* are the most interesting portions of a good record, giving more than a hint of Charlie Parker's style, which crystallized more than a decade later. The rhythmic flow and riff settings in the Blue Devils became the basis of the best Moten band, and of Count Basie's own band of the late 1930's. Blue Devils drummer Alvin "Mouse" Burroughs was to spark Earl Hines' great band in the later 1930's, with the tenor solos and arrangements of another Kansas City veteran, Budd Johnson.

The reorganized Blue Devils still had Buster Smith, and also had Lester Young on tenor sax. Lester may have joined the band as early as 1930, while Walter Page was still the leader. The 13 Original Blue Devils, as they were now known, managed to stay together until 1933, when a string of dates they had booked all the way to Virginia went through the hands of a crooked agent who collected their salaries in advance and then skipped town. They finally broke up in Virginia, where their horns impounded nightly, after each dance, to insure their staying in town long enough to work off their debts. Buster Smith joined Bennie Moten, and Lester Young joined Andy Kirk for a time, while the others scattered far and wide.

While the Blue Devils were going under, Andy Kirk's career was on the rise. He had assumed leadership of T. Holder's band in early 1929, and went on location in Oklahoma City. In the change-over, Andy lost the services of Holder's superb alto man, Alvin "Fats" Wall, who went on his own. John Williams took Wall's chair, and Gene Prince took Holder's job.

On location at Crystal Lake Park, Kirk ran into George Lee, who was scouting suitable locations for his band after they finished their run at Kansas City's famed Pla-Mor Ballroom. Lee recommended the Clouds of Joy, as Kirk's band was known to the Pla-Mor management, and worked out a business arrangement with Kirk, to exchange jobs at above-scale prices whenever possible, which they did for a long while thereafter.

During the time Andy Kirk was in the Pla-Mor, a group of record executives from Brunswick, headed by Jack Kapp and Dick Voynow, came to Kansas City looking for new bands to place under contract. They heard Lee, Paul Banks and Andy Kirk, and later went on to Oklahoma City to hear Walter Page. They came away most impressed by the Clouds of Joy, and scheduled a series of sessions at KMBC's studios.

On the afternoon of the Clouds' first session, pianist Marion Jackson failed to show up, so Andy made a call to Mary Lou Williams, piano-playing wife of his altoist, John Williams, who was then in Kansas City but not playing music. Mary Lou came over and made the date, knocking out the musicians and recording people alike.

Andy rewarded her for her fine work by giving her the privilege of making the balance of the Kansas City sessions, so she sat up with Andy and worked out some arrangements, which they used on the sessions. Some time later, when the band was scheduled for another session in Chicago, Marion Jackson was back at his piano chair. When Kapp heard them rehearsing, he didn't like what he heard, and told Andy it didn't sound like the same band, and that he had to have Mary Lou. She came up from Kansas City and continued to make all the recordings at Kapp's insistence, and not with Andy's reluctance. She finally joined the band in 1931, after they had come back from their first trip East.

Fletcher Henderson had played a date in Kansas City early in 1930, and was on the lookout for a suitable band to fill in at Roseland during the summer when he came out. He decided to use Andy's band. They played the Savoy as well, and toured all over New York State, Pennsylvania and New Jersey before returning home in the fall. Fletcher had wanted to take Andy's drummer, Edward "Crackshot" McNeil, away, but he wouldn't leave, and remained with the Clouds until he died in 1931. Ben Thigpen came in from Cleveland to take his place, staying with the Clouds until they broke up for good in 1948.

They returned East for another tour in 1931, and went into the Pearl Theatre in Philadelphia as the house band, backing up Blanche Calloway and other name acts. Trumpeter Edgar "Pudding Head" Battle was now with Andy, and at one point the manager of the theater, Sam Steiffel, attempted to maneuver Blanche into leadership of the band. Bennie Moten also happened to be playing in the vicinity and told Andy of a forthcoming job at Winwood Beach, a local resort back home, that the union wanted him to fill for the summer, so Andy managed to return home with his band intact. Battle stayed on and lured five men who wanted to come East out of Jap Allen's new band in Kansas City. Among them were Ben Webster and pianist Clyde Hart.

Jasper "Jap" Allen was born in 1899 and raised in Kansas City, graduating from Lincoln High during the same period as Walter Page. He started on tuba with Paul Banks in 1925 and stayed with him through 1927, then went out and organized his own group. By 1929 they were organized and playing well, and were thought to be the best young band in their part of the country. Clyde Hart was doing the arranging, copying McKinney's Cotton Pickers recordings, and they had fine soloists in trumpeter Eddie "Orange" White, trombonist Alton "Slim" Moore, and alto man Booker Pittman. Bennie Moten gave them encouragement and turned over some of the jobs he couldn't fill to them. They began traveling all over the Southwest and Midwest and did well until the end of 1930, when bookings started to dwindle down to nothing. Five men left to join Blanche

Calloway in 1931; Jap went down to St. Louis to get replacements, and the band toured the Midwest with vocalist Victoria Spivey from New York. Jap disbanded after the tour and went to St. Louis, where he worked with Fate Marable and Dewey Jackson during the 1930's.

Southwestern musicians were anxious to be recognized on the basis of their musical abilities, and took the battles of bands very seriously for many years. They were just as serious about the jam sessions that took place for individual soloists, as they began to break away from the earlier and comparatively simple solo work that was prevalent during the 1920's. Arrangements that came from the pens of Eddie Durham, Jesse Stone, Mary Lou Williams, Budd Johnson and Tommy Douglas began to make the bands sound more flowing, eliminating the staccato and jerky feeling of earlier years. The solo's possibilities were opened up by the same arrangers, who were themselves proficient soloists, as well as by musicians like Eddie Tompkins on trumpet, Snub Mosely on trombone, Booker Pittman on alto sax and Count Basie on piano. Their conception involved more notes, complex phrasing and better musicianship. Buster Smith and Lester Young were pointing the way to the jazz of tomorrow.

The best example of the evolving style that was taking place in the late 1920's and early 1930's is the Bennie Moten band. When Moten first organized his big band in 1926, jazz was all but dead in New Orleans, dying out in Chicago, and undergoing changes in New York and other parts of the country.

Moten's first period of big-band recordings is from 1926 to 1929, and the band's style was then relatively simple, with loose section work and uncomplicated solos, some of which tended towards the novelty vein (Woodie Walder's clarinet solos, for example).

In 1929, Eddie Durham, Bill Basie (not then known as "Count") and Jimmy Rushing joined Bennie Moten, and Lips Page was to join the next year, bringing the brass section to five men, two more than anyone else used in Kansas City during the same period. Written arrangements were introduced to the band by Durham and later by Basie, and their section work had improved considerably. By 1930 they were beginning to break away from the simple patterns of previous years. Recordings like *Boot It* feature more complex brass phrasing and tighter section work, and guitar breaks by Eddie Durham. *New Vine Street Blues* tends to set a mood, with the rhythm less noticeably two-beat than before, and has a fine blues solo by Basie and more guitar work by Durham. *Won't You Be My Baby,* with a vocal by Jimmy Rushing, is written in the McKinney Cotton Pickers style, and flows as much as a tuba-driven rhythm section can.

On his tour East in 1931, Bennie purchased some forty arrangements by Horace Henderson and Benny Carter, and proceeded to use them in place of some of his earlier, time-proven hits. That winter he gave notice to four of his men, and two others left shortly after. Their replacements included Walter Page on string bass, Ben Webster on tenor sax, and Eddie Barefield on alto and clarinet. For a while trumpeter Joe Smith also joined the band. Their arrangements were being written exclusively by Durham, Barefield and Basie now, and new riff originals like *Toby* (based on *Sweet Sue*) and *Moten Swing* (based on *You're Driving Me Crazy*) became standards. The tuba was thrown to the winds, and Page's bass played even fours. Moten's final recordings, made in December, 1932, produced the driving powerhouse that was later to be heard in Count Basie's band.

The change in personnel improved the band musically but hurt their commercial prospects, since their public, on tour and back home, had been accustomed to their delightful bounce, which few other bands in the country played the way they did, and their novelty solo work. The tour preceding their last session was a disaster, and they barely made it back to Kansas City. Eastern audiences had been used to four-four rhythm since the middle 1920's, through Fletcher Henderson, Duke Ellington, Chick Webb and many others, and thought Moten's new band to be just like the rest, and therefore nothing original. Buster Berry, the banjoist from the old band, who switched to guitar, recalled people asking specifically for their old novelties and for Woodie Walder's clarinet specialties. Before the tour, they had suffered a humiliating defeat back home, at the annual Musician's Ball, held every May at Paseo Hall. Every band in town played at those affairs, and some eight, including those of Moten, Andy Kirk, George Lee, Paul Banks and Clarence Love, and a new band called the Kansas City Rockets, led by trombonist Thamon Hayes, played that year.

The cast-offs from Moten's band—as well as some men from George Lee's band, which reorganized around the same time—got together and formed the Kansas City Rockets. Harlan Leonard's mother-in-law helped finance the band with uniforms and they rehearsed daily at Hayes' home. They had a dozen arrangements made by pianist Jesse Stone, who also directed the band. They played locally a few months before the Musician's Ball, and had gained sufficient popularity to be accorded next-to-last place, directly before Bennie Moten.

Six bands had played for forty-five minutes each, and the crowd was at fever pitch, when Hayes' group took the stand. They played their top dozen arrangements and left the stand, taking half the dancers outside the building with them, before Bennie Moten began to play. Moten had very rough going after that, and at one point lost his entire band to Basie, with the exception of Herschel Evans and Jack Washington, who wouldn't leave.

Basie went on location in Little Rock but didn't last very long, because he didn't have a name or publicity at the time, and one by one the men returned to Kansas City and Moten. By late 1934 Moten had pulled them together and they returned to favor locally and got some good work. Talk of bookings in the Grand Terrace never materialized, but they were on the rise when they went into Denver's Rainbow Gardens, an important stop for all name bands in the 1930's. Bennie himself stayed behind for a minor tonsillectomy. He was said to have had a cold at the time and he was unable to take ether, necessitating a local anaesthetic. He was a nervous person and had put off the operation for a long time, until it became necessary for his health; and he apparently moved at a crucial moment, so that the surgeon's scalpel severed his jugular vein. Bennie's surgeon was a prominent man in the Midwest, and he was forced to give up his practice and move to Chicago as a result of the accidental death. Irreparable damage was done to the morale of the men on the job in Denver, and they were barely able to finish the engagement. Walter Page and Bus Moten each tried to rally the men and keep the band together, but it was no use; they disbanded for good in the summer of 1935.

The Kansas City Rockets went on the road after their victory at the Musician's Ball. They did well the first year or so, and were pointing to Chicago and the East. They managed to get some good work in Chicago and proved so popular that they drew some of Earl Hines' business away from the Grand Terrace. Hines is said to have put pressure on Jesse Stone to write and arrange for his band. The gangsters backing the Grand Terrace had union pressure put on the Hayes band and kept them from remaining in town. They appealed the union's decision, and even had a long-term offer from a good club, but were unable to get a reversal. Jesse Stone quit in 1934, remaining in Chicago, and Thamon Hayes gave up in disgust and turned the band over to Harlan Leonard the same year. Stone organized a fine band in 1935, which featured Jabbo Smith and Budd Johnson, while his place was taken by Roselle Claxton, another good arranger, who later worked with Ernie Fields in Tulsa.

The Rockets had tough going after that; they had to return to Kansas City in 1936 and soon disbanded. In 1938 Harlan Leonard was to assume leadership of a young band that had been built up and drilled by another unsung musical giant, reedman and arranger Tommy Douglas.

Douglas was born in Eskridge, Kansas, in 1911 and went to school in Topeka. He began playing locally and studying music by himself. He became proficient enough to win a scholarship to Boston Conservatory and spent four years there, becoming close friends with Johnny Hodges, Otto Hardwick and Harry Carney, all around Boston at the time. During vacation periods, in order to help meet his expenses, he giged with territory bands led by Captain Wolmack in Buffalo; Jelly Roll Morton, touring the Midwest; and George Lee and Jap Allen in Kansas City.

Douglas wrote and sold arrangements to Casa Loma and other popular bands, and received numerous offers from well-established leaders, such as Fletcher Henderson, which he turned down. He did join Duke Ellington in 1951, replacing Hodges, but left after a few months.

He formed and disbanded many fine bands all during the 1930's and 1940's. They were advanced in conception and used many top men, such as Jo Jones, Paul Webster, Eddie Tompkins, and his brothers Roy and Bill, both fine reed soloists. But he lacked proper financing and promotion, although, at one point in 1935, he had a shot at a measure of fame which he was unable to profit by.

Douglas had absorbed a high-school band fronted by tenorman Jimmie Keith, and drilled them daily, much in the same manner Don Redman employed earlier while building McKinney's Cotton Pickers. He took the younger men because he could train them to play in the style he wanted. Until they were able to phrase and solo well, he had them playing whole notes as backgrounds while he took all the solos on every reed instrument. After spending some months on the road, he got some choice location work at Tulsa's Casa Loma Ballroom. He made friends with Allen Franklin, then program director for radio station KVOO, who was enthused about the band and put a radio wire in for two daily broadcasts. Franklin promised Douglas a national hookup within thirty days if he would remain at the Casa Loma Ballroom. Douglas felt his break was here and wanted nothing more than to stay put for a while.

Meanwhile a local druggist named Crawford had come around, talked to the men in the band without consulting Douglas, and persuaded them to sign an agreement with him. He promised them they would see the country, and when Douglas found out, there wasn't anything he could do, since he had made the band a commonwealth outfit, which meant he had an equal vote with them in any matter, and was only the nominal leader. Crawford took them out of Tulsa over Franklin's protests and they went on the road, winding up in Coffeyville, Kansas, deep in the red. Franklin had obtained the promised national hookup, and finding himself without a band, turned to a local entertainer, Bob Wills, and gave him the air time, which helped him gain national stature.

Crawford was sent to jail for selling his landlord's furniture in order to pay some of the mounting debts, and the incurrent publicity forced Douglas to take the band down to Louisiana, where they worked one-nighters for several months before returning to Kansas City. Douglas was fined by the union for using nonunion men (none of Keith's men had been in the union), and he soon gave the band back to Keith, who kept them going until Harlan Leonard took them over in 1938.

Douglas continued to build bands. One featured trombonist Fred Beckett (later with Harlan Leonard) and another at the College Inn in 1942, featured vocalist-trumpeter Julia "Tiny" Davis. He recorded for Capitol during the middle 1940's, through Dave Dexter, but he felt his association with them to be a failure, since he wasn't allowed to record the songs he wanted, which showed him and his men to good advantage. The recordings show little indication of Douglas' talents; in fact, he rarely solos on them. Charlie Parker also worked with him at one point, and it is said that Parker came under his influence to some degree, since Douglas had always been considered an advanced soloist. He is still active today.

Down in Texas, reedman Troy Floyd began to build a reputatation with a combo in the early 1920's, and began expanding his band until he had twelve men by 1930. He helped put a night club called the Shadowland in business, and stayed there several years. One of his first great musicians was trumpeter Claude "Benno" Kennedy, a musician with a tremendous range and freak style, quite similar to that developed later by Rex Stewart with Fletcher Henderson in New York. Kennedy left to take out his own band in 1927, and eventually went to California. His place was taken by New Orleans trumpeter Don Albert, who had studied under the Pirons and Tios.

Floyd's band recorded for Okeh in 1928 and 1929. The first piece, *Shadowland Blues I,* has an opening trumpet solo by Don Albert, and a soprano chorus by Si-Ki Collins, another fine musician. *Dreamland Blues* has an unusual vocal by Kellough Jefferson, whose style would indicate classical training. The records are unavailable today.

Floyd wasn't much of a musician, but he knew how to please his audiences and how to hustle tips. Tenorman Herschel Evans joined in 1929, and Buddy Tate came in on alto in 1930. Floyd disbanded in 1932 as a result of the Depression, which cut down business in the Shadowland and in many of the hotels (such as the Plaza) where he worked for long periods of time. He had smaller combos for several years and wound up in San Diego as a pool-hall operator. He died in 1951.

Drummer Gene Coy's Happy Black Aces took jazz out of Amarillo in the middle 1920's and played all over the United States. Ben Webster began with Coy on tenor; trumpeter Edgar Battle and trombonist Eddie Durham were with him during the 1920's; and his wife, Ann, was an excellent pianist. During the early 1930's, tenorman Dick Wilson worked with him, and bassist Alvin "Junior" Raglin and tenorman Maxwell Davis were in his band later in the decade. He played in Canada, Washington, Mexico and all over the Pacific Northwest, and was very popular into the middle 1940's. He never recorded with his bands, and lives in California today.

Among the many fine bands and large combos working in Texas

throughout the 1920's were saxophonist and arranger Ben Smith's Blue Syncopators. They were in El Paso in 1927 and 1928 and had trombonist Dan Minor and drummer Debo Mills, among others.

A kid band called the Blue Moon Chasers, in Dallas in the mid-1920's, featured a number called *Country Picnic,* on which drummer Budd Johnson played drums, piano, tenor, alto and trumpet. His brother Keg Johnson was on trombone.

Trumpeter Edgar Battle's Dixie Stompers worked out of Greenville, Texas, from 1926 to 1928, with Eddie Durham on trombone. This band is supposed to have recorded for Gennett or Brunswick.

The DeLuxe Melody Boys in Austin, with pianist Lloyd Glenn; the Singer Brothers in Fort Worth in 1919; The Royal Aces, with trombonist George Corley and tuba player Gene Ramey in Austin in 1930; Johnson's Joymakers, with trumpeter Joe Keys in Houston in 1928, are some of the many groups which had local popularity and many fine musicians, but whose reputation never enabled them to tour or record.

Individual musicians like trombonist Bert Johnson, pianist Sam Price, clarinetist Buster Bailey (not the Henderson star), saxophonist Willie Lewis (who led one of the most popular American bands in Europe in the 1930's) and pianist Edgar Perry are all remembered as being well above the average. One of the most popular musicians in Texas during the late 1920's was a New Orleans trumpeter nicknamed "Frenchy." His real name was Polite Christian and he recorded with a string trio for Columbia in 1928. Both Buddy Tate and Budd Johnson remember him well, and recalled that he had a very powerful tone which could be heard nearly twenty blocks away.

By 1932 Texas' best band was the one led by trumpeter Don Albert, who left Troy Floyd in 1929 and returned to New Orleans to get his musicians. They hit the road as Don Albert's Ten Happy Pals, played the Texas Centennial Fair and a local night club known as the Chicken Plantation, and then went on the road for a while. They went into the Shadowland when Troy Floyd came out and stayed there for nearly a year before traveling again. Lloyd Glenn joined in 1932 and wrote most of their arrangements until he left in 1937, and trumpeter Billy Douglas came to the band from a territory outfit in the Carolinas in 1934. Don had given up playing before that to concentrate on business details. Most of the trumpet work was handled by Douglas, who was an exceptional musician, originally from New Haven, where he lives today. The band stayed on the road and became very popular all over the South and along the Eastern seaboard. Eight titles recorded for Columbia in 1936 indicate the fine qualities of the band; good rhythmic drive; fine solo work from tenor, baritone, alto and clarinet; and exceptional trumpet solos from Douglas. It is interesting to note that this band, composed largely of New Orleans musicians, was perhaps the only one operating successfully within the swing framework and not in the New Orleans tradition.

Tenorman Jimmy Forrest and pianist Jay Golson were in the 1938 band, and Don kept going until 1940, breaking down combos until recently. He has a night club known as the Keyhole which is still operating today.

The absence of Don Albert from the local scene in San Antonio paved the way for drummer Clifford "Boots" Douglas, whose career began in the late 1920's, and who organized a band to play locally during the early 1930's. They were well known as Boots and His Buddies and were popular locally until the war years, recording many titles for Victor between 1935 and 1938. The band was frequently out of tune, and sounded more like a rehearsal band than one which worked regularly, but their versions of *How Long Blues,* in two parts, and *Blues of Avalon,* with good trumpet solos by Charlie Anderson and good tenor by Baker Millian, are worth while. Al Hibbler sang with them for a while before joining Jay McShann in 1942.

A full decade passed before another group in Arkansas came up to rival the popularity that Alphonso Trent had had in the early 1920's. The new outfit was formed by pianist Chester Lane, who had worked earlier with Brady-Bryant's Peppers, a local outfit of the late 1920's. Lane started with a trio, working locally around Little Rock, and had eight pieces by 1934, with Al Hibbler's vocals as a feature. He called the group the Original Yellowjackets, and they featured head arrangements of riff tunes and pops like *The Hour of Parting,* one of eight titles they recorded after Lane himself left the band.

The Yellowjackets built up a local restaurant called the Chat N' Chew, where they worked regularly during the 1930's. Tenorman Buddy Tate, working with vocalist and leader Ethel Mays in 1934, remembered them well, and thought they were a fine, jumping outfit.

Their recordings bear that out, particularly *Swinging at the Chat N' Chew* and *Yellowjackets Get Together*. These titles are out of print, and pianist Lane is now playing Dixieland with Teddy Buckner in Hollywood.

Lane left the Yellowjackets to join the Jeter-Pillars band in St. Louis in 1937, and they were the most popular band in the Mound City in the 1930's. They were formed in 1934 by altoman James Jeter and tenorman Hayes Pillars, both veterans of the Trent band. They went into the Club Plantation on a trial basis and stayed nearly ten years, playing for dancing and the huge floor shows. Walter Page and drummer Sid Catlett were with the band in 1935, and Hawaiian guitarist Floyd Smith was featured on their recording of *Lazy Rhythm*. Trumpeter Walter "Crack" Stanley and bassist Jimmy Blanton were with them during the late 1930's. Primarily a commercial band, and later featured on the Fitch Summer Bandwagon radio program, they could play good jazz.

St. Louis was a river town, and the Streckfus Brothers, a German family of five, some of whom were trained professional musicians, operated a fleet of riverboats. They brought pianist Fate Marable out of Kentucky at the end of World War I, to organize a dance orchestra. Two years later Marable went to New Orleans and brought out Louis Armstrong, Johnny and Baby Dodds, Pops Foster and others, and drilled them into a crack outfit. From that point until the early 1940's, his bands were considered the equal of any playing, and he always used top musicians.

Fate was a college graduate, but somewhat lazy and relatively unambitious. He had numerous offers to go to New York and Chicago, but he always turned them down, preferring to work on the boats. He never bothered to write down any of his arrangements, just taking the time out to show each musician his part, until tuba player Cecil White began writing them down in 1926. Marable's 1924 band recorded for Okeh, although the music is not indicative of his best efforts. He wouldn't stand for poor musicianship, and often fired men who couldn't read, unless they showed unusual promise. Before he retired to supper clubs, Zutty Singleton, Charlie Creath, Dewey Jackson, Red Allen, Harold Baker, Tab Smith, Jock Carruthers and Jimmy Blanton were among many who went on to greater fame after having learned the rudiments of music from him. He died in 1947.

St. Louis was a trumpet town, and some of this undoubtedly

came from Louis Armstrong's impact in 1919, although the many municipal brass bands and lodge organizations drilled into young musicians an instinct for trumpet. A Major McElroy, who had the Odd Fellows Brass Band for many years, drilled musicians like Leonard Davis, Charlie Creath, Dewey Jackson, and Irving Randolph, all of whom later had choice jobs with name bands or led their own outfits. St. Louis also had excellent trumpet teachers in the German community, who had military and classical training.

Charlie Creath, the blues expert, was born in 1890 in Ironton, Missouri, and became the first great trumpet soloist in St. Louis, after having worked with brass bands and the famed Hagenbeck-Wallace Circus band in 1916. His own bands were of varying size and lasted from the early 1920's until the mid-1930's. Recordings made between 1924 and 1927 show an increasing tendency towards the use of arrangements, although Creath's own solo work was always blues-based.

A better all-around musician was trumpeter Dewey Jackson, who was born in 1900. He began with Fate Marable and recorded four rare titles for Brunswick in 1926, all of which have fine samples of the Jackson solo ability. Dewey had bigger bands in the 1930's, which were always a jazz fan's delight, since they featured plenty of his trumpet work and largely head arrangements. He recorded again in 1950 for a now-defunct local label; and, according to all who have heard him in recent years, he still has plenty of power and good ideas.

Another good brassman was Eddie Allen, whose solos in the many small groups fronted by pianist Clarence Williams in the 1920's were often mistaken for the work of King Oliver. He had bands on the riverboats in the early 1920's, before he came to New York.

During the late 1920's, trombonist Willie Austin was popular with an entertaining band that worked the Chauffeur's Club and other local spots. He never recorded, although he was active for many years.

A St. Louis band became the first to work New York's Cotton Club in 1925. They began as Wilson Robinson's Syncopators, and came to New York in 1924 under violinist Andrew Preer's baton, recording for Gennett with him. Eli Logan, a Kansas City sensation on alto, was the band during this period, although he never recorded with the band and died at the end of the 1920's.

The band became known as the Missourians after they left

New York in late 1927, when Duke Ellington came in. They toured with Ethel Waters and went under MCA's management, recording a dozen titles for Victor in 1929 and 1930, eight of which were released on the now-defunct "X" Label several years ago. Their records indicate kinship with the Kansas City bands of Jesse Stone and Bennie Moten. Stone's *Boot to Boot* became their *Ozark Mountain Blues,* and Moten's *South* became their *You'll Cry for Me When I'm Gone.* They had plenty of drive, and fine brassmen in trumpeters Lamar Wright and R. Q. Dickerson.

They were fronted by vocalist Lockwood Lewis until Cab Calloway's manager engineered him into the leadership of the band. Cab's career began to soar with the Missourians behind him. Oklahoma-born tenorman Walter "Foots" Thomas was featured regularly in 1930 and 1931.

Another trumpeter, Oliver Cobb, was prominent as leader of small combos and larger bands in which he was primarily featured, until his accidental death by drowning in 1931. He recorded for Brunswick and Paramount and had a style and vocal sound similar to Louis Armstrong's. His band was taken over by his pianist, Eddie Johnson, who formed Johnson's Crackerjacks, the top band of the early 1930's in St. Louis.

Several different bands used the Crackerjack name during the 1930's, and two recorded—Eddie Johnson's in 1932 and Chick Finney's in 1936. Johnson's band used to battle every band that came through St. Louis in the early 1930's, and he usually won his battles. He was helped considerably by the exceptional trumpet solos of Harold "Shorty" Baker, currently with Duke Ellington; and tenor soloist Ernest "Chick" Franklin. Baker's early brilliance is preserved on a cut-out Victor recording of *Duck's Yas Yas,* a popular St. Louis party song written by pianist James "Stump" Johnson, who recorded regularly for Paramount, D.R.S. and other "race" labels in the 1920's; and *Good Old Bosom Bread.* Baker was sought after by all the leading bands, but didn't leave town until 1936, when Don Redman finally got him to join his band. His brother Winfield, a trombonist, had taken over the majority of Eddie Johnson's band by this time, although Johnson reorganized with other men.

Chick Finney was the pianist with Winfield Baker in 1934. Afterwards he took over the lead of the Crackerjacks and renamed them the Original St. Louis Crackerjacks. They became quite popular, with vocalist Austin Wright in front. Eight titles, now cut out on Decca, range from the moody *Echoes in the Dark* to the jumping *Crackerjack Stomp,* with good arrangements by guitarist William "Bede" Baskerville.

Trumpeter George Hudson, who had been with Jeter-Pillars, had a big band during the 1940's and is still active, while Buggs Roberts and Eddie Randall—the last named had Miles Davis in his trumpet section at one point—were active in the 1930's and 1940's. Clark Terry was also active before World War II.

Promoter Jesse Johnson was the biggest single entrepreneur St. Louis has ever seen. He booked all the bands; owned a restaurant, a hotel, a poolroom, a barbecue stand, a publishing company and several other enterprises; and became quite a wealthy man before he died. He is also credited with many popular compositions.

Oklahoma became a boom state as a result of many oil discoveries and other profitable industrial enterprises. Tulsa became the head-quarters of the Southern Serenaders, a fine group of the early 1920's, led by an advanced pianist, Salva Sanders. His style was similar to that of Earl Hines, and he is said to have helped Basie in later years. Trumpeter Hiram Harding (later with Don Albert) was featured. The band changed personnel frequently and was taken over by trombonist Ernie Fields in the early 1930's. Sanders died in 1937, and his place was taken by arranger Roselle Claxton, who did most of the band's scores, with guitarist Rene Hall.

John Hammond heard Fields' band in 1939 and arranged to bring them to New York for recordings and a theater tour. They had strong commercial potential in vocalist Melvin Moore (later with Lunceford), and some good soloists in trumpeter Amos Woodruff, tenorman Roy "Buck" Douglas, and altoman Hunter Garnett. Fields later went into rhythm-and-blues work.

Another prominent Tulsa resident, who led some jumping bands, was Kansas City-born Clarence Love. Love's first combo had trum-peter Milton Fletcher (later with Earl Hines), and played Murphy's Egyptian Club in Omaha in 1928, before going on an extended road tour for the next two years, playing all over the Southwest and the Pacific Coast region. Love's band played along fairly sophisticated lines and found regular work in hotels and ballrooms in Kansas City until 1933. He often worked the Blue Hills Gardens and the swank El Torreon Ballroom. Joe Smith, Lester Young and reedman Tommy Douglas all worked with Love during these years, and his regular guitarist, "Jim Daddy" Walker, is said to have influenced Charlie Christian later on.

Love was forced out of town in 1934, when his father and union president William Shaw, both barbers, had a dispute over ownership of a shop. Love worked down into Texas and began rebuilding in Dallas. By 1935 he had good bookings at the Samovar Club, and Eddie Heywood joined the band. They signed a contract with Dave Kapp of Decca, to record whenever they got to New York.

Ex-Kansas City vocalist Orlando Robison, who had gone to fame singing with Claude Hopkins in the early 1930's, was to take Love's band on a road tour starting in New York. No sooner did Love bring the band into New York than Robison jumped them right into Danville, Virginia, to start their tour, and Love never got back to record. The tour broke up later that year in Lansing, Michigan, and only a few of the men returned to Dallas with Love.

He formed another band and took it through the South for several years, winding up in Indianapolis, at the Sunset Terrace Club, in 1941. His band was being directed by ex-Andy Kirk vocalist Pha Terrell, and had J. J. Johnson on trombone, before a crooked agent duped Love out of the lead.

He joined the Ferguson Brothers agency in Indianapolis and booked all the leading territory bands for the next year. He fronted an all-girl orchestra, the Darlings of Rhythm, until 1946; then he settled in Tulsa, opening a lounge there which had all the name bands.

A large number of fine bands and individual musicians came out of Omaha from the middle 1920's into the war years. Trombonist Charlie "Big" Green, a star with Fletcher Henderson in the 1920's, began in brass bands around Omaha. Clarence Derume, from New Orleans, an organizer of parade bands, worked around Omaha for years.

Among the first jazz combos were the Omaha Night Owls— later taken over by vocalist Red Perkins, to become his Dixie Ramblers band—and Sam Turner's group. Turner was a banjoist and entertainer who featured a fine early trumpeter, Willard Chew, and for many years worked at the Grotto, one of the first clubs associated with jazz in that part of the country.

Red Perkins was probably the most popular single entertainer ever to come out of Omaha, and his Dixie Ramblers became a pretty good big band in the 1930's. His popularity was built around elaborate floor shows and entertainment within his band, and he wasn't challenged musically until trumpeter Lloyd Hunter organized Hunter's Serenaders in 1927.

Hunter had been active since the early 1920's, but the Serenaders did not make a dent in local popularity until 1927, when trombonist Elmer Crumbley and pianist Burton Brewer stood out. Crumbley recalled, ". . . the first time we went to Chicago Brewer moved Earl Hines right off the piano stool, and this was when Earl was the hottest thing in jazz. . . ." Brewer died of tuberculosis in 1929, shortly before Hunter recorded, in the spring of the following year.

The popularity of the Serenaders enabled them to form a mutually profitable union with New York vocalist Victoria Spivey, who became their director in 1930. They managed to get as far East as Boston, but never down to New York. Their one, rare recording, made for Brunswick in March, 1930, has the sharp drive associated with Midwestern territory bands. *Sensational Mood,* a fast stomp written and arranged by composer Henri Woode and saxophonist Noble Floyd, has solos by every instrument, with trumpeter George Lott's work outstanding. The Spivey vocal on *I'm Dreaming About My Man* is excellent and has fine trumpet backing and a moody banjo solo. Jo Jones began his professional career with Hunter's band and worked with him off and on until 1933.

Hunter had bands active all during the 1930's, and later ones were patterned on the Basie model. Trombonist Dan Minor, saxophonist and arranger Ben Smith, and Sir Charles Thompson, then just starting on piano, all worked for Hunter.

Omaha's top outfit during the 1930's was bass player Nat Towles' band, formed in Texas in 1935. Towles was born in New Orleans in 1905 and played with the local bands of Jack Carey, Punch Miller, Buddy Petit and Henry Allen, Sr. He took his own bands out in the early 1920's, trumpeter Herb Morand accompanying him on one of his first ventures. He worked around Texas, New Mexico and Oklahoma and built a reputation which enabled him to take over the Wiley College band in Austin. He brought them to Dallas in 1935 and soon built them into the state's best outfit.

Choice location work in Omaha prompted him to bring the band there the next year, and he took over the Dreamland Ballroom, the top spot in town, elbowing Red Perkins and Lloyd Hunter, the previously established leaders, out of the number one jobs. From that point on through the war years, the Towles band had the best dates in the Southwest and the Deep South. They played the best night clubs and ballrooms, with some of the top musicians in that part of the country, including Buddy Tate on tenor; C. Q. Price, arranger and alto; Sir Charles Thompson, arranger and piano; Fred Beckett and Henry Coker (now with Basie) on trombones; Paul King (featured soloist with Andy Kirk 1936–37) and Nat Bates on trumpets; and popular vocalist Duke Groner. They missed being able to work in Chicago or farther east until the war years had taken their best men, although every musician who heard the band felt it to be the equal of any playing in the country.

At one point in 1940, arranger-pianist Horace Henderson scrapped the band he'd been leading in Chicago and took over most of the Towles group, keeping only trumpeter Emmett Barry, bassist Israel Crosby and drummer Debo Mills from his own group. He managed to get some good work and brought them to New York, where they recorded four sides for Okeh in the fall. Two titles, *You Don't Mean Me No Good,* a Towles feature written by tenor-man Bob Dorsey, and *Smooth Sailing,* written and arranged by Sir Charles Thompson, preserve the verve and drive the Towles band had. Each has fine solos and full ensemble drive, the entire band working off the firm bass of Israel Crosby. Trumpeter Nat Bates, then compared stylistically to Buck Clayton, and altoman C. Q. Price (later with Basie) are outstanding.

Buddy Tate, a ten-year Basie veteran (1939–49) is insistent that the Towles band was superior to Basie's: ". . . we would have torn his band apart. We caught his [Basie's] broadcast from the Grand Terrace and believe me, there was no comparison. We were swinging all the time, could entertain and play pretty, and had as many as five different arrangements on one tune. . . ." Towles' band was undoubtedly a fine outfit, and the cut-out Horace Henderson recordings lend credence to that statement.

The battles of music Nat Towles had with another fine Texas crew were legendary. The band was trumpeter Milton Larkins' from Houston. They battled every Sunday for years at the old Harlem Square Club in Houston. Larkins could boast of having started Arnett

Cobb and Illinois Jacquet on tenor; Eddie Vinson, altoman and fine blues vocalist; and guitarist-pianist Bill Davis, who was also chief arranger.

Larkins was born in Houston in 1910. He took his inspiration from Bunk Johnson, and started working in the early 1930's with D. Johnson and Chester Boone, before organizing his own band at the Aragon Ballroom in 1936.

The noted arranger, Sy Oliver, then with Jimmie Lunceford, recalled the rough time Larkins' band gave them whenever they came through Houston. Cab Calloway—then featuring Dizzy Gillespie, Jonah Jones and Chu Berry, among others—also got rough treatment from the Larkins crew. Gillespie used to sit in with Larkins' band every time they came through Houston.

In 1940 Larkins received an offer from the College Inn in Kansas City and worked there for several months, attracting another offer, from Chicago's Rhumboogie, for a two-week trial run. The Rhumboogie job lasted nine months, and veteran drummer Alvin Burroughs, trumpeter Jesse Miller (both formerly with Hines), and trumpeter Clarence Trice (formerly with Andy Kirk) also joined the band. They never recorded, although they managed to get good work until Larkins was drafted in 1943.

A few years earlier, in Oklahoma City, a young electric guitarist named Charlie Christian was the talk of the whole Southwest. Born in Dallas in 1919 and raised in Oklahoma, he started playing bass with Alphonso Trent in 1934, and then worked locally on bass and guitar with his brother Eddie's band, and a band led by Anna Mae Winburn, later director of the Sweethearts of Rhythm. He received a great deal of help from Eddie Durham, perhaps the first electric guitarist in jazz, and from "Jim Daddy" Walker, another fine, unsung guitar wizard. By 1938 he was again working with Alphonso Trent, in a septet with tenorman Henry Bridges (later with Harlan Leonard) and trumpeter Harold Bruce (later with Jay McShann) at the Dome in Bismarck, North Dakota, and in Casper, Wyoming, as well. Musicians who heard the group recall his wonderful solos, and the many new ideas he had cropped up later in his work with Benny Goodman's sextet of 1939–41, after John Hammond had brought him to New York. His early death in 1942 robbed jazz of another brilliant and inspirational soloist.

To return to Kansas City, night life was running full blast as the Pendergast régime became more and more open in its association with criminal elements. Most of the bigger bands finished up their jobs around one o'clock, and all the top soloists would come over to Twelfth Street or Eighteenth Street to jam at the Sunset and Subway Clubs. The Sunset was at Twelfth and Highland; it was owned by Felix Payne, and managed by Piney Brown. Joe Turner tended bar and shouted the blues in accompaniment to the driving house band, led by pianist Pete Johnson. A fabulous altoman, Walter Knight, and a dependable ryhthm drummer, Murl Johnson, rounded out the band, which often enlarged to ten men in the course of an evening's jamming. A full roster of the greatest soloists of the Southwest could be heard any evening in the early and middle 1930's and the sessions in which Coleman Hawkins and Chu Berry attempted to cut Ben Webster, Herschel Evans, Dick Wilson and Lester Young are legendary. The musicians from the Southwest competed on a friendly basis, but often laid a trap for their Eastern counterparts with the big reputations. A Ben Webster or a Dick Wilson would start off blowing against Hawk or Chu Berry and hold his own, until Lester Young, who had been waiting in the wings, would come out and wear them all down. Alto soloists and clarinetists always got rough treatment at the hands of Tommy Douglas and Buster Smith, and trumpeters could expect plenty of action from Eddie Tompkins, Hot Lips Page, Carl Smith, Bob Hall and Hugh Jones. The last named was considered "a phenomenal solo man, who couldn't read, but was hired by all the bands to sit out front and solo. He later learned to read and lost his lip."

As Piney Brown was considered the musician's friend, so was Ellis Burton, known as the "Chief," who ran the Yellow Front Saloon during the early 1930's, where Bus Moten, Julia Lee, drummer Baby Lovett, Sam Price and even Bunk Johnson worked. He was raided regularly by the police, but was always open for business the very next day. He died in 1936.

Other clubs, such as the Vanity Fair, the Blue Hills Gardens, the Cherry Blossom, Wolfe's Buffet, the Lone Star and the Spinning Wheel, all had fine combos led by top local musicians, and during the 1930's jam sessions took place which sometimes lasted to noon of the following day.

The beginning of the end of Kansas City's high life began when public indignation mounted over open flouting of the law. The Union Station massacre of 1933, in which Pretty Boy Floyd and his cohorts killed four policemen, began a rumble of protest from public-minded citizens, which didn't calm down the following year, when local ganglord Johnny Lazia was machine-gunned to death. The fraudulent election returns of 1936, coupled with rumors of a statewide insurance payoff by Tom Pendergast, put a sharp focus onto Pendergast's machine activities. His addiction to gambling eventually led to his conviction for income-tax evasion in 1939. Just four years earlier, Bennie Moten had died on the operating table at the age of forty-one.

Contrary to many stories, Count Basie didn't take over the Moten band, but worked as a single until he was able to build a following at the Reno Club. By early 1936 he had nine pieces. Drummer Jo Jones was working across the street with Tommy Douglas at Amos N' Andy's.

There was some talk of merging Basie's and Douglas' bands when John Hammond entered the picture and arranged to have Basie sign with Willard Alexander of MCA. Lips Page and Buster Smith quit before Basie left town in 1936. Buck Clayton and Herschel Evans had come back from California, where they had been with Lionel Hampton's first big band, and Basie took thirteen pieces into the Grand Terrace in Chicago.

Critical and public reception to Basie was indifferent for almost two years, although Basie had Billie Holiday singing with his band until early 1938. Fletcher Henderson helped Basie with some of his own arrangements, because Basie was not allowed to use many of his originals on the air until later on. Basie laid eggs at Roseland, the Savoy Ballroom and Pittsburgh's William Penn Hotel, but early in 1938 the band won a well-publicized victory over Chick Webb in a battle of music at the Savoy, which helped them immeasurably. John Hammond came to their aid again when he put them in the Famous Door that summer, and they were on their way after that. Billie Holiday never recorded with the band, since she was with Columbia and Basie was then with Decca, although several quite good broadcasts that feature her vocals with the band have been bootlegged for years. Helen Humes took her place and stayed for several years. But before Basie achieved commercial success, Andy Kirk had found another niche that paid off.

Kirk had gone East before Basie, and recorded for Jack Kapp on Decca early in 1936. Kapp wanted Kirk to make *Christopher Columbus,* the hottest band tune of 1936, and Kirk did a good job with it. He wanted Kapp to listen to a few bars of a new ballad they had, which Pha Terrell sang and which was well known in the Kansas City area as *The Slave Song.* Now it was called *Until The Real Thing Comes Along,* but Kapp didn't want to hear it; he wanted *Moten Swing* and *Froggy Bottom,* insisting that Andy leave the top tunes to the white bands, who he felt couldn't play jazz. Andy got Kapp to listen reluctantly to a few bars of the song, and he flipped. From that point on, the Kirk library was expanded to include many pop tunes in a similar vein. Andy was assured of commercial success and went into rotation with Louis Armstrong, Earl Hines and Fletcher Henderson at the Grand Terrace. His band always had its quota of fine jazzmen, including Don Byas, Harold Baker, Ken Kersey and, later on, Fats Navarro, Charlie Parker and Howard McGhee.

Back in Kansas City, two other leaders were attracting local attention. Harlan Leonard had taken over the Jimmie Keith band in 1938, and with several additions made it into the new Rockets. He went on the road, did good business all over the Midwest and went into the Century Room, the biggest ballroom for Negro bands in Kansas City, in 1939. Some of his best arrangements were then done by Gus Wilson and Richard Smith, and later by pianist Tadd Dameron from Cleveland. Fred Beckett on trombone and Henry Bridges on tenor became the featured soloists, while Myra Taylor and Ernest Williams handled the vocals. Jazz experts Dave Dexter and Marshall Stearns were astounded by the band's attack as early as 1938.

Recording for Victor in 1940, they had a hit with *Hairy Joe Jump,* later known as *Southern Fried,* and made many fine jazz sides, including *A La Bridges, 400 Swing* and *My Gal Sal,* all of which feature Beckett's superlative trombone. Bassist Winston Williams was a fine musician, and the only one who dared challenge Jimmy Blanton to a duel, although he usually came off second best. Billy Hadnott replaced him later in 1940, and Charlie Parker had come and gone over to Jay McShann earlier.

Leonard was booked into the Golden Gate Ballroom, opposite the Savoy, in 1940, but flopped and never came back, working around the Midwest until 1946. He lost some of his following in Kansas City to Jay McShann.

McShann came out of Muskogee, Oklahoma, and joined two minor territory bands, led by Al Denny and Eddie Hill (Howard McGhee and Billy Hadnott were in this band in 1935), although he could not read music very well. By chance he was in Kansas City in 1937—en route to Omaha, where he expected to find work—when he ran into Bus Moten, who encouraged him to stay in town, and helped him get set with Prince Stewart's eight-piece band. McShann stayed with Stewart for three months and attracted the attention of Sharon Pease, then writing for *Down Beat,* who rated him a fine, individual soloist. He began gigging locally and took a quintet into Martins-on-the-Plaza, a new club right in the center of town. Charlie Parker and Gene Ramey were with him that fall. Parker left town to go to Detroit and eventually to New York, and didn't come back to Kansas City until 1940. McShann built a solid following at Martin's over a year-and-a-half stay, and was aided by local radio executives and businessmen in building his band to twelve pieces by 1940.

He started touring the Southwest and did terrific business, battling and cutting better-established bands like those of Nat Towles and Jeter-Pillars. The band went into the Century Room after Harlan Leonard left to go to New York, and Jay happened to hear Walter Brown sing the blues one night in a side-street bar. Jay hired him and they went down to San Antonio, Texas, in 1941 to record for Dave Kapp. Although McShann's book had many fine arrangements by William Scott, Ramey and Parker, Kapp wanted only the blues. He accepted *Swingmatism,* after being thoroughly satisfied with Brown's vocals on *Confessin' the Blues.* Al Hibbler joined the band shortly after that, and by February, 1942, they were in the Savoy in New York, opposite Lucky Millinder's popular band.

Millinder had vocalist Trevor Bacon, a very commercial singer; trumpeters Freddy Webster and Archie Johnson; and a strong rhythm team in Bill Doggett, George Duvivier and Panama Francis on piano, bass and drums respectively, but they were no match for McShann's band, which blew them out with regularity. Brown's and Hibbler's blues shouting, McShann's fine piano, the terrific rhythm team of Gene Ramey on bass and Gus Johnson on drums, and Charlie Parker's magnificent alto solos became the latest sensation in New York.

Arranger-pianist Skip Hall joined the band and wrote many fine things for McShann, while musicians like Paul Quinichette, Jimmy Forrest, trumpeter Willie Cook and others all went in and out of the band before McShann joined the service late in 1943.

For all McShann's rave notices, his band had tough going and had to be helped several times. Don Redman came to their aid on two occasions, when they were on the verge of going back to Kansas City. He was then free-lancing, selling arrangements to all the top bands, and didn't have his own band any more. He kept getting offers to take bands out, and used the McShann band, once in Trenton, New Jersey, and again in Boston at the Tic Toc Club, where he began paying attention to the band, and particularly to Charlie Parker.

Parker was already known as "Bird" when he came to New York because of an incident on the road. One of the band's cars ran over a chicken, which Parker called "yardbirds." He got out of the car, wrapped the dead chicken carefully in old newspapers and took it to the next town, where he insisted their cook prepare it for dinner that night.

Redman woke to Bird's potentialities when he heard an up-tempo arrangement of *The Whistler and His Dog,* on which Bird took four choruses. Don flipped and urged Bird to do whatever he could to remain in New York, assuring him he would have little difficulty finding work with his talents. Bird soon accepted Budd Johnson's tenor chair in Earl Hines' bop-oriented band of 1943.

McShann came out of service in 1944 and reorganized his band, working on Fifty-second Street and going on the road. Singers Crown Prince Waterford and Jimmy Witherspoon worked with him then. He broke up the band in 1949, and returned to Kansas City, where he is still top man today.

The hottest combo in Kansas City during the war years was trumpeter Oliver Todd's. They worked at the College Inn for a long while, although they never recorded. Todd came up in the middle 1930's, in bands led by Charles Green and a fine pianist, Margaret "Countess" Johnson, who once subbed for Mary Lou Williams with Andy Kirk before her death from tuberculosis. Todd's trumpet had an easy flow and lyrical sense which made him much in demand. A good sampling of his style can be heard on one track by Jay McShann, *Moten Swing,* on the Capitol *KC in the Thirties* LP. Todd doesn't play too much trumpet these days; he works mostly on piano.

Thus far the white musician's story has been ignored, although many fine white jazzmen—Jack and Charlie Teagarden, Peck Kelly, Pee Wee Russell, Harry James and Benny Strickler, to mention just a few—were working in the Southwest before moving on, in some cases, to greater fame. With the exception of Jack Teagarden and St. Louis altoman Frankie Trumbauer, whose careers have been well documented, the other musicians seem not to have been influential or to have had much contact with their Negro counterparts in the Southwest, although further research might contradict that statement. Theirs, apparently, is a separate story, which should be written.

A full evaluation of the contribution made by the Southwestern musician and the difference in regional styles cannot be made at this writing, since all the research data is not at hand; but this chapter may help point out that a great deal of activity took place all over the Southwest, an area which is by no means musically inactive even today, and that Southwestern musicians contributed greatly towards furthering musical developments, right up through modern jazz.

The value in any style of music, as always, lies with the individual musician. For the writer, the music of Kansas City and the Southwest has been a source of constant stimulation.

THE ELLINGTON STYLE: ITS ORIGINS AND EARLY DEVELOPMENT

∧∧∧∧∧∧∧∧∧∧∧∧∧∧∧∧

Gunther Schuller

Gunther Schuller is a leading contemporary classical composer, who has received several commissions. He is also a first French horn player at the Metropolitan Opera, and teaches the instrument privately and at the Manhattan School of Music. He was in charge of the jazz section of the late David Broekman's stimulating "Music in the Making" series at Cooper Union, New York.

In jazz, Schuller participated in the influential Miles Davis Capitol records (on the 1950 sessions), and has been closely associated with the Modern Jazz Quartet as friend and occasional adviser since that group's start. He has written for the Modern Jazz Quartet, and has conducted works by John Lewis, Jimmy Giuffre and J. J. Johnson in *Music for Brass* (Columbia CI-941), which also contains his own non-jazz *Symphony for Brass and Percussion*, conducted by Dmitri Mitropoulos.

Schuller was largely responsible for the unprecedented concert that was part of the 1957 Brandeis University Festival of the Arts. It was the first time jazz works were commissioned by a university—three by classical composers, including Schuller, and three by jazz writers (*Modern Jazz Concert*, Columbia WL 127).

Schuller has written on jazz for *The Saturday Review, Musical America* and *The Jazz Review*. He has long been intrigued by the music of Ellington, and has composed *A Tribute to Duke Ellington*, based on a number of Ellington themes. Schuller proposes to continue his analytical study of Ellington's music, begun here, in a future book.

Nearly two decades ago Duke Ellington gave the world of music his masterpiece, *Ko-Ko,* and four years later his long-planned "musical history of the Negro," *Black, Brown and Beige.* Despite many and varied efforts on the part of a host of younger musicians, the perfection of the former and the scope and stature of the latter have as yet not been surpassed and only rarely equalled (if at all). It may come as a surprise, then, to realize that practically nothing has been written about Ellington and his works in terms of their musical and stylistic essence, nor about the even more fascinating question of how the leader of a band which, in its earlier days, played primarily show and dance music came to create such compositional landmarks.

The musicologist in jazz, unlike his colleagues in the world of classical music, must of necessity base his analyses primarily on recordings. This has both advantages and disadvantages. On the one hand, it eliminates the vexing problem of interpretation which faces the classical musicologist. Even the most exacting notation—and let it be noted that many composers were (and are) not very exacting, relying rather often upon the tradition and current interpretational styles to complete what they have left unwritten "between the lines"—leaves room for interpretation and the injection of a performer's personal feelings and musical attitudes. In a jazz recording, on the other hand, we have a single specific interpretation by the creator *himself*—a frozen image, as it were, of the player's creative impulse, an image which contains *both* that original impulse *and* its realization. It seems to me that once the artist involved has given his approval to a recording, it must be considered as a valid, analyzable version of his intentions. But this is, on the other hand, precisely the disadvantage—the other side of the coin. For in a music where spontaneity, not only of performance but of *creation,* is such a vital element, any single performance is apt to give less than the complete picture. Recording conditions being what they are, 1) recorded performances are rarely able to capture the excitement of a live performance, where the vital element of audience reaction plays its important role, and 2) for a variety of reasons countless jazz recordings are made before the performances have jelled into an over-all unified concept, and too many are recorded in a decidedly under-rehearsed state.

In any case, the jazz musicologist has practically no choice. He must turn to recordings, especially in the case of Ellington, where many performances were the result of head arrangements—collective experimentation on the part of Ellington and the whole band—while, in some other cases, what scores and parts were eventually copied out have seemingly been lost. And in a band where the personalities of the players contributed so heavily to its sound, its style and quality, even if scores existed, they would tell us very little.

The Beginnings

The Ellington discography starts theoretically in 1924, [1] but for all practical purposes, the first more or less presently available re-cordings [2] date from April, 1926.[3] At that time Ellington had al-ready been leading a number of small groups for some five or six years, first in Washington and later in New York. In the late years of World War I, when Washington—Ellington's birthplace—was a bee-hive of activity, bands providing music for dancing and all manner of social and political functions flourished in great numbers. Elling-ton, by the time he was seventeen or eighteen, had developed a considerable local reputation as a ragtime and party pianist, and often played with some of the more famous Washington orchestras. I think it is of great importance to any investigation of Ellington's development to note that most, if not all, of these were more or less commercial orchestras—large groups, generally led by well-known ragtime pianists but otherwise consisting primarily of reading or "legitimate" [4] musicians, since the "best gigs in town" were for society and embassy affairs. However, some of the rougher, smaller

[1] Benny H. Aasland, *The Wax Works of Duke Ellington,* a discography.
[2] *The Birth of Big Band Jazz*—Riverside 12–129.
[3] Two old acoustical records, *Trombone Blues* and *I'm Gonna Hang Around My Sugar,* recorded (according to Aasland) in late 1925, are inconse-quential items that sound like any number of bands of the period, and certainly not as good as the Fletcher Henderson band of the time, which, of course, had Coleman Hawkins and Louis Armstrong, as well as Don Redman as alto and arranger. Both Ellington sides are typical numbers for dancing, with little "Charleston" touches and a goodly collection of the syncopated clichés of the time. The personnel, I venture to guess, consists of Hardwick on alto, Prince Robinson on clarinet and tenor (he plays what for the time was a fair solo on the second side), Charlie Irvis on trombone, Ellington (piano) and Fred Guy (banjo). The trumpet and tuba are less individual and therefore harder to identify.
[4] Barry Ulanov, *Duke Ellington,* pp. 15–17.

outfits undoubtedly played more rags and what was then beginning to be called jazz than waltzes and tangos.

Later in 1922, when Duke and his Washington friends, Otto Hardwick and Sonny Greer, came to New York, it was to play for Wilbur Sweatman, a leader who fronted a large orchestra that played production-type theater dates and acts, although some of the music was categorizable as jazz. And in 1924 Ellington made the first of several financially unsuccessful forays into the world of musical shows, when he wrote the music for an ill-fated show called *Chocolate Kiddies of 1924.*[5] In between, of course, the Washingtonians, as Duke's group called itself, played at jam sessions, house hops, rent parties and an assortment of odd jobs, enough to develop a small repertoire of their own.

Even at its most indigenous, the jazz music that was developing in New York and the whole Northeast was something quite apart from what the more blues-oriented Louisiana (and other Southern) musicians were playing. A functional music, geared specifically to social dancing and theater shows, the Northeastern jazz music, whose inspirational centrum seems to have been Baltimore (with Washington not far behind), revolved primarily around ragtime. Ragtime and the fox trot were the rage of the country, and bands, large or small, tried to embody in orchestral versions at least the spirit, if not actually the style, of the leading ragtime pianists. As late as 1927, when Ellington was still trying to forge an individual style, there exist examples (*Washington Wobble,* for instance) which are fairly literal transcriptions for orchestra of Duke's piano playing. In this they differ drastically from the work of Jelly Roll Morton, for example, whose orchestrations are not mere transpositions of a given set of notes from one instrument to several others, but are true orchestrations, reworked to fit the requirements of orchestral instruments. In Ellington's case, however, this purely transcriptive approach had far-reaching consequences in relation to voicing, about which I shall have more to say later.

In any case, by 1923 Duke's little band had made enough of a reputation to be offered a steady engagement at the Hollywood Club, Forty-ninth and Broadway, soon to be renamed the Kentucky Club. And it was about two and a half years later that Ellington's

---

[5] Although this show never got to Broadway, it enjoyed an extremely successful two-year run in Berlin, played by the Sam Wooding orchestra.

Washingtonians, as they were still known then, made a number of recordings [6] which in toto are surely of slight musical significance, but historically quite important.

The earliest of these seem to have been two sides for Gennett. Primarily a "race record" company, Gennett wanted blues, and got *You've Got Those "Wanna Go Back Again" Blues* and *If You Can't Hold the Man You Love,* which strictly speaking, weren't blues at all but fairly catchy blues-ish tunes. The band consisted at the time of Bubber Miley (trumpet), Otto Hardwick (alto and baritone sax), Charlie Irvis (trombone), Sonny Greer (drums), Fred Guy (banjo), Bass Edwards (tuba) and Duke on piano. For the record date Duke enlarged the band to twelve men, adding Jimmy Harrison on second trombone and vocal; Don Redman, George Thomas and Prince Robinson (reeds); Leroy Rutledge and Harry Cooper (trumpets), the latter substituting for Miley. Harrison was just starting his brilliant, short-lived career, while Cooper had played briefly with the Bennie Moten orchestra in Kansas City. Redman, of course, was beginning to exert considerable influence as an arranger. And yet, though studded with these budding names, the two sides are no more than partial attempts at imitating the King Oliver Creole Jazz Band, with which Gennet had had great success a few years earlier and whose playing had been setting styles ever since. *If You Can't Hold the Man You Love,* for example, has a trumpet duet (Ex. 1) in the manner

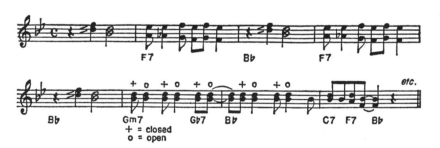

Example 1

of Oliver and Armstrong, although it lacks their stylistic grace and precision. It also has a similar full-band collective-ensemble sound on the out-chorus—but again, with almost none of the unanimity and continuity of the Creole Band, and with rather less of a beat.

[6] On the aforementioned Riverside LP.

If one searches for embryonic Ellingtonian elements, the pickings are very lean indeed, but there is at times the characteristic separation of the reeds and brass which marks the entire early Ellington period. There is also, in *Wanna Go Back Again,* the first of the nostalgic train-whistle imitations [7] which were to creep into Ellington's work from time to time; and there is, in *If You Can't,* a characteristic harmonic progression which—although in this case neither by Ellington nor altogether new—he was to use continuously in ensuing years (Ex. 2). *Wanna* also features Hardwick on baritone

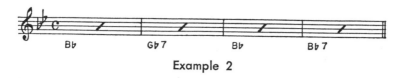

Example 2

and some rather good-natured Irvis trombone, with only a touch of growl (on one note). But on the whole, these initial sides sound more like some of the white bands of the period than the other great Negro bands, such as those of Jelly Roll Morton and King Oliver.

Animal Crackers and *Li'l Farina,* recorded two months later, with Miley back and only Charlie Johnson (trumpet) and Prince Robinson (tenor and clarinet) added to the original personnel, already have a shade more distinction, although the tunes themselves are rather undistinguished but typical music-hall material. While on the one hand these records prove (as many others do), that Duke's piano was at the time a very sloppy, helter-skelter sort of party piano, and that he and certain other members of the band had a tendency to rush tempos, the records also reveal much clearer (possibly better-prepared) ensemble work and, most important of all, a first-rate Miley solo.

Much has been written about Miley's plunger and growl technique. This is understandable, but it has tended to obscure the fact that Miley's solos are often great from the point of view of the *actual notes* played. His solo on *Animal Crackers* is a good example of what I mean. Notice the daring intervals of his opening two measures, and later on in the twenty-fifth bar of his solo the D flat

[7] By 1926 this was a well-established tradition among the orchestras that played the so-called "symphonic jazz." Entire train rides were depicted musically, evidently with considerable realism. Ellington's own efforts in this genre, of course, culminated in the virtuosic 1934 recording of *Daybreak Express.*

(flatted fifth!) and B flat (minor third against the major third B natural in the accompaniment) (Ex. 3a and 3b). Miley uses the growl or plunger with great restraint in this solo. It is unfortunate that he pushes the tempo too hard, but it does give that part of the

Example 3a

Example 3b

performance a kind of headlong, devil-may-care feeling, which, it seems to me, is less annoying than the more characterless remainder of the record.[8] *Animal Crackers,* the less steady of the two records rhythmically—by coincidence both pieces are in the same tempo—fluctuates between dragging (in ensemble passages) and rushing (in solos). It is important to note this because rhythmic unanimity and collective swing were not a strong point of the Ellington organization [9] until Jimmy Blanton joined the band in 1939.

The next two recorded sides present us for the first time (except for *Li'l Farina*) with Ellington the composer; both tunes are his. *Rainy Nights* has that already-mentioned chord progression in the first three measures (see Ex. 2). It also contains a full chorus each

[8] The A natural in bar two of Miley's solo could have been accidental. It is possible that Miley tried for the sixth of the chord (G) and overshot the mark, since on a trumpet the fingerings for G also give you an A. The history of jazz improvisation on brass instruments is full of such chance moments, often with very fortunate results.

[9] One of the most solid players rhythmically in the early Ellington days was Bass Edwards, the tuba player (1926), who had not only a remarkably expressive tone, but a strong pungent beat. Unfortunately he is heard to good advantage only on four or five sides, some of which, like *Immigration Blues* and *The Creeper,* are very hard to obtain.

by Irvis and Miley, both of which are paraphrase improvisations.[10] Irvis' solo is expansive, big-toned, basically simple and at times quite tender. Behind both solos the rhythm section plays chords on the second and fourth beat of each bar, leaving the first and third empty, which gives the whole section a slightly halting, suspended feeling. (Since the playing of the band in those years was more the result of collective thinking than of anything written down, it would be rash simply to ascribe the idea solely to Ellington.) The record ends on a ninth chord, a device that had become "hip" in the middle 1920's, after seventh-chord endings had begun to pale with much overuse.

Choo-Choo, taken as a whole, is the best of these six earliest sides. It is an Ellington tune with a lovely set of chords on which Miley, again sticking close to the melody, fashions a disarmingly simple "paraphrase" solo with little touches here and there of playfulness and nostalgia, and a very discreet use of the plunger and growl (Ex. 4). *Choo-Choo,* as might be expected, ends with the inevitable train whistle, manipulated by Greer.

Summing up these first recordings, we find rather ordinary material, a modicum of organization, one lovely tune and two fine Miley solos. Although the Ellington historian is apt to look with a kindly eye on these early efforts and find little glimpses of future developments, there is no gainsaying the fact that they cannot stand up in comparison to such contemporary masterpieces of both orchestration and formal structure as Jelly Roll Morton's *Black Bottom Stomp* or King Oliver's *Froggie Moore.*

Of course Ellington was only twenty-seven, while both Morton and Oliver were just turning forty and in their prime. This accounts, certainly, for part of the difference in quality. But there were also fundamental differences in musical backgrounds, as I've already implied. Some of the older musicians, who were maturing in the early 1920's, verify the impression that the Negro music of the South (from Texas to the Carolinas) was slow in reaching New York, and generally reached it indirectly, via Chicago and St. Louis. Furthermore, there seems to have been a greater effort on the part of Northeastern Negroes to assimilate with the whites, especially in the field of music.

[10] I am using this term in the sense that André Hodeir has applied to it, namely a type of improvisation based primarily on embellishment or ornamentation of the original melodic line.

Example 4. The Diagonal Lines Through the Stems of Some Notes Indicate
the Use of the Growl

This accounted for the fact, for example, that in the early 1920's there were several large orchestras, like Sweatman's and Sam Wooding's, that played what was then called "symphonic jazz." In an interesting process of cross-fertilization, these orchestras at first tried to emulate the big white organizations (Whiteman, Hickman, etc.); while, in turn, by the middle and late 1920's the big white orchestras reciprocated by trying to capture the more Negroid strain which began to infiltrate the eastern bands with the spread of the New Orleans style (notably through Oliver and Armstrong). Moreover, many colored bands of the time had two kinds of music in their repertoire, one for Harlem (uptown) and another for Broadway (downtown). If a rough generalization can be made, one can say that the New

York bands, small and large, were pretty showy, "dicty" outfits that catered primarily to white audiences and were slow in shaking off the ragtime milieu and adopting the New Orleans style (which, paradoxically, was already in its decline, as shown elsewhere in this book by Hsio Wen Shih).

Ellington was part of this Northeastern tradition, as were the others in his band at that time. It was not until Miley had heard Oliver in Chicago that he began to feature the growl and plunger. Both Irvis and Nanton (who was to replace Irvis in late 1926) learned these same techniques from Miley and a now-forgotten St. Louis trombonist, Jonas Walker, who was probably the first (though not necessarily the best) to apply the New Orleans "freak" sounds to the trombone.

As discussion of succeeding records will show, it was the influence of Miley as the leading soloist of the band [11] and as author (or co-author) [12] of many of the Ellington numbers of 1927 to 1929, as well as the influence of the "jungle style" as practiced by Miley and Nanton, that actually brought to full realization the early "Ellington effect." [13] This quality has too often been credited entirely to Duke. As leader, of course, he had the opportunity to promote or discourage these stylistic developments. It is a mark of his talent and vision as leader that he let his *musicians* lead the way, until years later, when he had learned to use his remarkable aggregation of sounds on a more purely compositional level. The evidence of the recordings and corroboration by contemporary musicians definitely indicate that Ellington was very dependent upon

[11] In this connection Ellington's own statement is very telling. "Bubber used to growl all night long, playing gutbucket on his horn. That was when we decided to forget all about the sweet music." (*Hear Me Talkin' to Ya*, Shapiro-Hentoff; p. 231.)

[12] The actual extent of Miley's authorship is still a matter for further research; but there seems to be little doubt that the works that bear his name along with Ellington's derive in basic content predominantly from Miley.

[13] In the one-year period, November 1926–December 1927, out of a total of seventeen pieces recorded, only four were written by song writers outside the band, and of the remaining thirteen five were authored by Miley, including the three most important ones of the period. (Six others were by Ellington and two by Hardwick. It may also be that some of the six by Ellington should be attributed to others in the band, because it was a common practice—and still is today—that titular heads of the organization often took full credit for a particular piece.) The "Ellington effect," incidentally, is a very accurate term coined by Billy Strayhorn.

his players, and that *they* knew it. But the fierce pride and communal attitude within each orchestra—an attitude sorely missing in present-day groups—took precedence over individual feelings and jealousies. The over-all collective spirit was based on the premise that what was good for the band as a whole was good for the individual.

The Influence of Miley

On the recordings of late 1926 and early 1927 we hear the fruits of this collective spirit, especially in pieces like *East St. Louis Toodle-Oo, Black and Tan Fantasy* and *Creole Love Call*. In all three Miley was involved to a considerable extent as co-author, and these records bear the stamp of his unique talent more than that of any other member of the band, including Ellington.

As I've already indicated, Miley's importance cannot be fully appreciated solely in terms of his growl and plunger technique. His melodic gift was equally great. One should not even separate the two, because they are inextricably one in concept. As with any great performer or composer, pitch and color derive *simultaneously* from the same initial inspiration. If I separate the two elements in this case, it is only to re-establish the pre-eminence of Miley's melodic gifts. To my knowledge, only Roger Pryor Dodge [14] has tried to show that Miley's importance goes beyond the fashioning of extravagant, bizarre muted effects. His contribution to jazz in the realm of pure classic melody has been unfortunately neglected.

East St. Louis Toodle-Oo is a fine example of his great gifts. The melodic line is so disarmingly simple that, except for the use of the mute and growl, it would sound like pure folk song; and it may well be, as Dodge points out, that this thematic material was "common musical knowledge" at the time. It is the way in which this melody is accompanied, however, that for its time adds a striking note to this piece. Underneath the trumpet solo, Ellington (I presume) arranged a moaning, sustained passage for the saxophones and tuba, that provides—whether it is pure jazz or not (see Dodge) —both framework and contrast to Miley's line (Ex. 5).

Ellington made many recordings of *East St. Louis Toodle-Oo* for various record companies, and when compared, these records tell us several interesting facts about the Ellington approach, in as

---

[14] *Jazz Monthly* (Volume 4, No. 3), May, 1958; p. 2.

Example 5

much as they span a period of thirteen months. The Vocalion and Brunswick versions, made four months apart, are practically identical in quality and format. A slightly livelier tempo and the rich tone of Bass Edwards on the earlier recording are the only differences from the better-known Brunswick performance.[15] The Brunswick and Columbia versions were recorded eight days apart, and although not identical, are still very similar in form and musical content. The latter is in general a bit more subdued, mainly because of differences in studio and recording equipment. The tempo is slightly faster on the Brunswick master, and Braud's tuba has less punch than Edwards', on the Columbia version. The solos are virtually the same, so much so that there is even a great similarity between Hardwick's and Jackson's clarinet solos (on Brunswick and Columbia respectively). Nanton's slightly stiff but good-natured solo is, except for minor technicalities, also the same, which indicates that once the "improvisations" were set, they remained unchanged for a certain period.

The later Victor version, however, shows some major revisions. The form has changed (Ex. 6), and so have the solos:

[15] At the time Vocalion was a subsidiary of Columbia; and since Columbia re-recorded the Ellington band in *East St. Louis* four months later, I suppose the parent company intended the new version to supersede the earlier one; this would explain why the two Vocalion sides (the first recording of *Birmingham Breakdown* is on the B side) were never reissued. The Vocalion *East St. Louis* version is therefore practically unobtainable.

Example 6

	Intro	A	B	A^1	B^1	B^2	A
Vocalion		32	18	16	18	8 + 10	8
& Brunswick		(Miley)	(Nanton)	(Clar.)	(Brass)	(Reeds-full	(Miley)
& Columbia						ensemble)	

	Intro	A	B	B^1	A^1	B^2	A
Victor		32	18	18	16	18	8
		(Miley)	(Carney)	(Nanton)	(Clar.)	(Brass)	(Miley)

(The small numbers qualifying the letters indicate variations of the material. The other numbers indicate the number of bars.)

Most important of all, the weakest part of the earlier versions, namely the trite polka-like phrase in the reeds, arranged by Ellington (the first part of B^2), has been eliminated. This was done by converting the arranged ensemble of B^2 into a Carney baritone improvisation, inserted between Miley's theme and Nanton's trombone solo to contrast a reed instrument with the two brass. The clarinet solo, which was in the high register in the earlier versions, has become a growly low-register solo. Unfortunately, though the format is improved, the performance on Victor (except for Miley's) is poorer. The tempo is draggy and slower, the intonation and balance are quite miserable, and Braud's bowed bass is cumbersome and too lugubrious for the occasion. Even Carney, still a bit green (he *was* only seventeen at that time), is excessively reedy in tone, and his loping, on-the-beat rhythm is a little dated. Only Miley survives the changes rather well. He *has* taken some of the humor out of the bridge of his theme (by slurring one phrase formerly tongued), but his final eight bars have become a little more aggressive and dirtier in the use of the growl.

One final point about the form of *East St. Louis Toodle-Oo.* Whereas most bands of the period ended each number with full ensemble (sometimes collectively improvised), Ellington—or Miley —chose to end quietly with a short reprise of the theme, a pattern Ellington was to develop thoroughly in the next decade. This recapitulation really saves *East St. Louis* from complete deterioration after the tawdry ensemble passages. And it seems to me that the importance of this ending lies not so much in the fact that a felicitous choice was made, but that such a choice was *possible*. It was possible because *East St. Louis* was not a collection of thirty-two- or twelve-bar "take your turn" solos, nor was it a totally improvised ensemble piece, but in its faltering way a *composition;* it had a two-part (A and B) form and a thematic statement which made such a recapitulation both logical and pleasing.

Basically the same points could be made about the other two Miley-Ellington masterpieces of the period, *Black and Tan Fantasy* and *Creole Love Call.* The former gives further evidence of the difference in artistic levels at that time between Miley and Ellington. The piece consists of Miley's twelve-bar theme based on the classic blues progression,[16] three choruses on the same (two by Miley, one by Nanton), an arranged ensemble passage, a twelve-bar Ellington piano solo, and finally a recapitulation with the famous tagged-on Chopin *Funeral March* ending. Of these segments only two can be attributed to Ellington, and they are not only the weakest by far, but are quite out of character with the rest of the record. Whereas Miley's theme, his solos—and to a lesser degree Nanton's—again reflect an unadorned pure classicism, Ellington's two contributions derive from the world of slick trying-to-be-modern show music.

When I first heard these records in my teens, I recall vaguely feeling a discrepancy between the Ellington and Miley sections, without at the time realizing (or analyzing) the exact nature of this discrepancy. I always found the arranged ensemble passage (with its characteristic move to G flat major, in the key of B flat the lowered sixth step) slightly cheap and the piano solo boring.[17]

Fortunately in *Creole Love Call*—famous for being Adelaide Hall's first attempt at an instrumentalized, wordless vocal—Ellington's role was limited strictly to orchestrating. The melancholy simplicity (again, blues chords) is unadulterated, though the ensemble parts cannot compare with Miley's or Rudy Jackson's radiantly singing New Orleans-styled solos.

A comparison of the three 1927 recordings of *Black and Tan Fantasy* again shows that over a seven-month span the "improvised" solos changed very little. Even when Jabbo Smith substitutes for

---

[16] As Roger Pryor Dodge explains, the melody of *Black and Tan Fantasy* is a transmutation of part of a sacred song by Stephen Adams which Bubber's sister used to sing.

[17] This is all the more annoying when one realizes that Duke's piano solo is in fact also based on the blues chords, but comes out in his typical stereotyped party-ish stride style.

Miley on the Okeh version, the over-all shape of the trumpet part does not change drastically, though in terms of expression Jabbo's richer sound and looser way of playing make this performance even more of a fantasy.[18] Miley's solo on the Victor version is, of course, one of his most striking recorded performances. It makes brilliant use of the plunger mute and the growl; but it is, to our ears, thirty-two years later, especially startling in its abundant use of the blue notes, notably the flat fifth in the first bar of the second chorus (Ex. 7). It is also a highly dramatic solo, equal to anything achieved up to that time by the New Orleans trumpet men. And perhaps none of them ever achieved the extraordinary contrast produced by the intense stillness of the four-bar-long high B-flat, suddenly erupting, as if unable to contain itself any longer, into a magnificently structured melodic creation.

Miley's contribution as composer and player in *Black and Tan Fantasy, East St. Louis Toodle-Oo* and *Creole Love Call* would suffice to place him among the all-time jazz greats. His influence on the emergence of the "Ellington effect," however, was not limited to these particular pieces. He had a hand in the composing of *Blue Bubbles* and *The Blues I Love To Sing* (both 1927); *Black Beauty* (1928); and, in his last year with Duke (1929), *Doin' the Voom Voom* and *Goin' to Town*. Miley also left an indelible stamp on the band's style with great solos on some of the above, as well as on *Jubilee Stomp, Yellow Dog Blues,*[19] *Red Hot Band, the Mooche, Rent Party Blues,* and the earlier *Immigration Blues* and *New Orleans Lowdown*.[20] Miley also played hundreds of nightly improvisations at the Cotton Club, forging (with Nanton) the "jungle style" that was the first really distinguishing trademark of the Ellington band.

If Miley was the prime musical inspiration of the early band, Tricky Sam Nanton was its most unique voice. Like Miley, he was a master in the use of the growl, the plunger and wah-wah mutes, and his style had a similar classic simplicity. But where Miley tended

[18] In a still later (1930) recording of *Black and Tan Fantasy,* Cootie Williams also adheres to the original Miley choruses.

[19] Miley's solo is based on the verse, rather unusual in those days.

[20] *Immigration Blues,* recorded December, 1926, contains one of Miley's very greatest solos. It is unfortunately a very rare collector's item. Miley's chorus is highly imaginative in its simultaneous use of growl and plunger, and is played with a penetrating, nasty tone that almost creates the illusion of speech. *New Orleans Lowdown* is another good Miley record, containing, in fact, two full choruses.

Example 7

Blue Notes: a = minor third

b = flat fifth

c = minor seventh

d = minor ninth

e is a bent tone which goes from a flat octave through the minor seventh to the sixth degree, anticipating the return to B♭.

to be dapper and smooth, Nanton had a rough-hewn quality in his playing which actually encompassed a wider range of expression. Whether plaintive or humorous, his wah-wah muting often took on a distinctly human quality. His open-horn work also extended from the dark and sober to the jaunty or bucolic. But whatever he was expressing, his distinctive vibrato and big tone gave his playing a kind of bursting-at-the-seams intensity and inner beauty that made every Nanton solo a haunting experience. Melodically or harmonically (it comes to the same thing) Nanton was not as advanced as Miley. But this did not prevent him from creating, over a period of twenty years with Ellington, an endless number of beautiful solos, many of them marked by completely original melodic turns (Ex. 8), all the more unforgettable because of their simplicity. As a matter of fact, Nanton's solo work, in its totality, is unique and perplexing. Here is a player whose solos rarely go much beyond a range of one

Example 8a. Jubilee Stomp

Example 8b. Yellow Dog Blues

Example 8c. The Blues I Love to Sing

octave; who has some real limitations instrumentally (compared, for instance, to a virtuoso like Jimmy Harrison); and who, in a sense, plays the same basic idea over and over again—but who, by some magic alchemy, manages to make each solo a new and wondrous experience.

In the period with which we are dealing at the moment (1926–1927), the reedmen did not exert as much influence on the "Ellington effect" as the two brassmen I've discussed. Otto Hardwick, Duke's right-hand man, although a distinctive stylist himself, with an unusual tone and a lithe staccato style, was to influence the Ellington sound not so much directly as *indirectly,* through his influence on Hodges and Carney, which was to be felt a few years later. Rudy Jackson, a fine player in the New Orleans Bechet-influenced tradition, evidently did not find the Ellington approach to his liking. The malleability and growth which Bigard, Jackson's successor in early 1928, had was not in Jackson's make-up, and he left to play with Noble Sissle and other bands.

But this imbalance between reeds and brass was soon to undergo changes. As Duke's band made a success of its historic Cotton Club engagement, it began to expand and attract new players, such as Bigard and Hodges. Soon Whetsol returned (after a leave of absence since 1924), replacing Metcalfe; and in late 1928 the brass were enlarged to four with the addition of Freddy Jenkins. From now on each player was to be chosen by Ellington for some distinctive or unique quality; and it was in 1927 and 1928—his imagination kindled by Miley and Nanton, and encouraged by the band's success—that Ellington began to have visions of future possibilities in composition and tonal color. From now on *his* ideas were to become, in increasing measure, the dominant factor in the development of the orchestra's output.

Ellington's Own Blossoming Sense of Color and Harmony

As important as the contributions of Miley and the others were, Ellington's influence was, of course, far from negligible. We have seen how, in some cases, it affected certain pieces negatively. But in the early years Ellington also managed occasionally to contribute wonderful little touches, which foreshadowed similar moments in later records (in some cases as much as a dozen years later!) or prophesied whole future developments.

Since the early Ellington records are often passed over in favor of the masterpieces of 1939 to 1942, it might be interesting to point out some of these early signposts of things to come. In *Birmingham Breakdown,* an Ellington composition, he uses for the first time phrases not based on either the thirty-two-bar song form or the various blues forms. The main theme, a jaunty twenty-bar phrase, consists simply of a succession of similar two- and four-bar segments. I think this odd assortment of measures came about because the theme really has no melody to speak of. It is simply a rhythmicized chromatic chord progression. As fetching as it is, especially in its initial exposition, with Ellington's sprightly piano obbligato, it is rather static thematically and wears thin after several repetitions. Ellington wisely switched to the twelve-bar blues for the last two (collectively improvised) choruses. In its simple way, *Birmingham Breakdown* broke the ice for the five-bar phrases of *Creole Rhapsody* or the ten- and fourteen-bar lines of *Reminiscin' in Tempo.* These in turn, of course, led eventually to the larger asymmetrical formations of *Black, Brown and Beige* and other extended works.

As was the case with *East St. Louis Toodle-Oo,* the Vocalion and Brunswick versions of *Birmingham Breakdown* are structurally identical. However, except for a badly muffed ending, the earlier performance (Vocalion) is superior. On the whole, the ensembles are better, and Bass Edwards plays a more interesting (and more audible) bass line than Braud. But what really makes the Vocalion recording unique is something that, to my knowledge, never occurs again in an Ellington record (in the Brunswick version it is already eliminated)—*i.e.,* a dual improvisation, in this case by two trumpets, Miley and Metcalfe. Of course, even the New Orleans or Oliver-influenced collective improvisation of the final choruses (on both discs) was already a rarity by 1926 and 1927, giving way to the arranged ensemble. Although one may bemoan the demise of collective improvisation, with its unpredictable excitement, it is obvious that Ellington, had he retained this course, would never have attained his later creative heights.

Immigration Blues contains, aside from the already mentioned Miley solo, an interesting organ-like opening section which at moments resembles *Dear Old Southland,* a later Ellington recording based on the spiritual, *Deep River*. Very likely *Immigration Blues* was based on similar gospel material. (The same material was also used in the middle section of the *Blues I Love to Sing*.) The performance features a touching Nanton solo and some fervently singing tuba by Edwards. The reverse side, *The Creeper*, is a spirited piece based in part on *Tiger Rag*. In fact, the four-bar break in the brass (incidentally, borrowed from King Oliver's *Snake Rag*) that we know from the Ellington record of *Tiger Rag* makes an early, rather frantic appearance on *The Creeper*. This side again features good Nanton and typical Hardwick, and in general is relatively well-organized for the time.

In *Hop Head*, an Ellington-Hardwick collaboration, one can hear in embryonic form the arranged brass-ensemble chorus which, with the gradual enlargement of the brass section, became another of the Ellington trademarks. In *The Blues I Love To Sing*, for the first time with Ellington we hear Wellman Braud abandon the usual two-beat bass line to double up in four beats to the bar.[21] (And once heard, who can forget Nanton's haunting eight-bar phrase, fluff and all, or for that matter this record's perfect evocation of the aura of the 1920's?)

On the final choruses of both *Blue Bubbles* and *Red Hot Band*, Ellington again uses the driving brass ensemble in a repeated, rifflike, wailing phrase that makes effective use of the blue minor third. On the orchestral version of *Black Beauty*, one of Ellington's most beautiful compositions,[22] he plays what could be considered his first good piano solo. For once, his playing is fairly clean and unhurried. The disarming charm of the melody, embroidered in a way reminiscent of Willie "The Lion" Smith, contrasts well with Braud's driving double-time slap-bass interpolations.

Jubilee Stomp (the Victor version, recorded on March 26, 1928, after Bigard and Whetsol had joined the band) is one of the few *great* early Ellington records. Except for Duke's frantic piano, it has a controlled, driving beat, rare in early Ellingtonia, and contains not

---

[21] In *Washington Wobble* Braud goes one step further and creates a "walking" bass line, the discovery of which is often loosely credited to Walter Page, despite the fact that Page admits his great indebtedness to Braud. (See *The Jazz Review*, "About My Life In Music" by Walter Page, p. 12, Vol. 1, Nov. 1958.)

[22] In his biography of Ellington, Ulanov asserts that Miley was responsible for the melody.

only some striking solos (especially Miley's puckish sixteen bars), but some greatly improved ensemble work. It also has an early, albeit very short, instance of unison saxophone writing, a rarity in those days. Above all the performance *builds* through these solos until Whetsol's sure lead-trumpeting takes the band through the final chorus with a surging momentum, capped in the final eight measures by Bigard's New Orleans-styled, high-riding obbligato.

In the introductions of *Got Everything But You* and Spencer Williams' *Tishomingo Blues,* Ellington experiments with "modern" harmonies. Through the highly popular piano playing of Zez Confrey, Rube Bloom and others, it had become very "hip" to use chromatically parallel ninth cords (Ex. 9) in introductions and bridges.[23]

Example 9. Tishomingo Blues (Introduction)

Both pieces start with these stereotypes. But in the fifth bar of *Tishomingo Blues* we hear for the first time something that, it seems to me, is one of the striking characteristics of Ellington's voice leading. In the C-ninth chord (Ex. 10), the baritone plays, not—as might

Baritone

Example 10

be expected—the root of the chord, but the B-flat directly below. This may seem a minor point to some, but it is, in fact, to this day

[23] To this day Tin Pan Alley sheet-music "piano solos" are filled with these dated clichés.

one of the two consistent characteristics differentiating Ellington's saxophone section from all others (the second being its distinctive tonal color). Ellington ingeniously avoids duplication and the wasting of Carney's very personal tone quality by keeping him away from the bass line and giving him important notes within the chord that specifically determine the quality of that chord. It is this seemingly minute detail of voicing which adds that unusual, rich, slightly dark and at times melancholy flavor to Ellington's saxophone writing.

Another remarkable moment occurs during Miley's muted solo in *Tishomingo Blues.* In an old tried-and-true pattern that was usually played as in Example 11a, Ellington changes the last chord (Ex. 11b). Miley, building an idea based on gradually enlarged intervallic skips, muffs the first two, and in stretching for a higher note than the G in bar three, comes up (perhaps accidentally) with a high B (see Ex. 11c and footnote 8). Thus Ellington's altered chord and Miley's luck combine to turn what would otherwise have been a routine break into a very special moment.

The new voice on this side and its coupling, *Yellow Dog Blues,* is Johnny Hodges', once more enriching Ellington's palette. The ragged brass work [24] points up by contrast the unusually clean and solid playing of the sax section, now dominated by Hodges' rich

Example 11a

Example 11b

[24] Nanton obviously had trouble maintaining the beat while turning from the microphone to blend with Whetsol and Miley.

Example 11c

N.B. As indicated in the text, Miley muffs the notes in the first two bars of 11c. For the sake of accuracy, I have notated the notes he actually played, whatever else his intentions may have been.

tone. *Yellow Dog Blues* has Hodges on soprano sax, which gives Ellington another chance to write (as in *Creole Love Call* and countless others) a very high reed trio, with Bigard and Carney on clarinets. Aside from the already-mentioned Miley and Nanton solos, the performance, a very good one from this period, contains another minute touch which was to become in later years one of the salient features of Duke's piano playing. In the twelfth bar of Miley's solo, Ellington superimposes over the three sustained clarinets a short figure

Example 12

which momentarily clashes with them in a very subtle way (Ex. 12). Again, this is the original predecessor of a long line of such harmonic clashes, most notably those in *Ko-Ko* (see Ex. 13).

Obviously an examination on this level of over thirteen hundred Ellington recordings could fill several volumes. A single chapter can only graze the surface. But I have gone into some detail regarding these early records because it is in them that the explanation for the entire musical development of Ellington and his orchestra is to be found. What emerges from even as limited and selective an analysis as the above are two important points. First, Ellington

Example 13

began a process of writing (or dictating to the band in head arrangements) [25] pieces which, in retrospect, turn out to be in five categories: 1) numbers for dancing; 2) jungle-style and/or production
numbers for the Cotton Club; 3) the "blue" or "mood" pieces; 4)
pop tunes (at first written by others, later in increasing measure his
own); and 5) pieces which, although written for specific occasions,
turned out to be simply abstract "musical compositions." [26] And
within categories Ellington was to work on specific musical ideas—
a certain progression, a certain voicing or a certain scoring—repeating them in successive arrangements in a process of trial and error,
until the problem had been solved and its best solution found. From
there he would move on to tackle the next idea or problem.

[25] A fairly informative account of this process is contained in *The Hot
Bach* by Richard Boyer, reprinted in *Duke Ellington,* edited by Peter Gammond, pp. 36–37.
[26] It should go without saying that a) these categories were not always consciously developed, and b) some pieces defy exact categorization and could
belong to several groups.

The second point gives us the answer to my original question: how did Ellington, at first a musician with a decided leaning towards "show music," [27] develop into one of America's foremost composers? It was precisely due to the fortuitous circumstance of working five years at the Cotton Club. There, by writing and experimenting with all manner of descriptive production and dance numbers, Ellington's inherent talent and imagination found a fruitful outlet. A leader playing exclusively for dances (like Fletcher Henderson in the 1920's, for example) would have very little opportunity to experiment with descriptive or abstract, non-functional [28] music; whereas the need for new background music, new material for constantly changing acts at the Cotton Club, in a sense *required* Ellington to investigate composition (rather than arranging) as a medium of expression, and he found in his band more than sufficient raw material to implement this idea.

Thus, from early 1928 to 1931, the greater part of his Cotton Club tenure, Ellington's recordings reveal a multifarious experimentation and intuitive probing. Except for hints of orchestration or of harmony that he garnered from Will Vodery,[29] the chief arranger for the Ziegfeld Follies, Ellington developed his ideas quite independently *within* his genre, with almost no borrowing from outside his specific field. There are certainly no traces of any influence from classical music, except perhaps very vague ones, which, in any case, had long before infiltrated jazz and popular music. It was in these years that the personalities and sonorities of his orchestra became the instrument upon which the Duke learned to play.

The ability to play this instrument could not, and did not, come overnight. Although Ellington made some 160 recordings between mid-1928 and mid-1931, all of them interesting, very few were completely successful artistically. Only one could compare in origi-

---

[27] To this day Ellington's overriding ambition is to compose a successful jazz musical or jazz "opera."

[28] I use these latter two words in their broadest meaning, synonymous with non-descriptive or non-representational.

[29] From Vodery, Ellington got an indirect knowledge of modern orchestration and harmony as practiced by Ravel, Delius and other composers, much favored in the twenties, albeit strained through the sieve of Broadway commercialism. The rather widespread notion that Ellington was influenced directly by Ravel and Delius is untenable, since he never heard or was interested in hearing these composers until years later when his own style had long been crystallized.

nality of conception with *Black and Tan Fantasy,* and that was *Mood Indigo.* Almost all the others suffered from one or more of several ailments. Some were thematically weak, some had poor or indifferent solos, others were too hastily thrown together and badly played; still others had some fine moment, but a bad introduction or an awkward bridge. In some cases mawkish pop-tune material, used in the Cotton Club shows or foisted on Ellington by Irving Mills' business associates, proved too much for the abilities of even these remarkable players.[30] But slowly and relentlessly, through a process of continuous reappraisal, of constant polishing and refining, the Duke's musical concepts began to crystallize.

In this welter of pseudo-jungleistic dance or production numbers—the kind of thing the "tourist," expecting to be transported to the depths of the African jungle, had come to look for at the Cotton Club—certain performances stand out like signposts along the way.

In the "blue" or "mood" category, Duke in 1928 penned *Misty Mornin'* and *Awful Sad,* both leading up to the immortal *Mood Indigo* of 1930. The man who primarily imparted that special nostalgic flavor to these pieces was Duke's old Washington friend, Arthur Whetsol. His poignant style and tone quality—probably unique in jazz, then or now—were the perfect melodic vehicle for these three-minute mood vignettes. Duke loved the melancholy, almost sentimental flavor in Whetsol's playing, and in speaking of *Black and Tan Fantasy,* Ellington once remarked that Whetsol's playing of "the funeral march" used to make "great, big ole tears" run down people's faces. "That's why I liked Whetsol." [31] In the two earlier pieces Whetsol's blue-colored tone and Bigard's low-register clarinet were still used separately, but in *Mood Indigo* Ellington combines their sounds, adding the even more unique tonal color of Nanton's trombone, and thus returning to the classic New Orleans instrumentation but in a totally new concept—a sound which

[30] Ellington was not above trying to hit the white market with established "pop" successes. An early instance of this was *Soliloquy* (1927), a Rube Bloom tune which had become a big hit with Whiteman. Ellington tried to cash in on the success of the tune. Without prior knowledge, however, it is barely recognizable as an Ellington item.

[31] This writer recalls a sleepless night—after a one-night stand in Quebec—during which Ellington delivered a lengthy and movingly simple eulogy on Whetsol, who died in 1940.

the Crescent City pioneers would never have imagined in their wildest fancies. From a compositional point of view, all three pieces have one feature in common which is important for the development of the Ellington style: namely, a kind of winding chromaticism *not* to be found in the faster dance numbers or stomps. Completely instinctively and very logically, Ellington found that chromatic melodies and chromatic voice leading gave these slow pieces just the right touch of sadness and nostalgia. *Awful Sad*, recorded in October, 1928, goes furthest in this direction, in its very unusual chord changes and especially in two of its two-bar breaks [32] (Ex. 14a and 14b). The first (in the trumpet) is in a shifting whole-tone

Example 14a

Example 14b

pattern; the second (with Bigard on tenor) momentarily goes quite out of the key (B-flat major) into a slightly "atonal" area, only to modulate suddenly to D major.[33]

Misty Mornin', based on somewhat altered blues changes, once again has that characteristic move to the lowered sixth step of the scale (B flat to G flat) which we have already encountered so often; and in the fifteenth and sixteenth bars of Whetsol's solo the unique inner voicings that helped to make *Mood Indigo* so special are tried out very briefly (Ex. 15). Such voicings were unorthodox and wrong, according to the textbooks. But Ellington did not know or care about the textbooks. His own piano playing gave him the most immediately accessible answer to voice-leading problems. Examples 15

---

[32] These breaks are unfortunately rushed in tempo every time.

[33] The chromaticism of the "blue" pieces became one of the most original contributions to jazz of the maturing Ellington style, leading Duke eventually to bitonal harmonies and to such masterpieces of the genre as *Dusk, Ko-Ko, Moon Mist, Azure* and *Clothed Woman*.

Example 15a   Example 15b

and 16 have the kind of parallel motion that a pianist would use, and what was good enough for the piano seemed good enough for his orchestra! It must be remembered that Ellington was an almost completely self-taught musician. As such, contrapuntal thinking has always been foreign to him; but the parallel blocks of sound he favors so predominantly are handled with such variety and ingenuity that we, as listeners, never notice the lack of occasional contrapuntal relief. To Duke's ears, reacting intuitively, and unfettered by preconceived rules, the effect of this kind of "piano" voicing, though novel, sounded good. As I've indicated, out of such almost chance discoveries, worked out mostly in this three-year "workshop" period, Ellington forged his unique style.

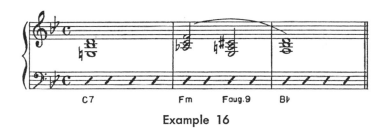

C7   Fm   Faug.9   Bb

Example 16

In the production- or show-music category, Ellington produced some two dozen numbers, ranging from such bits of dated exotica as *Arabian Lover* or its companion piece, *Japanese Dream* (pentatonic melodies, ominous "Charlie Chan" gongs and all) [34] to more original pieces, such as *Jungle Jamboree* or *Rocky Mountain Blues*. As a category, it was perhaps the least fruitful in this period (except, of course, for the outright pop tunes); but, as I have indicated, it led to experimentation with different programmatic ideas that Elling-

[34] Undaunted, the Victor labels continued to read "Hot Dance Orchestra"!

ton might otherwise never have chanced upon. It produced, among other things, a whole line of heavily stomping four-beat pieces—a genre for which Duke had a special predilection, especially after the success of the prototypical *Black and Tan Fantasy* and *The Mooche*. In *Harlem Flat Blues, Rent Party Blues* and parts of *Saratoga Swing, Mississippi, Haunted Nights, Jazz Lips, Lazy Duke,* and *Jolly Wog,* Ellington tried to recapture the success of the two earlier medium-tempo stomps. Some of these were also attempts at conscious jungle evocations—pieces like *Jungle Jamboree, Jungle Blues,* or *Jungle Nights in Harlem,* the latter one of the most patently dated pieces in the band's repertoire. It is easy to imagine how such a number complemented the pseudo-jungleistic, "primitive" murals on the walls of the Cotton Club.

But as we have noted, in almost every piece—whether bad or good—Ellington and his men tried to work out some new sound, some new musical idea. *Saratoga Swing,* for instance, was an early, successful attempt to employ a combo within the big band. Played by a septet consisting of Hodges, Bigard and Cootie Williams, plus the four rhythm, *Saratoga Swing* became the forerunner of many similar small-band recordings, notably the series made in the late 1930's under the leadership of various Ellington sidemen. Two other early septet recordings—among the finest of this period, though unfortunately not as well known as many lesser sides—were *Big House Blues* and *Rocky Mountain Blues*.

Rocky Mountain Blues is an especially good example of the inability of the Ellington musical mind to be satisfied for long with the tried and true. Basically founded on the twelve-bar blues progression, Ellington finds a very imaginative alternative for the fourth bar, which by rights should have been a B-flat seventh chord. As can be seen in Example 17, a subtle shift of two notes (the expected

Example 17

B flat and a half tone higher D to C flat and E flat respectively) results in a wondrously new sound. The three "horns" thus end up in the key of A flat minor, while Braud's double-time walking bass holds on to the basic B-flat chord, thus creating a delightful bitonal combination—this in 1930!

Primarily, the jungle pieces offered Duke a more or less legitimate excuse to experiment with "weird" chords and sounds—as, for instance, in *Jungle Blues*. Similarly, *Harlem Flat Blues* gave Nanton his first opportunity to produce a lengthy "talking" solo. He was to return to this idea hundreds of times in his career, but this early fantasy, evoking a not-quite-human language, stands out as one of his best. During this period Ellington also learned to use Nanton (mostly cup-muted) with two low-register clarinets, a very unusual sound; and when he made the practically unheard-of move of adding a second trombone in the person of valve trombonist Juan Tizol, Duke had at his disposal not only another color, but a highly chromatic instrument that could be used interchangeably with the trumpets or reeds, as the occasion demanded. An early example of Ellington's use of the chromatic-trombone line can be heard in the final eight-part ensemble of *Jazz Lips* (Ex. 18).

Example 18

On some of these sides, guitarist Teddy Bunn appeared as guest soloist. His simple, lean melodic style stood out in contrast to the now-enriched, more and more vertically conceived tonal quality of the band. In *Haunted Nights* this contrast is most apparent. In this piece, an obvious attempt to effect another *Black and Tan Fantasy,* only Bunn's guitar is able to recreate the expressive simplicity of Miley's playing.

By and large, the most successful pieces in terms of jazz came out of the category of music written for dancing. Among these, the best were a whole series of up-tempo stomps, headed by *Old Man*

Blues (especially in its first recorded version). Others, almost as good, were *Double Check Stomp, Cotton Club Stomp, Stevedore Stomp, Wall Street Wail, Duke Steps Out, Hot Feet, Ring Dem Bells* —all of them direct descendants of earlier "flag wavers" like *The Creeper, Birmingham Breakdown* and *Jubilee Stomp.* All were very similar in intent and content, and some—like *Double Check Stomp* and *Wall Street Wail*—were even based on the same chord progressions. They were mostly head arrangements, thematically rather noncommittal. But they inspired the major soloists, most notably Carney and Nanton, to create a profusion of fine improvised solos. Interestingly, time and time again in these pieces, Nanton teams up with Braud. The great trombonist seemed to thrive on the near-slap-bass punch of his colleague, and together they produced some of the hottest and most swinging moments on these sides of the late 1920's and early 1930's. Bigard, during this time, seemed to be coming gradually into his own, although he had not yet quite found the liquid quality of later years, and more often than not he relied on old New Orleans clichés that he remembered from numbers like *Tiger Rag.* Also, his time was still rather shaky during this period. Cootie Williams was developing with rapid strides, especially in the use of the growl and plunger, a heritage left him by the departure of Miley. His best solos —*Saratoga Swing, Ring Dem Bells, Echoes of the Jungle,* to name but a few—already show a considerable mastery of this difficult style, at times even glimpses of a more imaginative use of it than Miley's. Hodges was used mainly in flashy, bubbling solos, not yet having discovered the subtly wailing style that was to make him famous in later years. As lead alto he added a tremendous solidity to the reed section; and his solo work, generated by an endless flow of melodic inspiration, was never less than reliable. His playing already had an inevitability about it—not to be confused with predictability—that seemed always to guarantee the right note in the right place. Hodges' solo, for example, on *Syncopated Shuffle*—otherwise a minor record—has this quality, and his solo break at the end is far ahead of its time in its freedom and perfect timing.

The solo capacities of these players were naturally considerably constrained by most of the show material and/or arrangements. A series of pieces based on the old standard, *Tiger Rag,* was probably intended to give the musicians a chance at some uninhibited freewheeling improvisation. The most cohesive of these was the two-part

Tiger Rag itself. The early *Creeper* and *Jubilee Stomp* had been based—in part, at least—on these same time-honored chords, and now *Hot and Bothered* and *High Life* were added to the repertoire. All of them were fast, hard-driving numbers, underscored by Braud's indefatigable though occasionally erratic bass. *Tiger Rag,* of course, as a staple of the jazz repertoire, had through the years been done to death by innumerable bands. "Inspired" by the Original Dixieland Jazz Band, this poor vehicle was customarily overloaded with a wide assortment of corny or humorous instrumental effects. The Ellington band's version suddenly changed all that by presenting a staggering array of non-gimmicky, highly individual solos. Even Bigard's brilliant chromatic run—under other circumstances a fairly tawdry idea —has in this context a propulsive drive that turns it into a high point of the record.[35] The two players who seemed to feel most at home in these *Tiger Rag* pieces were Bigard, who suddenly found himself returned to a thrice-familiar mold, and Freddy "Posey" Jenkins, whose bent for the flashy, high-stepping solo happily coincided with the obviously ostentatious nature of the pieces. Jenkins' solo became a regular fixture of the *Tiger Rag* numbers. Not only did he virtually repeat it in *High Life,* but in a later version of *Hot and Bothered,* for the obscure Velvetone label, we find Cootie Williams (according to Aasland's discography, at any rate) playing the same solo. Still later it was arranged for trumpet ensemble.

It was the original *Hot and Bothered* recording, incidentally, made in October, 1928, and issued later on English Parlophone, that so excited the British conductor-composer and Ellington enthusiast, Constant Lambert. He likened it to the best in Ravel and Stravinsky, which not only seems somewhat exaggerated, but ignores several other Ellington sides that surpass *Hot and Bothered* in terms of both conception and performance. Indeed, the performance leaves something to be desired, a fact which Lambert in his enthusiasm failed to notice. Admittedly, it is emotionally rousing, again due largely to Braud's excitable bass. But the wrong entrances of Miley, vocalist Baby Cox and Braud, as well as the ragged saxophone ensemble work in the final chorus—which Lambert incidentally found so

---

[35] Hearing this record, one also tends to suspect that Juan Tizol was already a member (or perhaps just a guest that day) of the trombone section. I find it fairly hard to otherwise explain the low B-flat trombone trill (!) just before Freddy Jenkins' famous chorus.

"ingenious"—indicate that the piece was not quite ready to be recorded. Also, Bigard had troubles with his timing, and even Hodges seems less assured than usual. The point is, of course, that a flashy virtuoso piece is very little without flashy virtuoso playing.

It was Lambert, too, I believe, who first compared Ellington to Frederick Delius, which in turn led to a kind of tacitly accepted notion that Ellington had indeed been influenced by the English impressionist. Aside from my point earlier about the *indirect* influence on Duke of certain European composers (footnote 29), I cannot see how the use of lush ninth and eleventh chords or the tendency towards an "impressionist" approach constitute sufficient justification for such a claim. It smacks of over-simplification and the kind of snobbism that implies a piece of jazz music is not very good until it can be equated with some accepted European compositions.

The fact is that Ellington's harmonic language is quite original, and as different from Delius' as Debussy's *Jeux* is from Ravel's *Daphnis and Chloe*—perhaps more so. To cite just two obvious differences, Delius' harmonic writing in his best works constantly features first, second and even third inversions of chords. The somewhat suspended feeling thus engendered allows him to drift in endless chains of unresolved modulations. Obviously this is not the case with Ellington, who rarely uses such inversions and whose phrase endings are quite clearly defined by resolutions of whatever has passed before. Furthermore, I do not find Ellington to be entirely the "impressionist" the comparison to Delius implies. True, there are dreamy landscapes like *Dusk* and *Misty Mornin'*, and atmospheric abstractions like *Mood Indigo* and *Moon Mist*. But what about the hundreds of vigorous, earthy, directly *ex*pressed pieces that make up the bulk of the Ellington repertoire?

It is the link to Delius, I believe, that has also fathered the notion that Ellington is a "rhapsodist" and most at ease in the looser form of the rhapsody. This again is only partially true. Ellington may be a rhapsodist in terms of musical expression (even this is debatable); but he certainly is no rhapsodist when it comes to form. In this respect he is a strict *classicist,* perhaps only surpassed by Jelly Roll Morton. And certainly Ellington's forms are more concise and symmetrical than those of any number of nineteenth-century romantic composers. In fact, when compared to the great formal achievements of a Beethoven—or even a Chopin—Ellington's form, in the majority of cases, seems almost hackneyed and naïve in its restraint. This was, of course, already inherent in the principle of linking twelve- or thirty-two-bar small forms into one single larger form. The fact that Ellington was able to infuse these stereotyped forms with such life and—by the late 1930's—such seamless continuity, is one of the measures of his genius as a composer. It is precisely because he is *not* a rhapsodist in the formal sense that Ellington has been largely unsuccessful in the big, extended forms. He is basically a miniaturist and lacks the control and discipline a good "rhapsodist" has—and *must* have—in order to contain his inspiration within a logical form. But the problem of Ellington's large works of the past fifteen years really requires a degree of discussion quite beyond the intended scope of this chapter.

Two oddities from this prolonged "workshop" period are *Oklahoma Stomp* and *Goin' Nuts*. In them the rhythm instruments outnumber the "horns" (Hodges, Cootie, Jenkins and Nanton). Teddy Bunn on guitar, and a washboard player by the name of Bruce Johnson, were added to the normal four-man rhythm section. *Oklahoma Stomp* is very aptly named, because, with its modern-sounding hard drive, emphasizing the second and fourth beats, it sounds very much like the kind of strong, rocking rhythmic music characteristic of the Southwest. In this respect the record is unique in the Ellington discography. The unusual rhythmic feeling is especially noticeable during Bunn's solos. Here the group sounds like some imaginary, superior multi-guitar hillbilly band from the Ozarks or some such place. Unfortunately the side also contains what must be Ellington's worst and most unintelligible piano solo on records.

Hot Feet is another fine record from 1929. After a very "jazzy" syncopated opening, designed to get the dancers on the floor, Cootie scat-vocals *à la* Armstrong, answered by Freddy Jenkins in a sort of chase chorus. A two-bar bridge, used later in *Reminiscin' in Tempo,* leads to a Hodges solo, followed by a chorus of some of the above-mentioned blistering Nanton-Braud teamwork. Brass riffs, embellished by some superb three-part sax ensembles, lead to one of the most startling endings Ellington ever created: a sudden brass pyramid followed by a major seventh chord on the already often-encountered lowered sixth step of the scale (Ex. 19).

Ring Dem Bells is a somewhat similar piece, slightly slower and again with a responsorial chorus, this time Cootie's vocal answering

Example 19

Hodges. Cootie then solos, with some wonderful "rolling" sax figures as accompaniment.[36] Fluent yet bursting with a kind of controlled excitement, these figures are the perfect contrast and complement to Cootie's jabbing solo. As in *Hot Feet,* the final chorus features five-part brass chords, through which one can hear the running sax ensembles. These brass figures are an expansion of the riff figures played earlier on the chimes (incidentally, by Charlie Barnet).

Perhaps the best record of this period (1928 to mid-1931), outside of *Mood Indigo,* is *Old Man Blues,* especially in its first version (Victor), recorded on the same session as *Ring Dem Bells.* This date took place in Hollywood, where the band had gone to make a movie called *Check and Double Check* (from which came *Double Check Stomp*). Listening to the results of that session, one gets the impression that the visit to movieland had an invigorating effect on the band. Certainly *Old Man Blues* was played with a verve and excitement that many of the previous sides had lacked. Musically, the record is most important because it crystallized for Ellington, to an unprecedented degree, the effectiveness with which a composition—be it head arrangement or an actually written-out piece—could form a framework, a point of departure for the talents of his particular group of soloists.

Earlier pieces, like *Black and Tan Fantasy,* bore the stamp of one particular musician—Miley, in that case—and we have seen how Bubber's personal solo talents were to some extent at odds with the prearranged musical framework fashioned by Ellington. One senses the lack of a uniform concept. Through the dominance of one soloist, the collective equilibrium that was such an integral part of jazz was temporarily disturbed; and with this discrepancy, the

[36] As I've indicated, a musical idea such as this was subjected to repeated experimentation. First used in *Stevedore Stomp* in early 1929, it was heard again in *Duke Steps Out,* and in 1931 in *It's Glory* and *Echoes of the Jungle.*

seams of the structure began to show. But here, in *Old Man Blues,* the collective excitement and the feeling that the performance was truly the sum total of all its parts were re-established, and the perfect balance between composition and improvisation was achieved. And this achievement is, of course, above and beyond everything else, Ellington's greatest contribution to the development of jazz. As Francis Newton summarized it so brilliantly in a recent issue of the *New Statesman,*[37] Ellington "solved the unbelievably difficult problem of turning a living, shifting and improvised folk-music into *composition* without losing its spontaneity."

Example 20

Introductory vamp	A	B (march)	A^1
8	16 + 8 + 6	(4 + 8 + 8)	(16 + 8 + 8)
	(Nanton, with Bigard obbligato)	(rhythm-saxes-tpt's)	(tpt's-Nanton-tpt's)

A^2	A^3	B	break	A^4
32	(16 + 14)	6	4	(16 + 8 + 8)
(Carney, with piano obbligato)	(Hodges-Jenkins)	(saxes)	(brass)	(brass-Nanton-full ensemble with Bigard obbligato)

The form of *Old Man Blues* (see outline in Ex. 20), though hardly revolutionary, was a perfect example of its kind, representing the high point of a long line of pieces attempting to solve the relationship between form and musical content. That is to say, a way was found to preserve for the musician the freedom inherent in jazz, while the piece in its totality satisfied the demands of organized or pre-determined form. To quote again from the Francis Newton article, Ellington produced a music which was *"both created by the players and fully shaped by the composer."*

Listening to the solos on *Old Man Blues,* it becomes clear that the musicians did not feel restricted by such seemingly conflicting demands. As a matter of fact, they were probably unaware of the large form, and therefore not inhibited by it. To them it was just another chorus, which would be good, bad or indifferent. As it turned

---

[37] October 11, 1958, p. 488.

out, the solos are of a high caliber, with Bigard—relying too much on his *Tiger Rag* routines—perhaps the least inspired. Certainly Carney and Nanton are at their very best: Carney in a rare rambunctious mood and Nanton in three separate, contrasting solo spots. *Old Man Blues* is also blessed with moments of fortuitous recording balance, as, for example, in the bridge of the first chorus, where Nanton's trombone somehow blends with Bigard's low-register clarinet embellishments in such a way as to make the two instruments jell perfectly into one sound—almost as if both parts were played by one man. Ellington's excellent background piano behind Carney, and Braud's walking four-to-the-bar bass, are also worthy of mention. Harmonically, too, *Old Man Blues* has its touch of originality. In a four-bar break before the final chorus, three trumpets and one trombone play a chord (Ex. 21), repeated in syncopation, which is

Example 21

similar to the chord at the end of *Hot Feet,* and once more placed on the lowered sixth step of the scale(!).[38]

On page 255 I mentioned a fifth category, namely that of more or less pure, abstract "musical composition." It was during the period of intensive experiment under discussion that Ellington began to create, with some consistency, pieces that were not *strictly* functional—pieces that, although perhaps originally geared to some specific function (as background music for a Cotton Club tableau),

[38] This chord, a commonplace today, was still daring in jazz at the time of the recording. The other early instance of its use, to my knowledge, occurs in the final chorus of Alphonse Trent's 1930 *I Found A New Baby.* Incidentally, the advanced writing and highly skillful playing of this great Southwestern band raises the intriguing question of whether Trent's and Ellington's paths ever crossed, and whether any influencing occurred. This would seem to be a fascinating subject for research.

had a life of their own, *independent* of that functional purpose. The great 1927 masterpieces, like *Black and Tan Fantasy* and some of Morton's better creations, had already shown that jazz was capable of this. From 1928 to 1931 a number of these compositions make their appearance. They were not merely arrangements or arbitrarily thrown-together chains of choruses, but disciplined musical creations which could be judged by standards of musical appreciation and analysis established for centuries in classical music, and which by their *character* as much as by their quality distinguished themselves from the other jazz-*Gebrauchsmusik.*

As a matter of fact, often it is only the *character* of a piece which establishes it in this compositional category. For numbers like *Take It Easy, Dicty Glide, Drop Me Off in Harlem* and even *Creole Rhapsody* are at times of questionable *quality.* On the other hand, high quality and purely compositional characteristics do go hand in hand in *Old Man Blues, Rocky Mountain Blues* and the incomparable *Mood Indigo,* for instance.

At any rate, as Ellington's control over his unique medium sharpened, he was able to create more and more works that assumed an independence aside from their original impetus. And it is this quality which has made them live beyond their time. As Ellington matured, his growing concern for the compositional element led him to write the later masterpieces, *Concerto for Cootie, Ko-Ko* and *Sepia Panorama;* and, still later, the orchestral suites and stage works, *Beggar's Holiday* and *Jump for Joy.*

Having perfected form on the level of the three-minute, ten-inch record in *Old Man Blues* and *Mood Indigo,* Ellington's restless and by now fully stimulated musical mind next tackled the problem of a larger form. By January, 1931, he had created *Creole Rhapsody.* This was recorded in two versions, half a year apart. Comparison is again very revealing as regards Ellington's methods, and I find it difficult to agree with the prevailing opinion that the second (expanded) version is inferior to the first. I have already said that the piece in general represents a step forward formally. In it Ellington also experimented with, among other things, asymmetrical phrase lengths [39]

---

[39] See an article by this writer on *"The Future of Form in Jazz,"* originally printed in *The Saturday Review Of Literature,* and reprinted in *The Saturday Review Treasury,* p. 561, Simon and Schuster, 1957.

and a trombone duet (perhaps the first in jazz). But it must be stated that most of the *playing* on the original *Creole Rhapsody* is second-rate. Unlike *Old Man Blues,* the form was rather haphazardly strung together. This, plus the fact that *Creole Rhapsody* was more of an Ellington composition than a collectively created head arrangement, made the players uncomfortably rigid. And Ellington's own dated piano interludes (happily changed and cut to a minimum in the second version) disjoint the piece even more. Furthermore, the disparate compositional material of the original really was not suited to being played at the same tempo throughout. In the half year that elapsed between the two versions, Ellington must have realized this. For in the Victor performance each section is played in different tempos. This is not to say that the composition is thereby improved, but the performance of it certainly is. As a matter of fact, it is obvious that the band had, in the meantime, learned to play the piece. The ensemble work is immeasurably improved, and the tempo changes—then as well as now a rarity in jazz—come off surprisingly well. The solos, too, are better, though not yet remarkable.

Furthermore, almost the whole second side of the first version has been scrapped in the second and replaced by added material in the dreamy, lyrical vein of *Mood Indigo,* incidentally making this the first ternary-form piece by Ellington. This new section is treated in loosely variational form, and Arthur Whetsol first states it in his inimitable fashion. It then returns in an incredibly creamy blend of saxophones and muted valve trombone (Tizol), and lastly in a free-tempo version by Bigard and Duke. It is startling to realize that the three saxophones accompanying Whetsol, in terms of both tone quality and voice leading, achieve a sound that Ellington may have equalled again but never surpassed—not even in the 1940 color masterpieces, *Warm Valley, Moon Mist* and *Dusk.*

It is also true that, unfortunately, in the second version the expansion of what was already an extended form proves too much for Ellington; and despite (or more likely *because* of) some subtle "borrowing" from Gershwin's *Rhapsody in Blue,* the last minute or so does not hang together too well. Despite this error in judgment, the greater part of the Victor performance (now available on LP) must be considered an improvement, and it is certain that in his quiet, noncommittal way Ellington benefited from the experience of *Creole Rhapsody.*

The First Full Flowering of the Ellington Concept

With this innovational experiment out of the way, Ellington returned to more conventional areas. After *Creole Rhapsody,* the Ellington orchestra recorded only four other sides in 1931, in striking contrast to the fifty-odd sides per year in the preceding period. These were *Limehouse Blues, Echoes of the Jungle, It's Glory* and *The Mystery Song.* All four not only rank among the finest of recorded Ellingtonia, but represent the full fruition of the aforementioned "workshop" period, and at the same time the starting point for a long period of consolidation and refinement. In these four 1931 sides the basic sound and approach of the great Ellington of 1940–42 is no longer embryonic. His style had achieved full individuality, needing only the further maturing with which youth mellows into full maturity.

The 1931 sides under discussion also belong to the "compositional" category. Perhaps the most limited of the four is *It's Glory.* The dated dance rhythm and slap bass detract from its value as pure composition. But this is counteracted by the quality of the writing for the brass and reeds—rich eight-part blended sounds that almost make us forget that we are listening to what is basically another arranged chorus. Moreover, the record contains two inspired moments. The first occurs in the bridge of the second chorus. Ellington has scored this for Nanton in the lead part—with a subtle touch of wah-wah—accompanied by a trio of two low-register clarinets and muted valve trombone,[40] creating a "blue" sound which must have amazed musicians in 1931. It is a sound which is not only pure Ellington, but still completely fresh and fascinating twenty-eight years later. The other fine moment comes in the next chorus, where Ellington once more employs the soft "rolling" sax figures behind Cootie Williams' solo.

Ellington's compositional talent had matured so fully by 1931 that he could even transform someone else's composition—a hackneyed standard at that—into a purely Ellingtonian opus. This was

---

[40] Ellington had tried this instrumental combination previously in *Lazy Duke* and *Creole Rhapsody*—further evidence that Ellington tested his ideas many times in different contexts, until his curiosity as to their potential was completely satisfied.

the case in the second of these four sides, *Limehouse Blues.* Again
we hear sounds that could never be confused with those of any other
band of the time. The brass shine with a rich yellow, and the blue
combination we just encountered in *It's Glory* is offered once more
as contrast. Ellington wisely refrained from any obvious Orientalisms
(tinkly pentatonic patterns on the piano, which all other bands used
on this tune and which the Duke himself had succumbed to earlier
in *Japanese Dream*). Again only the dated, vertical two-beat rhythm
limits the experience of this record, but I feel this is more than
counterbalanced by the flowing horizontal lines of the ensemble passages.

   Echoes of the Jungle, credited to Cootie Williams, undoubtedly
came into being as a production number for the Cotton Club, designed
to give the customers their glimpse of darkest Africa. But as the
English writer, Charles Fox,[41] has pointed out, it is "paradoxically
an extremely sophisticated" piece of music. In its haunting originality,
aided by a superb performance, it is the least dated of these sides.
It is, indeed, as fresh and timeless today as it was in 1931. Again
we marvel at the incredibly rich blend of the brass, this time muted
and embellished by Hodges' full-toned alto. Cootie solos twice—first
open, with a sensuous urgency; then with the plunger mute, in what
is still one of his most imaginative improvisations. And once more we
hear the chromatic, rolling sax figures behind him—an instrumental
combination Ellington seemingly never tired of. The succeeding
connecting passage, featuring Bigard in low register, answered by
Fred Guy's rustling banjo blissandos, is like the ominous lull before
a storm. And in the final three measures Ellington creates a big-
band sound and harmony which predict certain passages in *Ko-Ko!*

   Without having been present at the Cotton Club in June, 1931,
it is difficult to visualize what tableau or act inspired the sheer magic
of the opening of *The Mystery Song.* A perfectly conventional piano
introduction suddenly gives way to one of the most inspired sounds
not only in Ellington, but surely in all music. It is one of those
moments, resulting from a flash of inspiration, that is so unique
that it can in no way be duplicated or imitated without remaining
pure imitation. The mixture of sustained harmonies; the distant, muted
tone color; and Guy's restless, subtly urgent banjo conjure up a
sound that must be heard to be believed. Unfortunately Ellington

---

[41] In *Duke Ellington,* edited by Peter Gammond, p. 83.

was unable to sustain this level of inspiration beyond the exposition. (This may have had functional reasons related to the particular dance routine.) At any rate, everything that follows this glorious opening is anticlimactic and routine. It is a pity that Ellington never returned to this bit of inspiration to give it the framework it deserved.

As we have seen, in basic concept as well as in many details, the five 1931 records I have discussed predict quite comprehensively the development of the succeeding ten years and its peak in the earliest 1940's. In record after record, Ellington polished and refined his technique. Through the many "blue" pieces of 1932–34, through programmatic works like *Daybreak Express;* ballads like *Sophisticated Lady;* large forms like *Reminiscin' in Tempo* and *Diminuendo and Crescendo in Blue;* solo pieces *like Echoes of Harlem* (Cootie), *Clarinet Lament* (Bigard) and *Trumpet In Spades* (Rex Stewart); Ellington purified but never changed the basic concept he had evolved by 1931. In those succeeding years the orchestra's scope was to be widened by important additions to the personnel: first the incomparable Lawrence Brown, then the singer Ivie Anderson, later Rex Stewart, and finally the two crucial additions of Ben Webster and Jimmy Blanton. The last two, especially, expanded the range and scope of the orchestra, and Ellington's unique harmonic, coloristic and formal gifts were elevated to another level by the swinging rhythmic impulse generated by these two men.[42]

From the high point attained in the early forties, the creative level of Ellington and his marvelous "instrument" almost *had* to drop. It certainly could not be surpassed. And, as fate would have it, the personal, social and musical revolutions that beset jazz during the war years took their toll on the Ellington band. The long, ascending line of development, which I have tried to trace in part, was broken off. With an entirely different "instrument" at his command, Ellington had difficulties in re-attaining his earlier creativity. Committed to a life of one-night stands—partially because it is now in his blood, and partially out of loyalty to his men—the tragedy of Ellington's life is that the American public has never accorded him and his musicians the recognition that they, as the collective creators of a distinctly

[42] It is significant, I think, that neither Webster nor Blanton were Eastern jazz musicians. Webster was long a mainstay of a dozen Southwestern and Kansas City-based bands, while Blanton was St. Louis-born and learned to play on the riverboats, notably with Fate Marable.

American form of art music, deserve. But then, jazz itself—except in its more pallid derivatives—has been largely ignored by the American public.

But perhaps the greatest disappointment to Ellington has been the fact that his insatiable desire to write *the* American musical or opera has gone unsatisfied all these years. The dilemma in this case has been that, on the one hand, the American public has not been able to accept jazz—one of its few wholly indigenous artistic expressions—in its native musical theater (again, except in strongly diluted forms), while on the other hand Ellington's own brand of sophisticated jazz has antagonized that segment of the jazz public that thinks of jazz as something rather more naïve and rough-hewn. In a sense these ambitious attempts on the part of Ellington have been caught between two fires, being neither the expected fish nor fowl. I would not think it unreasonable to assume, however, that Ellington's music—be it for the night club, for concert or for the stage—has indicated the possibilities for future developments in these directions, at least as basic concepts which, perhaps soon, another genius may develop successfully into the kind of vision Ellington has dreamed of all these years.

CHARLIE
PARKER

∧∧∧∧∧∧∧∧∧∧∧∧∧∧∧∧∧∧∧∧∧∧∧

Max Harrison

A great deal, some of it quite fanciful, has been written about the life of Charlie Parker and his posthumous influence. Not too much of value has been printed as yet concerning the actual music of the man. There have been valuable essays in this respect, however, by André Hodeir, Ross Russell and Tony Scott. Max Harrison's appraisal of Parker on records complements these previous studies by offering an introduction towards the placing of Parker's recorded work in perspective.

Throughout its existence jazz has changed continually, yet several features have remained as common denominators over the years. One of the most significant of these is that each new development has been, not the work of one man, but rather a collective creation. New Orleans jazz was a synthesis that resulted from a particular combination of circumstances around the turn of the century, and similarly modern jazz is the product of a meeting of like minds in New York in the early 1940's. Kenny Clarke may be credited with the rhythmic foundation of the new music, while Charlie Christian and Thelonious Monk were responsible for its harmonic basis. Dizzy Gillespie clarified some of the ideas produced in abundance by the little group, and was one of the very first to develop a solo style based on them. It is appropriate that no one particular innovation can be attributed to the other vital member of the group, for Charlie Parker was to prove the leader of the whole movement.

Parker's beginnings were not very promising, and there was little in his youthful work to suggest that he was one of the most remarkable of all jazz musicians. In his early professional days in Kansas City he was a barely competent player; more than one story has been preserved of his disgracing himself at jam sessions. He seemed destined to become at best a mediocre sideman in undistinguished Midwestern bands, a musician whose chief merit lay in his participation in the Kansas City tradition. Yet Parker's creative potential was such that when, in his early twenties, he contacted the other key musicians of his generation, he showed himself to be the man in whom modern jazz was to find its most perfect expression.

Parker's mature style was of considerable complexity, and although its constituents may be categorised under melody, harmony, rhythm, tone, etc., it should be understood that these elements are in practice mixed indissolubly. Thus melodic idiom and harmonic style are intimately related, one conditioning the other. The freshness of the best modern-jazz improvisations was often partly due to the soloist's basing his melody on the higher intervals of the chords or on passing chords, which were implied in his phrases but were not stated by the rhythm section. This broadening of the harmonic structure gave the soloist a wider choice of intervals and led to a richer melodic vocabulary. Such techniques had, of course, been employed before, but never as systematically as in modern jazz, nor with such mastery as Parker's. Phrasing is as much conditioned by rhythm as linear structure, but an essential feature of Parker's melodic style was his freedom from the traditional four-bar unit. Other moderns interpreted this very freely, but the diversity of his phrase-lengths defies generalisation, as each solo tended to be a law unto itself. Linked with this was the diverse character of Parker's phrases. Ideas that were in turn angular, flowing, harsh and elegant would be thrown together in a seemingly arbitrary fashion; yet in performances like *Dexterity, Ah-leu-cha* and *Swedish Schnapps,* their differences were made to complement each other and a solo of complete cohesiveness was formed. It is probably the most remarkable single aspect of Parker's melodic style that he was able to retain this element of discontinuity within a framework of logical development. Discontinuity was a positive feature of some of his solos, and in such recordings as *Klactoveedsedstene* he demonstrated his ability to impart shape and coherence to improvisations made up of short, apparently unrelated snippets.

The basis of the rhythmic qualities of Parker's work was the division of the beat. Whereas older musicians generally stressed the four-to-a-bar pulse, with certain definite syncopations, Parker would sometimes place accents on the beat and at other times between beats. Thus the bar was in effect divided into eight parts. By creating an opposition of on-and-off beat accentuations, he sometimes obtained the effect of two streams of rhythm. Playing a melodic instrument, he could only suggest this polyrhythmic element, and he relied on his accompanists to actualise the opposing rhythms. A rhythm section of the traditional type was unsuitable for Parker, but bop innovations resulted in the maintaining of continuity by the bass and cymbals while the pianist and drummer deviated from the beat with an endless variety of patterns. The polyrhythms this produced were Parker's natural element, and on records like *Segment* and *Ko-Ko,* Max Roach, the most sympathetic accompanist he ever had, can be heard providing ideal rhythmic counterpoint to Parker's improvisations. Bud Powell's piano chording in *Buzzy* and John Lewis' in *Marmaduke* are also noteworthy in this respect.

A style that incorporated such devices was complex of necessity, but it is a sign of the integration of Parker's art that emotional expression remained its foremost quality. In forming a communicative style from such complex elements, he was aided by his background.

The early days in Kansas City and membership in bands like Jay McShann's determined that Parker was fundamentally a blues musician. Blues remained the basis of everything he played—this is true even of such elaborate ballad improvisations as *Embraceable You*—and ensured the solid emotional content of even his most daring flights. It is further indicative of the real nature of his music that he was able to play such simple blues as *Cheryl, Cool Blues, Bluebird* and *Funky Blues* without either losing contact with the parent idiom or departing from his own involved and highly personal melodic language.

Parker was not a conscious innovator to any significant degree. The growth of his style was natural and unforced, and although he adopted the new musical ideas current among his associates, he did so not to draw attention to his skill or to shock with a carefully contrived originality, but because the old language could not express the many new things he needed to say. Again, when at about the age of twenty-five he had forged an idiom adequate to his needs, he did not "progress" towards greater purity or amplification of style. Once he had freed himself from the conventions of the older jazz, the expression of his unique musical personality was his only concern.

In Parker's finest moments the emotional content of his work was communicated with rare directness. Performances like *Warming Up a Riff* and *Meandering* have an immediacy of expression unsurpassed in any music. This could be achieved only by an artist whose language was perfectly adapted to the character of his message, and probably this integration of style and idea is the greatest single part of his achievement. His tone was another aspect of this unity. A jazz musician's sound is one of the most revealing parts of his work and, in the case of the major figures at least, tells us much about the personality behind it. Parker's tone was one of the most singular jazz timbres and remains unique despite its wide imitation. In contrast to such great predecessors as Benny Carter and Johnny Hodges, his sound was often hard and cutting. Indeed, so strong was the drive informing his most inspired work that his tone could become harsh, even brutal. Yet it was always completely appropriate to his angular melodic inventions, and the occasional roughness enhanced the unabashed intensity of his playing. Parker's was essentially a blues sound, as has been indicated; and the vocalisation of his tone in such performances as *Dark Shadows* and *Parker's Mood* is as marked as in the work of much earlier jazzmen. Yet another sign of the unity of this amazing man's playing is that, without losing the essential qualities of this sound, he could, when his ideas demanded it, produce an unruffled, almost elegant tone. The smoothness of such highly wrought solos as *Cheers* and *Stupendous* manages to be just as expressive of its creator's personality as the hoarseness of *How Deep Is the Ocean?*

A few musicians, such as Jimmy Yancey, were able to express themselves movingly with a very limited amount of musical material, but so highly cultivated a technique as Parker's could only have an enormous power of invention as its vehicle. Many jazz musicians have had a fine inventive facility, but almost any half dozen of Parker's solos show he possessed it to a very singular degree. Once again, it is difficult to separate this fecundity from the other elements of his work. The fluency in melodic invention is inseparable from the varied character of his phrases and his rhythmic virtuosity. It is our loss that Parker was never able to take full advantage of the long-playing disc and record lengthy solos of the kind that became common in the years following his death. The effortless proliferation of material in solos like *Visa* and *Passport* shows how well he could have exploited the opportunity. Perhaps the most outstanding examples of his inventive powers we do have are such deeply moving ballad improvisations as *Don't Blame Me* and *My Old Flame*. Yet the surest indication of the strength of his imagination was his ability to find new ways of expressing himself on the same theme. This did not always involve the invention of new material, for he would sometimes improvise one solo after another in which the same seminal ideas were employed in new ways each time. This can be verified by comparing the different versions issued of *Blowtop Blues, Carving the Bird, Donna Lee, Bongo Bop, Hot Blues, Relaxing at Camarillo* and many other titles. The five versions of *Billie's Bounce* form a particularly clear illustration. Any two or more solos on the same theme are almost certain to have some resemblances, but the relationship seems to be particularly close in this instance. After take one, the following solos produce comparatively few fresh ideas, despite inevitable differences in detail. What happens is that the same ideas are expressed in new ways, so that each solo appears to be a deliberate variation on its predecessor, rather than an improvement or a search for fresh inventions. In this respect Parker stands close to Jelly Roll Morton, of whom Roy Carew said, "a dozen ways of expressing a musical idea were always flashing through his mind."

Parker's first records were made in Wichita, Kansas, while he was a member of the McShann band. They were cut for the local radio station and must be presumed lost. His earliest solos available to us are on some of McShann's 1941 Deccas. Years ago, before one was familiar with Parker's mature style, his contributions to these performances seemed to be imperfect echoes of Lester Young's ideas. In the light of subsequent developments it can now be seen that this was not the case. Obviously the rudimentary hints of his later path contained in these solos must have become more pronounced in the following years; it is particularly unfortunate that the Earl Hines band in which he worked with Gillespie during 1943–44 left no recordings.

The first records on which Parker emerged as a distinct, if still not mature, solo personality were made at Tiny Grimes' 1944 Savoy session. These find him in a small jump band—a not inappropriate context for his work at the time. In comparison with his 1941 solos, they show him to have developed into a very promising and articulate soloist during 1942–44. His work is not yet wholly individual by any means, and is still shaped in the main on traditional swing patterns, but the outlines of his mature ideas are obvious enough. The fluency and invention are already evident, though the melodic contours do not yet have the angularities and vivid contrasts of the following years. The tone, although not fully characteristic, in readily identifiable.

It is again interesting to compare the different versions of each title. On the three takes of *Tiny's Tempo* and two of *Red Cross* issued, Parker improvises solos that are distinctly different in each case but evince a marked sureness of conception. This latter point is worthy of note in view of the uneven nature of some of his later work. In the following year, 1945, he recorded more often—notably on sessions led by Gillespie, Sir Charles Thompson, Clyde Hart and Red Norvo —but seemed less certain of his direction. Thus the alto solos on *Shaw 'Nuff* and *Hot House* with Gillespie, or *Hallelujah* and *Bird Blues* [1] with Norvo, foreshadow his subsequent achievements; while *20th Century Blues* with Thompson is almost a reversion to his McShann manner. This is largely because, when he recorded with Grimes, Parker was still a conventional if accomplished soloist; while throughout 1945 he was moving towards the fresh and personal mode of expression in which he would be able to say new things. It is not surprising that, during so crucial a phase of his career, he faltered and did not always play in a perfectly defined style.

The first records made under Parker's own name were cut in

[1] This is an alternate take of *Slam Slam Blues*.

November, 1945. It was appropriate that this was not only his best session thus far but the earliest at which he played with complete confidence in what was wholly his own idiom, the first to preserve his fully characteristic utterances. By that time he had entirely absorbed the innovations of his colleagues into his playing, and *Now's the Time, Billie's Bounce, Thriving from a Riff* and *Ko-Ko* were the first conclusive demonstrations of his creative fecundity and unique imagination. Tone, phrasing and above all the particular emotional climate of the music are here recognisable as his alone. On this session with Parker were Miles Davis (trumpet), Argonne Thornton (piano), Curley Russell (bass) and Max Roach (drums). On some titles Gillespie played trumpet and piano. This quintet instrumentation was used on many of Parker's sessions, and seemed to provide him with the musical context in which he was most at ease.

The thematic material Parker recorded can be classified under three headings: blues, such as *Barbados* and *Bird Feathers* [2] ; ballads; and original compositions based on the chord sequences of standards, such as *Quasimodo* (from *Embraceable You*) and *Charlie's Wig* [3] (from *When I Grow Too Old to Dream*). However, some performances were improvised without any attempt at initial thematic construction. *Bird Gets the Worm* and *Bird's Nest* are two such cases, one using the chords of *Lover Come Back to Me* and the other a variant of the *I Got Rhythm* sequence. Indeed, at times Parker seemed to be a "pure" improvisor, to whom the character and quality of the theme made little difference. He was in this respect very different from musicians like Ellington and John Lewis, for whom the theme and its presentation are of great importance. Parker was usually able to express himself with equal readiness in carefully worked-out pieces like *Hot House* and *Groovin' High* and on trite, mechanical themes like *Cool Blues* and *Constellation*.

Parker had extraordinary instrumental virtuosity in the widest sense. He was not only at ease at any tempo, but in any kind of performance. The vivid angularity of the *Klaunstance,* the double-time phrases of *Dexterity,* the elegance of *Relaxing at Camarillo*—all find him equally relaxed, and this is because his virtuosity was an essential part of his mode of expression and not a vehicle for gratuitous display. In the 1940's the boppers made a feature of ultra-fast tempos, and

---

[2] Also issued as *Schnourphology*.
[3] An alternate version was issued as *Bongo Beep*.

Parker seemed particularly at ease and articulate in them. Headlong improvisations like *Constellation, The Hymn,*[4] *Ko-Ko* and *Dizzy Atmosphere* almost form a special category in his output, and he left no solos more characteristic than these. At such times the ideas welled up from his imagination with such speed, consistency, drive and absolute confidence that one is tempted to compare the effect to that of an erupting volcano. The suggestion that such performances are particularly characteristic of Parker is strengthened by the fact that they were the most incomprehensible of his records when first encountered. They seemed to be not much more than inchoate groupings of notes, with little meaning and no continuity of thought. A constrictive tightness appeared to make the swing at best uncertain. Closer acquaintance revealed how complete was Parker's control, and that, along with the unpredictable accents and phrase lengths, was a swing as fundamental as that in earlier jazz.

Almost all the titles mentioned above were recorded for the Dial or Savoy companies in the 1940's, using the quintet instrumentation with occasional additions, such as J. J. Johnson (trombone) or Wardell Gray (tenor sax). It is safe to say that the larger part of Parker's greatest work was recorded between 1946 and 1948. For the remainder of his life he was under contract to the Clef (now Verve) company and, musically at least, the association was not always a happy one. Throughout his life there were only a comparatively small number of musicians with whom he enjoyed playing, because the highly concentrated nature of his work made greater demands on his associates than most could meet. Yet the frustration he suffered in earlier years from the musical inadequacies of others could have been little compared with what he had to support at many of his Clef sessions. The object of some of these sessions appeared to be to display his work in as inappropriate a setting as possible. He was recorded with choirs and with string orchestras, playing light-music arrangements of the salon type.

Even in such insipid surroundings Parker managed to achieve something, and his tone had an astringency that set him apart from his accompaniments. Often his solos decorated the surface of the music rather than exploring it in his usual manner, but on some of the titles with strings—*I Didn't Know What Time It Was, Summertime, I'll Remember April* and *East of the Sun*—he played with his

[4] Also issued as *Superman*.

accustomed intensity. The object of such sessions was to make Parker acceptable to wider audiences, yet he was an artist incapable of making commercial concessions, and the uncompromising honesty of his work contrasted harshly with the triviality of these settings.

In some cases a sympathetic ensemble was spoilt by the inclusion of one totally inappropriate musician. The 1949 date that produced *Passport* and *Visa* had the ideal rhythm section of Max Roach, Al Haig (piano), and Tommy Potter (bass), with Kenny Dorham on trumpet—and the vulgar, raucous trombonist, Tommy Turk. Similarly, the session with Gillespie in 1950 included Monk and Curley Russell. This was a very promising combination, and the alliance of Parker and Monk might have resulted in something altogether exceptional; but the drummer, Buddy Rich, was completely out of contact with their music. Critics of the New Orleans purist school have emphasised the importance of having groups of temperamentally compatible musicians to produce the finest music, implying that this is exclusively a requirement of the parent style, yet the inclusion of just one unsympathetic player can spoil the work of *any* small improvising group. Its complexity renders this especially applicable to modern jazz, and although Parker produced some fine work at both the above sessions, Turk and Rich induced a kind of tension that prevented him from being quite at his best.

Parker's final years did include a few happy occasions in the recording studio, however; and when he was not hampered by inappropriate accompaniments or inadequate associates, he created music as fine as anything that had gone before. The best of his Clef records show how false was the generally accepted view that he produced little of value in his later years. Successful small-group sessions resulted in thoroughly representative performances, such as *The Song Is You, Kim, She Rote, Chi Chi, Laird Baird, K.C. Blues, Loverman, Back Home Blues* and *Si Si*. Other tracks fully worthy of Parker were *Cosmic Rays, Confirmation, I Remember You, Au Privave, Ballade, I'm in the Mood for Love* and *Star Eyes*. Unique in Parker's career were four excellent titles with a big band: *Night and Day, What Is This Thing Called Love?,* and the very fine *I Can't Get Started* and *Almost Like Being in Love*.

Even before Parker's death, it was clear that his influence had been enormous and that he stood in much the same relation to his generation as Armstrong had to his. Armstrong was the first to demonstrate the real potentialities of the solo, while Parker showed that it was possible to assimilate complex techniques into improvisation, and that basic forms like the blues were as valid for modern as for earlier jazz. Both men changed jazz radically and both gave shape and direction to the work of the rest of their generations.

As early as 1946, altoists Sonny Stitt and Sonny Criss entered jazz with styles based on Parker's ideas. Before long the influence spread to other instruments; the motivation of Serge Chaloff's work was an attempt to adapt Parker's methods to the baritone saxophone. Parker's rhythmic subtlety was the quality that most completely escaped his followers, and it is certain that jazz has not benefited as much as it might from what he had to teach in this sphere. The "cool" jazz that followed bop may be regarded as a reaction against bop's complexities. Its exponents employ simpler rhythmic and harmonic patterns and play with less attack. There is no doubt that the music of this school—typified by Stan Getz and the playing of Miles Davis from 1949 onwards—whatever its other qualities, altogether lacks the rhythmic richness of Parker's work. Despite this, he had many disciples and their number appeared to indicate that his influence was even greater than Armstrong's. But in fact his influence, though more widespread, was in some ways not as great as it might have been. Most of his followers were little more than imitators, who mastered certain of the technical ingredients of his style without approaching his essential qualities, which stem from the central tradition of jazz. Throughout his mature life and even after his death, Parker inspired countless musicians, but the great majority of them quoted rather than understood him.

From about 1945 onwards it was almost impossible for anyone to play the alto saxophone without showing Parker's influence; and so, after his death, every altoist who made an impression on the jazz world was hailed as his successor. It is manifestly absurd to look for a man's successor among his imitators, and Parker could no more have a direct successor than Armstrong or Ellington. Such men are unique and usually do everything possible in their field so well that there is nothing left for their imitators to accomplish, even if they had similar gifts. The music Charlie Parker created was the product of a unique combination of gifts and circumstances that is unlikely to occur again.

The leaders of jazz after his death, his true successors, are to be found in men like John Lewis, Thelonious Monk and Sonny Rollins. Such musicians do not attempt to reproduce their predecessors' discoveries, but rather seek to express their own vision by exploring the further possibilities of jazz.

BEBOP
AND AFTER:
A REPORT

~~~~~~~~~~~~~~~~~~~~~

Martin Williams

Martin Williams' report on *Bebop and After* is more an attempt to assess in retrospect the main developments of a movement than to make a detailed, chronological study. It tries to extract from all the various modern-jazz activities of the past two decades the main insights into jazz making that have been discovered. It also tries to indicate which of them, according to Williams, are most likely to endure, either for themselves or on the basis of their influence—or both.

When bop arrived, it seemed a shocking revolution in jazz, much more shocking than jazz had seemed after ragtime (where the differences are almost as great), or the innovations of Armstrong. It seemed so for a number of reasons, but the first of them is unquestionably the war and the ban on recordings declared by the American Federation of Musicians. Almost two years of documentation, of transition and refinement were lost to people not in constant attendance during wartime at just the right clubs and dance halls. After the ban was lifted, it might have been possible to indulge in a bit of light puzzlement over Dizzy Gillespie (and over Max Roach, if one could hear him back there) in the context of a Coleman Hawkins date, or over Charlie Parker with a Sir Charles Thompson group or a Tiny Grimes quartet; but they were only a couple of players. It was not until late 1945, when truly bop-style records were made by bop musicians, that it became obvious that a *movement* was here and needed to be dealt with as such.

For the public, it was dealt with. And the way it was dealt with was strange indeed. There were journalists galore to beat the drum at any price—or, as is the case with Leonard Feather's *Inside BeBop,* keep useful journals—but to say that there was much to help a puzzled listener would be wrong. And the drum-beating itself was largely delivered with a defensive arrogance and press-agentry almost guaranteed to alienate a man who believed in the achievements of a Morton, an Oliver, an Armstrong, a Teagarden, a Henderson, a Hines, a Lunceford or an Ellington.

But that problem was really much older than the bop style; it was a problem that style was merely heir to. Although Roy Eldridge, Teddy Wilson, Jo Jones, Count Basie, Walter Page, Jimmy Blanton, Lester Young and Charlie Christian were praised or damned, there was little discussion of the innovative qualities in their work. A relatively naïve listener (whether he sat by a phonograph in Cedar Rapids or wrote for a fan magazine in New York or Chicago) could accept their work in the context of the style of the time, and like it or not on a rather primitive emotional level of his own. If he were adept at rationalizing his reactions, he might do so, however relevantly. If he were a bit more sophisticated, he might speak of Wilson's relationship to Earl Hines, Christian's "single-string" technique, Eldridge's "fire,"

Lester Young's "unusual" tone, Jo Jones' "high hat," etc. But of the real departures of these men in rhythm, line, harmony and instrumental function, little or nothing was said, and few followers of jazz were prepared to hear what they did.

Not that there was any lack of real critics or good commentators on jazz, but many of the best of them were more interested in its character and its past. One would have to wait until 1948–49 and Ross Russell's series in *The Record Changer* to find a criticism of bop on a level with William Russell's earlier analyses of blues pianists like Meade "Lux" Lewis or Cripple Clarence Lofton. (And it was not until the 1950's that anything of real perception was said in print about ragtime.) At the same time, the promoters of the kind of impressionistic enthusiasm (most of it coming first- or second-hand from Europe) that passed for "serious" criticism in jazz suffered from the same "conservatism" and reaction to the earlier "modernists" (such as Young, Christian, Eldridge and Wilson) that those same writers had accused the academicians and moralists of the 1920's of leveling against jazz itself.

At any rate, to defend the "real art of jazz" by awarding it much the same kind of naïve enthusiasm that Paul Whiteman had gotten from third-rate academicians was no solution for jazz. Simply to emote about Christian and Young was easy, and if they really were artists and innovators, a bit useless. And to enthuse over bop was much the same.

But if the advocates of bop were both critically intemperate and defensive, they were also a bit ignorant and naïve about the facts of jazz. They spoke of "new" harmonies, as if bop had suddenly discovered harmony and as if there had been no change since Oliver; and they compared Bartók and Stravinsky to Parker as though the latter's harmonic conception were based on theirs. They mentioned Lester, but not Bix and Trumbauer. They spoke of the new "melodic" role of drummers like Kenny Clarke and Max Roach as if Baby Dodds' work had not also been comparable in this respect, in a way that Jo Jones' was not. They spoke of the boppers as having "invented" the practice of composing new melodic lines on old chord sequences (or alterations thereof)—a practice as old as ragtime and one which had not only given, say, the Bennie Moten band half its book, but had given the Ellington and Basie bands a large part of theirs. And the practice of improvising on chord sequences rather than themes is as old as the blues, and was almost standard by the mid-1930's.

The writers spoke of long lines in solos rather than four-bar units, but they did not mention *Shreveport Stomp* or Lester Young in that context. They spoke of "tunes" without repeats after eight bars, but they mentioned neither Ellington nor the simplicity of *Cool Blues, Now's the Time, Bluebird,* etc. They spoke of the "polytonality" of one recording of *52nd Street Theme* and not of Ellington. They spoke of "atonality," as if these basically early-nineteenth-century harmonies of bop had much to do with atonality. A reader earnestly wrote to *Metronome* that in fairness he went to the Jade Palace in Los Angeles to hear Kid Ory, but took a copy of the magazine along to announce his loyalty to Eddie Heywood, who was playing down the street!

It was as if this bop style had swept away almost everything that had gone before it, no matter how well or how badly the writers knew and understood what *had* gone before it. It was as if the formal achievements of an Ellington could be forgotten because of what some young imitator of Gillespie had played the night before at the Onyx Club. And Dizzy was declared to be greater than Armstrong, whereas the contest (if there were one) would obviously be between Armstrong and Parker. Somehow, Bud Powell could not be important unless Morton and Hines couldn't play. Young, Christian and Jimmy Blanton might be allowed in, but only it seemed, for what they had contributed to bop.

Perhaps what bop's opponents said was even more naïve. The boppers used "European harmonies," as if there were any other kind of harmony, and as if jazz had not found itself almost from the very beginning in a unique and continuing interpretation of the resources of Western music. They said that the style exploited techniques for their own sake, an accusation that would better apply to Buster Bailey, Jabbo Smith or the Charlie Shavers of the mid-1940's than to Gillespie, and one that (happily for the artistic truth of the matter) had not been leveled at Hines or Wilson. Erroll Garner was rejected as a "modernist," but now that it is clear that he is not, they praise him as a giant—which he may well be.

Behind it all was undoubtedly a question of expression. As music imitates emotion and feeling, so a greater range of techniques enables it to handle a greater range of emotion and feeling. But techniques are an effect of an emotional cause, and so they were in bop. There were new things that jazz had to say and it learned to say them. To claim that bop was not jazz was perhaps to say that jazz should not learn to express these things. To say that it expressed them formlessly was really to say that nearly all intuitive improvisation in any jazz style is "formless"—and, indeed, from Armstrong forward, a great deal of it is (in an academic sense) and is bound to be. Jazz makes and remakes its own forms, and in bop, it was continuing to do so. A relatively sophisticated and trained artist must play that musical sophistication. If he attempted to do otherwise, attempted to unlearn, he could be no artist.

Certainly one great trouble was the inevitable number of pseudo-boppers who seemed to be accepted indiscriminately, and the number of them who were simply bad musicians. Hawkins was and is a great jazz improviser; he knew what the young modernists were doing harmonically and could play with them, but in rhythm he was and is often less free than even Red Allen. And for one Hawkins there were many, many almost absurd amateurs of the style, like baritonist Leo Parker, or bumbling drummers to whom frantic and disconnected off-beats were modern drumming. And, it seemed, if one were to accept the authentic artistry of Charlie Parker, Bud Powell, Gillespie, Max Roach, Kenny Clarke, Ray Brown, etc., he had to swallow Boyd Raeburn and the posturings of a Stan Kenton; he had to see something starkly innovative in the 1945 Herman bands' mélange of Lunceford, Basie, Ellington, and an occasional dash of Gillespie; he had to accept re-statements of 1938 Lester Young by a legion of tenormen as daring innovations; and he had to reject the major talent (perhaps genius) of Thelonious Monk as of minor importance, and reject Tadd Dameron as having written only one or two things. And from the relative amount of ink spilled, it seemed that a popularizer of bop like George Shearing was at least as important as Bud Powell—indeed, although bop was praised as something "new," the question of individuality and orginality within the style was seldom raised.

Analyses of the style of the bop rhythm section as a matter of simplifications in which the duplication of functions had been eliminated were instructive, and were an excellent counter to the usual statements, which seemed to depict the work of these men as pointlessly rococo gimmickery on the style of the Basie men. But one had to wait for André Hodeir's excellent (if overstated) explication of the rhythm of bop for the greatest insight: the rhythmic basis of the style is a subdivision of the quarter-note swing style into an eighth-note pulse. Once grasped, the accentuation of the weak beat, accents between beats, the runs of short notes, the delays—all fall into place as functional, direct, unadorned expression. So do other things: it is provocative to see the history of jazz, granted that it involves simplifications, in terms of a rhythmic evolution: the whole-note rhythmic basis of the cakewalk, subdivided into halves by ragtime, subdivided with syncopated quarters in New Orleans, subdivided fully into quarters by Armstrong, made into even fours by Basie, subdivided into eighths (possibly inspired by the popularity of boogie-woogie, by the way) by a bop style which, partly because of a wartime tax on dancing in clubs, could play for the listener.

One could hardly hear the swing of a Lionel Hampton and not sense that, for the future, some kind of rhythmic crisis was at hand, and that the implicit rhythmic monotony simply had to be broken through. For what has now happened to that kind of "jivey" beat, a great deal of rhythm-and-blues playing will provide an answer. And from what one could hear in the early 1940's among the younger players who were not seeking the way out but were emulating the more conservative riff-mongers among their immediate predecessors, a kind of jazz as melodically dull as a set of toned drums and as rhythmically monotonous as possible was at hand. In Christian, one can hear both the problem and the basis for its solution. It was a solution which Lester Young had helped provide him with, but Young's playing had long been exceptionally free of the mechanics of the beat, and held rhythm, line and harmony in a special balance.

If an emphasis on harmonic evolution dominates in an explication of jazz, it immediately causes troubles because, aside from what the individual improvisers might do, the chord changes in a blues like *Shoe Shiners Drag* occur more frequently at some points and are more complex than the basic patterns of many a Basie blues; and because a Beiderbecke, a Trumbauer, an Earl Hines or a Pee Wee Russell might imply passing chords one would not hear in a Chu Berry, or because the momentary crossing of polyphonic lines in a New Orleans ensemble might actually make such passing chords.

If one is looking for masterpieces from the bop years of 1945–48, he will find a *Shaw 'Nuff*, a *Ko-Ko*, a *Hot House*, a *Salt Peanuts*, a *Klactoveedsedstene* . . . but it will be difficult to name more than, say, ten or so recordings. This difficulty would not be found with

Ellington or Armstrong. As surely as jazz has had any "geniuses" (whether of form or of intuitive improvisation), Parker was one. There can be no question of his authenticity, his brilliance, his expressiveness, his importance; but, even understood as that of a "blowing" improviser, much of Parker's work seems daring, exciting, and, finally, unsatisfying. One feels that so many of his statements are incomplete, unfinished; and one seldom feels this about an Armstrong, a Hawkins, a Young or a Ben Webster, whether they are being brilliant or merely (for them) competent.

Like the New Orleans style, bop, for all its recording activity, left few masterpieces. Both styles are more difficult for improvisers to play well than the style of the 1930's. If a "New Orleans" record is not by a major figure or group, it is apt to be only a curiosity by a Louis Dumaine or a travesty by a revivalist. The same sort of thing might be said about bop. But could hardly be said about swing.

Conservatism was inevitable, and it came with something called "cool jazz." The cool style was "in the air," divergent and coincidental: a group of tenormen whose basic inspiration was Lester Young; the work of Lennie Tristano and some of his pupils; and a series of recordings led by Miles Davis for Capitol in 1949–50, and arranged by Gil Evans, John Lewis, Gerry Mulligan, Johnny Carisi, and Davis in a style owing a great deal to the lush manner that Claude Thornhill had set for his dance band nearly ten years earlier.

If Parker's *style* (aside from his artistry) is a yardstick of modernity, then much of cool jazz is regressive; and to call the Davis records, as one man has, a summary of all that had preceded them in bop, is to admit to an essential misunderstanding (or at least a very harmonic interpretation) of both styles.

None of the work of the cool tenor players is as important as the innovative work of their master, Young; none of it really strays far from him; nor is much of it as good. The best of the tenormen is certainly Stan Getz. His fluency—he never seems at a loss for ideas when improvising—is undeniable, but it is often based on his direct use of a stock of riffs and runs that many use and have used for a long time. For every *Lover Come Back to Me,* Getz has a few dozen performances where these licks may fall one after the other with little attention to continuity or development, and with an ease more on the surface than in the depths. He knows that one is now required to make transitions from chorus to chorus, so he does not begin at bar one and stop at bar thirty-two. However, Getz may stop at thirty or thirty-one, then play off that phrase which ends him in the second bar as if it were the result of overflowing inspiration rather than mechanics of style. But always there is his swing, and he can bring off a *tour de force* of excitement like *Getz at the Shrine* and show that one can achieve the effect of a Lionel Hampton without the banalities.

Tristano is the kind of musician who presents problems of category, and he is bound to be called, as he has been, "a dubious jazzman." Certainly, whatever the label, his groups have produced a charming music and a valuable attempt at ensemble improvisation, but there is more to art than charm or an attempt. Tristano's point of departure was, again, Basie and Young. He complicated their approach harmonically but (except for occasionally imposing other values on a basic "four") not rhythmically; and the waste of notes and apparent decorativeness that resulted may again lead one to the proposition that there is in jazz an innate and intrinsic relationship among melodic line, harmony, and rhythm; and that, if one attempts to explore one without an interrelated reshuffling of the others, he risks contrivance and failure. Perhaps, indeed, the basic approach is rhythmic. Certainly some of the youthful solos of Bud Powell with Cootie Williams show that he was learning the rhythmic lessons of Parker, Monk and Clarke well; and the work of Freddy Webster (as well as some of Gillespie's transitional solos recorded at Monroe's) shows, for all its brilliance on "ballads," that a harmonic grasp of the modern idiom alone can lead to a near preciosity of rather bloodless sound patterns.

The most important cool recordings in the Davis Capitol series (the group made one public appearance) risked the same imbalance in some of their percussion, but enough of the instrumentalists involved understood and could at least sometimes imply the bop idiom rhythmically and override the limitation. The scoring and improvisations on these records have been justly celebrated and analyzed, best by M. Hodeir. Certainly, their kind of orchestration often brilliantly risks exhibiting an effete succession of sounds-for-their-own-sake without ever falling into failure. [But I cannot agree that all of Evans' later work on *Miles Ahead* avoids the trap.] Davis was by the time of the Capitol sides finding a superb and individual solo voice, partly by acknowledging his technical limitations and working within them, and also through an ability to imply bop rhythms in his time without stating them directly; Lee Konitz was breaking away from the rigid lessons of his teacher, Tristano; and J. J. Johnson was continuing to show himself an exceptional and inventive instrumentalist—by themselves, the solos on these recordings might make them classics.

Their progeny was great and curious. In the mid-1950's, Davis seemed to begin again as a soloist where he had stopped after the Capitol recordings were made. Konitz, on the other hand, has not always played so well since that period. Johnson can seem, alternately, determinedly slick and glib and strongly expressive. Pianist John Lewis went on to direct the Modern Jazz Quartet. Then, there is Gerry Mulligan and the West Coast.

The public successes on the West Coast were hardly the artistic ones, but among those men who showed promise of artistic success there is a frustrating lack of fulfillment.

Mulligan's is clearly a case of unfinished business. As an improviser, Mulligan is "conservative" (*i.e.,* again, he owes most to Young and Christian and, as he proclaims, Red Nichols); he has many of Getz's compulsive problems; and his edginess, especially at fast tempos, sometimes prevents swing. Clearly he was once a man with a music, a form, an ensemble style to offer, but since his first work with a quartet, little has happened to that conception except that it hardly exists any more. His best work begs comparison with the previous trumpet-reed-pianoless recording group of Lester Young and Buck Clayton's Commodore sessions, and the comparison certainly points to the need for a degree of maturity in instrumentalists, in whatever context.

Notoriously, the West Coast had few really good soloists. Its chief virtue was that it promised form. Alas, it largely failed to deliver. It did have some very good instrumentalists (Red Mitchell, Curtis Counce, Shelly Manne, Barney Kessel) and *some* very good soloists (Paul Desmond, Art Pepper and the reluctant Joe Albany).

Aside from the more recent rebirth of Miles Davis, the most significant progeny of the cool records has been the Modern Jazz

Quartet. Foremost, its members (Milt Jackson; John Lewis; Percy Heath, replacing Ray Brown; and Connie Kay, replacing Kenny Clarke) are all superbly expressive players and improvisers, who either helped form the bop style or assimilated it; learned from the cool style; and are capable of musical discipline, responsiveness and spontaneity. But the group and musical director, Lewis, had intentions that went beyond "playing." The quartet's work is the first after the Davis Capitols, or perhaps the first after Ellington's—and parallel to Thelonious Monk's—to achieve meaningful form. A large part of that form was not won easily. As a great deal of even the most recent activity on both coasts could demonstrate (from Stan Kenton to Teddy Charles, Dave Brubeck to Teo Macero), a conscious attempt to borrow wholesale from Western concert music is not necessarily either successful or even musical. To arrive at his forms, John Lewis turned to the eighteenth century and at least by the time of the *Sait-On Jamais* (*No Sun in Venice*) score (1958) had transformed and assimilated his forms so that they were jazz; and the quartet had worked out a style wherein improvisation, the pre-arranged score, integrated discipline and spontaneity were held in balance. (Probably none of this could have been achieved with such authenticity if the quartet's members had not had the guiding and perhaps restraining influence of a feeling for the blues.) The group has performed a "conservative" act, but a large and important one.

Reactions to cool jazz were inevitable and, when one remembers some of the derivative claptrap and pretentiousness produced in its name, to be wished. The reactions centered in the East, and they soon acquired the names "hard bop" and "funky." They were inevitably called "contrived" and "regressive."

In part, the funky idiom represented an attempt by the jazzman to rediscover his emotional roots at a time when cool jazz seemed to be jeopardizing them in favor of preciosity and contrivance. He turned to gospel music and blues, and, if he was reluctant to inspect Bessie Smith or King Oliver, he was willing to hear Ray Charles, Mahalia Jackson and Bo Diddley.

The talent of trumpeter Clifford Brown provided an early focal point: he was a brilliant technician who seemed to be reinterpreting cool jazz (*i.e.,* Miles Davis) in terms of bop (*i.e.,* Gillespie and

Navarro). Brown was, at his death an immature soloist, limited in tempos, rhythm, and originality of line, but he had been an inspiration in less than a year.

The funky style was announced by the group led by Art Blakey and directed by Horace Silver in 1955. There was "regression." The *stated* chords in the funky bass line were few, compared not only to those in bop but to those of some earlier styles; the soloist implied his own. The melodies were usually riff-like, rhythmically and melodically not quite like swing riffs, but rather simple compared to some bop lines. Piano styles, including Silver's, soon tended to degenerate into disconnected, interpolative four-bar fragments. Running chords and splicing arpeggios, became for some as common as it had been among pseudo-boppers. One spoke of "cooking," "wailing," "soul," "feeling," "swing," "tension"; but seldom of melodic invention, mood or release.

Blakey, obviously an important drummer, seemed to accompany as if the way to inspire was to coerce, and his followers, like "Philly Joe" Jones and Elvin Jones, seemed to do the same thing, but with a greater rhythmic complexity that bordered on chaos.

Within the movement and around its edges was undeniable change: it had taken up several problems where bop had left them in the late 1940's. In bop the rhythmic lead had been awarded to the bass. The pianist's left hand, and the drummer's left hand and right foot, were released to improvise punctuations and polyrhythms as the soloist dictated. In one respect, Jimmy Guiffre and Lucky Thompson (on one recording date, ABC-Paramount 111) had carried things further than both bop and Mulligan's groups; they dropped all of the rhythm section except the bass.

At the same time that Charlie Mingus had, on *Pithecanthropus Erectus,* dropped the pretentiousness of some of his early recordings to work within the materials-at-hand of jazz, he had developed a virtuosity probably rivaled only by Red Mitchell, and he could maintain a beat firmly and cleanly while providing a polyphonic line behind ensemble and soloist.

In an opposite direction, Wilbur Ware approached the bass as a stringed rather than a percussive instrument and, in a style potentially revolutionary, played solos of singing melody, with freedom in time, harmony and fingering technique.

The style that Blakey played and that the two Joneses were

developing was not really one of over-loudness and interference. It was a drum style that implied not so much a "push" behind the improviser as almost a parallel, interplaying but separate percussive voice, improvising within and around the horn lines on an almost equal footing. It is ironic that so far the only complete break with time-keeping has been made by Max Roach in *Bemsha Swing,* on Thelonious Monk's *Brilliant Corners* LP.

Some hornmen were dealing with the problem of structuring long improvisations and coming to unique solutions in an area that few earlier jazzmen except certain pianists had attempted. Because of a unique ability to disintegrate (and later rebuild) a melodic line gradually and to invent complementary melodies; and an ability to set, sustain and build a mood with great power, Miles Davis could not only improvise a long blues solo like *Walkin'* but play on ballads without at all resorting to the stalling cliché-mongering, banality, or trickery of others. Tenor saxophonist Sonny Rollins, with more virtuosity but a less complex harmonic sense than Davis, could keep the longest solo interesting by both distilling and developing melody, gradually revealing and diminishing a Parker-inspired virtuosity in notes, rhythm and line length. Even when he used a freely harmonic variational approach, he showed a relaxed and constant inventiveness.

There was a time in late 1957 and early 1958 when John Coltrane (who could not sustain a long solo) was placing the notes in his rapid tenor runs so as to imply that he wanted the eighth-note rhythms further subdivided into sixteenths.

But one of the most significant events that resulted from the reaction to cool was the rediscovery of Thelonious Monk. The ingenious use of time, the development over several choruses of a single motif in his *Bags' Groove* solo, and his very personal use of thematic material on such recitals as *The Unique Thelonious Monk* lead to several realizations: that his recordings between 1947 and 1950 were, with Parker's, the most important and abiding of their time; that Monk was a major composer, perhaps the first in jazz since Ellington; that Monk's technique was all musical and that he was a virtuoso of the basic materials of jazz: time, metre, accent, space; that Monk's was an original and entirely authentic talent; that Monk was a strikingly expressive and inventive player; and that Monk was what no jazzman before him had ever been: after more than fifteen years, still an innovator and legitimate experimenter, who at the same time was rediscovering form directly in terms of the materials of jazz. Again, he was looked to by the young jazzmen for hints about what to do next.

Besides Wilbur Ware and Sonny Rollins, others were getting answers from him.

Probably as a result of the simplification of the funky bass line, and certainly with inspiration from both Miles Davis and Monk, several pianists seemed for the first time in the *avant-garde*. Bill Evans and Martial Solal, in France, were working on styles which seemed to have almost as much relationship to Earl Hines as to Bud Powell. That is, they depend for melodic grounding less on the rapid and thick succession of chords in bop (which can easily lead to faking in hornmen, of course) than on scalar language. And Cecil Taylor's assimilation of resources from Stravinsky, Bartok and Schönberg into jazz (by way of an apprehension of Ellington and Monk) was obviously the most provocative and authentic attempt to deal with the devices of twentieth-century concert music *en masse* that jazz had produced.

Inevitably, jazz has attracted, and will continue to attract, all sorts of peripheral pretentiousness and spuriousness. At the same time, more and more, it will attract the concert composer, who will not only borrow occasional devices but in the future will use its improvisers in a way that will seem to swallow jazz up as only an occasional interlude in the tradition of Western concert music. And such attempts at understanding can be even more difficult to deal with than the patronizing attitude that formerly emanated from the academies. On the other hand, the critic's complaint that the jazzman could learn invaluable things by a more careful and sympathetic attention to his heritage than he has been willing to make is entirely legitimate. But, as the critic does not always understand, a part of the jazzman's task has been to *re*-interpret that heritage, or as much of it as he wishes. In 1938 Duke Ellington said in an interview that what jazz needed was something new. It was several years in coming, but it came. And recently one jazzman said, "Don't worry, it will continue, it will spread, and it will grow. It is going on and on." Hearing the conviction in his voice and knowing how jazz has grown so far, one could hardly doubt that a music that has produced a Morton, an Armstrong, an Ellington, a Young, a Parker, a John Lewis and a Monk will continue to flourish—and that a Mahalia Jackson, a Muddy Waters, a Ray Charles and an Art Farmer will all continue to work within it.

Bibliography

Ross Russell, "Be Bop" (a series). *The Record Changer,* 1948–49.

André Hodeir, "Charlie Parker" and "Miles Davis," in *Jazz: Its Evolution and Essence* (Grove Press, 1956).

Martin Williams, "A Look Ahead," *Music '58* (*Down Beat* Yearbook).

Max Harrison, "Looking Back at the Modern Jazz Quartet," *Jazz Monthly,* April, 1958.

Bobby Jaspar, "Philly Joe Jones and Elvin Jones," *Jazz Hot,* translated in *The Jazz Review,* January, 1959.

Gunther Schuller, "Sonny Rollins and the Challenge of Thematic Improvisation," *The Jazz Review,* November, 1958.

THE RE-EMERGENCE OF
TRADITIONAL JAZZ

Albert J. McCarthy

Although the history of writing on jazz could be subtitled, "Studies in Polemics," there has never been as irate a body of material as that which accompanied the re-emergence of traditional jazz in the 1930's and early 1940's. There follows an assessment of that movement and its significance that seems to many of us balanced and reasonable; but for the partisans involved, attaining a definition of what is "reasonable" may be as difficult as writing a "balanced" history of the I.R.A. In any case, this is the first history of that phenomenon written by a close observer who is not a camp follower.

Semanticists would probably find the analysis of jazz styles an interesting if somewhat confusing field of study. For two decades critics have attempted a rigid categorisation of the various schools, but as soon as one has finally thought that a written definition could be produced, the innumerable exceptions to the rule come to mind. It is not surprising when one considers that jazz itself has never been satisfactorily defined, and even if one were to omit the fanatical partisans of a certain style or musician, it is unlikely that the most tolerant critics, with the widest range of taste, could agree on any written definition of the music. It is necessary to state this by way of an introduction to this chapter, for the words "traditional jazz" have emotive qualities for many followers of the music, and there may be some who would dispute the interpretation that I use.

Traditional jazz means, for most critics and fans, the music played by the pioneer New Orleans artists. It conjures up an image of a polyphonic style which utilises a front line of cornet (or trumpet), trombone and clarinet, with a rhythm section using three or four of the following instruments—piano, guitar (or banjo), string bass (or tuba), and drums. There may, of course, be variants, for two trumpets might be used, or a saxophone added; but at least there can be little disagreement on the essentials of the style.

Our knowledge of much of the early history of New Orleans jazz is still rudimentary, and it may be that a great deal has been lost to the jazz historian; but even though certain definitions may be based on insufficient knowledge, they have grown to be widely accepted. Terms like "Dixieland" are common currency today, and while the purist may object that the bulk of the music that is played under this tag is merely a bad copy or a secondhand derivative of the original, he will usually concede that it at least has its roots in what he would define as traditional jazz. For the purpose of this chapter I am using the term fairly broadly, but the widest possible definition within reasonable limits is necessary if one is not to be sidetracked into constant explanations of why a certain group or artist is mentioned.

It is claimed of English law (not always correctly) that it is not only necessary for justice to be done, but that the stock figure of the "reasonable man" should be able to perceive at once that such is the case. In the same way, I use the words "traditional jazz" in such a manner that not only does one see in the abstract that a case can be made for accepting a certain music as coming within its scope, but that the "reasonable man" of jazz (even more of a myth than his counterpart in law) can see that the music referred to has its roots in what is generally known as New Orleans jazz.

It may appear somewhat arbitrary to say that traditional jazz re-emerged during the late 1930's and early 1940's, for in some form or other it was played throughout the whole of the 1930's. It is possible to point to the music of the Chicagoans; the records which the French critic, Hugues Panassié, supervised for Victor in 1938; or the Muggsy Spanier band of 1939. One could also mention the Bob-Cats, a small group within the Bob Crosby band, which made records from around 1937, or the innumerable small units which were playing in obscure clubs in New Orleans and Chicago during the 1930's. However, the fact remains that the dominant jazz of this period was swing, using the term in an all-embracing sense to include not only the music of the white popularisers like Benny Goodman and Artie Shaw, but that of the great Negro orchestras of Count Basie, Duke Ellington, Earl Hines, Bennie Moten, Jimmie Lunceford and many others, both known and unknown. The public, if it recognised jazz at all, associated it with musicians like Goodman and had only the vaguest idea of the music of the New Orleans pioneers.

Such ignorance was by no means confined to the public, for I can recall that when I first started to collect records in 1935, the now-accepted classic items by the Louis Armstrong Hot Five and Hot Seven were dismissed as merely crude, and Jelly Roll Morton was a shadowy figure who had made a few obscure "race" records. I still have periodicals in which quite well-known critics speak slightingly of records which are now virtually revered as jazz classics, and they are compared very unfavorably with long-forgotten sides by mediocre swing bands. It is possible that this attitude may be partly responsible for the violent nature of the reaction when it did come.

It is no longer possible to pinpoint any single event as the starting point for the revival of interest in the traditional form. What did happen was that a series of factors led to a realisation that jazz history, as it was accepted, was largely a myth. Perhaps the most important point about the sudden rediscovery of the work of the great traditional musicians is that it was largely due to the increase in record collectors. Until this time there had been only the few isolated individuals who took jazz seriously enough to form representative record collections, but now they had reached such a number that they were able to make the companies reissue important sides and even occasionally record a few sessions featuring some of the earlier musicians.

Magazines like the *H.R.S. Rag* and *Jazz Information* acted as a stimulus to research into personnels of older records, and as the names of musicians who had previously been unknown came to light, there was a natural tendency to try to trace their present whereabouts. The few years from about 1938 to the middle of the 1940's saw more information on earlier jazz become common knowledge than was the case during the previous two decades. It is true that some of the more partisan followers of New Orleans jazz tended to replace one set of myths with another, but the reasons for this will be discussed later.

In 1939 the book *Jazzmen* was published. It consisted of a collection of essays, edited by Charles Edward Smith and Frederic Ramsey, Jr. It was the first book to deal with New Orleans history in any objective manner, and although many of the views expressed in it are no longer accepted and certain information has proved to be incorrect, it would be difficult to overevaluate the impact that it had on collectors throughout the world.

Someone has said that it is not really correct to speak of a revival of interest in traditional jazz, for it was not so much a revival that the collectors of the period were faced with, but a revelation. The suggestion is not without point if one considers the prophetic language that was to become commonplace in the writings of many of the traditionalist spokesmen during the next few years. It is perhaps easy to assume that only in jazz historical research is it very unusual to document activities when they are actually taking place; but it is certainly true that the jazz historians have a tendency to overlook what is under their very noses and that they later have to go back and obtain their information in circumstances made difficult by the deaths of many who could have helped them, by the faulty memories of others, or by the desire of certain musicians to claim a greater share of credit for their own contributions than is actually justified. The current picture of the 1930's, for instance, is almost certainly a false one, and the pattern of regional activities that was so important to the development of the big bands is only now being investigated. Even closer in time are the first few years of the bop era, and yet it is surprising what gaps there are in our knowledge of records and musicians' activities in this period. One also needs to take into account the fact that it is the art of the immediately preceding period that suffers most when a new school arises, but that it is also a common pattern for that art to be rediscovered at a later date and for it to be hailed just as immodestly as it was once denigrated. Something of the sort may be happening to swing at present.

Although one can see the chain of circumstances that led up to the renewed interest in traditional jazz, in retrospect one is still mildly astonished at the violence of the dissensions that split the jazz world for over a decade after the early 1940's. It is somewhat interesting to speculate upon the different course the jazz revival might have taken had it not coincided with the growth of the modern-jazz movement, although it is difficult to see that the artistic outcome could have been any different. The propagation of the merits of traditional jazz was not enough for the collectors of the period, for by a curious freak of history there arose from the new schools of bop and modern jazz a group of critics and some musicians who dismissed the earlier forms as artistically worthless, or at best a necessary evolutionary step towards something more valid.

Faced with this criticism, the purist followers reacted in kind, accusing the modernists of falsely taking the name "jazz," and denying that modern jazz had any roots in the genuine music. As one who has never been partisan to the music of either the revivalists or many of the modernists, it has always seemed a miracle to me that the former attacked the boppers on completely false grounds when, in fact, there are many areas in which the modernists are particularly vulnerable. The history of the 1940's, as far as criticism is concerned, is not edifying; but, although the absurdity of the extremist viewpoints is generally accepted, the scars have by no means healed. It is also unfortunate that so many of the traditionalist writers have marred a perfectly valid case by wild overstatement, for some listeners who might otherwise enjoy some of the music these writers extoll have been deterred by the polemical nature of much of their writing.

The most famous purist book is Rudi Blesh's *Shining Trumpets,* published by Alfred A. Knopf in 1946; but, although Mr. Blesh can write very well on traditional groups and blues singers, the book as a whole is virtually worthless as jazz history. One could quote endlessly the absurdities contained within the volume, but it would probably be better to regard it less as a history than as a polemical weapon in the war between the purists and the modernists. In England similar views were expressed in Rex Harris' *Jazz,* which, because it was published in the cheap Pelican Books series, must have caused endless confusion to the newer enthusiast, who had no means of knowing that the views expressed were slanted to an extreme extent. I do not propose to quote more than one or two passages from such books in this essay, but the messianic nature of much of the traditionalist thinking in the 1940's is demonstrated in the following extract:

> The band sails from here on out, showing adequately for the first time on records the terrific rock with which Kid Ory and his band, night by night, are steadily undermining the foundations, not merely of the Jade Room [the Hollywood night club where the band was playing at the time] and its surrounding segment of Hollywood but, as well, the trembling bastions of the commercial music fortress. March on 'round the walls, Kid Ory!

This review of *1919 March,* by the Kid Ory band, was printed in Blesh's *Shining Trumpets,* and while it is easy enough to make fun of the book today, it has to be remembered that such views were not all that uncommon during the 1940's. It would be out of place to dwell any longer on the critical situation at the time, but unless one realises the conditions which prevailed, much of the subsequent course of traditional jazz would seem incomprehensible.

It should, without doubt, be clear that, although the rediscovery of many of the earlier New Orleans musicians was made possible by these critics—who were also concerned with the revival of the traditional form as a whole—the music of the pioneers and that of the white "revivalists" must be considered apart. In the first instance, the pioneer musicians were playing as they had done throughout their lives and with a thorough background in the traditional field. The revivalists, on the contrary, were attempting the far more difficult task of recreating a form of which they had no first-hand experience, and one which had arisen as the result of a set of social circumstances not likely to be duplicated several decades later. Apart from the task involved in re-establishing traditional jazz, the revivalists also hoped to enrich the form, but their failure to do so could have been predicted by any objective critic. The revivalists will be considered later in this essay, but for the moment it is necessary to consider those New Orleans musicians who did find their way onto records during the 1940's and 1950's.

A key figure in the history of current New Orleans jazz is the collector and critic, William Russell. Russell became interested in jazz in the 1930's, when, as a schoolmaster, he asked some of his pupils to bring along their favorite records to play. His intention was to point out the defects in popular music, but instead he became interested in some of the jazz records he heard and commenced a serious study of the subject. We owe it almost entirely to Russell that we are in a position to hear recorded examples of New Orleans jazz of the 1940's, and were it not for the items on his American Music label it is unlikely that even a tentative summary could be attempted.

The earliest documentary recording made in New Orleans is the set featuring Kid Rena, but this was not successful. Russell systematically recorded as many musicians as he could find, and while the results are uneven, many of the items released are of considerable musical as well as historical value. It is unfortunate that Russell's American Music label has followed a somewhat eccentric course, with records being allowed to go out of circulation within a week or two of issue, while many sessions which promised much have never been issued at all; and it is to be hoped that a more stable policy will be followed in the future. However, although Russell's reluctance to make his records generally available may be irritating to many, without him our admittedly sketchy knowledge of later New Orleans music would be virtually nonexistent.

The first reaction of older collectors to the initial records released, nearly all featuring trumpeter Willie "Bunk" Johnson, was one of scepticism. Johnson had been rediscovered by a group of collectors during the research for the book *Jazzmen;* subsequently he was fitted out with a new set of false teeth and a trumpet, and for the next few years, until his death in 1949, he became an extremely controversial figure. He will be dealt with in more detail shortly.

The great problem in any consideration of Russell's American

Music recordings is to assess their historical and musical worth. To many collectors they are so different from the classic New Orleans items of the 1920's—the Oliver Okeh and Gennett sides, the Armstrong Hot Five and Hot Seven releases, or the Morton Red Hot Peppers items, for example—that they find it difficult to accept the records seriously. Such collectors tend to advance the theory that these records are by musicians who remained in New Orleans because they were inferior to those who left, and that it is impossible to judge their music in the same way as that of earlier and greater artists.

The flaw in such an argument is that it is all too easy to assume that the greatest musicians would necessarily leave New Orleans to seek fame elsewhere, whereas the evidence seems to prove that quite a number, who were considered among the greatest of their day, preferred to remain at home. Chris Kelly, Buddy Petit and Henry "Kid" Rena were three trumpeters who enjoyed considerable reputations in New Orleans, but only Petit played elsewhere, and he was away for a very short time. A theory that sets out a dogmatic principle that an outstanding musician *must* follow the general trend to move on to Chicago and New York is hardly a convincing one.

Another theory that was quite widely held is that the music of Bunk Johnson, George Lewis, "Shots" Madison and others represented an earlier phase of jazz than that of Oliver and Morton, for example, and that it had links with the pioneer efforts of such musicians as Buddy Bolden. In its most extreme form the theory held that this music was a type of "folk jazz," whereas Oliver, Morton and Armstrong had been corrupted by alien influences. The whole reasoning seems to break down if one takes into consideration the ages of the players on the American Music recordings, and also the difference between the style of Bunk Johnson and most of the other musicians who recorded with him. When a music is as functional as New Orleans jazz, it would be extraordinary if men of Armstrong's generation should consciously return to an earlier tradition, and the theory is so unlikely that it can be discarded. It seems probable that the "folk jazz" suggestion may have received an unconscious impetus through the desire of certain admirers of the Johnson band to explain away the fluctuations in pitch which are so apparent on many records.

It is true, as Bruce King has remarked, that pitch, like scales and keys, is only a convention, which our ears have learned to accept. It may also be true that the retention of African roots in New Orleans jazz *might* have some bearing on the matter, but even if one accepts this, the fact remains that the abnormal pitch used on many of the New Orleans records of the last decade and a half seems to represent a fairly recent development. One can only theorise on the subject, but the answer, I am inclined to feel, lies with the evolution of brass-band music. As recent an LP as that by the Young Tuxedo Brass Band (Atlantic 1297), which was recorded in 1958, shows this somewhat eccentric concept of pitch to the full, even in those numbers which were written and have no improvisation. Virtually every musician who has played in New Orleans groups during the last twenty years has had brass-band experience, and the few records available of these bands all show a disregard for conventional pitch, particularly on slow dirges. The objection to this view is that Louis Armstrong and King Oliver, to name two obvious examples, also played in brass bands and did not pitch out of tune for effect. However, we have no examples of brass-band music in New Orleans before the 1940's, and it is possible that changes took place during the twenty years after the pioneer musicians left the city. This is a field of research that might be worth following up. What makes so untenable the view of the critics who maintain that the unusual pitching is merely the fault of poor musicianship is that many of the men who use it on slow dirges, hymns and some blues revert to more orthodox pitch on the bulk of their jazz performances. It is necessary to distinguish between the fluffs and faulty intonation that certain older musicians are guilty of—presumably as a result of their age and irregular playing opportunities—and the deliberate use of abnormal pitching by George Lewis and others on funeral numbers. It is also noticeable that a trumpeter like Avery "Kid" Howard uses a much more pronounced vibrato on these numbers than he does on stomps and rags. The general effect is somewhat displeasing to listeners who insist on the observation of European musical conventions, and it must be admitted that at times the results appear somewhat melodramatic; but whatever the individual's reaction may be, it does seem certain that faulty musicianship is not the cause. One can but hope that when Samuel B. Charters publishes his work on the styles of New Orleans jazz during different periods, he may throw some light on the whole subject.

Interesting as this subject of pitch may be, it is of less importance than the question of the total value of the American Music
records and the attempt to place them in some perspective. One of
the most illuminating essays to have appeared on the subject was
printed in *Jazz Monthly* during March and April, 1959, and I propose to give a lengthly quote from that source, the writer being Bruce
King:

> For the meantime, however, I should like to suggest that these
> records generally represent a slightly corrupted version of New
> Orleans jazz as it was played after the migration of Ory, Oliver, and
> Louis to the West and North. Other periods, however, are repre-
> sented by the playing of such musicians as Bunk Johnson and Big
> Eye Louis Nelson. What little we know of New Orleans jazz style
> would seem to indicate that even after Golden jazz was still played
> fairly straight, with a rather metronomic concept of beat. Swing, in
> the modern sense, probably didn't exist in those days; tempos were
> probably slow in the early ragtime style (which may explain Baby
> Dodds's comment that the early blues were played slow with a
> rumba rhythm. He probably meant with the three-against-four
> syncopation of ragtime).
>
> Bunk's style on these records may be as close as we can now
> get to this period of New Orleans jazz history. However, Bunk's
> style is markedly different from Lewis's or Madison's; Bunk belongs
> to a different age group. Bunk was born in 1879, while Lewis was
> born in 1900 and Madison in 1899. In between was the generation
> of Ory (1889) and Oliver (1885), which played hotter than Bunk
> with more emphasis on improvisation, but with a somewhat similar
> concept of rhythm. Their ensembles were full, somewhat heavy,
> without great shading in dynamics; and they often played complex
> three and four strain rags. They were probably influenced in their
> rhythm by the fast ragtime style which developed after Bunk. While
> these musicians were often the cream of the New Orleans jazzmen,
> and created some of our greatest jazz recordings, their style seems
> to have followed its own development in the North, independently
> of the changes which were occurring in New Orleans. Occasional
> records made in Chicago indicate an awareness of the trends in New
> Orleans; but on the whole Oliver's style (which I am using as a
> standard) had to break down of its own weight, for it was too rigid,
> too intense, with little space, except in solos, for musicians to de-
> velop fuller lines.
>
> In New Orleans, by way of contrast, a third stage of develop-

ment seems to have been reached. As Charters remarks, the tricky rags were replaced by simple one-strain tunes, and a slow teasing swing replaced the more metronomic beat of earlier jazz. I do not know why this happened; but most people to whom I have spoken suggest that Buddy Petit was influential in this. Perhaps more important—if records are any indication—the New Orleans ensemble style became more fluid or flexible. Whereas Oliver's band style is thick in texture, the third style seems lighter. Lead voices are switched around, and there is more breathing room for each player. This, then, seems to be the basic style of the American Music records, which reflect the developments within New Orleans jazz by musicians born around 1900. Many more of these musicians had less formal training than the earlier ones, and this may explain both their preference for simple melodies and the exciting liberties they take with the bar line, and tune structure. Earlier musicians probably had a better idea of written parts, while less well trained musicians are more likely to treat the ensemble in an experimental manner.

In general, I incline to agree with Mr. King in most of the views he advances. However, it is necessary to state that many musicians have claimed that the music the Oliver band recorded is not representative, leaving aside the question of poor sound quality. It appears that Oliver, faced with the three-minute time limitation of a ten-inch record, tightened up the ensemble considerably, and that the bands which played at clubs utilised textures which were much looser. It is, of course, impossible to make an absolute judgment on such matters, but it certainly seems very likely. There is also the point that the musicians who remained in New Orleans were almost sure to hear those who had left when the latter returned for concerts or dance engagements, and that there was very likely an influence towards a swing pattern as a result.

The only band from New Orleans that was heard by enthusiasts in other cities was the one led by Bunk Johnson. In 1945 it came to New York City, playing at the Stuyvesant Casino, and was hailed by the purist critics as all that was holy in jazz. Bunk himself has been ill-served by his admirers, whose fantastic claims on his behalf were easy targets for the detractors of the band. Generally, his playing was straightforward, and after stating the melody he would go on to play a series of variations that seldom showed any outstanding originality. However, his better recordings show him to be the possessor of a very good tone, and his work is usually interesting. His final recording session, made in the winter of 1947, was the only one where he selected the musicians and tunes played, and it amply demonstrates the difference between his concept and that of the other members of his regular band.

Since Johnson's death the band has continued under the leadership of George Lewis, and is now virtually the only genuine New Orleans group in regular employment. Lewis has had an immense influence on the young revivalists, but few have been able to approach him in the authority and merit of his music. In the essay by Bruce King, which has already been quoted, there is a paragraph which serves as an excellent description of Lewis's style, as follows:

> Lewis's style basically consists of a series of arpeggio runs in wide intervals up and down the chords. Lewis, however, develops his runs in terms of the melody, rather than of the chords, so that they are a set of variations, rather than mere fill-ins. On *Ice cream* (American Music LP 639), Lewis's part is almost continuous throughout, being based on an eighth note rhythm, with shifting accents. All his phrases contrast, modify, or develop this pattern which echoes Baby Dodds's drum work. Lewis not only creates a wide variety of rhythmic ideas, but his playing exhibits a remarkable placing of accents between the beats at such a fast tempo. His accents, however, are integrated with his phrasing and are used for contrast.

It is also necessary to observe that Lewis swings a great deal more than many of the earlier New Orleans musicians. Essentially a blues player, his music, as reflected also in his band, is extrovert and essentially communicative, even when the number is a slow blues. The musical lapses of such members as Avery Howard and Jim Robinson are apt to be forgiven when one hears the band in person, for the immense vitality and sheer *joie de vivre* of the playing is extremely impressive. Recently the band has been featuring Thomas Jefferson, a comparatively young trumpeter in the Armstrong tradition, whose playing is very good both as a member of the ensemble and as a soloist. Mention must also be made of the seventy-year-old bass player, Alcide "Slow Drag" Pavageau, who is not only superb in his role of keeping the beat but also plays effective rhythmic patterns as a springboard for the front-line men to create their own accents. Age must shortly take its toll of the Lewis band, but it remains as a splendid example of a fine musical tradition.

It is not possible to deal with individual musicians in more than a general fashion in this context, but mention must be made of a few of the more outstanding players who appear on the American Music label. Of these, trumpeters Wooden Joe Nicholas and "Kid Shots" Madison, clarinetist Albert Burbank and pianist Dink Johnson are the most notable. Nicholas, who also plays clarinet in a somewhat contrasting manner, is a remarkable musician. He appears on one LP record (American Music 640) and proves that he has a considerable range, exceptional freedom as far as time values are concerned, and tremendous contrast in the use of smears, growls and phrasing. He plays a set of variations on *Careless Love* that reveals considerable imaginative gifts, while his work on the other tracks of the LP is worthy of study. Madison, a boyhood friend of Louis Armstrong—with whom he appeared in a band in the Waif's Home, to which Armstrong was confined when fifteen years of age—is a more melodic player than Nicholas, but his work has something of the form associated with Armstrong and his variations are notable for their logic. It is unfortunate that he recorded very little prior to his death in 1948, but his work on the beautiful slow blues, *Dumaine Street Drag,* and the faster *Bucket's Got a Hole in It* is noteworthy.

Burbank has not received the same attention as George Lewis, but he is a fine musician, whose sense of continuity in the development of his choruses repays careful listening. He is at his best on the Wooden Joe Nicholas LP already mentioned. Dink Johnson really hardly belongs in this essay, but the series of rags and stomps he recorded for William Russell are among the most delightful on records. At one time Johnson played clarinet with Jelly Roll Morton, and Russell has unissued sides by him on which he plays this instrument. The interesting factor in Johnson's piano recordings is that he plays rags in a far less rigid manner than is usual without destroying the inherent form of the compositions. In view of this, it is surprising that more of the revivalist musicians have not studied his work.

The concentration on certain musicians in this essay may be somewhat unfair to others who have recorded for American Music and other labels, but these were the men who played the major part in the revival of interest in traditional jazz. It is somewhat unfortunate that certain individuals had no opportunity of recording when they were in their prime, but it is not true, as certain critics have maintained, that nearly all these records are of only historical interest. During the past two decades in particular, jazz has become a highly sophisticated music, but the ensemble style of the New Orleans musicians can still be rewarding when the players are of a high calibre. In these records by a later generation of New Orleans men than those of the classic period, the ensembles are much lighter, allowing more freedom for each individual, with the result that an astounding variety can be discerned in the instrumental roles from one chorus to another. It is very unfortunate that this aspect of these recordings has been almost totally rejected by the revivalists.

If the American Music records by New Orleans musicians played a major role in reviving interest in traditional jazz, Kid Ory's share is nearly as great. There is, however, an important difference between the records by the Ory band and those on American Music. Ory himself is a veteran of many early traditional groups, including the famous Louis Armstrong Hot Five and Hot Seven, and Jelly Roll Morton's Red Hot Peppers. In the spring of 1922 he made the first records by a traditional New Orleans group, and for many decades he has been resident of Los Angeles. He had retired from music in 1931, and it was not until the late 1930's that the renewed interest in traditional jazz brought him out of this retirement. His big chance came in 1944, when Orson Welles was running a broadcast series for Standard Oil and invited him to form a band. Ory's first group had Mutt Carey on trumpet, Jimmie Noone on clarinet, Buster Wilson on piano, Bud Scott on guitar, Ed Garland on bass and Zutty Singleton on drums. All these men had been famous during the 1920's and early 1930's, and had left New Orleans in the general exodus to seek their fortune in Chicago and elsewhere. Their names were already familiar to collectors from innumerable recordings, and for them it was more a question of resuming from where they had left off.

In the case of a musician like Noone, there could be no shadow of doubt as to his technical proficiency—he had, in fact, influenced clarinet players like Benny Goodman and Jimmy Dorsey—and he had a tone that was much more legitimate than that of most New

Orleans clarinet players. For this reason the music of the Ory band was much more acceptable to many collectors than that of a Bunk Johnson or George Lewis. It is unfortunate that Noone died during the period of the broadcasts and, as a result, only a few rather poorly dubbed acetates remain by which one can judge the original band. However, the first records that the Ory band made for a small company are justly esteemed, with Omer Simeon or Darnell Howard in place of Noone, and Minor Hall replacing Singleton.

For the past fifteen years Ory has continued to lead a band, and while many good records have resulted, none have equalled the 1944/45 sessions. Mutt Carey, who died in 1948, was not a trumpeter of any startling imagination, and his technique was not great, but as a lead man he was exceptional. His ability always to play the right notes and to fill in correctly made him a very great asset to the band, and since his death nobody has fitted so well in the trumpet role. Ory himself has changed little in thirty years; his rough-hewn solos are effective but his main strength lies in his ability as an ensemble player. Omer Simeon and Darnell Howard are both fine clarinet players, but in more recent years a succession of less talented musicians have been with Ory. Both Wilson and Scott died some years ago, and much of the strength of the rhythm section lies with the talented Minor Hall. Hall must be the finest traditional drummer playing today; his sense of dynamics and ability to vary his role to fit each soloist seems uncanny at times, and he swings well. During the past decade there have been many LPs by the Ory band, often of a variable quality, but the veteran trombonist has that rare ability to make competent musicians sound better than they really are, and once or twice has achieved astonishingly successful results with the most unlikely of combinations. At its worst, the band may sound like the many run-of-the-mill "Dixieland" groups that are popular today, but every so often Ory can still surprise one by producing an LP that has some of the depth of the true New Orleans jazz. Now over seventy years of age, his great days are past, but by comparison to the revivalists, he remains a zestful performer.

Leaving aside the Dixieland bands, which have, in the main, replaced depth with a somewhat synthetic heartiness, the number of regular bands that have played traditional jazz well during the past two decades is limited. For social as well as musical reasons, the young Negro musician has tended to reject jazz of this type, and while one may deplore this, it is understandable at one level. The few worth-while bands have been made up of older musicians, who play the style naturally, and time has taken its toll of these men. The three remaining groups to be mentioned are somewhat outside this category, for the leaders are all musicians who are associated with the swing era. The most notable is, perhaps, Wilbur de Paris.

Wilbur de Paris has led a band since 1943 that has included his brother, Sidney de Paris, on trumpet; Omer Simeon on clarinet; and a less stable rhythm section. Although Simeon is a New Orleans musician who is perhaps best known for his outstanding work on many Jelly Roll Morton records of the late 1920's, he has also had considerable big-band experience. Wilbur de Paris defines his music as *New* New Orleans Jazz, and claims that he has followed a logical development which would have been paralleled by the New Orleans men he knew in the past. The records that the band has made have been somewhat uneven, and at times have shown an uneasy compromise between the old and the new. Thus, one might find an excellent version of one of the leader's Latin-American-influenced numbers, followed by a track featuring a clanking banjo solo; but at its best the band has produced some of the freshest jazz in the traditional field of the past few years. It is ironic that its output should be dismissed by one purist critic as that of "malcontent professionals."

Teddy Buckner, greatly influenced by Louis Armstrong, is a trumpeter who until 1949 had played in swing bands. Kid Ory was left without a trumpeter one night and called Buckner in as a last-minute replacement, and since then he has played with traditional-style bands, leading his own group since 1954. Buckner is probably the best trumpeter around who is basically using the Armstrong style of the late 1920's and early 1930's, and his records are interesting without being exceptional. The personnel of his groups varies, but of late he has featured an excellent trombonist, John Ewing, whose own experience was also gained in big bands. At times the music of this group is close to the stereotyped Dixieland units; but with the decline of the authentic New Orleans music, it is probable that this is the form that traditional jazz will take in the next decade. At least a band like Buckner's combines a high degree of technical proficiency with a certain amount of individuality in solo work, and unless one tightens the definition of traditional jazz to exclude such a group as the Armstrong Hot Seven, it is difficult to see that a musician such as Buckner can be considered in any other idiom.

The final regular group to be considered is unusual in many ways. The leader, Franz Jackson, was an arranger and tenor saxophonist for Earl Hines' large band in the late 1930's, and had never played until a year or two ago in any other setting than swing. Late in 1956 he sat in for George Lewis when the latter was ill during the course of a club engagement, and shortly afterwards he formed a traditional group, which has been playing for the past two years at a club on the outskirts of Chicago. His companions in the front line are Albert Wynn, a trombonist who was popular in the late 1920's and whose professional experience covers many fields, and trumpeter Bob Shoffner. Shoffner has played with Charlie Creath, King Oliver, Earl Hines, McKinney's Cotton Pickers and many other bands, large and small. The rhythm section features a tuba and a banjo, played by Bill Oldham and Lawrence Dixon respectively, and is filled out with drummer Richard Curry and pianist Little Brother Montgomery. The latter is a blues pianist who has only recently had much experience with bands. This somewhat heterogeneous collection of stylists is not one that, at first glance, seems likely to produce very cohesive music, but the one LP that the band has made (Replica 1006) at the time of this writing shows ensemble playing of a high order. The band returns to the classic mould of earlier New Orleans jazz, showing no influence of later developments, although Jackson himself denies that he is attempting to copy New Orleans jazz. What is probable is that the musicians would all have heard bands of the calibre of Oliver's and Noone's, and that their thinking would be influenced by this. I wrote Franz Jackson, asking him a number of questions about the formation of the band, with particular reference to the use of the banjo and tuba, and his answers are worth quoting:

> In the early 40's when everyone seemed to be stressing the four beats, I found it more convenient in my playing to think in two. Consequently, when I formed this band I could never forget the impressive beat that one absorbs from the playing of two beats as we find in all marches. That is the reason I chose the tuba and the banjo, as the two go together in my conception as do the string bass and guitar. Therefore, in numbers of a festive nature I pur-

posely had the recording engineer accentuate these two instruments. In this idea, the piano as a solo instrument becomes like the old-time recording, an instrument that stands by itself with only the thesis accentuated by the drums. Also, in piano solos I found that the timbre of the piano is lost when these instruments are playing (tuba and banjo). I guess, I more or less, backed away from the modern concept of rhythm as I found it very difficult to play rhythmically against such complicated background that is now being offered by many modern drummers today. So I can very well say that I feel "at home" with two beat, which is a question that is asked by those who know that I more or less came up in the Swing Era.

I am not trying to copy New Orleans jazz, though I do play numbers that are characteristic of that style—if anything comes out like it, it just seems to fall natural.

The essential point about the few remaining traditional bands that still turn out creative music is that the members are, in the main, men who grew up with the idiom or, in a few instances, musicians who turned to the traditional form after varied careers which would have brought them into contact with many of the pioneer stylists. There are a number of individuals who are certainly creative musicians of a high order (until his recent death, Sidney Bechet was one obvious example) still playing in the traditional field, but they no longer lead regular groups. The few bands made up of old-timers are heavily outnumbered by the Dixieland units—which utilise the outer shell of the traditional form and reduce everything to a slick formula—and the revivalists. The commercial success of the latter is one of the most interesting and, to most professional musicians, inexplicable factors of the current music scene.

The history of the revivalists is well enough known not to need detailed repetition. The impact of the Lu Watters band, which started playing a repertoire of rags, stomps, blues and ragtime in what they considered the authentic style, had world-wide repercussions during the early 1940's. Similar bands sprung up throughout the U.S.A., Europe and Australia, some achieving considerable public acceptance. Despite the derision of many critics, the popularity of such groups has hardly waned—in Europe at least—and one has recently witnessed the astounding fact of a British band— Chris Barber's—selling a million copies of one record in the United States. This same band, with a formula as slick as George Shearing's in his field, can outdraw almost any other band in the British Isles, and its records outsell those by the men from whom it drew its inspiration. No single factor explains the success of such bands, but the causes are numerous.

Initially, bands like Watters' had as their object the dissemination of the style and repertoire of the great traditional groups of the past, and it was claimed by some partisans that after a while individual development within the idiom would take place, leading to an enriching of that tradition. It is a truism to remark that little creative art has followed a re-creation in any sphere, for such attempts ignore differences of social environment and the long period of gestation that takes place before a style is likely to reach maturity. New Orleans jazz, more than any other form, was the product of a unique environment and the stimulation of diverse musical influences, and it had a strongly functional role within the community in which it was fostered. It is sometimes overlooked that what has made jazz so interesting is its lack of rigidity, but the revivalists attempted to apply strict classifications within their idiom and paid the inevitable penalties of ossification. The revival has produced a few minor musicians of merit, but several of these have since left the narrow traditionalist field. Lacking the stimulus of a social environment that would give life to their music, the revivalists turned inwards, and later groups were reduced to copying the first generation of copyists. Quite where the Watters and similar bands got their ideas on the function of the rhythm section in a traditional performance, I cannot say, but the heaviness and lack of flexibility of these sections is quite inimical to swing. The revival started out with very praiseworthy motives, but it lacked one necessary element—creative performers.

In recent years the revivalists have probably gained their success, as far as public acceptance is concerned, from the surface extrovertism of much of their music. The young are seldom interested in complex music, and the individual creativity of the players is of little moment to them. Revivalist bands do produce quite good dance music, and in Britain, which lacks a swing-band tradition, it is obvious that such music has a greater functional appeal than modern jazz, which cares little for dancers as a rule. A number of the revivalist musicians gained a reasonable technical proficiency; and if they happened to hit on a successful formula, they ceased to bother about ultimate objects—or, more precisely, the ultimate object was altered. Despite the claims of certain critics, there is, after all, no magical formula about traditional jazz that prevents commercialism in the pejorative sense of the term.

In Britain, at least, and probably elsewhere, there was a further strong element that led to the success of the revivalists. Among jazz enthusiasts there has always been a strong left-wing political trend that is hostile to commercialism in the form of the music industry. The magic word which exorcises commercial intent is "folk music," and revivalist jazz seemed to these people to have strong folk elements. The more rabid saw the day when the commercial structure would collapse and folk songs would replace the abominations of Tin Pan Alley. What they did not foresee was that Tin Pan Alley publishers are not committed to issuing trash *per se;* if folk songs sell, then they will unblushingly release the most "socially conscious" item, preferably with a few bars altered so that someone can claim credit and draw composer royalties. One has witnessed the success of a Lonnie Donegan (a rock-'n'-roll singer who came out of the revival) using Leadbelly numbers, and the disillusioned left-wingers are finding that there is nothing sacred from the predatory hands of the commercial music world.

It has taken many years, though, for the lesson to sink in. It has been left to Professor William L. Grossman, in his book, *The Heart of Jazz,* to fall back on a theory that traditional jazz (including the revivalists) has a Christian content; but it would need more than the biggest dose of Christianity to inject some creativity into revivalist jazz at this late date. That the content of jazz has received little attention is certainly true, but facile theories are hardly adequate replacements for serious research, and the latter-day pundits of revivalism have been singularly unconvincing in their views. It is probable that the one aspect of revivalism that is good is that it has helped to popularise jazz. Many of the youngsters who listen and dance to the revivalist bands have probably become interested in the genuine form as a result, and it is certainly healthy that people should sometimes make their own music. The important point is that it should be recognised for what it is—amateur music making.

The future for traditional jazz does not look promising. The great exponents are retiring or passing on, and there seems little likelihood of finding new talent of the same calibre. It is unfortunate that jazz tastes are so much dictated by fashion, but one has to remember that the traditional form had only a minority status by the end of the 1920's. Nothing can lesson the achievements of great pioneers like King Oliver, Jelly Roll Morton, Johnny Dodds and Jimmie Noone, and their music retains its validity irrespective of changing styles and fashions. It contains lessons that a later generation can benefit from, but slavish copying is not a real tribute. What is essential today is that the few remaining traditional musicians of worth should be heard, both musically and otherwise. Any art that totally rejects tradition is likely to be as sterile as one that can only view it with servility. What jazz needs most at present is the middle course.

WHOSE ART FORM?: JAZZ AT MID-CENTURY

∿∿∿∿∿∿∿∿∿∿∿∿

Nat Hentoff

Surprisingly little has been written about the conditions in which jazz is played. This last chapter attempts to set the past two decades' musical developments in jazz, and its growth in public "acceptance," in the context of the way the jazz musician exists from night to night. Jazz may be an "art form" in the Sunday magazines, but it is still vulnerable to a Greenwich Village policeman pointedly advising a night club-owner not to rebook a particular group because "it attracts too much of a mixed audience."

The headline and subhead of a feature article in *The New York Times Magazine,* August 24, 1958, illustrates a prevalent image of the state of jazz at mid-century:

JAZZ MAKES IT UP THE RIVER

was the head, followed by:

The long voyage from New Orleans barrelhouse to public respectability ends in a triumph.

This sanguine viewpoint is shared by most writers on jazz; most of the jazz public; and increasingly by those listeners and readers who are not basically interested in the music, but who see more and more references to jazz in "respectable" places, note its inclusion in year-end roundups of cultural affairs, and observe other evidence that jazz is no longer in context only in gin mills and brothels.

The resultant consensus is that jazz has indeed become triumphantly accepted and honored, and perhaps may even be an "art form," as its more fervent proselytizers claim. Many, incidentally, use the term "art form" as a pennant, without substantial knowledge of what it means.

Musicians who see proclamations similar to that of *The Times* are not so sure of the extent or the quality of the "acceptance" they're receiving. Musically, as I hope this book has indicated, jazz has achieved a depth and range of content within the past half century that does merit—and reward—serious attention. It is true, moreover, that never before has jazz had so large an international audience, and never before has so much been written about it throughout the world.

Within the community of jazz musicians, most young players feel that jazz has become a music primarily to be listened to rather than a background for dancing or drinking, or both; and it is, therefore, "art music" in that sense. The facts of nightly jazz life, however, hardly indicate to them that an era of triumph, respectability, or artistic fulfillment has yet arrived.

The jazz musician, to begin with, continues to work mostly in night clubs. There are several players, young and older, who prefer the informality of the night club and see as its alternative only the cold, intimidating concert hall. But the majority of the younger musicians do not enjoy playing in night clubs, and will welcome whatever feasible ways are eventually realized to liberate them from a setting in which the music may have been the main attraction for some, but not for all.

It is unrealistic—whatever else one may feel about the direction of jazz—to expect that much of jazz from now on will be made for dancing. And the night club is hardly an optimum place for listening. There are the egregiously noisy distractions of bibulous customers, chattering customers, rude customers, waiters, cash registers and other insistently competitive sounds indigenous to the night club. Without attempting to equate or even to compare the two kinds of music aesthetically, it is as disturbing and ultimately as frustrating for many jazzmen to sustain invention in the middle of infinitely varied degrees of inattention as it would be for a string quartet to play Mozart at Birdland.

There are further ingredients. "I have few enough clothes as is," said a young musician who is serving his apprenticeship in the clubs; "and I come from the club with my clothes stinking of cigarette smoke and sweat, and my ears echoing with the conversation while I was trying to play."

There are the hours. A jazzman is required more or less to improvise five or six nights a week (seven in a few cities), from nine or ten at night to two or four in the morning. His sets usually run thirty or forty minutes, with maybe twenty to forty minutes in between. In most clubs, he can spend the time when he's not playing either in the turbid room or at a nearby bar or restaurant. There are usually no dressing rooms worth the name.

In view of the nature of even the best-behaved and most attentive night-club audiences, the musician is also often limited as to what he can play in a club. Longer and/or more complex jazz works are being written, but hardly any of them get played in night clubs. The compositions may be performed once or twice a year at a concert or at a record date, and then they're abandoned so far as club work is concerned. The musicians, accordingly, don't get as much opportunity as they should have to familiarize themselves with the particular disciplines required by these attempts to increase the resources of the jazz language; and the player-composers get little chance to hear and learn from having their works played.

Nor are the older players (who are not usually interested in "modern" attempts to expand and vary the forms of jazz) served any better by the night-club setting for most jazz work. While they are, in fact, more comfortable in a night club than most of the more self-conscious younger players, the jazz elders no longer work the best—or often, any—jazz clubs. They are, particularly in this decade, the victims of the night clubs' needs to turn a weekly profit; most night-club owners' corollary unwillingness to "take chances" and their lack of knowledge of how best to promote their attractions. John Levy, manager of George Shearing and several other jazz leaders, and a former bassist himself, said at a Newport Festival symposium in 1957: "Nearly every jazz club owner I've met should have been a wholesale grocer or a butcher, and some were."

When a period comes—as in the past few years—in which the older players appear to be "unfashionable" with that part of the jazz audience that goes to night clubs, their chances for work and their incomes are severely curtailed. Properly presented in concerts, on a TV series or on recordings, these older men could still remain in the center of jazz activity, but none of these alternatives yet exists consistently to a sufficient extent. Like the young players, the elders depend mostly on night clubs, and if the booking offices and club owners become convinced that the older jazzmen have fallen from favor with the drinking public, they do not work except perhaps in rhythm-and-blues bands, neighborhood bars or raucous weekend concerts.

There are other negative factors involved in the general confinement of jazz to night clubs. While a youngster can learn about chamber and symphonic music firsthand at a concert hall, he isn't old enough to attend a jazz club. And if he has come of liquor age, he may well not have the money—in view of the prices at most night clubs, jazz or not—to go as often as he'd like. Older listeners who have lost the habit of night club-going—an easy habit to lose—are likely to prefer records and concerts to the frequent indignities of night clubbing. A jazzman's "live" audience is thereby diminished. What is often left for him to play to are conventioneers; call girls; a nucleus of jazz listeners; boozers; and the curious tabloid readers who are waiting for a man to appear on the stand with a needle in his arm. As a result, the two-way communication essential to all music is considerably delimited and distorted for the jazzman in a night club.

It is not enough for a musician to be aware that a recording of his may be bought by thousands of listeners; there is the further dimension and learning process involved in speaking directly to an audience that is present at the moment of communication, preferably an audience that is really concerned with receiving and reacting to what he has to say.

The prognosis for removing much of jazz from night clubs is uncertain. The basic obstacle is the omnipresence and power in jazz of the booking agents. The jazz musician may read that he is triumphantly respectable and is "accepted" by the State Department and even "jazz priests," but he is booked and treated by most of the agents and most of the club owners as if he were a comic, an "exotic dancer," or minister to a dog act.

The agents are of another time but unfortunately of this place. With very few exceptions, they care little about jazz, have small knowledge of it or respect for the players, and thus can hardly be expected to want or know how to guide the careers of their charges from any long-range perspective. They'll book a jazz group anywhere they're likely to be sure of their commission, often with Brobdingnagian jumps in between dates, and with little if any concern for the kind of room the group is to be baited in, its acoustics, or the state of its piano.

By contrast, the major booking agencies for talent in classical music are hardly paragons of virtue and intelligence (as this writer tried to indicate in "Lost Soloists Along the Concert Trail" in *The Reporter,* April 3, 1958); but they at least do know something about classical music, about their artists, and about minimal physical requirements for concert halls.

The jazz bookers, with very few exceptions, are crude and prehensile. As Ralph J. Gleason has observed in the *San Francisco Chronicle:*

> That the booking agency field might be termed a racket, and that entertainers, bandleaders and musicians have been looted for years, is no news to anyone inside the trade.
>
> Personal managers have founded fortunes on the backs of

successful artists. Booking agencies have built empires by sharp practices. And many a band manager bought his house by cheating on the take on one-nighters because, as all bandleaders have learned to their sorrow, you can't play music and watch the door at the same time.

Honesty and integrity in the booking and managerial field is almost as rare as imagination and good taste. Erroll Garner, for one, is lucky in having a manager who possesses all four virtues, plus the courage of a tiger when it comes to fighting for him.

But lots of artists haven't been as lucky as Garner. I know of a famous bandleader who was regularly mulcted of thousands of dollars a month by a cheating manager who went into cahoots with promoters to falsify box-office reports.

The American Federation of Musicians licenses managers and bookers and when promoters fail to pay off talent they are put on the "unfair" list and musicians are not supposed to work for them. But it's a situation that's easy to dodge . . .

It's a jungle, pure and simple, and what laws there are only work now and then. Mostly it's jungle law and a respectable night [club] owner (and the more respectable the better) apparently thinks nothing of making a deal for less than union scale whenever he can.

The only ones who really beat it are the lucky ones like Garner, blessed with honest managers, or the strong ones like Tommy Dorsey, who was his own manager. The rest take a licking to a greater or lesser degree.

And Norman O'Connor, a Catholic priest who lectures and writes on jazz avocationally, wrote in the *Boston Globe:*

> Too many (booking agents) still have a country fair mentality, in which there is no concern for the public, no interest in what is best for the business, but only a delight in how much can "we make and let's get out of here fast."

It is a frequent practice, for example, to block book. A club owner will be told by a powerful agency that he will be allowed to have a currently "hot" attraction if he'll take three or four others who are not as much in demand. The resultant onus on both the successful group (which must now really bring in the receipts) and the combos which have been let in on sufferance is obvious. It is also a practice at times for an agency to lend money to club owners and thereafter dictate their booking policies. There are other shoddy agency practices, all of which illustrate the feeling of most bookers that they indeed "peddle flesh."

Like the classical music performer, the jazz musician—unless he has a personal manager—is relatively helpless in dealing with the agent, on the one hand, and the buyer of his music on the other. There are exceedingly few people in the jazz world of enough integrity, intelligence and perseverance to function valuably (for the musician) as jazz managers. As a result, most jazzmen, including most of the biggest in terms of public appeal, allow themselves to be exploited by the booking agencies.

"I know what's going on," says one world-famous jazz leader wearily, "but what can I do? How else will my men and I work regularly?"

"They don't believe," Dizzy Gillespie says of the booking agencies, "that they work for *you*. They think you work for them. And if you let them, they'll prove it."

The jazz player so far sees few ways of doing without the bookers and the club owners. There seemed to be at least summer hope in the burgeoning festival movement that started to grow rapidly after the first Newport Jazz Festival in 1954. But, as Whitney Balliett wrote in *The New Yorker* after the fifth annual Newport non-profit bingo game:

> Since its beginnings in 1954, the Newport Jazz Festival has, like a contented city dog, slowly grown sleeker and rounder. The first Festival consisted of two modest concerts attended by some fifteen thousand people. The latest Festival, held over the Fourth of July weekend in an endless arena called Freebody Park, was a statistician's dream: There were seven concerts (afternoon and evening) and two musically illustrated morning lectures, all of which amounted to over thirty-five solid hours of music and talk; approximately two hundred and fifty musicians, including five big bands, sixteen singers and a welter of small groups; and a total attendance of sixty thousand.

"About the only thing missing," concurred *Newsweek,* "was the elephants."

Newport has been depressingly representative of most of the other festivals. The "festivals" have turned out to be no more than inflated package shows which do not allow the musicians enough time to be heard in other than *Reader's Digest* terms; they are, in fact, much more limiting to self-expression than the average night club.

The jazz-concert experience has been little better. Most of the concert work in jazz continues to be of the "25-Big-Names-Count-'Em-25" variety. There, too, there is insufficient time for each musician and group, and relentless pressure to perform one's most "popular" recording rather than try newer and/or more challenging works.

These "concert" packages are products of the booking agencies and promoters (often doubling as club owners) who are vastly uninterested in esthetics.

The alternatives to the night-club, festival and packaged-concert-show situation are so far difficult of execution. The alternative, for example, to the night club need not—and should not—be the large concert hall, except perhaps for a large jazz band. In any case, I would tend to agree with those classical composers and musicians who are convinced that the concert hall as such is anachronistic and that a new architectural conception of the listening place can result in markedly improved acoustics, comfort, and communication.

For most jazz, in any case, the small concert hall is preferable, and best of all is a theatre-in-the-round or three-quarters-in-the-round. If the concert is limited to one to three groups, if the surroundings are warm, there is no reason why the concert setting *need* by hypertensive or arctic.

There have, of course, been instances of jazz concerts that were successful both artistically and financially. There is Erroll Garner's practice—made possible by the fierce battles his manager, Martha Glaser, has had for years with booking agencies and promoters—of appearing in concert with his trio only. Usually there are no other units on the bill. Garner's impressive concert record prompted Sol Hurok in 1958 to add the pianist to his list of concert attractions. Hurok may not be precisely Prince Valiant, but he's a light-year away from Joe Glaser, head of the Associated Booking Corporation, the world's largest handler of jazz talent.

The Modern Jazz Quartet has managed to perform by itself in concert programs at small auditoriums, museums, and other small concert halls throughout this country and in Europe with rewardingly consistent success. So have the Dave Brubeck quartet and other small combos in circuits of college concerts. One answer in the future may be for colleges, high schools, and other institutions with music programs, such as museums, to include in their music seasons a few jazz units as well as classical chamber groups and solo recitalists. In the proper city and with intelligent organization, there is likely to be room in time for a separate jazz-subscription series. Such a series could present, for example, the Modern Jazz Quartet, Coleman Hawkins, Thelonious Monk, George Lewis and composer-conductor George Russell in the course of a season.

If such a series existed in enough cities—with a further network in Europe—the jazz musician's economic dependance on night clubs would be considerably decreased. It already has been for the Modern Jazz Quartet, Dave Brubeck and Erroll Garner. In the process of getting away more and more from night clubs, all three have benefited —musically, financially and in terms of their own emotional fulfillment.

By and large it will require a competent personal manager, more than any other force, to lead the jazz musician at least partially out of the stifling control of the agencies and those who deal in the musician as chattel.

One of many ways in which a personal manager can protect a musician is guidance in setting up a publishing company for the musician's original works. It's becoming clear, in view of the direction of jazz, that the better jazz player-writers can have an annuity, to some degree, on the basis of performance fees and record royalties from their compositions. The writer, however, should place his work in his own firm, both to safeguard his rights and to increase his take. A few of the younger writers—Quincy Jones, George Russell, Gigi Gryce, among them—have done this, but many more remain prey for those A&R men who are carnivorous. There are still some record companies whose session directors insist that a musician place his composition with their own *sub rosa* publishing firms (or the record company's legitimate firms), or they will not allow the musician to use that original on the record date.

As jazz has become big business, in fact, the successful jazz musician finds himself in a jungle similar to the grim terrain of pop music. Note, for example, the number of bands and combos who worked regularly at New York's leading jazz club, Birdland, in 1958– 59—and who also, in time, left their record labels to join Roulette, of which Morris Levy, Birdland's head, is president. There was a time earlier when one of the major record firms had a tie-up with a club owner-entrepreneur. The latter constantly pressured musicians to sign with that particular label or risk not getting work in his club or on his tours.

The price of "acceptance" for jazzmen in the music business is often bitter and always requires contant caution on the part of the musician or his manager.

As for television—in a period during which most writers on jazz are congratulating themselves, the musicians, and the public for having elevated jazz from the whorehouses of New Orleans, Memphis, etc.—"respectability" for jazz has meant in many cases bringing the musicians back into prostitution, a more direct prostitution than jazzmen have ever previously participated in. At least, in the bordellos, they played interlude and background music. On TV "specials" like the Timex series, as at some of the "festivals," they are the main event.

There was, to return to the festivals, the Randalls Island New York Jazz Festival in the summer of 1958. There, a tie-up between the Festival promoters and various liquor companies resulted in jazz leaders being presented with ormolu figurines (the kind usually available at carnivals) as "appreciation" awards by the distillers. There was also a Festival queen, carefully not Negro that year, because, said the press agent, "The pictures would break only in Harlem if she were Negro."

The irony of much that has happened in this decade of "acceptance" is that the jazzmen (who has presumably chosen his vocation because of its freedom of self-expression) compromises his music for the money, the exposure, and the delusion that by reaching thousands (and in television, millions) he's helping to open the way for jazz—in however distorted a form—to gain initial acceptance. Later, so the theory goes, it may be possible for presumably more "honest" jazz to reach even more millions. This wishful reasoning is based on an incomprehension of Gresham's Law as applied to the entertainment world: You can't be a half virgin.

There is so much of value in the music, and so much likely to come, that I do not believe—despite several of the Hieronymus Bosch aspects of the jazz scene at mid-century—the future of jazz need necessarily be flabby and decadent. It should be possible for jazz musicians to achieve acceptance on their own terms. After all, jazzmen have been in a socio-economic jungle for half a century, and surprisingly many have survived without their music having been diluted. Although the temptations that have arrived with the greater popularity of jazz are themselves larger and more diversified, at least part of the mid-century acceptance of the music is genuine enough to provide a firmer base for the jazz musician than he's ever had—although much more building has to be done. The numbers of serious jazz listeners (and serious can also be synonymous with joyful, as those in love will attest), to whom the musician can communicate fully and with fair expectation of being understood, are also growing, and they are the most solid ground for the future.

I am not arguing, by the way, that all forms of "acceptance" automatically taint. Some critics—and fewer musicians—have constructed a neat and untenable theory that once a jazzman has attained some financial and popular success, he becomes excommunicated, or at least ostracized, by many of the critics. All the theory lacks is evidence to support it. There have been, to be sure, musicians such as George Shearing, who *have* sacrificed continuing self-searching for a mechanical formula which ensures them continued high box-office grosses and "acceptance" among certain kinds of audiences. This kind of capitulation has been rightly condemned. But most— perhaps not all—writers and musicians have been gratified at the growing acceptance and success of the Modern Jazz Quartet, for example, because these musicians have *not* compromised their music while on the ascent, nor have they stopped growing musically.

The future of jazz, so far as one can predict the future or understand the present of anything, should continue to be worth serious attention musically. Efforts like the Timex TV shows (one of which was described by Miles Davis as "a Christmas tree on a plantation") and the Newport Jazz Festival are alien to that part of the future of jazz which is creative and involved with the quality of "acceptance" that jazz deserves. As I wrote at the end of a magazine article, "Jazz: Sideshow or Culture" (*Rogue,* May, 1959):

> The Newport Festival has nothing to do with the future of jazz. It is a last if large gasp of the more expendable show-biz, con-man, fast-talking-agent, tent shows, musicians-come-in-the-back-door past of jazz.

The point, too, is not that jazz must inevitably become devitalized or overly formal in the process of leaving the clubs, the Newports, the booking agents. Freedom from parasites, after all, does not portend emasculation, but rather just the opposite.

There is, however, a bittersweet myth, especially in Europe, that if the working and living conditions for jazzmen are improved, they'll lose their "souls." John Martin writes in an article, "Culture Conscious Cats," in the February, 1959, issue of the British *Jazz Journal:*

> Musicians have always accepted the fact that to produce music of any lasting value a person must have, first of all, experienced the hard knocks of life. In the wider field of classical music both Chopin and Beethoven, together with many others, fought all their lives against illness and great personal handicaps. The almost unbearable anguish of King Oliver's horn playing the blues gives testimony to the poverty and prejudice of his times. The legend of Charlie Parker is a story of battle against the inevitable and is an expression in music which might never again be equalled. Parker would never have produced this contribution to jazz had he been assured of protection from the reverses of living. A cottonwool world of respectability would have strangled Parker.

What of Bach, Stravinsky, Ellington, Basie? As commercialization tries to compress jazz into molds safe enough for the mass-communications media and large profits *now* at the festival gates, so the lay brothers of the "hard-knocks-of-life" sect are suspicious of most attempts to treat the music more "seriously" and to place it where it can be heard without smoke screens. The *faux* Baudelaires fail to realize that by staying in clubs, Newports or with the bookers —and generally "suffering" in other ways—the jazz musician will lose more and more of his freedom and will find himself conforming more and more to what he thinks or is told will sell.

John Martin adds:

> The idea of teaching jazz seems to me to be completely incongruous if the past is to be accepted as evidence. For it cannot be denied that the hard school of life is the proven breeding ground for future greats. Jazz is the musical expression of a personal out-

look and, unlike knowledge, which can be transmitted, the art of
expression in music must be acquired individually, otherwise the
musician's work will represent a mere parody of life, or worse, a pale
imitation of a more eloquent exponent.

As The School of Jazz in Lenox, Massachusetts, with its faculty of working jazzmen, has indicated, Mr. Martin's thesis is absurd. Certainly one cannot teach a man "soul," but one can, especially
in jazz, teach him a great deal about the "art of expression." As
John Lewis, Executive Director of the School, explained:

> A great many elements indigenous to jazz are not entirely
> based on what you can learn in a music school. These are elements
> music schools can't account for; they are instrumental, composi-
> tional and orchestrating techniques based on uniquely individual
> contributions to the jazz language, and these techniques can be most
> directly and valuably learned from the contributors themselves.

Or, as faculty member Kenny Dorham said during the 1958
semester, "If only there'd been a school like this when I first came
to New York, I could have saved so much time."

Though John Martin is British, his viewpoint is a characteristic
part of the murky anti-intellectualism concerning jazz still evident
among that small percentage of American intellectuals who know
or care anything about jazz. These intellectuals—there are exceptions, who do understand jazz's organic need for growth—realize
that knowledge of form and technique does not extinguish feeling in
their own absorption or practice of poetry or painting. Nonetheless
they usually prefer their jazz to remain "primitive" and will not
accord it the right to develop in complexity—and in the challenges
it makes to the listener, emotionally as well as intellectually—as any
form of expression must develop. Its language and the variety and
subtlety of its techniques must inevitably grow as its players grow in
their desire to say more, in different ways than their predecessors
have.

In any case, there are still hardly any articles about jazz in
the "little magazines," and no major fiction writer—except for
James Baldwin in sections of his short story, "Sonny's Blues,"
(*Partisan Review,* Summer, 1957)—has yet handled the jazz life
with insight. Similarly, although beginnings have been made in socio-

economic and psychological writing about jazz (an example is Howard Becker's "The Professional Musician and His Public" in the *American Journal of Sociology,* September, 1951) not too much of a body of valuable material has been printed in those areas at the time.

What, for instance, has been written so far about the reverse segregation in parts of jazz—the conviction on the part of some Negro jazz players that the white musicians are interlopers and unqualified to play jazz? What has been written of the white jazzmen who succumb to greed and practice their own economically motivated segregation in forming all-white units so as to be able to play "all kinds" of clubs? What has been written about the economic life of the jazzman, the psychological context of his life, the composition of the jazz audiences, etc.? And when will someone do some serious research on the social history of jazz taste; the reason for the remarkably small number of Negro writers on jazz; the ambivalences concerning jazz among Negroes and how these ambivalences differ in the various Negro classes? *

As for the academies, it is true that several colleges and universities have begun to offer courses in jazz history and "appreciation," but one wonders how—if at all—jazz figures in courses in the history of American civilization. As music, jazz is not yet included in the curricula of most of the major music schools and conservatories, although a few—like the Manhattan School of Music—are making provision for jazz courses. It is likely that, in the next decade and after, there will be more jazz instruction in the music schools, although it's also likely to remain true that the jazz student will still absorb most of value to him in institutions like The School of Jazz —unless the regular musical schools do hire working jazz players as teachers.

It will be at least a generation, if not more, before a jazz unit-in-residence is likely to be appointed—as already occurs with classical composers, pianists and string quartets—by a college or university. One area in which jazz musicians and composers could be particularly well used is in the regular secondary-school systems. There has already been strong evidence at this writing that band-

* John Steiner notes in an earlier chapter in this book that in their study of Negro South Side Chicago life, *Black Metropolis,* Drake and Clayton make "no mention of Jazz or Jazzmen."

masters throughout the country are utilizing more jazz material and, in some cases, are inviting jazz musicians to teach at band clinics. But what the Ford Foundation has done for classical composers could be equally desirable and productive for jazz player-writers and the students who'd be under their influence.

As announced in *The New York Times,* February 19, 1959:

> Twenty-five composers will be established as "composers in residence" in secondary public school systems throughout the United States during the next three years. . . . Each composer will take up residence in a selected community. He will have no teaching responsibilities, but will compose music written specifically for performance by the orchestra, chorus and band of the school system. . . .
>
> According to Dr. Hanson [Howard Hanson, president of the National Music Council], the purpose of the project is "to encourage composers, to enrich the musical life of the communities and to expand the repertory of secondary music school music throughout the United States."

Unfortunately, it's unrealistic to expect foundation money for jazz projects in the near future. For one thing, jazz is still suspect at the foundations. If jazz is misinterpreted or not really known at all by most younger intellectuals, it is certainly misunderstood by nearly all their elders, to whom jazz is synonymous with pop music and is considered a particularly loud aspect of juvenile delinquency. Yet there is some hope. Once in a while, a legitimate jazz scholar like Fred Ramsey has received aid, as from the Guggenheim Foundation, and it is also true that in 1958, the Ford Foundation did grant seventy-five thousand dollars to Tulane University for a five-year jazz project concerned with the history of New Orleans jazz.

Later in 1958, Ralph Gleason wrote in the *San Francisco Chronicle:*

> I would like to suggest that the successful launching of this work be followed by projects for Kansas City, Chicago, New York, the South Atlantic seaboard, the Southwest and San Francisco. Very little has been done with Kansas City, almost nothing with the Southwest and the Atlantic Coast. There is a great body of material available on San Francisco jazz history, too. Perhaps this can all be brought together as a National Jazz Archives under some university's

sponsorship which would then be a great and valuable center for further study.

Considerable research funds are needed, and quickly, because many of the available sources of material—the older musicians and their contemporaries—are dying. It is unfortunate, for example, that Newport did not take the fifty thousand dollars it expended on the International Band gimmick of 1958 and use it instead for research grants. It's also unfortunate the Institute of Jazz Studies in New York is so limited an operation that it is of value only as a reference library for what others have already done. It's unfortunate that the jazz record companies—let alone the booking agencies—have never felt the responsibility to underwrite research grants. As a result, although there are a few researchers who somehow support themselves while gathering whatever material they can, much valuable data concerning jazz history will never be known, because it will be too late by the time jazz does indeed become "respectable" enough for the foundations.

The foundations, of course, cannot be entirely blamed for wondering whether much jazz scholarship is worth subsidizing. There'd be practically no evidence in that direction were foundation staff members to read only *Down Beat* and *Metronome*. Only towards the end of 1959 did two magazines start—*Jazz: A Quarterly of American Music,* 2110 Haste St., Berkeley 4, California, edited by Ralph Gleason; and *The Jazz Review,* Box 128, Village Station, New York 14, N.Y., edited by Martin Williams and this writer—which began to show some of the areas of jazz research and criticism that have been largely neglected in this country, and to a lesser extent in Europe (where several valuable magazines do exist).

A few books have also indicated what can be done. Among the most notable have been: William Broonzy's *Big Bill Blues,* the blues singer's story as told to Yannick Bruynoghe (Grove Press, 1956); Alan Lomax's *Mister Jelly Roll* (Duell, Sloan and Pearce, 1950, also available in Grove Press paperback, 1956); Rudi Blesh and Harriet Janis, *They All Played Ragtime* (Knopf, 1950); Sidney Finkelstein's *Jazz: A People's Music* (Citadel, 1948); André Hodeir's *Jazz: Its Evolution and Essence* (Grove Press, 1956, also available in Grove Press paperback); Frederic Ramsey, Jr., and Charles Edward Smith, *Jazzmen* (Harcourt, Brace, 1939, now available in

Harvest paperback); and *The Art of Jazz* (Oxford University Press), co-edited by Martin Williams.

Hodeir's book was the first major achievement in musical analysis of jazz. Two other important workers in this field are Gunther Schuller (whose study of early Ellington is contained in this book) and Louis Gottlieb, a regular contributor to *Jazz: A Quarterly of American Music.*

With all of the reservations previously noted—and more— concerning the connotations of some of the ways jazz is currently being "accepted," it is true nonetheless that working conditions for the jazzman are improving and his music is, to some extent, being heard and even understood by more and more people and by a wider range of listeners. More listeners are beginning to continue their interest in jazz into their thirties and forties and beyond, so that gradually, a jazz audience is being built which has had experience of more than one era of the music, and accordingly is less inclined to be parochial in its tastes and in its encouragement of new developments than previous generations of listeners have been.

That there are dangers for the music and the musicians in certain *kinds* of acceptance has, I hope, been made evident. It is not enough for partisans to proclaim that jazz is an art form. It's also essential to know *whose* art form—the bookers', the festival promoters', or the musicians'.

SELECTED
DISCOGRAPHY

West African Music

African Coast Rhythms (Riverside 4001)
Tribal, Folk and Café Music of West Africa (Riverside 4001–4003)
Folk Music of Senegal (Folkways P 462)
Music of Liberia (Folkways P 465)
Baoulé of the Ivory Coast (Folkways FE 4476)
Malinké and Baoulé Music (Counterpoint 529)
Musique d'Afrique Occidentale (London TWBV 91105)
Music of Dahomey (Esoteric 537)
Drums of the Yoruba of Nigeria (Folkways P 441)
Music of the Cameroons (Vanguard 7023 and 7032)
Music of the Bulu of the Cameroons (Folkways P 451)
Music of Equatorial Africa (Folkways P 402)
Music of the Western Congo (Folkways P 427)
Congo Music (Riverside 4002)
Denis-Roosevelt Expedition to the Belgian Congo (General Album G-10)
African Music recorded by Laura C. Boulton (Folkways 8852)
Congo Songs and Dances (English Decca LF 1172)

Other African Music

Africa South of the Sahara (Folkways FE 4503)
African Drums (Folkways FE 4502)
African Folk Music (Stinson SLP 89)
African Music Society's Best Music for 1952 (English Decca LF 1171)
African Music Society's Best Recordings of 1953 (English Decca LF 1225)
African Tribal Music and Dances (Counterpoint 513)
African Zulu Music (Capitol T 10114)
Bantu Choral Folksongs (Folkways FE 6912)
Bantu Folk Music (Columbia KL 213)
Belgian Congo Music (Commodore 30005)
East African Drums (English Decca LF 1120)
Ekonda Tribal Music (Riverside 4006)
Ethiopian Folk Music (Folkways FE 4405 and FE 4442)
French Colonies (Columbia KL 205)
Guitars of Africa (English Decca LF 1170)
Ituri Forest Music (Folkways FE 4457 and FE 4483)
Kenya (English Decca LF 1121)

Negro Music of Africa (Folkways FE 4500)
Talking and Royal Tutsi Drums (English Decca LF 1169)
Tanganyika (English Decca LF 1084)
Uganda (English Decca LF 1173)
Watutsi Songs of Ruanda (Folkways FE 4428)

78-r.p.m. Discs

It is often thought that African records are rare. This is not so. There are easily 6,000 to 7,000 good African recordings available on 78-r.p.m. discs. The main sources are Galatone in South Africa; the HMV LON series for the Belgian Congo, the HMV GV, JL, JLC, JP, JZ and MA series for other parts of Africa; the Odeon PL and PO series; the Parlophone EZ and UTZ series; the Decca (British) WA series for West Africa; the Columbia (British) EO and WE series; the South African Trek DC series; a huge catalogue of modern, urban West African music on Melodisc (British); the Philips ACP series; Pathé Marconi's CPT series; the Boite à Musique (Paris) BAM series; and Africa Vox in France.

For specialized research and collectors, records are also obtainable from the Musée de l'homme, the Phonotèque Nationale and the UNESCO International Archives of Music—all in Paris.

American Negro Work Songs

B.B. and Group: *Black Woman* (Nixa NJL 11)
B.B. and Group: *Ol' Alabama* (Nixa NJL 11)
Boykins State Farm Group: *Look Down That Lonesome Road* (LC * AAFS 14)
Bradley, Jesse & Group: *Hammer Ring* (LC AAFS 39)
C.B. and Group: *Rosie* (Nixa NJL 11)
Cumins State Farm Group: *It Makes a Long Time Man Feel Bad* (LC FM 2)
Hill, Clyde & Group: *Long Hot Summer Days* (LC AAFS 13)
Ironhead & Group: *Go Down, Ol' Hannah* (LC AAFS 38)
Ironhead & Group: *Grey Goose* (LC AAFS 15)
Ironhead & Group: *Ol' Rattler* (LC AAFS 38)
Jimpson & Group: *No More, My Lawd* (Nixa NJL 11)
Jordan, Frank & Group: *I'm Goin' to Leland* (LC AAFS 14)
Leadbelly: *Black Betty* (MU 224 or Folkways FP 241)
Leadbelly: *Bring Me a Li'l Water, Sylvie* (Folkways FP 4 or Stinson SLP 19)

    * LC-Library of Congress.

Leadbelly & Golden Gate Quartet: *Ham an' Eggs* (Victor 27266)
Leadbelly: *Line 'Em* (Folkways FP 34 or Stinson SLP 19)
Leadbelly: *Looky, Looky Yonder* (Musicraft 224 or Folkways FP 241)
Leadbelly: *Ox-driving Song* (Folkways FP 24)
Leadbelly & Golden Gate Quarter: *Pick a Bale of Cotton* (Victor 27268; alternative FP 4)
Leadbelly: *Take This Hammer* (Asch 101, Folkways FP 4 or Capitol LC 6597)
Leadbelly: *Yellow Women's Doorbells* (Musicraft 224)
Lightning & Group: *I Wonder What's the Matter* (LC AAFS 39)
Lightning & Group: *Long John* (LC AAFS 13)
Pace, Kelley & Group: *Jumpin' Judy* (LC AAFS 13)
Pace, Kelley & Group: *Rock Island Line* (LC AAFS 40)
Parchman Farm Group: *Katy Left Memphis* (Nixa NJL 11)
Tangee Eye & Group: *Jumpin' Judy* (Nixa NJL 11)
Twenty-two & Group: *Early in the Mornin'* (Nixa NJL 11)
Twenty-two & Group: *It Makes a Long Time Man Feel Bad* (Nixa NJL 11)
Twenty-two & Group: *Old Dollar Mamie* (Nixa NJL 11)
Terry, Sanders & Group: *Pick a Bale of Cotton* (Folkways FP 28)
Turner, Willie & Group: *She Done Got Ugly* (Folkways P 417)
Webb, Jeff & Group: *Rosie* (LC AAFS 14)
Williams, Ernest & Group: *Ain't No Mo' Cane on the Brazos* (LC AAFS 13)

In addition, work songs of some interest can be found in the following collections and anthologies:

Take This Hammer (Folkways FP 4)
Rock Island Line (Folkways FP 14)
Leadbelly's Legacy, Vol. 3 (Folkways FP 24)
Leadbelly's Legacy, Vol. 4 (Folkways FP 34)
Leadbelly's Last Sessions, Vol. 1 (Folkways FP 241)
Leadbelly's Last Sessions, Vol. 2 (Folkways FP 242)
Leadbelly Memorial (Stinson SLP 17, 19, 48, 51)
Leadbelly Party Songs (Stinson SLP 39, 41)
Horace Sprott, Vol. 1 (Folkways FP 651)
Horace Sprott, Vol. 2 (Folkways FP 652)
Horace Sprott, Vol. 3 (Folkways FP 653)
Music from the South (Folkways FP 654)
The South (Folkways FP 53)
Negro Music of America (Folkways P 500)

Alabama Negro Folk Music (Folkways P 417, P 418, P 471, P 472, P 473, P 474)

Worksongs (Stinson SLP 87)

Chain Gang (Stinson SLP 7, SLP 8)

Negro Prison Camp Songs (Folkways 4475)

Negro Prison Songs (Tradition 1020)

Negro Hollers, Work Calls and Street Cries

Bama: *Levee Camp Holler* (Nixa NJL 11)

Brooks, Samuel: *Quittin' Time Song* (LC AAFS 37)

Brown, Enoch: *Complaint Call* (Folkways P 417)

Butler, Charlie: *Diamond Joe* (LC AAFS 16)

C.B.: *Whoa, Back* (Nixa NJL 11)

Dodson, Annie Grace: *Children's Call* (Folkways P 417)
                                 Father's Call   "
                                 Field Call   "
                                 Greeting Call   "

Hall, Vera: *Another Man Done Gone* (LC AAFS 16)
                Boll Weevil   "

Hazel, Sam: *Heavin' the Leadline* (LC AAFS 36)

Henry, Jim: *I Don't Mind the Weather* (LC AAFS 16)

Jimpson & Group: *The Murder's Home* (Nixa NJL 11)

Leadbelly: *Ain't Goin' Down to the Well No Mo'* (Mu 224 or Folkways FP 24)
           Dick Licker's Holler (Folkways FP 241)
           Go Down, Ol' Hannah (Mu 224 or Folkways FP 241)

Lowry, Irvin: *Joe, The Grinder* (LC AAFS 16)

Marshall, Thomas J.: *Arwhoolie*   (LC AAFS 37)
                  Mealtime Calls "   "   "

Prothero, Allan: *Track Lining Song* (LC AAFS 40)

Shores, Joe: *Mississippi Sounding Calls* (LC AAFS 36)

Tangle Eye: *Tangle Eye Blues* (Nixa NJL 11)

Thomas, Edna: *Street Cries of New Orleans* (English Columbia 4196)

Truvilion, Henry: *Come on, Boys* (LC AAFS 37)

Truvilion, Henry: *Come on, Boys* (LC AAFS 37)
                  Tamping Ties   (LC AAFS 38)
                  Unloading Rails "   "   "

Various: *Street Cries of Charleston* (Stinson SPS 13 & 14)

Williams, Willie: *O Lawd, Don't 'Low Me To Beat 'Em* (LC FM 2)

Ring Shouts, Moans, Spirituals, Gospel Songs and Sermons

Amerson, Rich & Group: *Rock, Chariot, Rock* (Folkways P 418)

Brown, J. W. & Coleman, Austin: *Run, Old Jeremiah* (LC AAFS 12)

Congregation of Shilo Primitive Baptist Church: *Prayer Meeting* (Folkways P 418)

Congregation of Silent Grove Baptist Church, Clarksdale, Mississippi: *I'm a Soldier in the Army of the Lord* (LC)

Congregation of the Church of God in Christ, Clarksdale, Mississippi: *I'm Runnin' for My Life* (LC)

Congregation of the Church of God in Christ, Moorhead Plantation, Lulu, Mississippi: *I'm Gonna Lift Up a Standard for My King* (LC)
      I've Got a Hiding Place (LC)

Gates, Rev. J. M. & Congregation: *Born Again* (Folkways FP 252)
      Oh Death   "   "   "

Griffin, Sin Killer & Congregation: *The Man of Calvary* (LC AAFS 48)
      Wasn't That a Mighty Storm (LC AAFS 48)

Hibler, Rosie & Family: *Move, Members, Move* (Folkways P 418)

Johnson, Blind Willie: *Jesus Make Up My Dying Bed* (Columbia 14276 D)
      John, the Revelator (Folkways FP 252)

McGhee, Brownie; Terry, Sonny; & McMahon, Coyal: *I Shall Not Be Moved* (Folkways FP 28)
      Midnight Special (Folkways FP 28)

Mitchell's Christian Singers: *The Bridegroom's Coming* (Columbia 37483)
      Jesus Going to Make Up My Dying Bed (OK 04357)
      Swing Low, Sweet Chariot (Mellotone 60464)

Moseley, Rev. W. M.: *The Gambling Man* (Columbia 14186D)

Pace, Kelley & Group: *Holy Babe* (LC AAFS 49)

Phillips, Sister Berenice: *God Leads His Dear Children* (Circle 3011)
      I Couldn't Hear Nobody Pray (Circle 3012)

Reed, Dock; Reed, Henry; & Hall, Vera: *Trouble So Hard* (LC AAFS 11)
      Handwriting on the Wall (LC AAFS 11)

Spirit of Memphis Quartet: *I'll Go* (King 5998)

Sturdivant, Bozie & Congregation: *Ain't No Grave Can Hold My Body Down* (LC AAFS 47)
Tharpe, Rosetta & Knight, Marie: *Didn't It Rain* (Engl Brunswick 04851)
Up Above My Head (Engl Brunswick 04554)
Williams, Willie & Group: *The New Buryin' Ground* (LC AAFS 11)
Collections and Anthologies (list)
Bahama Gospel Songs and Spirituals (Folkways FE 4440, FS 3845, FW 6842)
Get on Board (Folkways FA 2028)
Harlem Congregation (Ducretet Thomson TKL 93119)
Music from the South, Vols. 2–10 (Folkways FA 2651—FA 2659)
South, The (Folkways FJ 2801)
Spirituals (Folkways FA 2038)
Swing Low, Sweet Chariot (Riverside 12–651)
Cat Iron (Folkways FA 2389)
Cotton, Elizabeth (Folkways FG 3526)
Fisk Jubilee Singers (Folkways FP 72)
Jackson, Mahalia (Vogue LD 067; Engl Vogue LDE 005; Philips BBE 12069)
Johnson, Blind Willie (Folkways FG 3585; Fontana TFE 17052)
Kelsey, Reverend (Brunswick E OE 9256)
McFerrin (Riverside 12–812)

Creole Roots of Jazz

All Star Stompers: *Dardanella* (London HAU 2035)
Barbarin, Paul: *Eh La-bas* (London LTZK 15032)
Ma Chère Amie (Jazztone J-1205)
Bechet, Sidney: *Ce Mossieu qui parle* (Vocalion E EPV 1020)
Les Oignons "
Marchand de Poisson "
Barnes, Emile: *Toute de Moi* (AM 641)
Eh la-bas (AM 641)
Carnival Three: *Creole Lullaby*
Celestin, Oscar: *Marie Laveau*
Creole Serenaders: *Les Oignons*   (London HAU 2035)
No Pas Lemme Ça "
Sale Dame "
De Paris, Wilbur: *Mardi Gras Rag*
Juba Dance (London LTZK 15086)
Gottschalk, Louis Moreau

Op. 2 *Bamboula, Danse des Nègres* (Vanguard 485; MGM E 3370)
Op. 3 *La Savane, Ballade Créole* "
Op. 5 *Le Bananier, Chanson Nègre* "
Op. 15 *The Banjo, Fantaisie Grotesque* "
Op. 37 *Ojos Criollos, Danse Cubaine* "
       Marche des Gibaros, Souvenir de Porto Rico (Vanguard 485)
Miles, Lizzie: *Bill Bailey* (Cap T 793)
Morton, Ferdinand: *Barbados* (QRS)
                   C'est l'aut' Cancan (LC 1684)
                   Crave, The (General 4003)
                   Creepy Feeling (JM 12; LC 1682; LC 1683)
                   Creola (QRS)
                   Fickle Fay Creep (Victor 23019; LC 1673)
                   If You Don't Shake (LC 1684)
                   La Paloma (LC 1682)
                   Mamamita (Gennett 3043)
                   Mama 'Nita (Para 12216; LC 1684)
                   New Orleans Blues (LC 1681)
                   Original Jelly Roll Blues (Victor 20405)
                   Spanish Swat (LC 1685)
Nicholas, Albert: *Moi Pas Lemme Ca* (Vogue V 2233)
Nicholas, Wooden Joe: *Ai, Ai, Ai* (American Music 534)
Original Creole Stompers: *Eh La-bas* (American Music 513, 535)
Ory, Edward: *C'est l'autre Cancan* (GTJ LDG 185)
             Creole Bobo
             Eh La-bas (Vogue V 2011)
Parenti, Tony: *Creole Blues* (Vi 19647)
               Vieu Carre (Jazztone J-1215)
Thomas, Edna: *Ai Suzette* (Co E 3526)
Wiggs, Johnny: *Chef Menteur Blues* (Golden Crest CR 3021)
               Camelia Gaspargeaux (Golden Crest CR 3021)

Anthologies

Cajun Songs from Louisiana (Folkways FE 4438)
Creole Songs & Street Cries (Folkways FA 2202)
Music of New Orleans, Vol. 1 (Folkways FA 2461)
The South (Folkways FJ 2801)

A catalogue of recordings available from the Library of Congress can be obtained by writing Music Division—Recording Laboratory, Library of Congress, Washington 25, D.C.

NEW ORLEANS AND TRADITIONS IN JAZZ

"To me there is no jazz music more enjoyable than that of several horns playing together, especially when each is listening to and trying to enhance the parts the others are playing."—Turk Murphy, quoted in Lester Koenig's introduction to *The Bay City Jazz Band.*

"Keep off my part!"—familiar plaint in Bolden Band (from Willy Cornish).

Brass Bands

We have Willy Cornish's word for it that the Buddy Bolden Band recorded at least one brass-band tune. Needless to say, this record, a cylinder, is not available, nor is such a recent brass-band album as the deeply moving funeral-parade music issued a few years ago on the Pax label. But a few albums, including brass-band music related to jazz, *are* available, and all are of interest. Of the following, the closest to traditions of oral improvisation are the country brass bands, whose harmonies have an awkward, almost ugly beauty, the rhythmic styles of which are among the most unique in jazz. The Kid Rena Band (*New Orleans Legends*) plays *Gettysburg,* and on *High Society* Picou plays the chorus he himself created (with perhaps more vigor) when he was much, much younger. The Eureka and The Young Tuxedo are bands still playing regularly for funerals and club events.

> *Music From The South* (vol. 1), *Country Brass Bands* (Folkways FA 2650)
> *New Orleans Legends, Kid Rena* (Riverside 12–119)
> *Music of New Orleans: Eureka Brass Band* (Folkways FA 2642)
> *Jazz Begins Sounds of New Orleans Streets Funeral and Parade Music by The Young Tuxedo Brass Band* (Atlantic 1297)

New Orleans Groups in Chicago and New York

In the development of San Francisco jazz, recorded jazz played an important role, but in Chicago in 1923, the one band that was pre-eminent amongst musicians was that of King Oliver. Thus, his ensemble style had an unforgettable impact on Chicago jazz. Later, Louis Armstrong's approach to improvisation, while still stressing the group, tended more and more towards the blowing-session type of jazz, trading of choruses and chase choruses, etc. In the early work of Jelly—along with his entertainer proclivity, which often included a tendency to corn it up— there are examples of some of the most interesting jazz of the period. These early records, which introduced a planned use of orchestral color, etc., sold widely on a national scale. Thus, a record made in a Chicago studio might (and did) influence musicians both on the West Coast and in Harlem.

> *Louis Armstrong: 1923* (King Oliver's Creole Jazz Band) (Riverside 12–122)
> *The Young Louis Armstrong* (Riverside 12–101), with Oliver, Fletcher Henderson, Ma Rainey, etc.
> *The Louis Armstrong Story* (Columbia CL 851–854). These four sets are among the indispensable albums of jazz.
> *The Incomparable Jelly Roll Morton* (Riverside 12–128)
> *The King of New Orleans Jazz* (Jelly Roll Morton) (RCA Victor LPM 1649). This album includes some of the best of the Red Hot Peppers series (*e.g., Black Bottom* and *Kansas City Stomp, The Chant.*)
> *Johnny Dodds and Kid Ory* (Epic 3207)

Early Traditional: I

Whereas many small groups (that should be nameless but aren't) were satisfied with creating shallow novelty jazz imitative of the Dixieland at its worst, two Chicago-based outfits, though influenced by Dixieland, were most forcefully related to King Oliver's Creole Jazz Band. Incidentally, if you discount the Bolden cylinder (on which a man who belonged to both the colored and the white local may have played!), possibly the first mixed recording date took place when the "creator of jazz, stomps and swing" (as Jelly modestly called himself on an engraved card) sat down in a studio with the New Orleans Rhythm Kings.

> *New Orleans Rhythm Kings, with Jelly Roll Morton* (Riverside 12–102)
> *Bix Beiderbecke and the Wolverines* (Riverside 12–123)

Early Traditional: II

As you'll learn when you look them over, none of the following sets provides Chicago-style jazz from first to last track. However, you'll

find that some of the best-known Chicago-style renditions are included
(*e.g.*, *Nobody's Sweetheart*). Both *Chicago Style Jazz* and *The Red
Nichols Story* on Brunswick include examples of Miff Mole, the first set
including Teschemacher With Mole's Molers. As is obvious, many of the
Nichols groups got together merely for recordings.

The nucleus of all Bix Beiderbecke's small-group recording dates (in
The Bix Beiderbecke Story) were men who worked with Bix in either the
Goldkette or Whiteman bands, or both. Paradoxically, there seems more
of a Dixieland flavor in this late-1920's period of Bix's than in his years
with the Wolverines. That Nichols was influenced by Bix should hardly
come as a surprise. That Bix admired the Nichols recording groups, and
especially the work of Miff Mole, is its corollary.

> *On-The-Road Jazz* (Bix, Wingy, Tesch, Muggsy, etc.) (Riverside
> 12–127)
> *Chicago Style Jazz* (Columbia CL 632). This includes some of the
> classics of Chicago as well as Tesch's recording with a New
> York group led by Miff Mole.
> *The Bix Beiderbecke Story* (Columbia CL 844–846). Bix, Eddie
> Lang, Frankie Trumbauer. Also, in one set, Bix with the
> Whiteman band.

Middle Traditional: Muggsy Spanier

Muggsy Spanier's Ragtime Band, including veterans of the Rhythm
Kings and the Chicago-style groups as well as younger men, opened at
Chicago's Hotel Sherman in 1939, and later that year broke things up at
Nick's in Greenwich Village. With Muggsy, Rod Cless and Brunis, this
band provided some great moments in group improvisation and deserves
a niche of its own.

> *The Great 16* (RCA Victor LPM 1295)

The Great Revival: Later Traditional Fare

The New Orleans men who had remained home or returned home
tended to play in an older style. When Louis and Bechet locked horns
in stirring choruses on *Coal Cart* and *Perdido Street Blues* in *New Orleans Jazz* (Decca) it was a thrilling display of two-way improvisation,
but when, in the same set, a Johnny Dodds group came along with
Gravier Street Blues, that was the sound and the ensemble. Indeed, like
some out-of-print records by Johnny, this is a superb example of group
improvisation, New Orleans style.

Of the many men who came out of partial retirement, among the best known are Bunk Johnson and Kid Ory. Unfortunately, many sides by Bunk (including those on the American Music label) are out of print. The set here included is Bunk's second, recorded under the usual primitive conditions by Eugene Williams in New Orleans in 1942. In the Riverside set, Kid Ory, the grandpappy of tailgate, begins to hit his stride after coming out of retirement (*New Orleans Legends*). "I'm an old man but I've got young ideas, and I like to swing," said Wellman Braud, the New Orleanian who swung the Ellington Orchestra for many years and joined Kid Ory for sessions on the Coast (Good Time Jazz). George Lewis (Blue Note) is one of the most talented of New Orleans men who stayed close to home. Paul Barbarin, now in retirement (almost), may be heard with Louis Armstrong (Vol. 4, above) and with the Young Tuxedo Brass Band.

New Orleans Jazz (Decca DL 8283)

Bunk Johnson and His New Orleans Jazz Band (Commodore 30007)

New Orleans Legends (Riverside 12–119)

Kid Ory's Creole Jazz Band (1954: Good Time Jazz L-12004; 1956: Good Time Jazz L-12016)

New Orleans Stompers (Blue Note 1205)

New Orleans Jazz: Paul Barbarin (Atlantic 1215)

Blowing Sessions, 1930's–1959

Informal sessions often featured exciting ensemble, such as that on *Mild and Wild* (with Edmond Hall). Pee Wee Russell, best known for his solo work, is also forceful in ensemble, and in *The Vic Dickenson Showcase* Vic, with the help of Ruby Braff and others, has no trouble getting the show on the road.

Mild and Wild, Wild Bill Davison (Commodore FL 30009)

The Roaring Twenties, Eddie Condon (Columbia CL 1089)

The Vic Dickenson Showcase, Vols. 1 & 2 (Vanguard 8520, 8521)

Jack Teagarden and Bobby Hackett (Commodore 30012)

Jam Sessions at Commodore, Eddie Condon (Commodore 30006)

Pee Wee Plays Pee Wee (Stereo-Craft RTN 105)

Portrait of Pee Wee Counterpoint 565

Documentary and Background

Jelly Roll Morton: Library of Congress Recordings (Riverside 9001–9012)

Satchmo and Me. Lil Armstrong's personally told reminiscences, including the period with King Oliver (Riverside RLP 12–120).

Music from the South (Folkways FA 2650–2659). Country music related to jazz, recorded by Frederic Ramsey, Jr.

Negro Folk Music of Alabama (Folkways FE 4417, FE 4418, FE 4471–74). An anthropologist examines the music of western Alabama, from African survivals to jazz roots.

Collections

Riverside *History of Classic Jazz* available in five-disc set (SPD-11) or in singles (12–112/12–116). See catalogue for details.

In the Folkways Jazz Series, volumes 1, 2, 3, 5, 6, 7, are specially relevant. Numbers are FP 53, 55, 57, 63, 65 and 67 respectively. (See catalogue for details).

The Encyclopedia of Jazz on Records Vol. 1 (Decca 8383)

History of Jazz, Vol. 1 (Capitol T-793)

Introduction to Jazz (Decca 8244)

Two sets of jazz related to New Orleans, traditional and mainstream are *A String of Swingin' Pearls* (RCA Victor LPM 1373) and *Guide to Jazz* (RCA Victor LPM 1393).

Reading references to discography

The New Hot Discography: the 1948 edition of Charles Delaunay's reference work, edited by Walter E. Schaap and George Avakian (Criterion Music, 1270 Sixth Ave., New York 20, N.Y. $7.50).

The Collector's Jazz, John S. Wilson's guide to traditional and swing. A Keystone paperback (Lippincott, $1.45).

A standard catalogue such as *Jazz' 'N Pops* (Long Player Publications, Box 346, New York 19, N.Y. 35 cents each or $3.00 a year.)

Catalogues of record companies cited above: Riverside Records, 553 West 51st Street, New York, 19, N.Y.; Folkways Records, 117 West 46th Street, New York, 36, N.Y.

JELLY ROLL MORTON

Jelly Roll Morton: Classic Jazz Piano (Riverside RLP 12–111). A selection of the Gennett-Paramount-Rialto piano solos, which unfortunately omits *Frog-i-More Rag, Mamamita, The Pearls,* but at least two thirds of which is excellent.

Jelly Roll Morton, King of New Orleans Jazz (RCA Victor LPM 1649). Fourteen of the 1926–28 Victor orchestral recordings. However, the take used of *Dead Man Blues* is not so good as the original, last available on Label "X" LX 3008 and on British HMV DLP 1071.

New Orleans Memories (Commodore 30001). Ten piano solos, five with vocals, some of which show the lyric side of Morton's talent uniquely.
NOTES: The Library of Congress series is currently available on twelve Riverside LPs, 9001–9012. The releases on Label "X" (LX-3008 and LAV-3028), now cut out, contain valuable additions to the Morton library. The series on His Master's Voice in England (DLP 1016, 1044, and 1071), also scheduled to be cut out, contains an excellent cross section of the Victor series. Two earlier Riverside ten-inch LPs (RLP 1083 and 1041) did contain some of the solo recordings which 12–111 omits.

BLUES TO DRIVE THE BLUES AWAY

This is a purely arbitrary selection of recordings illustrating some aspects of the above chapter and the work of some of the blues singers and artists mentioned therein.

Items Quoted in the Text:

1. Walter Davis *Worried Man Blues/M. & O. Blues*   (Victor 23333)
2. Peetie Wheatstraw *Hearse Man Blues/Bring Me Flowers While I'm Living*   (Decca 7886)
3. Barbecue Bob *Bad Time Blues/She's Gone Blues* (Columbia 14461)

Formative Influences on the Blues:

4. "Murderers' Home": Group work songs, hollers, penitentiary songs
(Nixa NJL 11) (English label)
5. "Negro Folk Music of Alabama—Secular": Hollers, field blues
(Folkways P417)

Southern Blues, Regional Forms:

6. Huddie Ledbetter (La.) *Packin' Trunk Blues/Honey, I'm All Out and Down*   (Melotone M13326)
7. Blind Lemon Jefferson (Texas) *Black Snake Blues/Match Box Blues*
(Okeh 8455)

8. Bukka White (Mississippi) *District Attorney Blues/Parchman Farm Blues*   (Okeh 05683)
9. Robert Johnson (Miss. North) *Last Fair Deal Gone Down/32-20 Blues*   (Vocalion 03445)
10. Charlie Lincoln (Georgia) *New Prison Blues/Fo' Day Blues*
                                                                                   (Columbia 14177D)
11. Blind Boy Fuller (N.C.) *Where My Woman Usta Lay/Put You Back in Jail*   (Decca 7903)

Vocal and Instrumental Quality:

12. Brownie McGhee *My Barking Bulldog Blues/Let Me Tell You Bout My Baby*   (Okeh 05812)
13. Tommy McClennan *Cotton Patch Blues/Baby Don't You Want To Go?*   (Bluebird B8408)
14. Lee Brown *I Can Lay It on Down/Low Down Feelin'*   (Decca 7626)
15. Sleepy John Estes *Broken Hearted, Ragged and Dirty Too/Black Mattie*   (Victor 38582)
16. Big Bill Broonzy *Prowling Ground Hog/C-C Rider*   (Perfect 0313)
17. Big Boy Crudup *Death Valley Blues/If I Get Lucky* (Bluebird 8858)
18. Joe Williams *Some Day Baby/Break 'Em on Down*   (Bluebird 8969)

Country Blues Bands and Juke Bands:

19. Peg Leg Howell and His Gang *New Jelly Roll Blues/Beaver Slide Rag*
                                                                                   (Columbia 14210D)
20. Cannon's Jug Stompers *Minglewood Blues/Madison Street Blues*
                                                                                       (Victor 21267)
21. Mississippi Jook Band *Barbecue Bust/Dangerous Woman*
                                                                                   (Melotone 61271)
22. Jim Jackson *Jim Jackson's Jamboree Parts 1 & 2*   (Vocalion 1428)
23. Hokum Boys *Sellings That Stuff/Beedle Um Bum* (Paramount 12714)

Classic Blues Singers:

24. Ma Rainey *Jelly Bean Blues/Countin' the Blues*   (Paramount 12238)
25. Bessie Smith *Nobody Knows You When You're Down and Out/ Backwater Blues*   (Columbia 3176)
26. Clara Smith *Daddy Don't Put That Thing On Me Blues/ It's Tight Like That*   (Columbia 14398)
27. Ida Cox *I've Got the Blues For Rampart Street/Chattanooga Blues*
                                                                                   (Paramount 12063)

28. Lillian Glinn *Where Have All the Black Men Gone/Shake 'Em Down*
(Columbia 14315)
29. Sippie Wallace *Special Delivery/Jack O' Diamonds*   (Okeh 8328)
30. Mamie Smith *Crazy Blues/It's Right Here for You*   (Okeh 4169)
31. Elzadie Robinson *The Santa Claus Crave/St. Louis Cyclone Blues*
(Paramount 12573)

Urban Blues in Chicago and New York:

32. Blind Blake *Seaboard Stomp/Hard Road Blues*   (Paramount 12583)
33. Charlie Spand *Soon This Morning No. 2/Lone Mother Blues*
(Okeh 05946)
34. Leroy Carr *Blues Before Sunrise/Mean Mistreater Mama*
(Vocalion 02657)
35. Bill Gaither *Bad Luck Child/Pins and Needles*   (Decca 7202)
36. Johnny Temple *Between Midnight and Dawn/Big Leg Blues*
(Decca 7547)
37. Memphis Minnie *Me and My Chauffeur Blues/Can't Afford To Lose My Man*   (Okeh 06288)
38. Washboard Sam *I Love all My Women/Out with the Wrong Woman*
(Bluebird 6794)
39. Sonny Boy Williamson *I'm Gonna Catch You Soon/Million Years Blues*   (Bluebird 8866)
40. Big Maceo *Kid Man Blues/Broke and Hungry Blues* (Victor 20–2687)
41. Lonnie Johnson *He's a Jelly-Roll Baker/When You Feel Low Down*
(Bluebird B9006)

Postwar Blues:

42. Cecil Gant *I Wonder/Cecil Boogie*   (Gilt Edge 501)
43. Joe Turner *Rocks in My Bed/Howlin' Winds*   (National 9144)
44. Wynonie Harris *Wynonie's Blues/Somebody Done Changed the Lock on My Door*   (Apo 362)
45. Sonny Parker *Disgusted Blues/My Soul's on Fire*   (Peacock 1620)
46. B. B. King *Three O'Clock Blues/That Ain't the Way To Do It*
(R.P.M. 339)
47. Muddy Waters *Louisiana Blues/Evan's Shuffle*   (Chess 1141)
48. Sonny Boy Williamson No. 2. *Mighty Long Time/Nine Below Zero*
(Trumpet 166)
49. Smokey Hogg *Baby Don't You Tear My Clothes/Highway 51*
(Modern 884)
50. Lightnin' Hopkins *Katie Mae Blues/That Mean Old Twister*
(Aladdin 167)

BOOGIE-WOOGIE

(The following list is not in historical order.)

Albert Ammons: *Shout for Joy* (included in Harmony LP 7104)
Boogie Woogie Stomp/Boogie Woogie Blues/Suitcase Blues/Bass Goin' Crazy/Chicago on My Mind (all Blue Note LP 7017)
Boogie Woogie (Solo Art 12001)
St. Louis Blues/Bass Gone Crazy/Monday Struggle (all included in Riverside LP 12–106)

Meade Lux Lewis: *Honky Tonk Train Blues*, 1927 version (included in Riverside LP 1009)
Yancey Special (included in Decca LP 5249)
Honky Tonk Train Blues (included in Camden LP CAL-328)
Bear Cat Crawl (included in Harmony LP 7104)
Melancholy/Solitude (Blue Note 1)
Mr. Freddie Blues (Decca 3387)
The Blues (Blue Note 8 and 9)
Messin' Around/Deep Fives/Blues de Lux/Closing Hour Blues (included in Riverside LP 12–106)
Honky Tonk Train Blues/Bass on Top/Six Wheel Chaser/Tell Your Story/Yancey Special/Chicago Flyer (all Blue Note LP 7018)
Denapas Parade/Boogie Tidal/Randini's Boogie/ Lux's Boogie/Yancey's Pride/Glendale Glide (all Stinson LP 25)

Jimmy Yancey: *The Fives* (Solo Art 12008)
Yancey Stomp/State Street Special/Tell 'Em About Me/ Five O'Clock Blues/Cryin' in My Sleep/Death Letter Blues/Yancey's Bugle Call/35th and Dearborn (all X LP LX3000)
Slow and Easy Blues/Mellow Blues (Victor 26591)
Bear Trap Blues/East St. Louis Blues (Vocalion 5464)
Eternal Blues/Yancey Special (Session 12–001)
How Long Blues (Session 12–002)
Pallet on the Floor (Session 12–003)
Rough and Steady (Session 12–004)
Jimmy's Rocks (Session 10–001)
Shave 'Em Dry (Session 10–005)

Midnight Stomp/Boodlin'/At the Window (all on Pax LP 600)

Jimmy's stuff (No. 2)/*Rolling the Stone/Steady Rock Blues/P.L.K. Special/South Side Stuff/Yancey's Getaway/La Salle Street Breakdown/Two O'Clock Blues/Janie's Joys/Lean Bacon/Big Bear Train/Lucille's Lament* (all on Riverside LP 12–124)

Pete Johnson: *Goin' Away Blues/Roll 'Em Pete* (Vocalion 4607)

Shuffle Boogie (Solo Art 12010)

Climbin' and Screamin'/Let 'Em Jump/B & O Blues (included in Riverside LP 12–106)

Boogie Woogie (Columbia 37334)

Holler Stomp/You Don't Know My Mind (included in Blue Note LP 7019)

Cripple Clarence Lofton: *Had a Dream/Streamline Train* (Solo Art 12003)

I Don't Know/Pinetop's Boogie Woogie (Solo Art 12009)

The Fives/South End Boogie/In the Mornin'/Early Blues/I Don't Know/Streamline Train (all on Pax LP 6005)

More Motion/Sweet Tooth/House Rent Struggle/Sixes and Sevens/Clarence's Blues/Lofty Blues/Juice Joint/Salty Woman Blues (all on Riverside LP 1037)

Charles Avery: *Dearborn Street Breakdown* (included on Riverside LP 1034)

Henry Brown: *21st Street Stomp* (included in Riverside LP 1013)

Henry Brown Blues (included in Riverside LP 1009)

Eastern Chimes/Deep Morgan Blues (included in Riverside LP 1034)

Cow Cow Davenport: *Chimes Blues/Atlanta Rag* (included in Riverside LP 1034)

Slow Drag (included in Riverside LP 1009)

Cow Cow Blues/State Street Jive (included in Brunswick LP 54014)

Will Ezell: *Mixed Up Rag/Heifer Dust/Playing the Dozen/West Coast Rag/Barrel House Man/Pitchin' Boogie/Just Can't Stay Here/Bucket of Blood* (all on Riverside LP 1043)

Lemuel Fowler: *Satisfied Blues/Blues Mixture* (Columbia A3959)

Leroy Garnett: *Chain 'Em Down/Louisiana Glide* (included on Riverside LP 1009)

Romeo Nelson: *Head Rag Hop* (included on Brunswick LP 54014)

Pinetop Smith: *Pinetop's Boogie Woogie/Pinetop's Blues/Jump Steady Blues* (included on Brunswick LP 54014)

Speckled Red: *Saint Louis Stomp/Doin' the Georgia* (Bluebird B7985)

Montana Taylor: *Detroit Rocks/Indiana Avenue Stomp* (included on Brunswick LP 54014)

Indiana Avenue Stomp/Montana's Blues/Rotten Break Blues/In the Bottom/Low Down Bugle/Sweet Sue/ I Can't Sleep/Fo' Day Blues (all on Riverside Limited Edition LP No. 2)

Hersal Thomas: *Suitcase Blues/Hersal Blues* (Okeh 8227)

Wesley Wallace: *No 29/Fanny Lee Blues* (included on Riverside LP 1009)

Jabbo Williams: *Fat Mama Blues/Polack Blues* (included on Riverside LP 1034)

Jab Blues (Jazz Information 3)

Charlie Spand: *Moanin' the Blues* (included on Riverside LP 1009)

Mississippi Blues (included on Riverside LP 1034)

J. H. Shayne: *Mr. Freddy Blues/Lonesome Man Blues* (Decca 7663)

Mr. Freddy's Rag/Chestnut Street Boogie (Circle 1011)

NOTE: It is very much regretted that so many of the above records are deleted from the catalogues, but it was impossible to cover the subject competently without reference to them. The following five twelve-inch LP's, mentioned above, are still obtainable from record dealers:

Piano Jazz, Vol. 1: Barrel House and Boogie Woogie (Brunswick 54014)

Great Jazz Pianists (Camden CAL-328)

Barrelhouse, Boogie Woogie and Blues (Harmony 7104)

Giants of Boogie Woogie (Riverside 12–106)

Yancy's Getaway (Riverside 12–124)

CHICAGO

In a surprising turmoil of reissue activity during the past decade, the record catalogues have added hundreds of early Chicago recordings by the bands of Albert Ammons, across the alphabet to that of Bernie Young (neither of these, however, has remained available). It seems likely that anthologies of early Chicago bands, Chicago stylists, Chicago blues and boogie-woogie, and of the major recording artists of Chicago jazz, such as Teschemacher, Condon, Hines, Ammons, Blythe and Keppard, will continue to reappear. It is also likely that the active Chicagoans, such as Hodes, Condon, Sullivan, Freeman, McPartland, the Franz Jackson

All Stars and the revivalists, will continue to produce frequent examples in the vein of Chicago musical styles. The jazz historian or musicologist must remain alert to these sporadic issues if he desires to acquire a broadly representative collection of the sounds of earlier times or their re-presentations. The following records are currently (1959) catalogued in either, or both, the U.S. and the U.K.

Retrospective Collections

Chicago Jazz (Columbia CL 632)

Early South Side Musicians:

Jazz, Volumes 2, 5, 6 (Folkways 2802, 2805, 2806)
Jazz of the 20's: Encyclopedia of Jazz Vol. I (Brunswick LAT 8166, English)
Young Louis Armstrong (Riverside 12–101)
Louis Armstrong Story, 4 12″ LP's (Columbia CL 851 to 854)
Jonny Dodds (Riverside 12–104)
Johnny Dodds (Epic LN 3207)
Dominique, Natty (Windin' Ball 104)
Art Hodes Trios—Dodds, Taylor, Howard, DeFaut (Paramount 113)
King Oliver Blues (Epic LN 3208)
No Saints—Franz Jackson's All Stars (Replica 1006)

Revivals of Early South Side:

Classics of the 20's—Doc Evans Band (Audiophile 50)
Jelly Roll's Jazz—Lawson-Haggart Jazz Band (Decca 8182)
King Oliver's Jazz—Lawson-Haggart Jazz Band (Decca 8195)

Early Chicagoans (Chicago Style, the Austin school)

New Orleans Rhythm Kings (Riverside 12–104)
Bud Freeman All Star Jazz (Harmony 7046)
Mutiny in the Parlor—Gene Krupa (Camden 340)
Classic Early Recordings—Muggsy Spanier (Riverside 12–107)

Revival of Chicago Style (or modifications, often Chicago-Dixieland amalgams):

Substantially all current recordings by Pee Wee Russell, Max Kaminsky, Eddie Condon, Jimmy McPartland, Bud Freeman and Muggsy Spanier. *Club Basin Street,* Danny Alvin (Stephany 4002)

Ashcraft Sessions (Paramount 104, 108, 110)
Chicago/Austin High School (Victor LPM 1508)
Hurrah for Bix—Marty Grosz (Riverside 12–268)
Windy City Jazz—Lawson-Haggart Jazz Band (Decca 8198)
Jazz Chicago Style—Art Hodes Band (Mercury 20185)
Jazz for Art's Sake—Art Hodes and groups (Dotted Eighth 101)

Chicago Piano:

Don Ewell Plays King Oliver (Tempo TAP 7, English)
Piano Solos—Jess Stacey (Brunswick 54017)
Mr. Piano Man—Joe Sullivan (Verve 1002)
New Solos by an Old Master—Joe Sullivan (Riverside 12–202)
Classic Piano—Jelly Roll Morton (Riverside 12–111)
Cass Simpson (Paramount 109)
Kansas City Frank Melrose (Paramount 103)
Earl "Fatha" Hines (Epic 3501)
Oh, Father! (Epic 3223)

Chicago Boogie Woogie:

Cat House Piano, Meade Lux Lewis (Verve 1006)
Meade Lux (Verve 1007)
Out of the Roaring 20's, Meade Lux Lewis (ABC 103)
Yancey Special—Jimmy Yancey (Paramount 101)
Albert Ammons (Brunswick oe 9325, English)
Powerhouse Piano—Tom Harris & Charlie Castner (Paramount 112)
Little Brother Montgomery (Windin' Ball 104)

Chicago Blues:

Folk Blues—Bill Broonzy (Emarcy 36052)
Classic Blues (Riverside 12–108)
Big Bill Broonzy (Phillips 7113, English)

Special:

Baby Dodds Drum Method (band, trio, solo examples) Dodds (American Music) 1, 2, 3

THE SPREAD OF JAZZ AND THE BIG BANDS

Absolutely Indispensable:

Jazz; Big Bands (1924–34) (Folkways FP 69)
Encyclopedia of Jazz on Records, Vol. II (Decca DL 8399)
Lester Leaps In (Epic LG 3107)
Count Basie and his Orchestra (Decca DL 8049)
The Music of Duke Ellington (Columbia CL 558)
In a Mellotone: Duke Ellington (Victor LPM 1364)
Lunceford Special (Columbia CL 634)
The Great Benny Goodman (Columbia CL 820)

Necessary but Rare:

Fletcher Henderson (Riverside RLP 1055)
Fletcher Henderson (Label "X" LVA-3013)
Fletcher Henderson Memorial Album (Decca DL 6025)
McKinney's Cotton Pickers (Label "X" LVA-3031)
McKinney's Cotton Pickers (Victor LPT-24)
The Missourians (Label "X" LVA-3020)
This is Duke Ellington (Victor LPT-3017)
Duke Ellington, Vol. I (Label "X" LVA-3037)
Jimmie Lunceford (Label "X" LX-3002)

Of Considerable Interest:

Blue Light: Duke Ellington (Columbia CL 663)
Charlie Johnson's Paradise Band (Label "X" LVA-3026)
Ridin' With Red Allen (Label "X" LVA-3033)
Oh, Father: Earl Hines (Epic LN 3223)
Basie's Best (Brunswick BL 58019)

KANSAS CITY AND THE SOUTHWEST

Ten-inch LPs:

Bennie Moten's Kansas City Jazz: Volume I ("X" Label RCA LX-3004) *
Volume II ("X" Label LVA-3005) *
Volume III ("X" Label LVA-3038) *

* indicates records now out of print.

Harlem in the Twenties, Volume I: The Missourians ("X" Label LVA-
    3020) *

Andy Kirk and His Clouds of Joy (Coral CRL 56019) *

Basie's Best: Count Basie Orchestra, 1937 (Brunswick BL 58019) *

The Old Count and the New Count: Basie, 1939–51 (Epic LG 1021) *

Rock the Blues: Basie, 1939 (Epic LN 1117) *

Kansas City Style: Kansas City Six, 1938–44 (Commodore FL 20,021) *

Count Basie at the Piano (Decca DL 5111) *

Jammin' at Rudi's, Volume II: Lips Page, Tyree Glenn, etc. (Circle
    L-410) *

Kansas City Memories: Jay McShann, 1941–42 (Decca DL 5503) *

Twelve-inch LPs:

The Boss of the Blues: Joe Turner (Atlantic 1234)

Little Jimmy Rushing and the Big Brass (Columbia CL 1152)

If This Ain't the Blues: Jimmy Rushing (Vanguard VRS 8513)

Goin' to Chicago: Jimmy Rushing (Vanguard VRS 8518)

Listen to the Blues: Jimmy Rushing (Vanguard VRS 8505)

The Odyssey of James Rushing, Esquire (Columbia CL 963)

Upright and Lowdown: Pete Johnson, Turner, Williams (Columbia CL
    685)

The Benny Goodman Combos: Charlie Christian (Columbia CL 500)

Charlie Christian w. Benny Goodman (Columbia CL 652)

Count Basie: 1937–38 (Brunswick BL 54012)

Count Basie and His Orchestra: 1937–38 (Decca DL 8049)

Lester Leaps in: Basie, 1939 (Epic LG 3107)

Let's Go to Prez: Basie, 1939–40 (Epic LG 3168)

Basie's Back in Town: 1941 (Epic LG 3169)

Blues by Basie: 1939–51 (Columbia CL 901)

Count Basie Classics: 1940–46 (Columbia CL 754)

One O'Clock Jump: Basie 1942–51 (Columbia CL 997)

Charlie Christian-Dizzy Gillespie: Minton's, 1941 (Esoteric)

K.C. in the Thirties: Lee, McShann, Brown, Webster (Capitol LP)

Kansas City Jazz: Kirk, Basie, Durham, Williams, etc., 1940 (Decca DL
    8044)

    These are largely reissues of various bands during their peak periods. Other representative samplings can be listened to today under Buddy Tate (Felsted), Buck Clayton (Columbia, Vanguard), Illinois Jacquet (Victor, Verve) and other stylists who retain the traditions brought with them from the Southwest years ago. The current Basie band is not included as representative of his original style.

    * indicates records now out of print.

THE ELLINGTON STYLE

Unfortunately many of the records I have discussed are only obtainable on shellac collector's items. The reissuing of early Ellington on LP has been extremely limited. Even some of the LPs listed below have been discontinued or are obtainable only in Europe. It is to be hoped that the immense wealth of early Ellington recordings will be made available in time by some of the major companies.

The Duke—1926 (10″ London LP AL 3551)
Early Ellington (12″ Brunswick LP 54007)
Saturday Night Function (10″ HMV LP 1094)
Duke Ellington— Early Recordings (10″ X-label LVA-3037)
Duke Ellington—Jungle Style (10″ French HMV FOLP-8001)
Duke Ellington (10″ Jazz Panorama LP-1802)
Duke Ellington at the Cotton Club (12″ Camden CAL-459)

CHARLES PARKER

1941 *Dexter Blues* McShann (Decca) *Hootie Blues* McShann (Decca)
1942 *Lonely Boy Blues* McShann (Decca) *The Jumpin' Blues* McShann (Decca)
1944 *Tiny's Tempo* Grimes (Savoy) *I'll Always Love You* Grimes (Savoy) *Romance Without Finance* Grimes (Savoy) *Red Cross* Grimes (Savoy)
1945 Reissued on Savoy are: *Groovin' High* Gillespie (Guild) *Dizzie Atmosphere* Gillespie (Musicraft) *Salt Peanuts* Gillespie (Guild) *Shaw 'Nuff* Gillespie (Guild) *Hot House* Gillespie (Guild). Reissued on Dial are: *Hallelujah* Norvo (Comet) *Get Happy* Norvo (Comet) *Congo Blues* Norvo (Comet) *Slam Slam Blues* Norvo (Comet). *Takin' Off* Chas. Thompson (Apollo) *The Street Beat* Chas. Thompson (Apollo) *Billie's Bounce* Chas. Thompson (Savoy) *Warming Up a Riff* Chas. Thompson (Savoy) *Now's the Time* Chas. Thompson (Savoy) *Thriving from a Riff* Chas. Thompson (Savoy) *Meandering* Chas. Thompson (Savoy) *Ko-Ko* Chas. Thompson (Savoy)
1946 *Moose the Mooche* (Dial) *Yardbird Suite* (Dial) *Ornithology* (Dial) *Night in Tunisia* (Dial)

1947 *Bird's Nest* (Dial) *Cool* (*Hot, Blowtop*) *Blues* (Dial) *Relaxin' at Camarillo* (Dial) *Cheers* (Dial) *Carvin' the Bird* (Dial) *Stupendous Donna Lee* (Savoy) *Chasing the Bird* (Savoy) *Cheryl* (Savoy) *Buzzy* (Savoy) *Dexterity* (Dial) *Bongo Bop* (Dial) *Prezology* (Dial) *Dewey Square* (Dial) *The Hymn* (Dial) *Bird of Paradise* (Dial) *Embraceable You* (Dial) *Bird Feathers* (Dial) *Klactoveedsedstene* (Dial) *Scrapple from the Apple* (Dial) *My old Flame* (Dial) *Out of Nowhere* (Dial) *Don't Blame Me* (Dial) *Drifting on a Reed* (Dial) *Quasimodo* (Dial) *Charlie's Wig* (Dial) *Crazeology* (Dial) *How Deep Is the Ocean?* (Dial) *Another Hair-do* (Savoy) *Bluebird* (Savoy) *Klaunstance* (Savoy) *Bird Gets the Worm* (Savoy)

1948 *Barbados* (Savoy) *Ah-leu-cha* (Savoy) *Constellation* (Savoy) *Parker's Mood* (Savoy) *Perhaps* (Savoy) *Marmaduke* (Savoy) *Steeplechase* (Savoy) *Merry-go-round* (Savoy)

1949 *Cardboard* (Clef—now Verve) *Visa* (Clef—now Verve) *Segment* (Clef—now Verve) *Passport* (Clef—now Verve)

1950 *Star Eyes* (Clef—now Verve) *Blues* (fast) (Clef—now Verve) *I'm in the Mood for Love* (Clef—now Verve) *Bloomdido* (Clef—now Verve) *An Oscar for Treadwell* (Clef—now Verve) *Mohawk* (Clef—now Verve) *Melancholy Baby* (Clef—now Verve) *Leap Frog* (Clef—now Verve) *Relaxin' with Lee* (Clef—now Verve) *Celebrity* (Clef—now Verve) *Ballade* (Clef—now Verve)

1951 *Au Privave* (Clef—now Verve) *She Rote* (Clef—now Verve) *K.C. Blues* (Clef—now Verve) *Star Eyes* (Clef—now Verve) *Blues for Alice* (Clef—now Verve) *Swedish Schnapps* (Clef—now Verve) *Back Home Blues* (Clef—now Verve) *Loverman* (Clef—now Verve)

1952 *Night & Day* (Clef—now Verve) *Almost Like Being in Love* (Clef—now Verve) *I Can't Get Started* (Clef—now Verve) *What Is This Thing Called Love?* (Clef—now Verve) *The Song Is You* (Clef—now Verve) *Kim* (Clef—now Verve) *Laird Baird* (Clef—now Verve) *Cosmic Rays* (Clef—now Verve)

1953 *Perdido* (Quintet of the Year) (Debut) *All the Things* (Quintet of the Year) (Debut) *Salt Peanuts* (Quintet of the Year) (Debut) *Wee* (Quintet of the Year) (Debut) *Hot House* (Quintet of the Year) (Debut) *Night in Tunisia* (Quintet of the Year) (Debut) *Chi Chi* (Clef—now Verve) *I Remember You* (Clef—now Verve) *Now's the Time* (Clef—now Verve) *Confirmation* (Clef—now Verve)

BEBOP AND AFTER

Lester Young-Buck Clayton (Commodore 30,014)
Christian/Monk/Clarke/Gillespie (Esoteric-Counterpoint 548)
Gillespie-Parker (Savoy 12020)
Charlie Parker (Roost 2210, Savoy 12000)
Bud Powell/Fats Navarro (Blue Note 1503)
Thelonious Monk (Blue Note 1509, 1510)
Miles Davis (Capitol T 762)
Gerry Mulligan (Pacific Jazz 1207)
Modern Jazz Quartet (Prestige 7005, Atlantic 1231, 1284)
Horace Silver-Art Blakey (Blue Note 1518)
Clifford Brown (Prestige 7038)
Miles Davis (Prestige 7076, 7109)
Thelonious Monk (Prestige 7027, 7053, Riverside 12–209, 12–226)
Sonny Rollins (Prestige 7079, Contemporary 3530)
Charlie Mingus (Atlantic 1237)
Cecil Taylor (Transition 19)
Bill Evans (Riverside 12–223)
Martial Solal (Epic LN 3376)
John Coltrane (Blue Note 1577)

THE RE-EMERGENCE OF TRADITIONAL JAZZ

Eureka Brass Band: *Panama/Trombonium/Just a Little While To Stay Here/Lord Lord Lord You Certainly Been Good to Me/Eternity/Maryland My Maryland* (all Folkways FA 2462)
Young Tuxedo Brass Band: *Lead Me Saviour/Eternal Peace/Medley of Hymns/Just a Closer Walk with Thee/Bourbon Street Parade/Lord Lord Lord/Just a Little While To Stay Here/Panama/It Feels So Good/Joe Avery's Piece/John Casimir's Whoopin' Blues* (all Atlantic 1297)
Bunk Johnson Band: *Big Chief Battle Axe/Dusty Rag/Franklin Street Blues/The Thriller Rag/Sobbin' Blues/Sobbin' Blues No. 2/When I Leave the World Behind/Sometimes My Burden's So Hard To Bear/Bluebells Goodbye/Shine/Yaka Hula Hickey Dula/Weary Blues* (all Commodore DL 30007)
Blues/See See Rider/When the Saints Go Marching in/Just a Closer Walk with Thee/Lonesome Road (all American Music 638)

Bunk Johnson Talking/Maple Leaf Rag/Make Me a Pallet on the Floor/When the Saints Go Marching in/Nearer my God to Thee/ Just a Little While to Stay Here/Baby I'd Love To Steal You/Dipper-mouth Blues/Ballin' the Jack (all American Music 643)

The Entertainer/The Minstrel Man/Chloe/Someday/Kinklets/Hi-larity Rag/You're Driving Me Crazy/Out of Nowhere/That Teasin' Rag/Some of These Days/Till We Meet Again/Maria Elena (all Columbia GL 520)

George Lewis Band: *Over the Waves/New Orleans Hula/Burgundy Street Blues/St. Philip Street Breakdown/High Society/San Jacinto Blues/ Ice Cream* (all American Music 639)

Ace in the Hole/It's a Long, Long Way to Tipperary/West End Blues/ Jambalaya/Wolverine Blues/Take My Hand Precious Lord/Mack the Knife/Yaka Hula Hickey Dula/Careless Love/Hindustan (all Verve 8277)

Wooden Joe Nicholas: *Shake It and Break It/Careless Love/Lead Me on/ Eh La-Bas!/I Ain't Got Nobody/Up Jumped the Devil/Blues* (all American Music 640)

George Lewis with Kid Shots Madison: *Bucket's Got a Hole in It/Dumaine Street Drag/In Gloryland/Sheik of Araby/When You and I Were Young Maggie/San Jacinto Stomp* (all American Music 645)

Kid Ory's Creole Jazz Band (1944–45): *Creole Song/Get Out of Here/ Blues for Jimmie Noone/South/Panama/Under the Bamboo Tree/ Careless Love/Do What Ory Say/Maryland, my Maryland/Down Home Rag/1919 Rag/Oh! Didn't He Ramble/Ory's Creole Trom-bone/Weary Blues/Maple Leaf Rag/Original Dixieland One Step* (all Good Time Jazz L-12022)

(1954): *Muskrat Ramble/Clarinet Marmalade/Gettysburg March/ Yellow Dog Blues/I found a New Baby/When the Saints Go March-ing in/Maple Leaf Rag/Wolverine Blues/That's a Plenty* (all Good Time Jazz L-12004)

Franz Jackson All-Stars: *Alabama Jubilee/Bill Bailey Won't You Come Home/South Side/West End Blues/Squeeze Me/Just a Closer Walk with Thee/Battle Hymn of the Republic/Sugar Foot Stomp/Runnin' Wild/Al's Strut/How'm I Doin'?* (all Replica 1006)

Teddy Buckner Band: *Potato Head Blues/Black and Blue/My Bucket's Got a Hole in It/Save It Pretty Mama/My Monday Date/Butter and Egg Man/Savoy Blues/Someday/Squeeze Me/High Society* (Dixieland Jubilee 505)

Paul Barbarin New Orleans Jazz: *Sing On/Eh La-Bas!/Just a Little While To Stay Here/Crescent Blues/Bourbon Street Parade/Sister Kate/*

Bugle Boy March/Someday Sweetheart/Walking Through the Streets of the City (all Atlantic 1215)

Wilbur de Paris New New Orleans Jazz: *Madagascar/March of the Charcoal Grays/Mardi Gras Rag/Are You from Dixie/Hot Lips/Yama Yama Man/Flow Gently, Sweet Afton/Milneberg Joys* (all Atlantic 1219)

Don Ewell with Darnell Howard: *South Side Strut/I Can't Believe that You're in Love with Me/A Monday Date/Love Me or Leave Me/ Squeeze Me/Bush Street Scramble/Old Fashioned Love/Blues Improvisation/Parlor Social/You Took Advantage of Me/Gee Baby Ain't I Good to You/My Honey's Lovin' Arms* (all Good Time Jazz L-12021)

Lu Watters Yerba Buena Band: *South/Chattanooga Stomp/1919 Rag/ Sunset Cafe Stomp/Copenhagen/Panama/Working Man Blues/Richard M. Jones Blues/Bienville Blues/Triangle Jazz Blues/Weary Blues/ Friendless Blues* (all Good Time Jazz L-12003)

NOTE: All the above are LPs. It is doubtful if the American Music items are available, but all others are in catalogue at the time of this writing. One or two items have been included for historical rather than strictly musical reasons.

Index